D1617454

All Can Be Saved

STUART B. SCHWARTZ

All Can Be Saved

RELIGIOUS TOLERANCE AND
SALVATION IN THE
IBERIAN ATLANTIC WORLD

Yale University Press
New Haven &
London

Published with assistance from the Kingsley Trust Association Publication Fund
established by the Scroll and Key Society of Yale College.

Set in Sabon type by Keystone Typesetting, Inc.
Printed in the United States of America by Thomson-Shore, Inc.

Library of Congress Cataloging-in-Publication Data
Schwartz, Stuart B.
All can be saved : religious tolerance and salvation in the Iberian Atlantic world /
Stuart B. Schwartz.
p. cm.
Includes bibliographical references and index.
ISBN-13: 978-0-300-12580-1 (alk. paper)
ISBN-10: 0-300-12580-1
1. Religious tolerance — Spain. 2. Religious tolerance — Portugal. 3. Religious
tolerance — Spain — Colonies. 4. Religious tolerance — Portugal — Colonies.
5. Spain — Church history. 6. Portugal — Church history. I. Title.
BR1025.S39 2008
270.09171'246 — dc22
                                                                    2007045562

A catalogue record for this book is available from the British Library.
The paper in this book meets the guidelines for permanence and durability of the
Committee on Production Guidelines for Book Longevity of the Council on
Library Resources.
10 9 8 7 6 5 4 3 2 1

For Fernando and Carmiña

Cada uno se puede salvar en su ley.
(Each person can be saved in his or her own religion.)
—*a traditional Spanish saying*

Contents

Acknowledgments

In researching and writing this book over the course of many years and in various countries I have incurred a long list of intellectual debts. I cannot list them all here, and I apologize at the outset if I have unintentionally forgotten anyone. Let me mention those people who had a direct bearing on this book. First of all, my Yale colleagues Paul Freedman, Jon Butler, Steven Pincus, Francesca Trivellato, Keith Wrightson, and Carlos Eire each read and critiqued various parts of the book and gave me the benefit of their command of their particular fields. Over the course of my teaching career at both the University of Minnesota and Yale I have had the privilege of working with outstanding graduate students who often taught me as much as I taught them. Some of them were very helpful in the research and preparation of this book, aiding me in the location and reproduction of documents, in passing along bibliographical leads, and in challenging me in continual conversations. I am particularly indebted to Daviken Studnicki-Gizbert, Martin Neswig, Raphael Folsom, Eric Myrup, Jeremy Mumford, Jennifer Ottman, Ryan Crewe, Casey King, and Tatiana Seijas for their help and the occasional reality checks they imposed.

In each country in which I conducted my research I benefited from the help and guidance of historians and other scholars. In Spain, I was especially helped by James Amelang, Jaime Contreras, Asunción Merino, Elda "Picchi" González, and Alfonso Moreno. Mercedes García Arenal gave me the benefit of her expertise on the Moriscos and provided generous suggestions to a bibliography unknown to me. I owe a special debt of thanks for his friendship, support, and encouragement to Fernando Bouza Álvarez, who has long been my *hermano español,* and to Carmiña Escrigas, his wife, for making Madrid a second home for me and my family. In Portugal, I have many personal and intellectual debts with my old friends Joaquim Romero Magalhães, António Manuel Hespanha, Francisco Bethencourt, and Pedro Cardim. José Pedro Paiva has been particularly generous with his time and his unparalleled knowledge of Portuguese religious history. In Spanish America, Pedro Guibovitch of Lima and Enrique Florescano of Mexico City encouraged the project in various ways. In Brazil, where I have worked so long, I owe thanks to many people, but I single out Laura de Mello e Souza, Ronaldo Vainfas, Anita Novinsky, José Jobson de Arruda, Iris Kantor, and Monica Dantas, all of whom contributed directly to this book. I also thank the Cathedra Jaime Cortesão and the Laboratory for the Study of Intolerance at the University of São Paulo for their invitations to share my findings with their members and students. In Paris, at the Ecole des Hautes Etudes en Sciences Sociales I had the opportunity to share my early research with colleagues as a visiting professor owing to an invitation from Nathan Wachtel and Serge Gruzinski. Other colleagues from the EHESS have also helped me, and I have benefited from the comments and encouragement of Bernard Vincent, Guilhaume Boccara, and Jean-Frédéric Schaub.

Over the years, I have asked for and received considerable help from many colleagues. David Nieremberg, Robert Lerner, Pamela Voekel, David Higgs, Wayne Te Brake, Erik Midelfort, Jonathan Israel, Henry Kamen, and Roberto González Echevarría all took the trouble to answer my queries. Criticisms and suggestions from Hispanists like Richard Kagan, Antonio Feros, and Teo Ruiz and from Latin Americanists like David Brading, Ada Ferrer, Tamar Herzog, Herbert Klein, William Taylor, Kenneth Mills, Eric Van Young, Father Stafford Poole, Clara López Beltrán, and Murdo McCleod helped me to clarify various arguments of the book and eliminate some errors. As is the case for almost any research scholar, my work was made possible by the competence and kindness of the professional archivists and librarians of the institutions noted in the bibliography. I owe a special thanks to César Rodriguez, Yale's outstanding Latin American bibliographer, for his help in locating new and obscure items. My daughter, Alison, and son, Lee, were always supportive and did their best to keep me aware of what tolerance really means. Finally, I wish to recognize the help and companionship of my wife, María Jordán Arroyo, whose own interest in the history of Spanish religion and culture was really the stimulus for me to undertake this project in a kind of history quite unlike any I have written before. At her side, the hours spent in the archives of Spain and Portugal and our incessant conversations about these subjects have made the years fly by. This book and my life have been enriched by them.

Introduction

This book was conceived in bed. I remember laughing out loud while reading Carlo Ginzburg's *The Cheese and the Worms* one winter night in Minneapolis and thinking how tolerant and modern its protagonist, the free-thinking Friulian miller Menocchio, seemed when in 1584 he told his inquisitors that no one really knew which religion was best; and that while he was, of course, a Catholic, if he had been born among the Turks, he would have lived in their religion and thought it best. Salvation was possible in any religion, he said, because God loves us all.[1] How curious, how commonsensical, how singular, I thought. Still chuckling, I turned off the light. Life moved on; the passage was forgotten. A decade later, while working in the records of the Spanish Inquisition on ideas about sexuality in Spain and its colonies, I began to encounter the cases of individuals whose attitudes toward other religions seemed quite close to those of Menocchio. Most were simple folk, but occasional clerics and educated laymen also expressed ideas of religious relativism and tolerance, often summed up in a common expression: *Cada uno se puede salvar en su ley* (Each person can be saved in his or her own religion). How was this sort of relativism or tolerance possible in early modern Spain and Portugal, the classic examples of the enforced orthodoxy of Counter-Reformation Catholicism? Who were these people and where did they derive this idea? My assumptions about the past of Portugal, Spain, and their American colonies were challenged and my curiosity piqued. This book was under way.

1

As will soon become clear, I have woven together the themes of salvation and tolerance because it was the question of salvation in both its spiritual and political dimensions that caused people to first consider the issue of religious tolerance. For men and women in the late Middle Ages and the early modern world no quest was more important than the search for salvation, or so they were continuously told by clergy and theologians. Life was all too short and eternity endless, and securing the soul's salvation was a matter of the utmost urgency. But soteriology, the understanding of salvation, was a contested issue. Whereas Christians in the East and West had accepted a single Christology (the idea of Jesus Christ as God and man), the interpretations of soteriology were several and sometimes overlapping. Was Christ's death an example for humankind, a ransom on behalf of humanity, a substitution for the punishment of everyone's sins, the satisfaction of the debt of all humans to God, or a sacrifice? And there were other interpretations as well.[2] Disagreements over how salvation could best be achieved lay at the very heart of the religious conflict and the process of confessionalization that eventually divided sixteenth-century Europe into Catholic and Protestant camps. Salvation raised many difficult questions. Was the key to salvation and eternal life God's divine grace and the sacraments of the Church or the good works of a just life? While in crude terms the Protestants, especially the Calvinists, stressed grace while the Church of Rome underscored human actions and merit, variations of emphasis could be found in both camps. And there were further questions. What of those people who had lived and died before Christ's coming or those who had never heard the Christian message? For Renaissance Europe, with its deep admiration for the learning and philosophy of classical authors, it was difficult for many people to accept the idea that Aristotle and Plato were condemned to eternal damnation, and as Europe's voyages of discovery revealed worlds and peoples previously unknown, theologians and laypeople alike began to question the idea that in God's divine plan all these gentiles, even those who had lived according to natural law, were damned.

The question of salvation had preoccupied the early Church fathers, and deviant positions like that of the Alexandrian theologian Origen (185–254), who thought a merciful God would ultimately save everyone (the heresy of apocatastasis), and that of the English monk Pelagius (354–420), who emphasized human goodness and the ability to win salvation through one's own efforts, led to their definition as heretics. Following closely the writings of St. Augustine, the position of Rome since the Middle Ages was that salvation was possible only after baptism within the Church and that it was restricted in various ways; but the doubts and questions remained and challenged the understanding and faith of many people.

The questions became even more immediate in the sixteenth century. The voyages of European expansion, the great global missionary effort, and the reform of the Church were all carried out in the shadow of the underlying question of God's plan of redemption and the appropriate road to individual salvation. The position of the Church summed up in the doctrine *extra ecclesiam nulla salus*, or "no salvation outside the Church," seemed to make clear the singular role and the exclusive validity of the Church of Rome, but historically this dogma continued to trouble theologians and laypeople, as it still does today.[3] What of right-living Muslims and Jews, or pagans, or members of other Christian churches? What about Chinese, Japanese, Hindus, and the peoples of the New World? Were all condemned? If not necessarily, then God's plan might be more ample and less exclusive. Other faiths might have some validity too (or all religions might have none), and if that was the case, then tolerance and acceptance of other ways might be not only practical but also within God's plan. Such thoughts were long considered heretical or heterodox within the Church, but they had existed in Christendom since its inception. This book argues that these old ideas never disappeared, and that while always a minority opinion, they eventually provided a context and in some ways the origin for the philosophical breakthroughs that led to the rise of religious tolerance and freedom of conscience, key concepts of the modern world. But ideas were not everything, and I will demonstrate that there was also a long tradition of indifference as well. There existed varying degrees of belief and varying degrees of indifference as well, and that too is part of the story. Of course, these ideas of religious tolerance, skepticism, and indifference were part of a broad range of heterodox ideas which were sometimes classified as heretical, but not all people who criticized some aspect of dogma or the excesses of Rome or who denounced the abuses of a particular priest or bishop were tolerant of other religions. Still, I hope to show that often dissidence in one area of dogma was accompanied by the questioning of other tenets so that religious tolerance sometimes was packaged with other doubts. By the eighteenth century Iberian defenders of orthodoxy saw religious toleration as the poisonous final product of doubt and freedom of conscience.

Scholars do not usually approach the history of toleration from the bottom up. The topic has long fascinated historians, and it has generated a vast and varied bibliography, including some outstanding works of historical scholarship, but one also marked by some peculiar characteristics. First of all, the study of toleration developed essentially as a branch of the history of ideas or as a subcategory of the history of religious doctrine. As the German scholar Heiko Oberman has written, there is probably no field of history that has remained so stubbornly in the hands of the intellectual historians.[4] Until the past decade, almost every study of toleration focused exclusively on educated elites, what came to be called the republic of letters, and on the great intellectual turning points in the development of toleration or, more recently, on their political contexts as well.[5] These studies usually concentrated on a particular thinker and his (or, more rarely, her) contribution to the general development of the theory of toleration. There are dozens of volumes which examine toleration, usually within the boundaries of Western Christendom. The cast of characters is somewhat predictable: John Wyclif, Christine de Pisan, Nicholas of Cusa, Bartolomé de Las Casas, Jean Bodin, Thomas Hobbes, Samuel Pufendorf, Baruch Spinoza, Pierre Bayle, G. W. Leibniz, Daniel Defoe, Jean Le Clerc, John Locke, and François-Marie Arouet Voltaire, to name only those featured in the recent miniboom of volumes of collected essays. Despite their obvious differences, most of these books have strong similarities in subject and approach, concentrating on the ideas of a single theologian, philosopher, or statesman, emphasizing philosophical or political considerations, and staying very close to particular texts.[6] These studies are in the main detached from any discussion of the reception of such ideas by the mass of the population and from any discussion of how similar ideas might have been shared or even generated by that population. But the best of the historians of toleration realized that something had been missed in this history. Joseph Lecler, a French Jesuit, whose two-volume *Toleration and the Reformation* (French ed., 1955; English ed., 1960) is a classic study, wrote a traditional intellectual history placing individual thinkers against the changing politics of a Europe torn by religious strife. Still, he perceived that there was something lacking in his work, and he ended his magnificent book with this observation:

> So this historical essay can hardly be concluded with a kind of prize-giving ceremony in honor of certain admirable men as "heroes of tolerance." I have tried not to underrate the outstanding personalities who contributed frequently penetrating observations on this theme. That is why their teaching has been carefully scrutinized; but I have also tried to point out that they themselves belonged to a particular social *milieu* as humanists, politicians, churchmen, and ordinary citizens, and that this whole *milieu* was already aware of the same issues. On this point history and sociology overlap in the study of tolerance.[7]

Lecler recognized that the history of tolerance and religious pluralism involved not just the intellectual elite, but society as a whole, the *milieu,* and that there was a relationship between society and the thinkers about whom he wrote. At that historical moment, he had neither the kinds of sources nor the method to get at this relationship. My book tries to do that in the unlikely context of the Hispanic world.

In all the historiography of toleration Iberia has had almost no place. For almost all historians of toleration as well as for intellectuals in the eighteenth century, Spain and Portugal and their Inquisitions seemed to be the epitome of intolerance, and as those countries slid into the status of second- or third-rate powers, they had a place in the history of toleration only as salutary examples of the dangers and costs of intolerance. Of course, some Spanish scholars have always disagreed with this assessment, pointing out how unity of religion helped Spain avoid the internal conflicts of the age of Reformation and arguing that the record of intolerance in Reformation Geneva, Elizabethan England, and Puritan New England should make foreign scholars slow to point an accusing finger at Spain.[8] An element of that defense appears in the work of the outstanding modern historian of toleration in Spain, Henry Kamen. He alone has concerned himself with the question in Spain, and he has argued at times that Spain was perhaps the "most tolerant" nation in Europe in the sixteenth century.[9] He makes this inversion by arguing that Spanish theologians were more willing than others to use persuasion, that Spain never committed itself to the terrible witch hunts that plagued northern Europe, and that Spain was less likely to burn its dissidents than were most other countries. Ultimately, however, while I owe a considerable debt to his scholarship and to our personal exchanges, we do not always agree in our interpretations. Now and then I find his definition of toleration, which at times has been limited to relations between Christians and which excludes relations with other religions, too limiting. Moreover, while not unaware of popular expressions of tolerance and other forms of dissidence, he has focused primarily on state policy and learned discourse. Still, he is one of the few historians who have given serious attention to this topic in the Iberian world.

To my mind and for my taste, the detachment of learned discourse from the cosmology of the majority of the population has made the historiography of religious toleration predictable, as scholars argue over the fine points of individual texts and the differences between authors in a history that moves from repression in the sixteenth century to enlightenment and increasing toleration in the eighteenth century. Within that chronology, the story then told is one of a rising attitude of tolerance born of three fundamental sources: practical necessity, self-interest tending to promote religious accommodation, and, finally, philosophical conviction. A Europe exhausted by religious strife began to seek accommodation by tolerating (in the sense of permitting something disagreeable) the practice of other religions. By the seventeenth century the possible economic benefits of religious toleration made clear by Amsterdam's attitude toward the Jews led politicians and rulers like Jean-Baptiste Colbert in France, Oliver Cromwell in England, Gaspar de Guzmán y Pimental, Conde-duque de Olivares in Spain, and Father António Vieira in Portugal to advocate some kind of toleration as state policy, and by the end of that century and the beginning of the next, practical considerations joined with the philosophical advances of Spinoza, Locke, and Voltaire. These writers formulated a cogent set of arguments that created the modern basis of religious toleration in which freedom of conscience became an inherent right, not a gift or concession, as it had been previously.[10] What has been lacking are the social and cultural contexts in which these changes took place and society's reception of these ideas.

My subject in this book is not the history of religious *toleration,* by which is usually meant state or community policy, but rather of *tolerance,* by which I mean attitudes or sentiments. The two terms have often been historically connected, but they are not necessarily related. Often toleration was a compromise born of practical political or economic considerations rather than of sentiments of tolerance. This, then, is a book about cultural attitudes. It is no longer common to use the term *history of mentalités* so popular in the 1970s and 1980s because that term seemed to project too much unity of thought on past societies, and in truth the main subjects of this book are people often at odds with the predominant ideas of their time. So I have conceived of this book as a social history of attitudes or cultural history of thought, but unlike the genre of history of ideas this is not a study of great thinkers and great ideas, but rather the stories of mostly previously unknown common folk, what they thought and said about their world and what they felt was right and just.

It is fair to ask, then, as my old friend the historian David Brading did on one occasion after hearing me lecture about these people, What, in fact, did these dissidents represent? Were they just a few cranks and discontents, the sort that every society produces, representing nothing but their own unhappiness and marginality? or did they stand for a deeper, broader discontent in their society? It is the old question: How many swallows make a summer? There is a real epistemological or methodological problem here. I am dealing with people whose dissident statements resulted in their arrest and often punishment. My research has revealed hundreds of cases of people who expressed some kind of attitude of religious tolerance, relativism, universalism, or skepticism. They were clearly not the majority in their societies; there was no thriving underground of village skeptics simply awaiting a chance to proclaim their creed. At the same time, however, given the dangers of making such statements and the commitment to intolerance of crown and Church, I believe it is fair to assume that there were many persons in these societies who held similar ideas but had the good sense or the discretion not to voice them. But even if their numbers were relatively few, I would argue that it is still important to tell their story. To write the history of "popular" culture does not mean that the common people in the past have importance only when they represent everyone else, or that one must always look only at normative behavior and find subjects who are just like their neighbors. Historians have long celebrated members of political and intellectual elites precisely because of their individuality. Desiderius Erasmus, Martin Luther, Spinoza, and Locke are interesting not because they were like everyone else, but because they were not and because their individuality and ability to create and represent ideas ultimately had an effect on the course of history. I wish to grant that same privilege to the obscure men and women who appear on these pages. Their vision of a society in which each person was free to believe as he or she saw fit without the threat of coercion won out, or at least provided a context for the development and success of policies of religious toleration, one of the central themes of modernity. They were in their way precursors of our world. Their doubts and tolerance created a soil from which modern concepts of freedom of conscience and toleration eventually grew, and their dissident views of a salvation possible for all were in fact in some ways closer to the position of the post–Vatican II Catholic Church than was that of the Inquisition which tried to correct them.

Writing about these people with the obvious sympathy I have for them carries with it various dangers. The first is the pitfall of a "Whig" interpretation, that is, a history written from the perspective of the present, in which toleration seems inevitable. To fall into that trap would be to assume that the past logically led to today and that present conditions and our own sensibilities are a kind of historical end point, even though events in the past decade have made it clear that toleration and freedom of conscience are still not universal values and that cultural and religious pluralism is still a matter of contention. Religious toleration and freedom of conscience have been viewed as fundamental outgrowths of the secularization of the modern world, but the resurgence of various fundamentalisms in our own times under the guise of nationalism or religious truth should make us cautious of any kind of teleological view of either secularization or religious freedom.

The question of toleration also presents another challenge to the historian. Modern Western societies have adopted freedom of conscience, pluralism, and religious toleration as positive attitudes, so that anything that smacks of control or censorship is seen in a negative light. Yet in early modern times almost no one believed religious toleration to be beneficial in either political or religious terms. Political stability was thought to rest on the unity of creed between ruler and subjects, and the tolerance of doctrinal error and heresy was thought to be destructive of the common good and of the souls of those in error as well. But not everyone held that opinion, and it is the story of these dissidents, whose numbers grew over time, that I wish to tell. The Iberian nations of Spain and Portugal and their American colonies, based as they were on state support for religious exclusivity and intolerance, serve here as a limiting case. I believe that the attitudes of tolerance I demonstrate were not peculiar to Iberia and were found throughout much of Europe but to a large extent have been ignored until quite recently.

If avoiding a supposed Whiggish stance is one challenge, surely another lies in what might be called the Schindler's List syndrome: the desire to find in the humane and tolerant actions of a few individuals a saving and exculpatory grace that gives one hope for the human condition. How much more pleasant and satisfying it is to concentrate on their humanity and bravery than to think about the vast majority who supported fully a regime of intolerance, discrimination, state repression, and extermination. The temptation to see the people who pass through these pages as heroes of tolerance would be facile and misleading. While some held their opinions with steadfast courage, others were lukewarm in their belief, and still others were indifferent to religion or principle altogether. Despite my personal sympathy for many of the people who are the protagonists of this story, I have sought always to see them in the contexts of their own times and to understand as well the motivations and thinking of those who opposed them, denounced them, and punished them.

This book goes against the grain in many ways. First of all, it is an examination of attitudes of tolerance among common folk, not philosophers or theologians. Second, it deals with both the Spanish- and Portuguese-speaking worlds, which are normally treated apart. While they have at times been studied together, as in the work of the remarkable conservative historian Marcelino Menéndez Pelayo (1856–1912) on heterodoxy in the Luso-Hispanic world, it is still relatively uncommon for scholars to deal with the complex histories and historiographies of Spain, Portugal, and their American colonies in the same study. Differences of language, history, politics, and viewpoint have usually required that separation. I seek to break down that barrier, but I recognize that what has been gained in scope by this approach has sometimes been at the cost of depth. This book, however, is particularly interested in the flow of ideas and practices from metropolis to colony, and so its perspective is transatlantic in that sense. Third, while the archives of the Inquisitions of Spain and Portugal form the documentary base and heart of this study, the Inquisition itself, its personnel, objectives, and history, is not the subject of the book. The Holy Office of the Inquisition was established in Castile in 1478 and in Portugal in 1526, and the records of its proceedings are a rich and seemingly inexhaustible mine of information. These documents present extraordinary opportunities and challenges. In arresting and interrogating people of all walks of life, but especially intellectuals, dissidents, and unlettered or semiliterate commoners, the Inquisition compiled records that are now one of the few sources in which historians can recapture the voice of common people in the past. But it would be naïve to think that these archives are not unproblematic, and they must be used always with caution. The very conditions under which testimony was gathered, including the disparity of power between the individual and the Church, the shadow of an omnipresent implicit threat of torture, the unequal dialogue between the learned inquisitors and their often unlettered prisoners, and the multiple strategies of accused, accusers, and witnesses, complicate the use of these records. Confessions were not necessarily expressions of true belief, nor were charges and accusations free of other motivations. Often the value of the records lies as much in what they reveal about the mental frameworks of inquisitors and accused as it does in the veracity of a specific charge or the accuracy of a defense. I have not exhausted all the materials of the more than twenty Spanish tribunals and the three Portuguese courts, but I have examined manuscript materials from Seville, Córdoba, Murcia, Toledo, Cuenca, Zaragosa, Valencia, Mexico, Cartagena de Indias, and Lima as well as those from the Portuguese tribunals of Lisbon, Évora, and Coimbra. In addition, I have made use of published documentation, especially the summaries of cases (*relaciones de causa*) from the Balearic Islands, the Canary Islands, Galicia, Granada, and Cartagena de Indias and the published *visitas* (tours) of the Inquisition in Brazil. I have also made use of a growing number of manuscript trials now available online through the efforts of the Archivos Españoles en el Red (AER).

I carried out the research for this book in a number of archives but principally in the national archives of Spain, Mexico, and Portugal, where the majority of Inquisition sources have been gathered. In methodological terms, although I have prepared a database to include those cases in which specific reference to religious relativism or tolerance was made and the results are included here at various points, my approach has not been essentially quantitative. Numbers seemed to me to be an inappropriate way to study dissidence and people whose distinguishing characteristic was inconformity. Instead, what results here is a sort of serial microhistory or a series of what are essentially case studies in which each presents peculiar individual characteristics, and my objective has been to find the patterns and contexts that help to explain the thoughts and actions of the people involved. I have tried to avoid the pitfall of using predetermined socioprofessional categories as a way of explaining cultural differences and perceptions.[11] The cases discussed here are many, but I believe that the richness of their details provides a key to the web of thought and practice that allows us to approach the beliefs of these societies. In the tradition of microhistory these details provide the contexts that allow one to understand individual behavior, but the scope of this book both

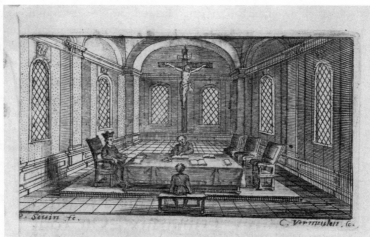

RELATION
DE L'INQUISITION
DE GOA.

CHAPITRE PREMIER.

*Motifs qui ont porté à donner cette Réla-
tion au Public.*

 OUT le monde fçait en
gros ce que c'eſt que
l'Inquiſition, & qu'elle
eſt établie en certains lieux,

A

An audience of the Inquisition.
This scene by Pierre-Paul Sevin, included in Gabriel Dellon's account of his encounter with the Portuguese Inquisition in Goa, conveys the disparity of power between the individual and the institution that frames much of the testimony recorded by those tribunals. Gabriel Dellon, *History of the Inquisition as it is exercised at Goa* (London, 1688). Beinecke Rare Book and Manuscript Library, Yale University.

geographically and chronologically exceeds the usual boundaries of microhistory.[12] Finally, I would emphasize that these cases drawn from Inquisition records are not like medieval exempla, didactic tales created and reported to admonish and instruct, but are, whatever their limitations of being recorded and archived by a powerful ecclesiastical institution, evidence of what people thought, said, and did and, if we read them carefully, a way of recapturing a furtive past.

Since this is a history of attitudes and culture it is not concerned with the institutional structures of religion or with politics per se, although both of those topics arise repeatedly in these pages. My understanding of culture includes attitudes, beliefs, rituals, and material culture, but I am enough of a Geertzian to recognize the importance of symbolic behavior as a crucial aspect of culture and to understand that cultures continually adjust. From Clifford Geertz I have taken the concept of the instability of meanings, and this is helpful in understanding how alternate interpretations of ideas, practices, or symbols might be made by people who considered themselves part of the same religious community. Heresy, we should recall, was always a matter of definition by authority.

I view cultures as being constantly in the process of change and adjustment and able to integrate conflict and difference. I personally have a strong materialist strain in my thinking, but I find myself more attracted to the interpretative strategies of Pierre Bourdieu than to the structuralisms of either Claude Lévi-Strauss or Karl Marx. My interest is in practice and specificity and in human actions within the limits imposed by cultural or economic structures. This book falls into the contested realm of popular culture, a concept whose very existence has been thoroughly and repeatedly analyzed and criticized, but a concept without which it is difficult to speak of the life and beliefs of ordinary people, even if it is difficult to define them or to distinguish their culture in many ways from learned or elite society other than in the specificity of their practices. I have no illusions about the common folk. The societies of Spain, Portugal, and their colonies were intolerant by definition, and I am cognizant that for every person who expressed tolerant ideas there were many ready to correct them or denounce them to authorities. Still, the question remains of how and why among the dissidents there were some who came to challenge conformity and the predominant values of their community on the question of tolerance. On these pages appear relativists, who thought that all religions might have some truth; universalists, who believed that all would be saved; skeptics, who doubted all or some truths; atheists, who denied God or at least divine providence; and people who while considering themselves good Catholics simply did not agree with the position of the Church on salvation outside it. These positions are obviously not all the same, but they did have a common thread in their tendency to promote tolerance of other beliefs and to question dogma. It is tempting to think that many who held these ideas formed a subculture within the Iberian world as a class of persons who were mobile and had traveled, had some access to print culture, and usually came from large towns or cities. But as I hope to demonstrate, there were exceptions to all these characteristics and also many examples of persons with these same social characteristics who remained orthodox in their belief in the exclusive validity of the Church and in their support of the politics of intolerance.

Finally, one of the most interesting questions that arises in the book is the complex relationship between popular and elite culture, or, as it is sometimes framed, between learned and semiliterate or oral culture. I have not assumed that ideas always flowed downward to the masses. The strains of tolerance that lay deep in Christian thought or that grew from a kind of simple common sense need to become part of the history of toleration. In that relationship, people of some education who could read and write and who, with the access to information that printing and cheap books gave them, increasingly de-manded the ability to know and to think for themselves played a crucial role as mediators and as agents. They were often the vectors between and within cultural divisions. They were increasingly critical of the failures and lapses of government and religion, and they often refused to accept the dictates of authority. They were the unwitting godparents of the secular future. The In-quisition was right to fear them.

I have organized the book both chronologically and geographically. Part 1, Iberian Doubts, examines in four chapters the tradition of religious dissidence and the idea of religious relativism in Spain. Chapter 1 examines the theologi-cal and social context for the crime of "propositions." Separate chapters are then devoted to the existence of these ideas, first among the population of converted Jews and Muslims and then among the so-called Old Christians. Finally, a chapter is devoted to expressions of tolerance in Portugal, especially in regard to the persecution of the New Christian converts from Judaism and their descendants. Part 2, American Liberties, examines for the same period of roughly 1500–1700 the development of heterodox and heretical ideas about sexuality and salvation. Two chapters are devoted to Spanish America, where the existence of native American populations raised both theological and practical challenges to Europe's cosmology. Here I demonstrate that universal-ist or relativist ideas were extended to Indians and Africans, in rare instances even producing opposition to the basic institutions of colonial control. I also argue that the integration of Indian ways and practices into a syncretic local culture was facilitated by religious relativism and by the seamless integration of the natural and supernatural worlds and of magic and religion that was part of early modern Europe's cosmology. A final chapter retraces a similar story in Portuguese Brazil, where because of the presence of African slaves, syncretism brought African elements into Brazilian cultural and religious practice. Part 3, Toward Toleration, includes two chapters on the eighteenth century in Iberia and America, respectively, which show how the ancient tradition of religious tolerance and the increasing demand for freedom of conscience became braided with the new philosophical currents of the Enlightenment in favor of religious toleration. The final chapter serves as a conclusion. It demonstrates that relativist ideas were not limited to Iberia but could be found elsewhere in Europe as well, and that in fact, a combination of historical and cultural forces eventually delayed the extension of religious toleration as state policy in Spain and Portugal, although it was achieved in the new nations of Latin America in the nineteenth century. The book closes with a brief reference to the still-debated question of salvation within the Catholic Church in the period since the Second Vatican Council and the continuing struggle of modern societies with the idea and practice of religious tolerance.

PART I

Iberian Doubts

Propositions

In science error is ignorance, but in holy doctrine ignorance is the sin of heresy.   —Pedro de Farfán (1585)

Diego Hurtado made his living as a copyist of books for the Church. He should have known better than to speak openly on sexual matters. In 1580, agents of the Inquisition of Murcia arrested him on charges that he had made statements that smacked of heretical beliefs. In a conversation with neighbors, someone had scolded him for breaking the sixth commandment by living with a woman out of wedlock, *amancebado,* as it was called.[1] Defending himself, Hurtado had said that God's prohibitions of sex referred only to "crimes against nature," that is, homosexuality or bestiality. Even worse, he had said that from what he had heard about the Lutherans and Muslims they had some good ideas about sex. He felt that those non-Christians suffered in no way for their beliefs, and he added, "God asks that each person save himself in his own law." In other words, there was more than one path to salvation.[2]

That Hurtado combined dissident thoughts about the body and the soul, about sexual satisfaction and salvation, is not contradictory or even strange. These ideas about the carnal and the sublime constituted a rationalistic, materialist, and skeptical approach to life which may have grown from a neo-Platonic philosophical heritage or may have reflected a kind of practical, commonsensical wisdom. In any case, they stood against the teachings of the Church and as such were potentially heretical and thus a matter of the Inquisition's interest.

From the Inquisition's prosecution of these ideas one can catch a glimpse of commonly held opinions often at odds with dogma that in their diffusion and repetition seem to have been broadly held. Along with superstition, astrology, and other readings of the supernatural, these ideas are gateways into belief and possibly unbelief, and they reveal the tissue of sureties and doubts that guided life. They were certainly not new. They had existed in Europe in general and in Iberia since medieval times. What they meant and how one should interpret them is a matter of considerable debate.[3]

The Church held that ideas in conflict with the revealed truth of dogma were "propositions" (*proposiciones*), that is, statements which potentially indicated thoughts that were in error in matters of faith and were thus sinful. These ideas placed an individual's soul in danger, but, even worse, their expression might cause others to be scandalized or influenced by them. Heresy lay not necessarily in the doubting of dogma or in statements at variance with the Church's position, but rather in the refusal to accept correction and in the stubborn persistence of error. The theologians who became the basis of authority on the topic realized that not all propositions were necessarily equally bad, and they eventually developed a system of classification which ran the gamut from the clearly heretical to the simply offensive.[4] Among the other types of propositions were those statements that smacked of heresy; others considered to be *temeraria*, that is, they argued positions in matters of faith that were unproven or without authority; the schismatic, those that caused a division within the Church; and others that were simply erroneous, blasphemous, offensive, scandalous, or ill-sounding (*malsonante*) to pious ears.[5] But the theological divisions between these categories were particularly ill-defined, and thus there was always considerable interpretative latitude in determining whether some expression was truly heretical or only offensive. This allowed the Inquisition an open field for its jurisdiction over thought and expression, and because of the insecurity of definition, it invited continual denunciation by people of each other for both serious expressions of disbelief as well as statements made in jest, anger, or desperation. As Juan Antonio Alejandre and María Jesús Torquemada, the two leading Spanish historians on the topic, have put it, "Anyone who risked his own opinion or expressed a discordant one was on the edge of an abyss."[6] That was made clear by the formal prosecution of such ideas by the Holy Office of the Inquisition, which with the support of the state served to correct and to eliminate any deviation from religious orthodoxy. Its great public *autos de fe* accompanied by the full panoply of ecclesiastical and royal authority served as instruments of instruction and theaters of power. And yet, there were still those who from carelessness or conviction spoke out.

The crime of propositions and the closely related offense of blasphemy covered a broad range of speech acts. Literally tens of thousands of persons were prosecuted by ecclesiastical courts and by the Inquisition for such expressions. Since propositions was a poorly defined miscellaneous category, it was always a problematical one. In theory, the Inquisition had jurisdiction only over those matters that implied formal heresy, and its gradual assumption of control and repression of such matters as blasphemy or opinions about various sex acts was contested by civil and episcopal courts. By the sixteenth century, the Inquisition, often with the support of the crown, began to arrogate to itself the role of social disciplining. Because an element of heretical content could be found in any statements or thoughts that contested dogma, even when they were uttered in anger, ignorance, or jest, the Inquisition gradually extended its control over all those who spoke them. It saw speech as the enactment of thought and the release of inner conviction, and it wanted to know the exact statement made and the conditions of its utterance because in its conceptualization, "speech guaranteed the reality of thought."[7]

The propositions themselves can be grouped in essentially four or five categories.[8] Somewhat apart was blasphemy, which was usually treated as a distinct category of offense but was closely related to propositions as an act of speech indicating deviant belief. Criticisms of the Church as an institution or those leveled against its officers and members also fell into the category of propositions. These might include questioning of the pope's authority or of the validity of indulgences or criticism of the moral habits or honesty of individual priests or bishops as well as complaints against the tithe or other aspects of the individual's ties to the Church. The complaints were sometimes expressed as common sayings like, "The friar who collects alms for God, collects for two." Heretical doubts about the sacraments, precepts, or liturgy of the Church and statements about sexual morality which were in conflict with Church dogma caused the greatest number of accusations under the heading of propositions. Finally, there was another category of speech acts that did not fall formally within the definition of propositions but was at times related to them. These were the offenses against the Inquisition, a potpourri of crimes ranging from impersonating officers of the Holy Office and giving false testimony to violating the tribunals' regulations of secrecy. This category also included spoken criticism of the Inquisition's principles, its mission, and its actions. It was not uncommon for people to say, for example, that the Inquisition was unjust, misguided, or moved by avarice rather than religion. Like most institutions in

An auto de fe in Madrid, 1680.

This scene of an auto de fe by Francisco Rizzi (1614–85) with the king and the court in attendance captures the impressive ritual and majesty of these public ceremonies, in which the accused were reconciled to the Church and in which the religious role of various groups in society was represented.

Courtesy of Museo del Prado, Madrid

early modern Spain and Portugal, the Inquisition had the power to censure and prosecute its critics and opponents.

While all of these ideas might be suspect because of their implied deviancy from dogma or their potential defiance of the authority of the Church and the Inquisition, the inquisitors tended to deal differentially with them. Blasphemy was especially common. A bad roll of the dice or deal of cards, a ruinous lack of rain, an affair of the heart gone sour were often enough to provoke it. Sometimes the blasphemy was jocular, contained in crude jokes about the sexual peccadilloes of the Virgin, the saints, or Christ himself. This was humor that displayed not necessarily disbelief but intimacy; it humanized the sacred, but it also represented a certain kind of resistance to doctrinal purity and the dictates of authority; "laughter degraded power."[9] But even sixteenth-century moralists recognized the potential social content of blasphemy, which, as Fray Luis de Granada commented, in the mouths of peasants not only showed disrespect to God, but revealed a discontent with their station in life.[10]

Despite that potential, this was a crime usually prosecuted among the lower classes, and the Inquisition usually took it for what it was: a demonstration of rusticity, coarseness, or ignorance; a practice born of habit, irony, humor, anger, or disappointment. While the theologians laid out the possible heretical content of such statements, the inquisitors usually limited punishments to admonishments, fines, and spiritual penance such as required prayers, confession, or attendance at Mass. In Galicia, for example, over 90 percent of the blasphemers were simply reprimanded and absolved. The inventiveness of expression, the variety of form made blasphemy a popular art. The Italians were famous for their creativity in it, but Spaniards were not far behind. In a way, the blasphemers seemed to have a profound faith, and in the midst of life's disappointments, their inversion of belief was a way of expressing the very depth of their despair or their integration of the divine into all aspects of their life. Blasphemy was perhaps one of the few areas in a world of religious control where an escape to fantasy was possible.[11]

Statements against the Church and its officers also tended to be treated rather lightly in most cases, so long as no real challenge to the Church's authority was implied. It was not uncommon to express doubts that confession to a priest who was living in sin with a woman, who sought sexual contact with his "daughters of confession," or who could be seen drunk in the local tavern was a sacrament of any value. As the historian Jaime Contreras has noted, however, in the period after the Council of Trent (1545–63), when the Church was seeking to dignify itself and its members within society, it sought not only to eliminate the abuses of a libidinous, blasphemous, and sometimes ignorant clergy but at the same time to limit popular criticisms of it.[12] In that regard, punishments of such criticisms were sometimes harsher: public shame, flogging, and stiffer fines.

Among the propositions, the statements about dogma or sexual morality which challenged the Church's teachings received far more serious treatment. It was here that the possibility of heresy seemed to loom and where the greatest efforts were made to punish and reprimand deviant thought. In the cases which came before the various tribunals of the Inquisition almost every point of doctrine and the validity of all the sacraments were questioned at one time or another. Doubts were expressed about the existence of the soul, the validity of baptism, the existence of heaven and hell, the reality of miracles or visions. While there was great variety in these statements, some of the propositions were repeated over and over; among them, doubts about the Eucharist, a denial of the possibility of an afterlife and of a need for confession, and a disbelief in the virginity of Mary. This last proposition was widely expressed and seemed to be particularly common in rural areas. Often it was expressed as a belief that Mary might have conceived as a Virgin, but that she had remained *virgo intacta* after the birth of Jesus was simply more than a rural population with its everyday experience of birth could fathom. Even though such thoughts were considered the result of ignorance, the Inquisition felt the need to take strong measures like sentencing offenders to the galleys in order to eliminate such a statement because "it greatly offends those who hear it and it makes the teachings of the Church as indicated by the Council [of Trent] more difficult."[13]

In the past thirty years, the many studies of the Inquisition in Spain, Portugal, and their empires have revealed certain patterns of activity which changed over time and which varied regionally. In the Castilian tribunals, the period prior to 1570 has been characterized as one of intense preoccupation with heresies, first that of the converted Jews, or Conversos, and then that of the Muslim converts, or Moriscos, and subsequently with the menace of Protestantism and with deviances within the Church. The historian Henry Kamen has argued that after the Council of Trent, by the mid-1560s, the Inquisition had perceptibly shifted its efforts away from Conversos and toward the habits and practices of the Old Christian population as part of the Catholic Reformation. During the century after 1560, about two-thirds of all those prosecuted by the Inquisition were, in fact, Old Christians, "unconnected with formal heresy or with the minority cultures."[14] He points out that in Catalonia between 1578 and 1635 about one-third of all those tried were prosecuted not for what they had done, but for what they had said, essentially for propositions and related offenses. This pattern is born out in other studies. In Galicia, from 1560 to 1600 the crime of propositions made up over 56 percent of all the cases heard by the Santiago tribunal, and even though that figure fell off to 17 percent for the next century, overall from 1560 to 1700 these cases constituted over a third of the tribunal's activities. In the Canary Islands about one out of every three persons tried by the Inquisition was accused of propositions or blasphemy.[15] In Toledo between 1540 and 1700 propositions and blasphemy were, as in Galicia, over one-third of all cases.[16] After 1570 propositions composed an even larger percentage of the total activity.[17] In Toledo, in the first years of the Inquisition (1483–1530), when the Inquisition's primary concern was still Conversos, propositions were involved in only 147 cases of the 2,874 heard, or about 5 percent of the total, but in the next century (1530–1620) there were over 1,500 cases examined, or just under 20 percent of the tribunal's activities. Then between 1621 and 1820 prosecutions dropped off to below the initial levels. By the eighteenth century, as the activity of the Castilian tribunals and the volume of cases declined, propositions and related offenses like blasphemy continued to constitute a significant part of the Inquisitions' business. In Valladolid, for example, they made up over 10 percent of all cases heard.[18] In the tribunals of Aragon, trials for propositions constituted about 23 percent of all cases processed, but the Aragonese tribunals were usually after bigger game, the formal heretics, and in these regions the prosecutions of Moriscos and Protestants preoccupied the inquisitors into the seventeenth century.[19] Portugal was another matter. The same propositions and expressions of doubt were also made in Portugal and its colonies, and people there were occasionally prosecuted for them, but because of the Portuguese tribunals' preoccupation with Judaizers, who overall constituted about 80 percent of all trials, those prosecuted for propositions constituted a smaller proportion than in the Spanish tribunals. It may also be the case that in Portugal these offenses were normally taken up by the ecclesiastical courts or during episcopal visitations rather than by the Inquisition so that there was a division of responsibilities between two branches of the Church's judicial machinery.[20]

I wish to make three observations about these patterns in the prosecution of propositions. First, while undoubtedly the vast majority of the persons prosecuted for this crime were Old Christians, that fact does not imply that these doubts and ideas were held only or even principally by them. The same doubts about the validity of the sacraments, the efficacy of the saints, the reality of apparitions, and various aspects of doctrine or dogma were expressed by Moriscos and Conversos. When a Converso or Morisco said such things, however, the charges almost invariably resulted in accusations of Judaizing or returning to Islam, sins which bore much stiffer penalties than did charges for propositions. The same doubts produced different "crimes" depending not primarily on the content of the statements made, but rather on the ethnicity or religious background of the accused. The Inquisitions' relatively benign treatment of such statements by Old Christians was not matched by any leniency when voiced by persons in the cultural minorities. This was also true when such things were said by foreigners since chances were that in those instances they would be prosecuted not for propositions but for Protestantism.

Second, the timing of the intensification of prosecutions for propositions was clearly tied to the desire to enforce the results of the Council of Trent after 1564, but it also was a response to the challenge of Luther and the rise of Protestantism in Spain.[21] After all, many of the doubts expressed as propositions, such as rejecting the authority of the pope or the validity of the saints, advocating marriage of the clergy or criticizing its abuses, denying the existence of purgatory or the value of indulgences, also formed a part of the Protestant critique of the Church.[22] Inquisitors were not unaware of the implications of these parallels, and they often spent considerable time in discerning if the expression of these ideas had come from the reading of books or discussion about theology or was simply due to ignorance and rusticity. Thus many clerics were accused under the heading of propositions, and their errors were treated more harshly than the expressions of rural folk or unlettered townsmen.

The real Protestant challenge in Spain, however, had been an elite affair for the most part. There had been the wide popularity of Erasmus's writings in Spain in the 1520s, but as criticisms began to appear, so too did the hostility of the Inquisition, and by the mid-1530s Spanish Erasmians were being prosecuted for erroneous theology. So too were Alumbrados, a sect that sought direct spiritual and ecstatic communication with God, sometimes through erotic acts.[23] These movements came to be associated with Lutheranism, partly because of the contacts between the followers of these various lines of thought and partly because they all smacked of heresy as far as the Inquisition was concerned. By the 1540s Lutherans were appearing in the autos de fe, some of them distinguished humanists and theologians like Juan de Valdés.[24] Two cells of Spanish Protestants, one in Seville and another in Valladolid, were crushed in 1559–60, but by far most of those prosecuted were foreigners, not Spaniards.[25] By 1570, the real threat of Protestantism in Spain was mostly gone, and the vast majority of persons subsequently charged as *luteranos* were foreigners, those who had lived abroad and wished to clear their slate with the Inquisition and had thus denounced themselves, or those who had no contact with any formal Protestant denomination but had simply expressed ideas that might be construed as such. Thus the campaign against propositions was a kind of prophylactic against the possibility of contagion, an attempt to choke off the weed before it bloomed into heresy.

Third, it has been argued that the campaign against propositions in the century 1560–1660 was part of the more general attempt to instill Counter-Reformation Catholicism in Spain and that overall it was relatively successful. This phase of Inquisition activity was directed toward the rural population. The major heresies had been a matter of towns and cities, and. at least in Castile, the period after 1560 witnessed a shift to the countryside. The intensity of activity from about 1560 to 1620 represented a program directed primarily toward the majority in this agrarian society, the rural Old Christians. Eventually, the diminution of cases of propositions in the tribunals can be seen as evidence that the orthodoxy desired by the Church was becoming implanted among the faithful. Scholars have differed in their opinions on the effectiveness of this program of instilling Counter-Reformation orthodoxy. Studies of Galicia, Cuenca, and Catalonia have demonstrated that the process was regionally unequal and depended often on the qualities of bishops, the character of the population, and local conditions as much as on the force of doctrine.[26] Then, too, there is always the possibility that what was learned during this campaign was not right thinking, but rather how to keep one's doubts private. During the late eighteenth century, when the winds of the Enlightenment blew through Spain, expressions of the old doubts were often interpreted as the "French infection" and were seen as imported heresies and "free thinking," but the similarity of language used to express them with the statements of the sixteenth century should make us reluctant to ascribe such ideas only to a reading of "Bolter" (François-Marie Arouet Voltaire), as the inquisitors were prone to do.

How these propositions might be related to broader dissident ideas is suggested in the rather strange case of Bartolomé Sánchez heard by the Inquisition of Cuenca in the 1550s.[27] Sánchez was a poor man, a day laborer and wool carder with a large family. He was what might be called today disturbed or unstable, and he eventually came to believe he was a messianic figure, the prophet Elijah. But in his "madness" he also spoke out a series of criticisms and condemnations that were in no way bizarre or uncommon. He had no confidence in priests, especially those who had violated their vows of chastity, and he wished to confide directly in God. He would not pay the tithe, nor would he worship the image of the cross or any other "idols." Sánchez believed that the Inquisition had killed people without cause. As he put it, "With good reason God, and I in His name, will damn you people of the Inquisition to hellfire for murdering and taking people's property in this fashion." Sánchez's theology was confused, and his criticisms of the Inquisition and the Church were sharp. Had he been of Converso stock he would surely have been burned as an apostate backslider, but because he was an Old Christian and it was considered unseemly for Old Christians to suffer such punishments for heresy, the inquisitor in charge of the proceedings was extremely patient and sought to convince Sánchez of his errors. After all, the propositions were common enough; the heresy lay in the stubborn persistence in their credence. For awhile Sánchez seemed to repent, and he was released, but the urge to speak was too great and his delusions reemerged, causing at least some to think he was a Lutheran. Arrested again, he was finally placed in a mental asylum. Mad perhaps, but in his theology was embedded a series of widely held and often stated dissident beliefs that the Counter-Reformation Church had found difficult to suppress and even harder to eliminate.

Sexuality and Thought

Of all the attitudes and beliefs expressed by the propositions, the ones which seemed most difficult to eradicate and most persistent in the face of the Church's campaign to ensure orthodoxy were those related to sexual morality.[28] Whereas in other areas of life and thought ordinary people were willing to cede authority to the "doctors," the learned men, in relations between men and women there was a popular understanding of what was right and wrong, of appropriate behavior, and considerable doubt that the supposedly celibate clergy were better informed on the matter than their parishioners.[29]

From the point of view of the Church, fornication was associated with a variety of other activities that implied immorality and violation of the sixth commandment. Bigamy, adultery, concubinage, and the solicitation of women by priests as well as homosexuality and bestiality were all condemned along with all impure acts and thoughts. The doctrinal emphasis on chastity before marriage, fidelity within marriage, and sexual relations as an obligation between husband and wife which should be directed not toward pleasure but toward procreation encountered a resistant permissiveness among the population which is documented by premarital sex, illegitimacy, acceptance of consensual unions, and prostitution.

Church doctrine on sexual practices both within and outside marriage had developed through considerable debate but had been codified to some extent by St. Thomas Aquinas in the thirteenth century. During the sixteenth century, and especially after the Council of Trent, Aquinas's synthesis enjoyed its greatest authority and became the theological guide on most matters of religion and morality.[30] From a Thomistic perspective, "simple fornication," sex between a man and woman which caused no harm to a third person, as in adultery or bigamy, was against the natural order in that reproduction should be within and limited to the state of marriage in order to educate offspring.[31] Moreover, it was harmful to one's own body to seek pleasure without constraint. Thus simple fornication, while not the worst of sins because it was not directly opposed to God, was nevertheless an aspect of lust (*lujuria*) and thus a mortal sin which excluded the sinner from the Kingdom of God.[32] By the mid–sixteenth century sins of the flesh by deed, word, or thought were considered mortal sins.[33] Unlike Dante, who had expressed a somewhat sympathetic attitude toward the sinners of the flesh, guidebooks on morality like Fray Luis de Granada's popular *Guía de pecadores* (Guide for sinners) ranked their seriousness behind only blasphemy and taking the Lord's name in vain.[34] By the sixteenth century, lust was ascending among the seven deadly sins and increasingly preoccupying priests and theologians.[35] But a residue of earlier practice remained. The pre-Tridentine concept was that marriage depended on the volition of the contracting parties, and thus the common practice of having sexual relations prior to marriage by a priest was widespread in many parts of Europe, including Spain.

The moral and theological campaign against sins of the flesh intensified during the century. The theologians were aware that controlling sexuality was a daunting challenge. As Luis de Granada's *Guide,* following Saint Bernard, stated, "Among the struggles of Christians, the most difficult battles are those of chastity, where the fight is daily and the victories are rare."[36] Despite the popularity of the *Guide,* its lessons were not universally accepted. The Inquisition, by finding the heretical content in the attitudes about sexuality, took over the labor of bringing the message to society with some force.

Autos de fe in Spain and Portugal as well as in the American colonies usually punished sexual sinners — bigamists, fornicators, those living in concubinage, those who held that the state (*estado*) of marriage was better than that of religious celibacy and other propositions which deviated from accepted dogma — as a kind of appetizer to be condemned and punished as a prelude to the more serious main course of executions for formal heresies. Punishments for simple fornicators were usually comparatively mild in comparison with those for formal heretics: public denunciation and embarrassment, the wearing of a *sanbenito* (penitential robe; see fig. opposite) confession, occasionally exile, and in more extreme cases public flogging, usually one hundred lashes, sometimes two hundred. But while fornicators tended to receive lighter punishments over time, in comparison to other propositions the Inquisition was rather harsh with them.

The Inquisition and episcopal courts, however, were concerned not so much with the actions as with the thought behind them. It did not seek to eliminate the act of fornication outside of marriage per se, but rather to inculcate the sense of sin implied by such activity. Thus, most of those prosecuted by it were denounced not for fornication itself, but for making statements that indicated beliefs or attitudes about it which deviated from dogma and contradicted the

Homme conuaincu d'hérésie qui s'est ac
cusé luy même auant que d'être jugé.

P. Sevin fe.   C. Vermeulen fe.

Sanbenitos, or penitential robes, worn by the condemned at an auto de fe. Those convicted
were sometimes sentenced to wear the robes for years thereafter as a mark of shame. The
sanbenitos of those condemned to the stake were later hung in their parish churches to serve as
a blot on the family's honor and a warning against heresy. From Gabriel Dellon, *History of the
Inquisition as it is exercised at Goa* (London, 1688). Beinecke Rare Book and Manuscript
Library, Yale University.

Church's position. The campaign against simple fornication was essentially ideological, directed against thoughts rather than actions. The Inquisition came to fear, and rightly so, that freethinking about sex might be linked to other heterodox attitudes or to heresies. A general order of the Inquisition in 1573 instructed local tribunals to treat as heretics those who believed that simple fornication was not a mortal sin, as it arrogated to itself jurisdiction over an area that had not traditionally been under its control.[37]

Studies to date of those prosecuted for propositions, especially fornication, have revealed that these ideas were not regional but were widely held across the Iberian world.[38] Those prosecuted were overwhelmingly males, mostly young single men, many of whom were transients, and in some tribunals many of them soldiers or mariners.[39] Such groups, along with peasants and artisans, were the most likely to be prosecuted for these ideas. Because many of the accused were rural people with little education, some inquisitors proceeded with leniency, arguing that the offending attitudes were due to ignorance rather than to a tendency toward heresy.[40] In fact, claims of ignorance and drunkenness were the best defenses thrown up by those accused, and surely this was a well-known fact.

Like the attack on propositions in general, prosecution for simple fornication by the Inquisition did not begin in earnest until the mid–sixteenth century, although there were occasional prosecutions, including a few in New Spain by ecclesiastical authorities in the 1530s.[41] People holding ideas on sex not approved by the Church became a regular feature of autos de fe in the second half of the sixteenth century throughout the Hispanic world. In Toledo, for example, between 1566 and 1591 such prosecutions ran between 15 and 34 percent of all cases, with 406 people accused.[42] In Lima, prosecutions for propositions were over a third (37 percent) of all cases heard before 1600.[43] Inquisitorial actions against such propositions intensified after the publication of a ruling in 1573–74 which identified deviant ideas about simple fornication with heresy and suggested that this opinion about fornication might be associated with Illuminism or Lutheranism because of the belief of those sects that carnality was not so great a sin.[44] The timing of this intensification of prosecution, therefore, coincided with the creation of the American tribunals of Lima and Mexico in the 1570s, so that the earliest American autos de fe usually included those prosecuted for simple fornication.

The most effective way to examine attitudes toward this most popular activity is to cite instances in which these sentiments were expressed or defended. Discussion of the fine points of many aspects of dogma was probably not common, but on the "matters of men and women" everyone had an opinion. The discussions took place "in the vineyard," "while harvesting the wheat,"

The conversation of common folk.
In such situations the discussion of life, death, sex, and salvation elicited opinions and sometimes denunciations. Diego Velázquez, "The Luncheon." Courtesy of the Museum L'Her-
mitage (St. Petersburg, Russia).

"at the fountain," "at the tavern," "on the road to Vera Cruz." The discussions
were not gender bound. Men and women testified against both sexes, indicating that the discussions were part of everyday interactions and conversations.
The phrase "Speaking of the things of men and women" appears continually in
the trials, testimony that it was a topic of constant concern and discussion.

Defendants of simple fornication took one of two positions. Some accepted
that it was, in fact, a sin but a lesser or not very serious one. They stated, like
Pedro Navarro of Granada, that "a man having carnal relations with a woman

was not a mortal sin, and it was [bad] enough to be venial because men have to go with women and women with men." Others took the more absolute position that it was no sin at all. Despite the teachings of the Church, many people could not believe that sex was a sin for which they would go to hell, and many men responded to criticism of their behavior with such defenses as a man who does not have sex is a faggot (*mariconazo*) or is not a good Christian.[45] There was also the widely held opinion and popular refrain that "the man who does not screw in this life, will be screwed by the Devil in the next one," or, in some variants, "screwed by the Devil with a horn in the next one."[46]

Others defended the more stable unmarried relationships. Juan de Torres of Murcia was eighty-four years old when he told his neighbors that the twenty years he had been *amancebado* were the best in his life, and in the face of their criticism he then denied it had been a sin. Inés Martín, in her forties and living with a man outside of marriage, had told her neighbors that "she also served God being *amancebada* just like the married women," equating the state of concubinage with that of marriage.[47] It was also apparently commonly held that cohabitation may have been a sin, but it was not a mortal sin unless the relationship lasted seven years. These statements constituted a popular critique of the Church's emphasis on monogamous, permanent unions as the only context for sexual activity. Generally, there was a feeling that the flesh was weak, that "men were made for women and women for men," that young men going to a brothel was "nothing to get excited about," and that God was very inclined to pardon the sins of the flesh.[48]

Popular Attitudes and Church Response

I have concentrated on the proposition of simple fornication for a number of reasons. First, in the sometimes Rabelaisian discourse of the accused one gets from these cases a sense of the practical rationality of common folk in the face of theology. As the historian Ricardo García Cárcel has stated, "The picturesque nature of their statements does not contradict a certain maturity in their thought."[49] Second, studies of propositions and of simple fornication have emphasized that the Inquisition's prosecution of this crime began in the mid–sixteenth century and crested before 1600. After that date, prosecutions in Spain, Portugal, and their American colonies were relatively few. This pattern might support the belief that the Church's campaign in conveying the message of Trent in this regard and in others had been relatively successful and that the populations of the Luso-Hispanic world had been successfully converted into conforming believers.[50] It is true that the campaign had some effect. The trials are filled with references to people who were admonished to hold their tongue by neighbors who warned them of their error and said that for such things people were burned or punished by the Inquisition. If it was not a mortal sin, his companions told Alonso de Cigales, an illiterate tailor in Toledo, why had they "brought people out onto the platform [*tablado*]?" in a reference to the autos de fe.[51] But it may be just as likely that people were learning discretion rather than proper thinking.[52]

Whereas the other propositions as speech acts left few traces that can be used to test the effect of the Church's attempt to instill orthodoxy, attitudes toward sexual practice can be measured in other ways. Considering sexuality along with other heterodox or heretical ideas allows us to approach a seeming epistemological dead end. One would like to know whether the diminution or disappearance of prosecutions for propositions, especially the idea of the possible validity of all faiths, represented a triumph of orthodoxy and an accomplishment of the Inquisition's program, or if it was simply a reflection of the Inquisition's slowing activity, a measure of change in emphasis and concerns, or perhaps even evidence of a growing caution on the part of the populace. The ideas on simple fornication present a parallel proposition, but one which often produced acts that left a human residue that allows us to measure the level of the Inquisition's activity against practice. The campaign against simple fornication chronologically paralleled the attack on all propositions, but there is little evidence that fornication outside of wedlock decreased in Spain.[53] In fact, rates of illegitimacy in early modern Spain ran between 3 and 7 percent of baptisms, although in cities like Valladolid they were as high as 20 percent, and as the age at marriage rose over time, so too did the rate of illegitimacy. These levels were higher than in Western Europe as a rule.[54] Even more significant, rates of illegitimacy in the Spanish colonies in the Americas were of a different order all together, often doubling the levels of Spain, and that was as true of the eighteenth century, after the Inquisition had been established, as it was of the sixteenth century before it was implanted in the New World. Of course, the Inquisition was not trying to eliminate fornication. It was much too practical to attempt that. Its objective was to make sure that the faithful knew it was a sin. The illegitimacy statistics, of course, can tell us about practice, but not about how people felt about what they were doing. Still, if post-Tridentine orthodoxy was being imposed, one would expect at least some reflection in practice as well. While fornication and toleration were two quite distinct activities, the evidence for the continual practice of fornication should at least make us wary of interpreting the sketchy documentary record of toleration as evidence of absence rather than absence of evidence or as proof of orthodox belief. Finally, what the inquisitorial inquests reveal is that the dissident attitudes about toleration and fornication often went hand in hand, and that people arrested for the propositions about sex often revealed under questioning a variety of other doubts about dogma.

How widely held were the attitudes expressed in the propositions and in what segments of the population? Here the Inquisition prosecutions are not necessarily an accurate guide. Some scholars have emphasized that these attitudes were held mostly by men of the lower class, ignorant or uninformed artisans, muleteers, laborers, and especially soldiers and seamen. Prosecution of men of the mercantile class or of hidalgos for simple fornication was extremely rare, but this did not mean that they were not fornicating or holding such views, only that they were rarely denounced or clever enough to avoid claiming that their actions were without sin.[55]

Those accused were usually artisans, rural laborers, and people of the lower classes, *la gente vil*. Rather than evidence of ignorance or rusticity, however, the discourse of those who defended simple fornication often displayed not only common sense, but also sometimes an acquaintance with, and at times a subtle understanding of, dogma and the hierarchy of sin. Numerous cases exist in which the defense of fornication was made with reference to the biblical injunction to multiply. In fact, a rather tired but often repeated joke appears across Spain as a cause for denunciation. Christ and Saint Peter or Christ and Pontius Pilate come to a bordello, and Christ goes in. After a while, his companion gets impatient and calls for him. "Wait a minute, I'm multiplying the world," Christ replies. Defenses of those accused of simple fornication based on the admonition to "cresite et multiplicamini terram" were common.

While it is true that constant denunciations indicate that many people accepted the Church's position on this issue, the sociology of accusations indicates complex patterns that reflect factors other than a conflict between popular acceptance or rejection of the idea of simple fornication as a mortal sin. Many of those denounced were transients, men not native to the place of their denunciation, unprotected by ties of dependency and reciprocity, and subject to close scrutiny by local society. Women were accused of these attitudes far less frequently, but not necessarily because they did not hold them. First of all, considered inferior, irresponsible, or as minors, women were prosecuted far less by the Inquisition not only for sexually related sins, but for all crimes (except for witchcraft or as false visionaries). Thus there is no reason to believe that lower numbers of accused females indicate that these were only male attitudes.[56]

Salvation: From Body to Soul

If the defense of simple fornication was among the most frequently prosecuted proposition against dogma, the idea that salvation was possible outside the Church was far less frequently made. The doctrinal error in defense of sexuality between consenting persons who were not constrained by the sacrament of marriage or by other impediments remained unclear in the minds of many people, even some clergy. Salvation was another matter altogether. Since the ninth century representations of the Final Judgment, the weighing of souls by the Archangel St. Michael, and the possibility of individual salvation through Christ had been a central theme of Christian art. Even the simplest parishioner understood that questioning this constituted a challenge to the Church's exclusive claim to validity. But as with ideas about fornication, the Church's position had changed over time, and the long debates of the early Church and through the Middle Ages had perhaps left some residue of doubt in common thinking about the issue.

The constant repetition of the refrain "Each person can be saved in his or her own law," the phrase Diego Hurtado had used, appears at first glance to be a commonsense interpretation and popular understanding of the diversity of belief in the world. The question had been, in fact, a central issue at the heart of early Christianity and one which Church theologians had struggled with mightily throughout the Middle Ages.[57] If God was an omnipotent force through whose grace humankind, no matter how sinful, could be redeemed, then how could the concept of salvation exclusively through the Church be reconciled with God's omnipotence? Could not an all-powerful divinity save whomsoever he chose? If, on the other hand, salvation could come only through Christ and his Church, then God had willfully condemned many good souls to eternal damnation. What about children who died before baptism, or the admirable men and women of antiquity, or those in faraway lands who had never heard of Christ? Christians were sometimes challenged to explain why God had waited for so long before sending his Son, thus condemning so many generations to eternal damnation? Why would God create so many people outside the Church? And, perhaps most troubling of all, why would a just God condemn to perdition persons who lived a good and righteous life according to the natural law that God had given all humankind even though they lived outside of the Church? As one convert to Christianity in Spain had put it, "God had failed in his office and if he wanted all to be Christians, he should have created them as such."

The Old and New Testaments were not clear on the question. There were those figures like Abel, Noah, Daniel, and Job who had lived before or outside the covenant with Abraham who had been just and whose lives had been pleasing to God. The righteousness of Noah and the patience of Job also figure in New Testament allusions as prefiguring the life of Christ. St. Paul's condemnation of the sins of the pagans in Romans 2:13–16 still left the possibility that

The imperative of salvation.

The themes of salvation and the inevitability of final judgment were constantly repeated and represented in popular books of devotion and in great compositions in the churches, in this case in a *retablo* from the Carthusian monastery of Portacoelli, Serra (Valencia), dated between 1470 and 1490. San Miguel selects those who will be saved while the devils overlook the multitude of the condemned. Courtesy of Museu de Belles Arts de Valencia.

those who lived by natural law could receive God's grace. The issue of salvation preoccupied the early Church fathers.[58] Drawing on the New Testament's universalism and elements such as Matthew's gospel, which emphasized the "expectation of the nations," but also recognizing St. Paul's emphasis that salvation was available to all through Christ, the lines of debate and disagreement on the issue were clear. As early as the second century, the Christian thinker St. Justin Martyr had argued for the possibility of salvation for those who lived before or outside the Church, if they had lived by reason (*logos*) or by natural law, which Christ and the Church had later come to represent. Such people were, in effect, Christians in essence, if not in practice, and thus could be considered within the Church as a concept rather than an institution and capable of salvation through it. This was a theme that later theologians would develop within the distinction of being part of the Church *in re,* in fact, or *in voto,* in desire, as expressed by intention and behavior. A number of the early fathers of the Church made similar statements. But there was also a counter and more restrictive position expressed, for example, by St. Cyprian, the third-century martyred bishop of Carthage. Cyprian had argued that "since there is only one house of God . . . there can be no salvation for anyone except in the Church." Not even martyrdom could save those who had separated themselves from the Church. Francis A. Sullivan, a modern Jesuit writer on this subject, has pointed out that many of the early statements on this problem were really directed toward Christian schismatics rather than at convincing or explaining the position of pagans or Jews, and that the earlier, more inclusive position was replaced by a more rigid theological stance after Christianity became the official religion of the state during the fourth century.[59] Once Christianity had become an official state religion, it was assumed that all could know its message and thus those who had remained outside the Church were not uninformed or ignorant, but stubborn and recalcitrant. Christ had died for them, too, he had done his part of the bargain, but by continuing to remain outside the Church they had rejected his sacrifice. Authors like St. Ambrose and even more so St. John Chrysostom took particularly strong positions against those who had turned a deaf ear to the truth as they saw it. For them, Jews and pagans were responsible for their own ignorance and error and thus their lack of salvation.

As in so many matters of dogma, it was St. Augustine who both codified existing thought and honed the position of the Church by his analysis. While he accepted the notion that some singular individuals who lived before Christ's message might find salvation, he also agreed that thereafter only through the Church could there be salvation. Augustine also held that those peoples who had not heard the true doctrine were ignorant of it because God had foreseen that they would reject the truth even if they heard it.[60] For Augustine and those later interpreters who followed him closely, the watchword became *extra ecclesiam nulla salus,* no salvation outside the Church, a formula that is not found in the New Testament, but that became an essential concept of Catholic belief.[61]

Augustine's position held that salvation was obtained by God's grace and thus given by God rather than deserved by people's efforts or actions. Salvation was not a prize to be won by actions, but a benefit bestowed by an omnipotent deity. Much of what Augustine wrote on this topic was directed against Pelagius, a teacher and ascetic who had settled in Rome in the late fourth century.[62] He and his followers took the position that the essential nature of humankind was good. It was given a choice by God to do good or evil, and people through their good works alone could merit salvation.[63] This position threw the issue of divine grace into question, and it raised a controversy over original sin, the condemnation of unbaptized infants, and a number of other matters of central theological importance. Pelagius and his followers were eventually denounced as heretics, and in the struggle against his ideas Augustine deepened his arguments about divine grace and about predestination and free will.[64] His position became the "official" position of the Church, but in truth, certain problems and inconsistencies remained unresolved. If grace alone was necessary for salvation, what was the role of the Church? One could imagine that God's salvific power could save anyone.[65] Various and sometimes contradictory attempts were made to explain Augustine's position. Moreover, the older tendency to recognize the validity of those who lived by natural law or who might, in Pelagian fashion, earn salvation had never really disappeared, either among theologians or in popular understandings of this point of doctrine. Traces of its emphasis on good works and human agency in the process of salvation are apparent among many of those accused by the Hispanic Inquisitions. These people rarely referred to the medieval theological debates on the issue, and so one is left to wonder about the influence of learned disputes on popular thought.

Pope Boniface VIII's bull *Unam Sanctam* (1302) emphasized the unity of the faith and the impossibility of salvation or the remission of sins outside the Church, which it compared to Noah's ark as a ship that had had only one pilot. Thus it should be in matters of the soul. The Church's position solidified in the thirteenth and fourteenth centuries. It was encapsulated in a decree of the Council of Florence (1442) which made it clear that pagans, Jews, heretics, and schismatics were all destined to burn eternally in hell. Since the churchmen at the council believed that God is just, this result could only be viewed as the fault of those condemned. Their separation from or rejection of the truth was the cause of their culpability. Good deeds, charity, and even martyrdom as steps toward salvation were of no use to those outside the body of the Church. This was the position that represented the orthodoxy defended by the Inquisition, but it was also a position that in fifty years would be directly challenged by the discovery and existence of the myriad peoples of the New World, whose culpability for their ignorance of the Church seemed dubious to many theologians and jurists, some of whom, like Juan de Palacios Rubios, would argue that the newly encountered peoples who lived according to natural law might be saved through the gospel even before they came to know it.[66] In any case, the European discovery of the New World raised a new dimension of concern for the theology of salvation and a challenge to the religious and moral understandings of the world.

The question of salvation and the related topic of justification, the forgiveness of sin and acceptance into communion with Christ made possible through his sacrifice became, of course, central issues for Martin Luther, John Calvin, and the other Protestant Reformers. Their strict adherence to the doctrine of grace left little role for the Church as a mediator and none whatsoever for such concepts as papal indulgences.[67] Catholic commentators like Juan de Valdés and Fray Luis de León sought to reconcile the idea of salvation by grace with the idea of free will, which disposed an individual toward receiving that grace. Among Spanish theologians the "controversy of Auxiliis" burned in the period 1580–1607 in a series of heated confrontations which often pitted Dominicans and Jesuits against each other, the latter being accused as Pelagians and the former as Lutherans. Only in 1607 with a papal order prohibiting these discussions were passions cooled for a while.

These debates within and between Christian confessional communities of Europe over the central truths of Christian doctrine had a distinct tenor within Iberia, with its multireligious traditions. The question of salvation and of its possibility of achievement through natural law or through merit was complicated by the long association with people of other faiths. The theologian Alonso Fernández de Madrigal, known as "El Tostado," had tried to explain that Jews and gentiles could be saved or at least go to purgatory prior to the spreading of the gospel, the Jews in their law and the gentiles through natural law; but after that time, Muslims, Jews, and gentiles all went to hell because they died in original sin.[68] Within Spain and Portugal, the overseas discoveries of the late fifteenth and early sixteenth centuries refocused the question and challenged theologians to explain God's design for the non-Christian peoples of the world, not only the Jews and Muslims, for whom a considerable theological corpus already existed, but for societies and civilizations like China, only barely known, or those of the Americas, completely new.

The challenge of soteriology was taken up principally at the University of

Salamanca in the mid–sixteenth century by Dominican theologians, particularly Francisco de Vitoria, Melchor Cano, and Domingo de Soto, all of whom grappled with the implications of the existence of whole continents filled with people who knew nothing of Christianity and were inculpable therefore. De Soto in particular had, by the time of his publication of *De natura et gratia* (1549), come to the belief that if the peoples of the Americas had not been brought to the true faith, it was not through any inherent fault, and that those who had lived prior to the arrival of Christians could, like the gentiles who had lived before Christ, come to an implicit faith in Christ which would be enough for their salvation. These ideas were put into practice by Bartolomé de Las Casas, another Dominican trained in the Salamanca tradition, for whom the defense of Indian rights and Indian humanity and thus their potential for salvation within the Christian community were paramount.[69]

The Dominicans of the Salamanca school had opened a channel that sought to reconcile the conflicts in the strict Augustinian position of no salvation outside the Church with the idea of a merciful and just God. The growing concept of "invincible ignorance," that those who knew no better might still be saved by an implicit faith in God, which also implied a desire for baptism and thus membership in the Church, left open considerable possibilities of inclusion. The Flemish theologian Albert Pighi (1490–1542) even went so far as to include the Muslims. God did not condemn them since "erroneous faith does not condemn, provided the error has a reasonable excuse and that they are invincibly ignorant of the true faith." This was a line of thought that Jesuit theologians and missionaries would explore in the following centuries. The great missionary to Japan Francis Xavier (1506–52); Francisco Suárez (1548–1619), a Spaniard who taught in Portugal and Italy; and the Spaniard Juan de Lugo (1583–1660), who became a cardinal, moved in varying degrees toward a position that an individual could be led to God by God's grace or by the observation of natural law and thus implicitly to baptism and through the Church to salvation. De Lugo's writings especially seemed to run against the old teachings of the Council of Florence because he went to the extreme of believing that even Muslims and Jews and heretics might be saved through a sincere faith in God and contrition for their sins and might be saved even in their own religion.[70]

Of course, this liberal interpretation confronted considerable theological opposition. Fray Alfonso de Castro, a theologian who served as confessor to Charles V and Philip II and a man who honed his attack on heresy during the repression of Protestants in Flanders, included the statement that salvation was possible outside the Church in his list of four hundred major heresies, the *Adversus omnes haereses* (Paris, 1534). This work was popular and by 1590 had gone through ten editions in Spain, France, Italy, and Flanders.[71] The issue remained unsettled however. The controversy over the possibility of salvation outside the Church and, even more so, over humans' possible role in their own salvation later lay at the heart of Jansenist reaction in the seventeenth century and their conflict with the Jesuits. Adhering to a strict Augustinian interpretation, the French Jansenists accused the Jesuits of being semi-Pelagians, and they denied any possibility that those who lacked an explicit faith in Christ or who had never been enlightened by the gospel might be saved.[72] Although the controversy was mediated by the papacy, the debates extended well into the eighteenth century, and echoes of them sometimes appeared in the trial records of the Inquisition. The Sevillian Franciscan Francisco Martínez told his colleagues in 1604 that "any infidel negative or contrary to the faith, like the Moor or the Japanese, keeping natural law can be saved, only needing to say to God, 'Lord, if I knew a better way or Law I would follow it.'"[73] Those echoes, however, were usually limited to clerics who had undoubtedly been exposed to the debates on salvation in their reading or discussions of theology. It is much more difficult to establish an archaeology of thought for laypersons, many of whom were illiterate or had only a rudimentary use of reading, or to determine the origins of the propositions they held. Juan Domínguez, a silk weaver from Seville, stated simply in 1630 that there was no hell and that if there was, only the soul of Cain was there and probably not even that of Judas, and he knew this from the Holy Scriptures.[74] Occasionally, there appeared a case like that of Stefano Mendache di Alcamo, who in 1575 stated to the Inquisition of Sicily that "a Moor or Turk if living well in his own sect or law, his soul will not go to hell but only to limbo." When questioned about the origins of this idea, he told the inquisitors he had read it in the poet Dante.[75] Mendache had read and understood. In the *Divine Comedy*, although Dante is orthodox enough to assign the pagan philosophers to hell, his preoccupation with the guiltless infidel who is perpetually condemned is apparent, and the poet could offer no satisfactory explanation for the condemnation. In canto 19 of *Paradise* Dante framed the dilemma that Christian Europe was to face repeatedly in succeeding centuries:

> Here's a man . . . born of some breed
> On Indus' bank, where there is none to tell
> Of Christ, and none to write, and none to read;
> He lives, so far as we can see, quite well,
> Rightly disposed, in conduct not amiss,
> Blameless in word and deed; yet infidel
> And unbaptized he dies; come tell me this:
> Where is the justice that condemns the man
> For unbelief? What fault is it of his?

Dante recognized that some outside the Church must have deserved God's favor, and so he placed at the very gate of purgatory a few righteous gentiles like the Roman Cato. But the citation of Dante's fourteenth-century epic as a source for understanding this dilemma in the late sixteenth century reveals that the question continued unresolved.[76] Still, there was a current of relativist thought that could be found in various places. Menocchio, the Friulian miller, had told his inquisitors in the 1580s that the righteous of all religions would be saved. He revealed that he had read about this in the famous parable of the three rings included in an uncensored edition of Giovanni Boccaccio's *Decameron*. The story of the three rings made by a father for his three sons so that they were indistinguishable from each other was a parable on the three monotheistic religions, implying that only God, the Father, really knew which was true. The story had circulated widely in medieval Italy and was included in the *Novellino*, a late thirteenth-century collection of short stories, the first of its kind composed in Italy. This was an idea not limited to Iberia, and one that had deep medieval roots.[77]

For many people, however, it was not reading but common sense that generated their ideas on this topic, and these were widely diffused and often repeated despite their heretical implications. An early inquisitorial record from the Canary Islands revealed a number of people who believed that "each person could be saved in his or her own law" or that "all those who do good go to paradise" or even that "there are two Holy Houses, one in Mecca and the other in Jerusalem."[78] For the most part, the proposition that salvation might be possible outside the Church, which implied a fundamental tolerance, like the idea that sex between consenting partners was not a mortal sin, seemed to originate as much from practical experience and observation as from theology. The fact that, in general, many heretical propositions were often held simultaneously by the same individuals and that these two specific propositions about soul and flesh were often found together suggests attitudes of skepticism in the face of authority. The peculiar context of Iberia's multicultural heritage created opportunities for interaction and observation and for the existence of dissident ideas. At the same time, the presence of a religious mechanism like the Inquisition, designed to suppress doctrinal error, allows one to recapture the voicing of this dissidence and to move from learned theology to popular practice.

Whatever the origins of such dissident thinking or the theological disputes on the issue, by the fifteenth century the position that there was no salvation outside of the Roman Church was a matter of dogma easily formulated in regard to Jews, Muslims, and pagans and perhaps less so with Eastern Christians. With the challenge of the Reformation in the sixteenth century and the political ramifications it implied, the question took on a new importance. In

Iberia, as in most of Western Europe, the question of freedom of conscience and religious diversity always had political implications. Enforcing religious unity seemed to run counter to the Church's advocacy of freedom of conscience, but there were strong doctrinal and practical reasons that made intolerance a policy supported by Church and crown. The theological position of the Church on its exclusive validity enforced by the Inquisition was supported by political theorists, who found religious unity the best security for the integrity and peace of the realm. Alternative religions seemed to promote dissent and discord and although elsewhere in Europe there were always some authors and courtiers, the so-called politiques, who argued that compromise was the best solution to religious difference and that loyalty did not necessarily grow from religious unity, in Spain and Portugal such thinkers had little effect. Instead, men like Diego Saavedra Fajardo, the most influential political theorist of his day, argued that internal peace was impossible without unity of religion.[79] The Church and the crown used their full powers to enforce this policy, but many people remained doubtful and unconvinced, and some were willing to risk an alternate view of salvation and society.

Conversos and Moriscos

I have kept the Holy Law of Moses. I have kept the law of Jesus Christ, and if right now Saint Muhammad appeared, by God! I would keep all three; and if all were to end tomorrow, I would not fear God because I had walked in all three laws.

— Simón de Santa Clara (Calatayud, 1489)

All men are entitled to redemption, each in virtue of his own religion — Jew, Muslim, and Christian are entitled to eternal happiness because all three religions have political aims the source of which lies in Natural Law.

— Juan del Prado (Alcalá, c. 1635)

Beginning with the Arab conquest of Iberia in the eighth century and continuing through the Middle Ages, the three monotheistic religions of Judaism, Islam, and Christianity survived side by side. To speak of them only as religions, however, is to miss the essential ways in which they really represented the ways of life of three communities in all the complexity of their legal, political, and social practices.[1] Over the centuries, Christian populations had sometimes come under the rule of Muslim lords, Christian princes often ruled Muslim subjects, and, depending on the place, Jews lived as subjects of both Christian and Muslim rulers. Through the recognition of communal rights, a modus vivendi was usually worked out between rulers and their multiethnic subjects, usually because it made good political and economic sense to do so. Considerable cultural interchange took place as Christian scholars gained access to classical authors through Arabic texts on everything from medicine to astrology. Linguistically, as a result of the continuing contact, the Latin-based languages of the peninsula added an enormous number of Arabic words; Muslims and Jews adopted the Romance languages, the Muslims eventually developing a separate version, *aljamiado,* as their speech of everyday. But, lest one take too rosy a view of this contact, interaction between the communities was often restricted and constrained, and laws prohibiting marriages, sexual contacts, and conversion (to the politically subject religions) or imposing distinctive clothing or taxes were used to mark the separation between groups.

This coexistence, then, was often conflictual, and the intensity of conflict and of cooperation varied greatly over time and space, but the continuing relationship between the three cultures gave a somewhat distinctive character to the nature of social, cultural, and political development in Spain and Portugal. This distinctive situation has sometimes been called *convivencia,* and it has become an issue of heated controversy among students of the culture and history of Spain. Half a century ago, this great debate raged between two erudite Spanish scholars, both of them exiles from Francisco Franco's Spain, and it continued among the schools that had formed around them. Claudio Sánchez-Albornoz, a medievalist and basically a historian of institutions, from his exile in Argentina took the position that the Spanish character was eternal and was forged in the political and cultural conflict of Catholic Spain with its traditional opponents, the Muslims and Jews. Américo Castro, a literary scholar, from his base at Princeton University, found in the dynamic interrelationship of the three castes, as he called them, the origins of modern Spanish culture.[2] The influence of both the Arabs and the Jews was everywhere in Spain. Castro went so far as to argue that even such traits as the concern with purity of blood (*limpieza de sangre*) and the Inquisition itself were elements of Jewish culture that Christian Spain had adopted.[3] The two views were in many ways diametrically opposed, but they were also similar in that they shared a tendency to essentialize Muslim and Jewish cultures and to overlook or minimize the effects of class and economic considerations on the relations between the groups.[4]

Whatever the differences between these two schools of thought, together they made the coexistence or conflict of the three cultures in the peninsula the central theme of the Iberian Middle Ages. Subsequently, some scholars have tended to see this period of coexistence as a golden age of cultural exchange and relative harmony which progressively broke down in the fourteenth and fifteenth centuries. The final acts in the story were the fall of Granada, the last Muslim kingdom, in 1492 and the expulsion or required conversion of the Jews in the same year. This movement toward political and religious unification was first supported by a policy of proselytization and conversion which preceded and followed 1492 and by a program of increasing discrimination, repression, and mistrust of Jewish and Muslim converts to Christianity. In Castile, Mudejares (Muslims living under Christian rule) were required to convert or leave in 1502. Once converted, they were considered Moriscos, that is, formerly Muslim Christians. Increasing limitations were placed on their dress, language, and customs. In the 1520s many Muslims in Valencia were forcibly baptized during the local popular uprisings, or *Germanías* ("brotherhoods," applied to those who rose against Charles V), that threw the countryside and towns into turmoil, and in 1526 conversion of Muslims to Christianity was required in Aragon. For a couple of decades the Inquisition proceeded slowly against the recent converts, but by the 1550s pressures were building to enforce Christian orthodoxy among the Morisco population. Harsh measures and civil as well as religious pressures then provoked Morisco resistance to these cultural, religious, and political impositions, resulting in a number of uprisings, especially in the mountains of Granada between 1568 and 1570. When the war of the Alpujarras, as it was called, ended, the Morisco population was removed from Granada and distributed to towns and cities across Castile. There, the rebels, many of whom had sought to maintain their Islamic traditions, now joined the old and somewhat more acculturated Castilian Moriscos. The alleged Morisco problem continued to preoccupy the Church while the crown cast a wary eye on the Morisco prophetic tradition, which looked to deliverance by a Moorish king. The more immediate threat came, however, from Barbary corsairs who raided the Spanish coast, and there was always the possibility that the Moriscos might become an internal enemy should the Ottomans attack Spain.[5] There were even fears that the Moriscos might make alliance with the Huguenots of France against their common enemy, Catholic Spain. Reformers like the Valencian bishop Juan de Ribera began to see them as incapable of assimilation.[6] Plans to expel the Moriscos had been discussed as early as 1582, but various interests, including municipal governments that would be financially harmed by their departure as well as powerful landowning aristocrats in Valencia who depended on a Morisco peasantry, had pleaded their case at court. Finally, in 1609, Philip III ordered their expulsion, and while many remained after that date embedded within the Christian population, estimates place the figure that departed from Spain for North Africa, Turkey, France, and other destinations at over three hundred thousand.[7] After 1492, those who had converted or who had been forcibly baptized were subject to the authority of the Inquisition. Between 1560 and 1615, some ninety-three hundred Moriscos were arrested by the various tribunals, and the prosecutions for Islamic practices and customs continued into the eighteenth century.[8]

Many historians have found in this story a sad tale of intolerance in which, through the expelling of some of Spain's and Portugal's most industrious inhabitants, the conditions of those countries' later decline were created. Other historians, usually of a more conservative persuasion, have viewed the creation of religious homogeneity and political unity in Spain and Portugal as essential to their survival and as a key factor in Portugal's success in the sixteenth century and Spain's to the end of the seventeenth century.[9]

Although historians of Christian Spain and Portugal in the sixteenth century were already creating an image of the previous centuries as a crusade against Islam, in fact, there had been long periods of peaceful, if not friendly, relations. Political and commercial relations were maintained between Christian and Muslim states, and within both there were resident populations of other faiths. Islamic law recognized the existence of *dhimmis,* religious minorities who believed in one of the monotheistic religions that the Koran recognized as legitimate revelations of God's word. These peoples, in return for a special tax, were allowed religious freedom and a certain amount of autonomy. Christian kingdoms often extended such protections and rights through charters and agreements made with conquered Muslim populations. These *capitulaciones* specifically recognized the continuity of the customs, religion, and laws of the new subject populations, and the references to the "law" of Mudejares was a recognition of their beliefs and practices.[10] Jews in Christian states also came directly under the protection of the ruler. They too had a distinct law, or way of life and belief. As Queen Isabella of Castile stated in 1477, "All the Jews of my kingdoms are mine and are under my protection and shelter, and it is my responsibility to protect, shelter, and maintain them in justice."[11] But what the ruler could grant, the ruler could also limit or take away, and being the monarchs' protected wards also made Jews and Muslims targets in struggles between royal power, noble factions, and local communities. As the historian Mark Meyerson has noted, the toleration of religious minorities was contractual and institutional and it by no means guaranteed the "harmonious intermingling of religious groups."[12]

One need not romanticize the relationship of the three Laws and their followers to accept their impact on each other, not only through books but through daily contact. This was especially true in religious matters, in which everyone knew and often discussed what was preached in the synagogues, churches, and mosques and in which trilingualism paralleled the existence of the three religions. Moreover, the theologians of the three faiths knew of the writings of their counterparts and sometimes even sought to translate or incorporate them. There was what the Spanish historian of theology Melquiades Andrés Martín has called "the interchange of a triple and difficult religious contrast," and the possibility of spiritual influences between the three faiths was always real.[13] Contact had been a reality of medieval life but so had conflict. The animosity and distrust generated by and during open hostilities did not disappear when the fighting was over. Contact between these groups may have been continual and intimate, but hostilities usually lay just beneath the surface.

Whatever the role of that convivencia in Iberia's overall development, the historical record shows it was often a confrontational and violent relationship as each of the groups sought to protect and further its interests and establish boundaries between itself and its neighbors that would guarantee its predominance or its survival.[14] Often this was done through an almost ritualized violence, such as the stoning or killing of Jews during Holy Week and the harsh punishments demanded by all the communities for those who had sexual relations with outsiders, and sometimes, such as in the urban riots of 1391 against the Jews that swept through much of Castile, it was random.[15]

It has now become popular in Spain and Portugal to emphasize the Muslim and Jewish heritage, partly in recognition of a supposedly more multicultural approach to the past and partly because it is good for the tourist industry. There is a certain irony, however, that the *barrio típico* of Seville or Évora is the old Jewish or Moorish quarter, or that the restored synagogues of Thomar or Toledo, converted into churches or warehouses when the Jews were expelled, are now celebrated as examples of an Iberian pluralism. Remembrance has become painfully selective and pragmatic.

Historians of Spain and to a lesser extent of Portugal have usually come down on one side or the other in examining this story, emphasizing either the cooperative or the conflictive aspects of these relations. There is plenty of evidence on either side, and certainly by the fifteenth century an increasingly clear story of conflict and of separation as the areas under Muslim control were reduced and as a drive toward religious and political unity took place in the principal Christian kingdoms. In 1480, for example, the Cortes of Toledo, a body representing the nobility, clergy, and commoners of Castile, required municipalities to establish *juderías,* or ghettos — separate, walled neighborhoods for the resident Jews — in order to prevent their pernicious influence on Christians and converts to Christianity. A change in social relations and conditions was under way, and an important element of it was the rapidly growing number of Muslim and especially Jewish converts to Christianity, the result of conquest, persuasion, proselytism, and coercion.

My purpose is not to review this fascinating central theme of the Iberian

Middle Ages, but rather to examine the situation after 1492 or 1502 or 1526, when, theoretically at least, there were no more Jews and only a limited number of Mudejares left on the peninsula. What remnants of the old coexistence and conflicts remained? how were they expressed? An intense century of war, conquest, conversion, and resistance often punctuated by bloody episodes of fanaticism and an accompanying discourse of condemnation of the minority religions had laid the groundwork for a new society in which religious unity and an absence of toleration of other faiths and of heterodox ideas would be the foundations. But the spiritual and mental edifice that arose on this base had cracks revealing the persistence of other ways of thinking. My purpose is to examine this countertendency and to present evidence of cultural understanding and tolerance. But in order to do so, I must first set the parameters of conflict that cut across class and religious divisions.

Names of Belligerent Intimacy

The process of living in close and often hostile proximity led to a familiarity and belligerent intimacy that generated feelings of superiority and distinction and a language of almost continual epithet between the different religious communities. Pride in status and in orthodoxy like that in Sancho Panza's famous self-defense as an Old Christian sometimes led to bizarre formulations.[16] The Inquisition rarely prosecuted hidalgos (nobles) for scandalous or heretical propositions, but one hidalgo, Bartolomé Vizcaino, found that his pride of status and dislike for the Jews got the better of him. He had said that "he was better than God, for God was a Jew from Judea and he, Vizcaino, was an Old Christian and a gentleman."[17] Such beliefs ran counter to the Church's teachings that all would be equal before God at the final judgment, but the belief in hierarchy was deeply engrained in social practice. Such ideas of rank also permeated the relations between the three faiths.

Over the course of the Middle Ages, the superiority of the Christian faith and the denigration of the other religions was established by law, theology, and everyday practice. Each of the communities established boundaries to distinguish, separate, and protect its identity and integrity. This could be marked out in restricted residence with the establishment of separated neighborhoods, in the prohibitions against sexual relations across religious lines, even with prostitutes, in the enforced wearing of distinctive clothing or badges by the Jews and Muslims, in prohibitions against office holding or occupations, and in the myriad aspects of everyday life.

One of the most common forms in which hostility was expressed was in everyday speech. Epithets were common. The term *dog* flowed easily and regularly from the tongues of almost everyone at moments of confrontation and anger. The biblical metaphorical use of *dog* to refer to the impure provided a guide. There was a long medieval tradition of bestializing heresy and using animal metaphors to describe human failings.[18] The *Refranero* of Correas, a collection of popular sayings, said, "Moors are called dogs for there is no one who will save their souls and they die like dogs."[19] Christians could hardly refer to Moriscos without the epithet "Moorish dog," and the compliment was generally returned. Leonor de Torres, a young woman from Jaén, got into an argument with an Old Christian neighbor who called her a Moorish dog. "It's worth more to be a Moor than a Christian," was her retort. Both sides, Moriscos and Old Christians, often deepened the insult by calling their opponents Jewish dogs as well.

The constant verbal aggression could sometimes provoke and ensnare the participants. Jerónimo Fernandez, an Old Christian agricultural laborer of twenty-eight from Villanueva de los Ynfantes, got into trouble with the Inquisition when he was denounced for calling Christ and the Virgin dogs. His problem was not theological but grammatical. He had been reciting couplets intended to ridicule the Moors. One went like this:

> One day in Algiers the Christians were having a fiesta,
> and they carried through the streets Christ and Santa Maria;
> and the Moors inquired, what bundles are those you sustain?
> Christ and his mother they are[,] dogs[,] came back their refrain.

An inversion of verb and subject and a missing comma or two caused him to be denounced as a blasphemer when his intention had only been to humiliate the Moors once again.[20]

The matter of common speech practices raises the methodological problem of the relationship between popular and elite culture. The invectives hurled and returned expressed deeply held popular ideas. Undoubtedly those who held firmly to their faith saw in the other religions falsehood and deception, but these popular manifestations cannot be entirely divorced from religious policies of the dominant institutions. With the foundation of the Inquisition, the increasing campaign toward religious unification, and the expulsion of the Jews and Muslims, an intense campaign was launched against the Conversos and *confesos* (an alternate term for converts) accusing them of insincere conversion, backsliding, and deception. Whatever the religious origins of this campaign, it soon was transformed into essentially racial terms in which the failures and defects of the Conversos and Moriscos were seen as inherent to the ethnic groups from which they came. The natural reaction was response in kind. Muslims and Jews found opportunities to demonstrate their rejection of

Christian practices and beliefs. The depth of feeling was profound. Whole literatures developed condemning or ridiculing the religion of the other faith. In this, Muslims seem to have been more active than Jews. Christian authors, of course, had the advantage of a state and a religious apparatus that supported the publication of their work and its diffusion. Morisco responses circulated in manuscript or by word of mouth.[21] The confrontation and hostility were never limited to words but enacted in a thousand ways. Morisco and Christian prisoners of the Inquisition of Cuenca took pains in the prison to humiliate each other, the Moriscos making crosses from the straw stuffing of their beds in order to step on them, and the Christians cooking pork simply to mock the Moriscos.[22] In Granada it had been even worse. There, a prison riot in which the townspeople had joined Christian prisoners against Morisco ones resulted in the death of over one hundred people.[23] But such bloody moments were only the crest of waves of animosity. It was a confrontation repeatedly enacted in the fabric of everyday life.

Christian attitudes toward Jews were in some ways even more negative. The conversion campaigns of the fifteenth century and the fear that converts were insincere in their professions of faith began to generate a literature of distrust and opprobrium and a discourse of invective aimed against Jews and by extension against converts from Judaism. A figure like Saint Vincent Ferrer (1350–1419), a pulpit preacher of rare talents, became a kind of lightning rod of intolerance. Wherever he preached, the potential for anti-Jewish rioting was very strong. Similarly, the famous Alonso de Espina, long thought to be a Converso himself because of his knowledge of Jewish practice but recently shown to be an Old Christian, used his *Fortalitium fidei* (1511) to spew forth opprobrium and invectives against the Jews and Conversos as obstinate, greedy deicides.[24] A series of such tracts, usually by clerics and created with either a denigration of the Jews and, by extension, of the Conversos or a defense of discriminatory policies such as the *limpieza de sangre* laws as the principal goals, came from the pens of writers in Spain and Portugal.[25] Some of these works were scurrilous, their essentializing racism barely beneath the surface.[26] A similar literature developed about the Spanish Muslims, although it was often framed within the question of the justice and utility of their expulsion after the civil wars in Granada, or, later, of their expulsion from the whole peninsula. The number and level of intensity of these writings varied in relation to the health and power of the Church and the perceived dangers that the Conversos and Moriscos presented.

Given this theological and institutional attack on the minorities and the power of the Church and state to sway and mobilize the population toward its objectives, it is not surprising to find that mobs could be raised by fanatical preachers or that thousands attended the autos de fe to watch, cheer, and ridicule the condemned as society was cleansed and order restored by the recantations, public floggings, and the flames. What should give pause, however, is that in the midst of this program and in the face of tremendous social, political, and religious pressures to fulfill its goals many people remained unconvinced that coercion was appropriate for conversion, that Conversos and Moriscos were always to be distrusted, or that only through the Church was salvation possible.

In the Iberia of the reconquest it had become common to refer to the three laws, that of Christ, that of Moses, and that of Muhammad. This was a shortcut used to refer to the three religions and the social and juridical systems to which they were attached. As the Christian reconquest spread, recognition of the rights of the newly subject Muslim and Jewish populations to live within their law were often extended through the *capitulaciones,* or treaties that were used to consolidate the new arrangements of rule. The idea of the three laws persisted long after the triumph of the Christian kingdoms and the eventual conversions and expulsions of Jews and Muslims; and it persisted among the believers in all three. Moriscos often expressed a belief that the law of Muhammad was a good one and still valid. They would not easily turn their backs on it. Diego de Mendoza, a Morisco blacksmith, when told by a neighbor that he was not a good Christian, responded, "If they made you a Moor by force, would you be a good Moor?" When the neighbor answered in the negative, Mendoza replied, "Well, then why do you want me to be a good Christian?"[27] Conversos from Judaism often referred to the old law, meaning Judaism, and in the privacy of their homes or in the heat of argument with Old Christians they sometimes claimed it was better than or at least the equal of the law under which they now lived. With the triumph of the cross, the discourse of the Church was to emphasize that the law of Moses was a *ley muerta,* a dead law, surpassed and replaced by the law of Christ, and there was no possible salvation through it. In the struggle for souls that these discourses represented, Conversos responded at a number of levels. One was to hold fast to the old law, at least in one's heart, and to seek to pass it along. Women may have played a special role in this regard. With the elimination of synagogues, rabbis, and the institutional aspects of Judaism, crypto-Judaism emerged and became by necessity a domestic religion, and women were perhaps best positioned to serve as its conductors.[28] Antonio Correa Nuñez, tried for Judaizing in 1663–67, explained how when he had reached the age of thirteen, his grandmother had spoken to him privately and told him that "out of her great love for him, she wished him to ensure the salvation of his soul and his happiness in this life. He would attain these things if he believed in Jewish law, observed the precepts and distanced himself from Christianity, which would not bring him salvation."[29] This concern for salvation and respect for the old law runs through the testimony of many Conversos who, even when outward worship was impossible, continued to "embrace the law of Moses in their heart."

For both Conversos who kept an attachment to the old law and for those who did not, the anti-Jewish discourse and policies presented a challenge to their status and livelihood within Christian society. These policies were expressed in the laws and regulations of purity of blood, which excluded the descendants of non-Christians from many aspects of life, including civil and ecclesiastical positions, university study, membership in the military orders, and a wide range of social life. By the seventeenth century, the Portuguese formulation of the exclusion was of those persons descended from "Jews, Moors, mulattos and other infected races." Even though *raça* (race) may not have had its fully modern meaning at the time, the intention and the depreciation were clear. Such persons intrinsically lacked honor, were devoid of noble sentiments and of nobility of lineage, and thus could not be trusted. These defects were inherent in their character as a matter of birth.

While there were those even within the Inquisition itself who were critical of the purity of blood exclusions and felt that Conversos could never be integrated into the Church so long as such distinctions were maintained, the response of some fifteenth- and sixteenth-century Converso authors is interesting.[30] They argued that related as they were to the Virgin and to Christ their lineage and blood were in fact noble. The Converso Pedro de Cartagena told his critics "he descended from a line of kings, and your ancestors were nobody." Diego de Valera, who wrote many works about the nature of nobility, in his *Espejo de verdadera nobleza* (Mirror of true nobility) (1441) argued that the Moors and Jews who had lived virtuously in their law and after conversion continued to do so lost none of their quality. Others, like Juan de Torquemada, rose to their defense and condemned those who refused to accept them fully into the Church.[31] There had been noble lineages among them. Who could doubt the nobility of the Moors with their many "kings, and princes and great men," and as for the Jews: "In what nation can one find as many nobles as among the Jews, among whom were all the Prophets, all the Patriarchs, and Holy Fathers, all the Apostles and finally our beloved Lady Saint Mary and her blessed child, God and our true redeemer, who chose this lineage for himself for it was the noblest?"[32] These learned defenses of the validity of the old laws were paralleled by the statements of simple and unlettered folk that the law of Moses and of Mohammad had been valid in the past and for many continued to be so, or, as we shall see, some believed that the God that had made one, made them all. What remains impressive is not that Conversos and Moriscos might hold onto these beliefs, but that Old Christians shared them as well.

Centuries of interaction, day-to-day contact, encounters in the markets and streets had created a common ground of understanding and acceptance, which provides an obverse to the common coin of conflict and violence between the communities. Some insight into these attitudes can be gained from a much-studied set of documents from the region of Soria and Osma in northeastern Castile. There, almost 450 persons made statements about themselves and their acquaintances and neighbors during visits of the Inquisition in the period 1490–1502.[33] Many, but by no means all, of the persons questioned and accused were Conversos, and the doubts or opinions they expressed have sometimes been seen as typical of those of recent converts.[34] Certainly some men and women expressed a nostalgia for their old faith and some hostility to their new one, but the doubts spoken about aspects of Christian dogma and practice and about the excesses or injustice of the Inquisition itself were not exclusive to converts: they were also made continually by Old Christians. Doubts about the power of the sacraments, the existence of an afterlife, the utterance of blasphemous expressions, and a lack of understanding or knowledge of what was required of the Christian faithful were common in this population. Among these unorthodox opinions and beliefs was the expression of sympathy for those who followed another law. An incident that took place in the 1480s makes this clear. In the town of Ausejo de la Sierra in the region of Soria, Gil Recio, a farmer, got into a discussion with the local miller, a man named Diego de San Martín. The military campaigns against the Moors in Granada were taking place, and when the miller complained of the great drought the region was suffering, Gil Recio answered, "How do you expect it to rain when the king is going to take the Moors' homes away, when they haven't done him any harm." The miller responded that the war was necessary to spread the true faith, to which Recio answered, "How does anyone know which of the three laws God loves best?"[35]

This expression of a religious universalism was among the ideas expressed by both Old Christians and converts. In 1488, Juana Pérez, a peasant woman from Aranda, made a statement that "the good Jew would be saved and the good Moor, in his law, and why else had God made them?"[36] The same concept of doubt about which of the three laws was best also came from the mouth of La Rabanera, an Old Christian peasant woman who in 1480 was praying in the home of a Jewish neighbor who had just died. When another Christian reprimanded her and said she was sinning, she answered, "May God forgive you. You are wrong. The good Jew will be saved and the good Moor in his law. Why else did God make them?"[37] Clearly this was a common expression. The case of La Rabanera is also instructive, not only for her relativist thought about salvation, but also because it reveals an intimacy in everyday life among Old Christians, converts, and Jews, an intimacy which allowed her to be praying in the home of the deceased Jewish woman, but also explained the presence of another Old Christian, the woman who had argued with her.

Not surprisingly persons of Jewish background expressed the same idea in the Soria inquests. The Converso priest Juan Rodríguez, whose parish was in the town of Tajahuerce near Soria, was accused of saying on various occasions that he did not know which of the three religions was best. He denied that charge, but he did not deny saying that each person could find salvation in his or her own law.[38]

The Soria and Osma investigations reveal a wide range of doubts about orthodox Catholic practice and dogma in the period just before and after the fall of Granada and the expulsion or conversion of the Jews. They provide a glimpse of Spanish life and belief at a crucial moment at the dawn of Spain's rise to power, and while they can admittedly be held suspect for their regional bias, the repetition of these beliefs from other regions of the peninsula suggests they were widely held. The Soria investigations imply that the long intimacy of the medieval convivencia had, despite confrontation and conflict and in the face of an active ideological campaign by the Church, nevertheless spawned sentiments of religious universalism and an attitude of live and let live.[39] But could such ideas, considered heretical or at least heterodox, implying as they did that other faiths might have some truth and that they too might be paths to God, continue as religious pluralism in Iberia came to its end in the early sixteenth century, after the expulsion of the Jews from Spain in 1492, the forced conversion of Jews in Portugal in 1498, and that of the remaining Muslims in Castile in 1502?

Jews and Conversos

I begin by examining statements of religious universalism made by individuals of the two principal minority groups within the societies of Spain and Portugal. One might expect that for various reasons those who had been converted would retain some sympathy for the validity of their former beliefs and way of life. It has even been suggested that such ideas of "tolerance" might be, in fact, a peculiarly Converso way of thinking.[40] I want to examine, then, each of the principal cultural groups that formed Spanish society in regard to these statements of religious universalism.

Although traditional Judaism placed little emphasis on salvation in a personal sense, the idea of some kind of punishment for the wicked and reward for the righteous was widely held.[41] This concept was also enmeshed in the belief in a Messiah and in deliverance, two beliefs that after 1492 flourished among those New Christians who kept some adherence to Judaism. New

Christians generally came to adopt the idea of individual salvation and in this they drew closer to Christian belief, but at the same time they, perhaps more intensely than others, also commonly expressed what might be called from an orthodox Catholic viewpoint heretical ideas about this concept. Nevertheless, as David Gitlitz has characterized this situation, "This conflation of the Jewish idea of righteousness through obedience to the Law and the Christian idea of salvation through belief is the single most powerful example of syncretism in the crypto-Jewish religion."[42]

Some distinction must be made between the converts of the first generation — those who had come under the heavy pressure of the state and the Inquisition after 1480 and those who had chosen to remain after the expulsion of 1492 — and the Conversos who were their descendants. As the generations passed, these New Christians were further and further removed from their Jewish origins and, for them, Christianity was the reference point against which their continued affiliation to Judaism could be measured. They were not Judaizers who were different from Christians, but "rather they were Judaizers insofar as they differed from Christians."[43] Despite a considerable level of syncretism among the later generations of New Christians, certain basic precepts remained as elements of their Jewishness, more deeply rooted and more ardently held, to be sure, among those more attached to their old faith. The ideas that God is one, that the Messiah has yet to come, that the Law of Moses is the path to salvation, that observance as well as belief is necessary, and that Judaism is the preferred religion existed in one form or another among those New Christians who still believed themselves to be Jews.[44] It was often the assertion of these ideas or, by extension, ridicule of contradictory concepts that caused New Christians to be denounced as secret Jews.

Here the concept of salvation and the validity of the "laws" of Moses and Christ came into play. Many Conversos adopted the Christian concept of salvation and heaven and even conceived of being united with Moses in paradise.[45] Some continued to hold that the law of Moses was the only means to salvation, but many felt that perhaps Judaism and Christianity might both be valid or acceptable to God. This was a position that recognized the universal truth of Judaism, but also that this truth was not necessarily exclusive. As one might expect, owing to the social situation and practices of New Christians some also came to believe that a mixture of the two faiths might also be valid. Statements that the law of Moses, or the old law, was better were common among the first generation of converts from Judaism, but such ideas stubbornly persisted. New Christians repeated such statements, sometimes in a joking sense, sometimes with complete theological seriousness.

From this position of surety and sometimes arrogance, it was not a great step to a more flexible and inclusive view of the validity of the different laws. The Converso Gonzalo de Torrijos's statement in 1538 that "God did exist, and the Moors were right when they said that they could be saved within their law as well as the Christians in theirs" expressed a relativism based on faith, but sometimes that relativism was also founded on a kind of practical skepticism. A couple of Conversos from the 1480s commended their souls to all three laws, expecting to cover all their bets in this way: "I have a God made of wood; I have kept the Holy Law of Moses, I have kept the Law of Jesus Christ, and if right now Saint Mohammed should appear, by God, I would keep all three; and if it were to end tomorrow I would not fear God because I had walked in all three Laws."[46] As people sought to reconcile themselves with their consciences and their social status with society, it is not surprising to find statements like that María de Zárate made to the inquisitors of Mexico in 1650: "God the Father did not get angry at those who served God the Son nor did God the Son get angry at those who serve God the Father; and that in cases of doubt the safest thing was to serve the Father, without ever mentioning the Holy Spirit."[47]

And so New Christians sought also to understand redemption and salvation, what was proper for themselves and for others. Here, traditional Jewish belief and Christian tradition were at odds. For the Church, salvation was personal and individual, and redemption was personal and internal. In Judaism, redemption took place "on the stage of history and within the community."[48] Jewish tradition tended to view the road to righteousness as one of adherence to the law of God, particularly that of Moses, compliance with its precepts, and the performance of good works and *mitzvoth*. Christian theology had long debated and struggled with the relative effect of human actions and God's divine grace and power on salvation and by the sixteenth century had taken a position within the Spanish church that grace above all was the determinant factor and that in any case without the intervention of the Messiah humankind's salvation was problematic, if not impossible. In fact, traditional Judaism did not give great attention to the idea of personal salvation or to the concept of a paradise in the afterlife. Righteousness was its own reward.

Nevertheless, the Conversos quickly adopted the idea of salvation and then applied it to their own situation. They came to believe that only by adherence to the law of Moses could they be saved, and they taught their children that the law of Moses, not the law of Christ, was their hope. Not surprisingly, even those Conversos who accepted their new faith and thought of themselves as Christians were not willing to believe that their beloved parents were denied eternal salvation, and so they held that by following the law of Moses, their ancestors had also found salvation.

Prior to the expulsion and forced conversions of the 1490s, Iberian Jews had often used the rhetoric of the competing laws, or religions. Statements that the law of Moses is the true law or that it is better than the Christian law were often made.[49] Like the Muslim converts to Christianity, Jewish Conversos were reluctant to believe that their parents and ancestors were suffering eternal damnation and preferred to believe that since they had lived by God's law, the souls of these relatives were saved. Such ideas were usually held within the family, and New Christians were less likely than Moriscos to confront Christians with such statements. Jews had constituted a minority in both Christian and Muslim Spain. Unlike the Moriscos, Jews could not look to any powerful empire of coreligionists to provide help or protection, and nothing parallel to the enslavement of Christians by Barbary corsairs put a restraint on Christian actions. New Christians may have had these ideas, but for the most part they remained interior to the community unless they were extracted in the Inquisition examinations or in special circumstances.

Moriscos, especially those from Granada, often acted quite differently. Muslims, after all, had in many places long been the majority population and had exercised political and religious control. They tended to be more confrontational in making open comparison between the three laws. They sometimes expressed these sentiments quite openly, even though they no longer held political power. Some Moriscos and Conversos adopted the relativist position that all of the laws were valid and that God had made them all. Others simply had doubts. Gregório Laínez confessed in 1500 that he sincerely did not know which law was better.[50]

An Interlude in Amsterdam

The variety of Converso belief and its complexity in relation to Christianity, Judaism, and universalistic concepts of religion can be best examined perhaps not in the constrained atmosphere of the Iberian world, where the expression of belief was dangerous, but in the relative freedom of Amsterdam. Spanish and Portuguese Conversos had fled there from the Inquisition beginning in the 1580s, and by the mid–seventeenth century the city had a thriving community of perhaps two thousand Conversos and their descendants, many of whom had reverted to Judaism, as well as an equal number of northern European Jews. Jews benefited from a policy of state toleration, and by the 1640s there were two synagogues functioning in the city. The Jewish religious authorities, or *Mahamad,* granted a certain autonomy by the city's government, sought to control public statements and writings among the community in order to diminish possible problems with the Christian population as well as to maintain orthodoxy among the Jews.[51]

But such orthodoxy was difficult to control among a varied and educated Sephardi population influenced by their Iberian experiences, their own dissimulation, and by their former contacts with Catholicism. Moreover, members of the community were also in personal or intellectual contact with a variety of Protestant confessions as well as with Christian skeptics, deists, and philosophical doubters. The story of Uriel da Costa (he died in 1647) is a case in point. Da Costa was a Portuguese Converso from Oporto who had studied theology at Coimbra and who had, with others in his family, fled Portugal for Holland. He lived for a period in Hamburg as a sugar merchant and eventually returned to Amsterdam. A man of unquiet spirit and broad theological interests, Da Costa was led by his self-questioning on a spiritual odyssey from Catholicism to deism with stops at crypto-Jewish *marranism* and more orthodox Judaism along the way.[52] Although not particularly well trained in Jewish biblical exegesis or law, he wrote in 1616 a tract contesting rabbinic authority, which led to his excommunication from the community. He continued publishing increasingly heterodox ideas and attacks on rabbinic authority. His life was made so miserable by his separation from the community that he sought and obtained reconciliation, only to be excommunicated a second time. He eventually committed suicide.[53] Da Costa, through his study of both Christian and Jewish theology, began to develop doubts about the claims of both, especially as regarded institutional authority and the divine origin of the Torah. He also came to doubt the immortality of the soul, and in this he held ideas in common not only with educated contemporary skeptics but also with many of the common people prosecuted by the Inquisition in the land of his birth.[54]

Da Costa and his ideas are sometimes viewed as a predecessor of that other, far more famous Amsterdam skeptic of Portuguese Converso background, Baruch Spinoza, and for the group of heterodox thinkers loosely associated with him in the Sephardic community.[55] Spinoza's *Tractatus Theologo-Politicus* emphasized the individual's freedom to judge and think as he chose and thus to be "by absolute natural right the master of his own thoughts." This was a major step in the history of toleration since it emphasized not toleration of religious expression or worship based on religious principles, but rather freedom of individual thought. Spinoza's concern was not religion per se but the relationship of freedom of thought and expression in the broad sense to the individual's relationship to the state, and the need for the state to recognize that freedom.[56] Underlying Spinoza's position that each person must be able to freely think and speak or write on matters of philosophy, politics, and religion was doubt as to the truth of any particular religion. His was a war on superstition and on religion as a source of public discord. In this sense, his skepticism was revolutionary, and his universalism in regard to religion quite unlike that of most of the Spaniards and Portuguese — Christians, Jews, and Muslims — whom I have been discussing. The Israeli scholar Yirmiyahu Yovel has called Spinoza a *marrano* (crypto-Jew) of reason who sought salvation neither in the law of Moses nor in that of Christ, but rather in rational thought itself.[57]

Spinoza's attack on religion led to his excommunication from the Jewish community, but around Spinoza within the Sephardic community were others with heterodox ideas about religion whose roots seem to grow more directly out of Iberian tradition or experience. Some were strange figures. There were men like Daniel de Ribera, not of Converso origin but a Spanish friar who had traveled to Italy and Brazil and had converted to Judaism in Amsterdam only to be driven from that community, eventually becoming an Anglican before returning to the Catholic Church; and the Andalusian poet and author Miguel (Daniel Levi) de Barrios, from a Converso family who moved to Italy, converted to Judaism, and traveled briefly to the Spanish Indies before arriving in Amsterdam. Barrios served as a Spanish captain in Flanders and apparently even maintained good relations with nobles and authorities there despite his professed Judaism. His writings were prohibited from publication in Holland by Jewish authorities for their lascivious content, but there is in them a curious combination of a celebration of Spain and some of its rulers who had most persecuted the Jews along with Barrios's own pride in his Judaism. The dichotomy underlined the ambivalence of the author.[58]

The life and career of Juan (Daniel) de Prado, widely known as a deist and skeptic of Converso origin and as part of the Spinoza group, are particularly interesting. Prado's story was a rather typical tale of the Iberian Conversos. His family lived near Jaén in Andalusia, and Prado was born there. He entered university at Alcalá in 1627 and in 1630–35 studied medicine at the same institution.[59] During that time he met Baltasar Alvares de Orobio (Isaac Orobio de Castro, 1617–87), another New Christian student who was also studying medicine and whose subsequent arrest by the Inquisition led to his own flight from Spain. As a defender of Jewish orthodoxy in the Amsterdam community, Orobio would later publish his work in Holland and conduct a public debate with Prado about matters of belief and theology. When the two had first met in Spain in 1635, they were both studying theology, and they became close friends. Their roads then separated, and by different paths they both eventually professed Judaism. The Inquisition arrested Orobio in 1654 and extracted information about friends and relatives from him by torture. In his statement he revealed that during a meeting in 1643 with Prado and his brother-in-law, long before either had left Spain or had publicly professed Judaism, Prado had revealed that his theological studies had led him to the conclusion that those religions which were in harmony with natural law could all lead to an individual's salvation. Orobio reported that Prado had stated, "All men are entitled to redemption, each in virtue of his own religion — Jew, Muslim, and Christian are entitled to eternal happiness, because all three religions have political aims the source of which lies in natural law, which in Aristotle's philosophy is styled *causa causarum*."[60]

Two days later in another meeting, Prado told Orobio that all the said religions have the capacity to bring their adherents to salvation, all of them having the same object, namely, to bring the believer to awareness of God.[61] Prado's brother-in-law supported his statements. Such reasoning seems to have been drawn from Prado's understanding of the implications of natural law, but his major argument was stated not only in a framework of scholasticism but in the form of the traditional Spanish proposition that each can be saved in his own law. Prado and Orobio later became bitter doctrinal opponents.[62]

While there were clearly differences between Spinoza, Prado, and other heterodox thinkers within the Sephardi community, I. S. Révah has argued that they shared a skepticism that had been growing among the Iberian Conversos since 1492, if not before, and that despite the differences among them, they shared a belief in the immutability of the divine order, a repudiation of conventional understandings of divine revelation, and a belief in a natural law common to humanity whose character was moral rather than religious. These positions served the roots of a deism that was common among them. Jewish defenses of Judaism and criticisms of Christianity have been identified as major contributing influences to the rise of Christian skepticism, but doubts about Judaism within the Jewish community itself had also developed out of the experiences of debate, persecution, and forced belief. The argument that Conversos were prone to dissimulation, to an emphasis on inner belief rather than outward profession of religion, and to a constant masking of thought has been suggested as providing a context for the rise of many things, from the picaresque novel in Spain to Spinoza's secular philosophy in Holland.[63] But the idea that such deism and skepticism might be a peculiarly Converso phenomenon, born of their experience of doubt, debate, dissimulation, and pressures upon their belief systems has been contested. Religious dissimulation among Christians, what was called Nicodemism, was common in early modern Europe, where Catholics in England and Protestants in Italy were forced to develop strategies of survival that produced similar divisions between public affirmation and private belief.[64] Even a scholar of the Sephardic community in Holland like Yosef Kaplan notes that such ideas were also circulating widely among the Christian population as well in the seventeenth century. In a curious way, the desire to find peculiarly Jewish or Converso roots for skepticism echoes the condemnations of the Conversos by contemporaries as a people with no real faith and committed to no religion whatsoever, ancestors of the "godless Jew."

These tendencies toward skepticism or "atheism" were, of course, more likely to surface in an environment such as the relative toleration of Holland rather than in Spain and Portugal, where belief in the old law's superiority, or at least equality, had given the Conversos an intellectual basis for their continued attachment to Jewish practice, even after adopting the Christian idea of salvation. Although there were good reasons this kind of relativism might be prevalent among them, in truth such statements were, as we have seen, also common among the Old Christian population. Such attitudes were not born only or primarily of the antipathy between Judaism and Christianity or as peculiarly New Christian beliefs. It well may be that New Christians were particularly prone to doubts and skepticism about certain aspects of Catholic faith and practice. That would only make sense. But they surely were not alone. There are literally thousands of cases in the Inquisition files of Spain, Portugal, and Italy of Old Christians who also voiced such propositions and who held similar ideas. They seem to have thought this way not simply because they had been infected by Jewish, Muslim, or Lutheran influences, but because their own doubts and questioning had led them to these conclusions.

Finally, an element has been overlooked in the scholarly search to identify the individuals, events, and contexts that influenced Spinoza's philosophical revolution, his expulsion from the Jewish community, and his emerging deism and toleration. Whatever the direct influence of Uriel da Costa, Isaac La Peyrère, Juan de Prado, and other Converso heterodox thinkers, many if not most of them had lived in Spain and Portugal, where there was a long popular tradition of religious relativism as well as an ancient theological discussion of the implications of natural law for the possibility of salvation. Prado, whatever his direct influence on Spinoza's separation from the Sephardi community, had as a young man expressed the old idea that all the faiths might lead to salvation. It was an idea that was familiar to all of the Conversos, whatever their orthodoxy or heterodoxy and whatever the faith they truly followed, and indeed it was familiar to Spaniards and Portuguese of all backgrounds. The step from universalism, believing in the possible validity of all faiths, to the atheism of the underground text the *Traité des Trois Imposteurs,* which drew on the skepticism of Spinoza and questioned the validity of all religions, was not large, and the Catholic theologians and inquisitors had recognized the danger all along.[65] Curiously, however, in Spain the peculiar proposition of the relative validity of all religions had not been associated exclusively or even particularly with the converts from Judaism, but rather with the Moriscos, the converts from Islam, whose experience with prejudice, forced conversion, and dissimulation had paralleled that of Conversos.

Moriscos

Even as the war against Granada, the last Muslim kingdom, had moved into its final stages after 1485, there were Muslim communities in many other parts of the peninsula, especially Aragon, Castile, and Valencia. These *mudéjar* enclaves were under increasing economic and cultural pressure, and after Granada's fall these pressures, especially that of conversion, became intense. The result was a series of large-scale conversions to Christianity, often under conditions that were just short of force. The resulting converts were, not surprisingly, often less than fervent in their new faith.[66]

While by the end of the sixteenth century there were perhaps only about three hundred thousand Moriscos in a total Spanish population of eight million, they were regionally concentrated in Murcia, Valencia, and Granada, forming in the first two regions about a quarter of the population, and in Granada perhaps half of the inhabitants.[67] Many had been born and had lived in conditions in which their former faith had been predominant and its validity in little doubt. Long after the fall of Granada in 1492, such sentiments had persisted, and for some these convictions had been resuscitated or reinvigorated in the Morisco revolts, the so-called Wars of the Alpujarras in 1499 and 1569–70.[68] Continual contacts with coreligionists in North Africa and the hope of support from Ottoman power in Constantinople gave Moriscos psychological and spiritual support in resisting the pressures of forced conversion and the threat, and later the reality, of expulsion, finally enforced in 1609.

There were, of course, regional variations. In Valencia, where the Moorish population had constituted a large rural peasantry controlled by the leading nobles, a certain protection and toleration had been extended to them until the second decade of the sixteenth century. Forced to convert or die during the popular uprisings of the Germanía, some Muslims maintained open revolt until the late 1520s. In Aragon, there was also a sizable rural population that had remained after the reconquest and continued to work the land, tend their flocks, and perform trades in the towns. Here too the Aragonese nobility had used them as retainers and dependents, and for this reason as well as for their religion they had been disliked, feared, and sometimes envied by their Old Christian neighbors. In both Valencia and Aragon there was always the fear that the Moors were a potential internal threat, disposed to collaborate, re-

Turning Moors into Moriscos.
"The Baptism of the Moriscos." Polychromed wood in the Royal Chapel of the Cathedral of Granada by Vignary Felipe (1470–1543). (Archivo Oronoz)

spectively, with Algerine or Moroccan corsairs and with Hugenots, and in both regions considered a potential Fifth Column for a Turkish attack on Spain.[69] Even after conversion, forced or voluntary, such fears and the Moors' persistent adherence to their language, dress, and customs caused their commitment to the Church to be questioned, and in truth many held stubbornly to their former beliefs.[70] In Castile, after Granada's fall there had been forced conversions, a short-lived rebellion in 1499, and an expulsion edict in 1502 that offered the choice of convert or leave. In Murcia and in parts of Andalusia, there were still scattered *mudéjar* communities living under Christian rule, remnants of the reconquest, but Granada was a different story altogether. There, in large parts of the kingdom Moors still predominated with their own patterns of life, structures of association, elites, and local authority still intact. After the conversion of 1502, they were still a community, and they resisted the economic pressures forced upon them by the "internal colonialism" of the Christian occupation of Granada as well as both the lenient policies and the repressive ones designed to make them firm in their new faith. In this they were aided somewhat by divisions and rivalries between Church and civil authorities and between noble factions, one of which, the Mondéjar family, was the hereditary captain-generals of Granada and the defenders of the Moriscos.

Continued suspicion of their collaboration with external enemies intensified as Ottoman expansion and victories increased in the 1560s, and in 1567 Philip II and his officers of Church and state, desirous of bringing the reforms of Trent to bear on Granada, sought to impose a series of laws that amounted to an open campaign to destroy any remnant of Arabic culture as a way of enforcing adherence to Christian dogma and practice. This included prohibition of the use of Arabic, the burning of books in that language, and prohibition of Moorish dress and of the use of Moorish names, ceremonials, and customs. All of these restrictions had been ordered before, but this time the intention of enforcement was serious. The community tried to buy their way out of their predicament, as they had in the past, but religious intransigence and the international scene now made this impossible. Pushed to the wall, the Moors reacted violently. The result was a two-year rebellion in the mountains of the Alpujarras (1569–70), in reality, a horrific civil war. The Moriscos proved to be effective guerillas, but the odds were badly against them, especially since Philip II saw this movement as a threat to the very heart of the kingdom. Brutally suppressed, the fighting was effectively over by 1570. While thousands found ways to stay in Granada, between 75,000 and 150,000 Moriscos were expelled from the region and distributed over the rest of Castile in an attempt to lessen their impact and threat by thinning them out over a broad territory. This policy created new problems. Moriscos now lived in many places as a minority; the new arrivals came to their new homes with understandable grudges and a faith hardened by adversity that they conveyed to the small *mudéjar* populations already in Castile.[71] Carefully watched, persecuted, and distrusted, they were especially sensitive to affronts to their honor and their culture. Still considered suspect in their political loyalty and in their faith, resented for their industry and economic success on one hand and denigrated for being bandits or beggars on the other, the Moriscos were finally expelled in 1609, at which time there were fewer than 100,000 left in Spain.

Given this history and the difficulties Moriscos faced in holding openly to their adopted faith, many of them sought a means to reconcile or accommodate the two religions and their place between them. Moriscos often expressed an opinion that "each person can be saved in his or her own law" and that the old law, that is, Islam, had been valid.[72] There were, in fact, Koranic passages and interpretations of the prophetic tradition that seemed to point to toleration in matters of faith. "To you your religion, to me mine" (Koran, 105.6) seemed to imply self-determination in belief, and in the text of Koran 5.59 there are echoes of the often heard argument that God had given each person a path to follow and had intended for people to follow it as part of his plan.[73] "To each of you God has prescribed a Law and a Way. If God [had willed], He would have made you a single people. But God's purpose is to test you in what he has given each of you, so strive in the pursuit of all the virtues, and know that you will all return to God, and He will resolve all the matters in which you disagree."

The Islamic concept of *fitra*, humankind's inborn religiosity, was fundamental. The Prophet had said all are born with *fitra*, and it is parents who make Jews, Christians, or Zoroastrians. Islamic theologians argued over the meaning of this statement, but at least some free thinkers believed it might imply more than one path to God.[74] Under the sway of these scriptural elements and also under considerable pressure, the converts from Islam became exponents of relativism in the face of coercion. Finally, the concept of *taqiyya* allowed for feigned acceptance of another religion when unavoidable, the Islamic equivalent of the strategy of Protestant Nicodemism or the dissimulation of the crypto-Jewish New Christians.

In 1560, a Valencian report to Philip II noted that Moriscos were in the habit of claiming that each person can be saved in his own law.[75] Some who had lived all their lives as Christians, when confronted with death revealed their doubts and their continued respect for the faith of their forefathers.[76] Forced or persuaded to accept the new faith, many Moriscos were reluctant to acknowledge Christianity's exclusive validity, and, as noted, they found it exceptionally difficult to accept the fact that their relatives and ancestors, who had lived in the law of Mohammed were, by that fact, condemned to hell, according to the precepts of their new religion. Often they sought parallels between the faiths. In 1525, María de Oro of Deza told a group of people who in discussion had noted that a certain Christian who had died fighting the Muslims had assured his soul in heaven that likewise the Muslims who had fought the Christians had also found salvation in this way.[77] The Granada Inquisition punished the elderly Leonor Tuniscia in 1577 for saying that her North African homeland was good because there the Moors lived in their law, the Jews in theirs, and the Christians in theirs. After all, God had created them all.[78]

Caught between faiths, Moriscos sought personal solutions and creative resolutions. Luis Borico Gajo, a laborer from Almansa and a convert from Islam, placed the blame for his predicament on God himself: "God has sinned and has not done his craft well, making some Christians and others Moors, and others Jews since all should be as one." These "pernicious" blasphemies earned him two hundred lashes in 1567. In that same year, his fellow Morisco laborer Gaspar Vayazan from Helche took a more comprehensive and practical position by claiming that he believed simultaneously in all three laws, "that of Our Lord Jesus Christ, that of Mohammed, and that of Señor Moses, for if one of them let him down, he could depend on the others."[79]

That the idea of the equality of the three laws and of the possibility of salvation in each was deeply held by the Moriscos is to some extent confirmed by the Inquisition itself. The proposition was general enough to merit inclusion in various edicts of the faith, the guidelines the Inquisition issued to instruct the faithful in the warning signs of heterodoxy and deviance. Curiously, in a number of the edicts there appears in the section warning of Islamic practices an admonition to be aware of the statement "to say that the Muslim can be saved in his sect and the Jew in his law."[80] This positioning of the admonition appears in a number of edicts issued in Castile, but also in an edict issued in Lima in the early seventeenth century.[81] The placement of the proposition indicates that in its origins inquisitors associated it with backsliding Muslim converts seeking to defend their former beliefs or those of their ancestors, but by the late sixteenth century that association was no longer so obvious, as the many cases of non-Moriscos who were prosecuted for these ideas indicate.

Still, the idea that this argument was viewed by the Catholic clergy as a peculiarly Muslim defense is apparent in the treatises written against Islam and against the continued adherence of Moriscos to that faith. For example, the humanist Bernardo Pérez de Chinchón, was from a Converso background. He overcame his family's religious origins and received support from the duke of Gandía in part by writing two texts critical of the Koran and Islam that were intended to convert Muslims to the true faith. In his *Diálogos cristianos* (1535), organized as a friendly discussion between the Christian Bernardo and his (former) teacher, Joseph Arabigo, who represents the Moriscos, Joseph at one point states, "Some of the learned men among the Moors say that each can be saved in his own law: The Jew in his, the Christian is his, the Moor in his; and it may be true what they say, for each will find happiness in his law and believe it is the truth."[82] Bernardo then seeks to prove to Joseph that such an argument is "false, mad, and stupid," for while there can be many laws made by men that differ from each other, some of them good and some bad, because men are men and subject to error either by evil intent or by being deceived, the law of God is never unjust, untruthful, or false. Since God is one, there must be only one law of God. The text then proceeds to explain by logic and metaphysics that two religions that hold contradictory opinions cannot both be correct, and Bernardo then attempts to point out the many errors of those who follow Islam. The question of Christianity's claim to truth is argued in a spirit of friendly persuasion, and the Muslim is chided for avoiding a reasoned debate of these matters or for insisting that there may be more than one path of God.

Many former Muslims, however, reacted to such argumentation at times more confrontationally than comparatively. Spanish Muslims and their descendants had developed a series of critiques and doubts about Catholicism and its practices. The cross was just a couple of sticks, the saints were only wood, and their veneration idolatry, for a real God could not die.[83] Such depreciation was not uncommon.

These direct affronts and confrontation, especially after the redistribution of the Granadan Moriscos across Castile in the wake of the rebellion, point to the texture of interaction between Old Christians and Moriscos, a relationship conflictive, continual, and often intimate. Songs seem to have been both a means of memory and affirmation as well as a way to provoke and challenge. When Martín de Murcia from La Roda overheard some Christians singing verses about the Morisco rebels of Valencia, he shouted that he lived in his law better than they did in theirs. In 1575, the Morisco slave Lope from Almería shouted, "Mohammed is better than you" and pulled a knife on a Christian who was singing verses about the victory over the Morisco rebels.[84] The case of Francisco Bocacho, a young Morisco of Alicante arrested by the Inquisition of Murcia in 1597, is symptomatic. He had been together with a group of Old Christians singing the *romance* of El Cid when he had lamented that the Cid had taken Valencia because "back then we were all Moors."[85] Upon being told there was no salvation except for Christians, he responded with the common refrain that the faith of his ancestors was good enough for him, and he reasoned with his Old Christian interlocutor, "Your mother and father were Christians and so you follow that law." He did not care about theology; "No, my mother a Moor, my father a Moor, I too am a Moor." The inquisitors were lenient, for he was deemed to be a rustic of little understanding, "raised in the countryside," and he had argued that what he said was, "Never Moor a good Christian, nor Christian a good Moor," apparently an inversion of the also common and more relativist expression, "Better a Good Moor than a bad Christian."[86]

Bocacho's story evokes the image of a society in which Moriscos and Old Christians rubbed elbows continually, knew each other by name, saw each other in church, and might even gather to sing the verses of the Cid, that traditional hero of Christian Spain who in fact had spent much of his career in the service of Muslim princes. Everyday associations and intimacy led to challenges, retorts, and discussions in which these opinions were expressed, leading then to denunciations to the Inquisition. Close association and intimacy produced the twin results of disdain and acceptance. Like sex, the question of the validity of the three laws was a matter of common concern, constant preoccupation, and continual discussion.

Given the history of the Moriscos and their difficult and sometimes confrontational relation to Christian society, the nature and variety of their responses on the issue of personal salvation, the true faith, and toleration are all understandable. At times, their arguments and positions, though lacking in instruction or knowledge, reproduced the old theological debates and humanist arguments about the nature of salvation and its possibilities. For example, Isabel de Torres, a fifty-year-old Morisca woman from Granada, had claimed that the Turks were not so bad and that they did many charitable acts (*limosnas*). When told they could not go to heaven because they had not been baptized, she took the old Pelagian position "that Heaven is open to all who do good works." Salvation depended on volition and action, not exclusively on grace.[87] The inquisitors wished to explore this further, for this went to the very heart of the issue of the Church's claim to exclusive validity. Isabel was subjected to torture, but even under duress, probably realizing the centrality of that point, she held that she had not claimed baptism was unnecessary.

While Isabel de Torres's argument had smacked of Pelagianism, in fact, her position was close to that of the Valencian humanist Fadrique Furio Ceriol, who had held that the world was divided simply into the good and the bad regardless of creed and had essentially argued for the equality of humankind. There is no evidence Isabel was aware of Furio Ceriol's work or even of the earlier theological disputes on the possibility of salvation outside the Church. Her position seems to have been arrived at not by the consideration of authority, but rather by the practice of reason. The question, in fact, may be better put: not did Furio Ceriol's writings or similar ideas of elite culture influence the thinking of people like Isabel, but rather how may such popular rationality or wisdom have created the context of life and understandings that emerged in the writings of some of the humanists.

Both convivencia and forced conversions could produce other results. Multiple and competing claims to religious truth might lead not to the fervor of the convert or the dissimulation of the forced adherent, but to skepticism and doubt about all faiths. Some scholars have argued that such doubts were inherent in the status of the Converso and explain the emergence of Spinoza's skepticism and the birth of rationalist philosophies. Perhaps the bishop of Sogorbe said it best when he complained that the Morisco converts in his diocese were "an ignorant plebe who don't know how to be either Moors or Christians."[88] Second, the transition from one faith to another would not happen overnight. Customs and practices so woven into the texture of everyday life that their religious content was no longer obvious persisted. Some theologians recognized that fact and called for leniency in the application of penalties for backsliding. That had been the approach of Bishop Hernando de Talavera (1428–1507) in Granada, and its replacement by the intransigence of his successor Bishop Cisneros provoked bitter resistance. In Portugal, after the forced conversion of the Jews in 1498, the Inquisition was prohibited from prosecuting New Christians until 1540 in order to give that first generation time to adapt to their new faith. Third, with so many competing claims to truth, a possible outcome was relativism, close to or born of incredulity. The Converso who could say, "In this land they do not live the life of Muslims, Jews, or Christians, and to live here it's best to live as Christians to be saved [from the Inquisition], like the little old lady who goes to her confessor, tells her [little] sin, and nothing else" was speaking with a sense of survival uppermost in his mind.[89] He was not alone.

Religion meant a great deal in this society but maybe not everything, and certainly not to everyone. In Andalusia, the African slave Alonso, who was ostensibly a Christian, admitted he wanted to escape to North Africa in order to see his parents and to die among his family. When asked by the inquisitors if he had also hoped to save himself in the law of the Moors, he answered from the heart: "He knew nothing of laws, and wherever they treated him well, there they had a good law; and if in Barbary the Moors treated him well and gave him what he needed to live, he would be a Muslim, as they were; and as far as going to heaven, he knew nothing, [he knew] only about having enough to eat and drink."[90] Relying on a similar rationale, the Morisco on his way to sell two rabbits in Gandía who, when questioned about which of the laws he followed, answered that "he had no law in his heart because he was too poor to permit himself such a luxury" should warn against tendencies to see the early modern world only in terms of religion and salvation.

3

Christian Tolerance

If God is so pleased, by doing good works and guarding God's law one can be saved, and it is not possible that such a mass of pagans could be damned. — Juan Sánchez de Escalonilla (Toledo, 1608)

It is wrong to take away the free will to believe what one wants and to obligate Christians to believe in the law of Jesus Christ by force . . . and it seems it is against what Christian doctrine teaches.
— Juan de Anguieta (Cuenca, 1662)

Given the history of contact and coexistence among the three religious communities in medieval Spain and the conditions of conversion which had brought many Muslims and Jews into the Church by the early sixteenth century, one can see why converts might have believed that other religions could be valid and that the Church did not have an exclusive claim to truth. Old Christians shared these ideas as well, but among them one must make some distinctions according to social status, nationality or place of birth, and life experiences, all of which influenced attitudes and orthodoxy. Perhaps the easiest way to make the transition from the minority groups of Conversos and Moriscos to the Christian majority is to examine Christians who were themselves of liminal status. One group of Christians who had lived beyond their cultural and religious frontiers, many of whom seem to have developed a certain permissiveness and sometimes even a sensitivity toward other peoples and other beliefs, were what the Spaniards called *renegados* and the Portuguese referred to as *elches,* that is, Christians who had converted to Islam.

There had been a good deal of cross-cultural military service in medieval Spain. Close contact had led by the thirteenth century to legislation aimed at restricting conversions. Throughout the medieval era, the continual contact between Christians and Muslims in Iberia, North Africa, and the Mediterranean created the conditions for such cultural crossovers, and the persistent if irregular hostilities produced willing converts and captives on both sides.[1] As Ottoman power expanded in North Africa in the late fifteenth century, the problem of Christian captives in Muslim hands intensified. Captives often converted, sometimes because of persuasion and conviction, sometimes to avoid mistreatment, and sometimes to live more freely and thus (so they claimed) gain access to the means to escape. This process continued in the early modern era.

Renegades

The numbers of Christians who as captives converted to Islam were not insignificant. Over 600 renegades appeared before the Inquisition tribunal in Sicily in the century before 1640; in the Canary Islands 232 were tried between 1579 and 1698. Hundreds of others appeared and sought reconciliation in the Inquisitions from Lisbon and Évora to Barcelona and Mallorca.[2] With the renegades, as with any other groups seen through the prism of Inquisition materials, one must proceed with caution. There are fine modern studies of the Iberian renegades prior to 1700 that, despite some overlapping, provide between six hundred and seven hundred accounts of intercultural lives and experiences.[3] The sample, of course, is far from representative. Only those who wished to return or who had the opportunity to do so or the bad luck to be caught came before the Inquisition. This meant that women rarely appear here, a situation created by the limitations on their lives in the Islamic world of that time and paralleled by less interest in them by the Inquisitors in general. Then, too, those returnees who did appear before the inquisitors understood that there were rules to the game of reconciliation. What they felt in their hearts, what they truly believed could often not be stated if there was to be hope of being accepted again within Christian society. In each inquisitorial investigation, a tale of captivity, hardship, escape, and redemption was spun out. Each renegade knew that in order to be welcomed back he could not say that he had abandoned the true faith in his heart or that if he implied that such was the case, it was a momentary lapse caused by love, the loss of the hope of rescue, or despair for other reasons. Most claimed they had converted to avoid punishment, torture, or bad treatment or in order to marry. While many *renegados* had become active in the endemic raiding by corsairs and other piratical activities in the Mediterranean and on the coasts of Iberia, they were usually very reluctant to admit their voluntary participation in hostile actions against Christians. The renegades told the inquisitors more or less what they wanted to hear: tales of unwilling prisoners who had to make some concessions in matters of faith in order to survive but who were now relieved to be once again in a Christian land and hopeful of being reintegrated within the Church.[4] The hundreds of cases are filled with fascinating details and glimpses into life on cultural and religious frontiers and zones of interaction, but because of the situation of their recording, the stories are predictable since their goal is almost always the same.

But despite the nature of these sources, the Inquisition trials of renegades provide an opportunity to examine belief and comportment of people at moments when the authority and power of their own state and the Church had been removed. Repeated over and over was the idea that many had eventually come to the belief that one could save one's self in "the law of the Moors" and that this law was a valid one. To what extent prior experiences and attitudes that predated the captivity itself facilitated such conclusions remains speculative, but as we have seen, such ideas were not absent from Christian society.

Force, conviction, and convenience may have all played a role in the conversion of the renegades to Islam, but the long-standing belief that "each can save himself in his own law" may have facilitated many of the decisions to convert. The phrase was repeated often in the depositions before the inquisitors. Catalans, Mallorcans, Greeks, Frenchmen, and Castilians all expressed some form of the old proverb in their stories as a way of explaining their acts of conversion.[5] In a world preoccupied with salvation, the idea that there be more than one path to it appealed to those faced with the travails of captivity and who sought some justification for improving their physical conditions without imperiling their souls. But there were sometimes cases of sincere conviction. A certain Joan Caules, a youth in his twenties from Mahón in Menorca, was held for almost four years in Algiers. He apparently had a taste for theology and listened to discussions between Christian clerics and Muslim scholars. It created doubts in his mind. On his return to Christendom, despite the admonition of friends, he spoke out, citing the usual propositions: How could Mary have remained a virgin after giving birth? It was wrong to paint images of God. If God is spirit which cannot die, then Christ could not die. But above all, he had come to believe that the law of the Moors and that of the Christians were the same. Only the prayers were different, the substance was the same.[6] Whatever the true nature of their beliefs, the *renegados* represented a large number of Christians who had been placed in situations of cultural and religious interaction.

While many of the renegades reported the ill-treatment and abuse they had suffered as captives, as was to be expected, many had also broadened their vision of the world and the range of their experience. From time to time, former renegades came to a cultural defense of their captors, noting various kindnesses, speaking of falling in love, and occasionally speaking of the religiosity of the Moors, for "they too believe in God" and "they pray four times a day" and "they are more charitable to one another than are we Christians to each other."

From the renegade stories, despite their universal desire to demonstrate a rejection of the otherness of the Islamic world, the permeability of cultural frontiers becomes apparent. In both the Indian Ocean and the Mediterranean, non-Christian cultures offered a variety of allures and opportunities that attracted Europeans. Take, for example, Francisco Rodrigues, an Old Christian of peasant stock who had gone with horse and arms to the African outpost of Tangier in 1582. Betrayal by his wife with a relative of his made him despondent, and he had then fled to Alcácer with the intention of converting to Islam. He was welcomed with open arms by the Moors. He told the inquisitors later that he had changed his mind and had never converted. Perhaps it was so, but there were many who went voluntarily into the service of non-Christian rulers and states and who seemed to make that cultural transition without great difficulty.[7] It was said some twenty thousand Portuguese renegades operated in the Indian Ocean beyond Christian control. They became cultural mediators, bringing European technology and ideas into their host societies. But their influence also moved in the opposite direction, and they became brokers and translators of other cultures for their societies of origin. Renegades could provide a point of contact with those who were still Christians. Pedro Fernández de Pastor, for example, a young man from Cartagena investigated by the Inquisition of Murcia in the mid-1580s, had been with some friends when they encountered a group of renegades who had arrived on the coast during a corsair raid. Pastor and his friends had asked the renegades why they did not return to their faith in Christ, to which they had replied, "They could also save themselves in that [Muslim] law." When one of the friends denied this, Pastor had told him to "shut up. What do you know about this?" An argument ensued. The friend held that learned doctors disagreed. Pastor said he knew more than all of them put together. The friend insisted that Moors went to hell and Christians at least went to purgatory, but Pastor remained adamant. The faith of the Moors was not a sect but a law, he said. They too had a purgatory, and he could not believe that their holy men who go to the hills to live a strict, holy existence are not saved by their good life. When told that they were damned, he replied that he had doubts since, "they also believe in God." The inquisitors proceeded. He denied the charges for awhile but was ultimately subjected to torture. He claimed that while Muslims might be saved if they lived a good life, he denied holding that they could be saved in their own law. Despite an escape attempt for which he received one hundred lashes, he got off relatively easily because "he seems to be a man of little understanding and has a big mouth."[8]

Old Christian Tolerance

The renegades in their liminal status and their broad cultural experience were a distinct element of the Old Christian population. Renegades along with the Conversos and Moriscos all had experiences, beliefs, or both that would make religious relativism or universalism attractive, but, as the Soria and Osma investigations discussed in chapter 2 revealed, such ideas were not limited to these minority or marginal groups. Other Old Christians shared these ideas.

Some cases from widely separated parts of the peninsula in the period 1570–1600 are instructive. In Portugal a visit of the Inquisition in the area of Porto revealed a number of people who believed in the old adage "each in his own law." The fisherman António Eanes denounced himself for having said, it's the same thing to be a Muslim or a Christian.[9] On the Mediterranean side of the peninsula, in Mallorca, Angela Ferrera, born in Moncada in Valencia and the widow of a tailor, had said that the Moors lived well in their own law. When admonished that there is no law except that of God, all other religions being but sects, she responded that God had made four laws, apparently including the Protestants along with the three traditional faiths. She was punished for these ideas, considered to be "manifestly suspicious of heresy," in 1591 and exiled from Mallorca for two years. The Catalan tailor Hierónimo Querols also ran afoul of the Mallorcan tribunal. He held a number of propositions that got him into trouble, and he was no friend of the Inquisition and its functionaries. Among his statements was that "there was more charity among Muslims and Lutherans than among Christians" and that "the law of the Muslims is better than that of the Mallorcans." His heterodox thinking got him five years in the galleys and a public flogging of one hundred stripes.[10]

Expressions of religious relativism for many Old Christians were part of a broader set of dissident ideas that set them apart from the dogma of the Church. We know about these propositions because their public expression often led to accusations and arrests by the Inquisition or because feelings of guilt caused people to confess their doubts and denounce themselves. From Inquisition records it is apparent that there were at least some doubters who expressed absolute disbelief; that there was only birth and death and all the rest — the existence of paradise, hell, and purgatory — was simply stories told by the priests to keep people in order. A Converso who stated that heaven was when you had enough money to give alms and hell was when you needed to accept them came close to a level of practical incredulity that would qualify him as a disbeliever. These skeptics approached the kind of atheism or doubt that Lucien Febvre in his classic book *The Problem of Unbelief in the Sixteenth Century* claimed could not have existed at that time, and which some Spanish authors have argued never existed in Spain. Part of the confusion is semantic. The term *atheist* was created in the sixteenth century. Its meaning then was broader than it is today and included not only those who did not believe in God, but also anyone who found God's presence to be irrelevant and thus might doubt the existence of heaven and hell or of the soul and its immortality. The fact that disbelief was severely punished by most societies led many people to dissimulate belief, and thus measuring the existence of disbelief is difficult.

But the possibility of atheism was already becoming a matter of concern among theologians at the close of that century. An edict of the faith asked people to denounce those who said that "there is no paradise, or glory for the good, nor hell for the bad. And there is nothing more than birth and death."[11] Both the French theologian Jean Bodin and his Spanish contemporary Fray Luis de Granada (in 1582) used the term *atheist* for such people. Gerónimo Graciano, in his *Ten Lamentations of the Miserable State of the Atheists in Our Times,* worried about the rise of nonbelievers, especially in the Low Countries.[12] In truth, however, Graciano's seven types of atheists were not really nonbelievers, but simply those whose actions or intentions violated true Christian belief or practice. Thus there were blasphemers, libertines, hypocrites, spiritual perfectionists (who created their own religions), political atheists (those who followed Machiavelli and put *raison d'état* above faith), and Christian atheists (who professed religion but privately lacked belief). Only these last and those whom Graciano called epicureans, who lived only for sensual appetites and who believed only in birth and death, seem to approach the level of disbelief in God that would make them atheists by modern standards. In the seventeenth century, writers like the Frenchman Michel de Montaigne, the Italian Giulio Cesar Vannini, and the Englishman John Toland would articulate views that were directly aimed as an attack on religion, while the New Science and post-Descartes philosophical trends would promote a rational questioning of religious belief. Nevertheless, even in the previous century there had been many people who had profound doubts about aspects of Catholic belief: the efficacy of the saints, the nature of the Eucharist, the concept of a God who dies, and the idea of the Trinity.[13]

Some of these doubters one might classify as skeptics or even agnostics, others were simply critical of the procedures and actions of the Inquisition or of the clergy in general, and still others were for various reasons attracted to other faiths. While some had reached their conclusions from exposure to "bad readings," others, often illiterates, had arrived at the same point through the lessons of life, brought to doubt and incredulity by exasperation, disappointment, or rational inspiration. It is important to place their stories into the discussion as a backdrop because the ideas of toleration, while usually not a negation of God's existence and in some ways an affirmation of a God whose power exceeded the constraints imposed by any one religion, were often packaged with other heretical propositions that indicated skepticism in some form. Take the case of Juan de Val, a fifty-year-old shepherd in the region of Cordoba, but originally from Raya (Burgos). A number of witnesses said he had questioned God's existence and had said he did not go to confession because it was just a way for monks and abbots to learn of his sins in order to make vulgar jokes (*chocarrear*) with the women. For him, God had not created religions or ordered churches to be built; those things had been done by men, and he did not believe in Jesus Christ. To these things he had added that the law of the Moors was good and that "each person should live in the law that he wanted." When challenged on these issues, he claimed that what he had meant was that each person should live according to his status (*estado*) — friar, priest, or married man — and that his status was that of bachelor (*soltero*). His defense was that of ignorance; he had never said the law of the Christians was better than that of the Moors or the contrary, and, after all, "he was no artist to know or understand which of the said laws was better."[14] This defense, that the accused was simply a poor, ignorant person, uninformed and unread, was a rather common one. "It is the 'lawyers' [*letrados*] or the 'doctors' or the 'doctors of Salamanca' who can answer that one" seems to have been a strategy employed by those arrested in this unequal dialogue between popular and learned culture that the inquests often represented. Those who employed it must have felt it would appeal to the men conducting the inquest, and in truth it was an effective strategy. Many of those who were punished relatively lightly received the inquisitor's mercy because they were "rustic and of little understanding."

But one cannot limit the analysis of such defenses to only the uneducated. The question of salvation preoccupied clerics, and the traditions and confusions of seemingly conflictive theological positions on the relative meaning of natural law, grace, and human agency often placed them before the Inquisition as well. They too argued ignorance. One of the standard defenses of these men was to say, "I am not a theologian" and "I will believe that which the Church requires me to believe." Their cases indicate that doubts on this central question of Christian faith were broadly held by lay and clergy alike and that there is little reason to distinguish between popular and learned culture in this regard. What remains unknown is whether the voyage of thought to these doubts followed similar routes, or whether the itineraries of the literate and illiterate diverged, or how experience and theology might have mutually reinforced the development of religious doubt.

Some detail is visible in another Old Christian case from Cordoba. The inquiry involved an investigation of Bartolomé de Jabalera, a weaver from Andújar who was about forty years old when he was arrested by the Inquisition. He had been denounced in 1573 for speaking too loosely on a number of matters relating to sexuality and religion. He had told an acquaintance that no one needed to go to hell for any sin, even sleeping with your mother. He also told the acquaintance, "Keep my secret, and I will tell you about the law of the Lutherans. They do not pay the tithe nor the church dues [*pimicias*], and he who has wealth gives it to him who has none. Don't you think this is good?" In another conversation someone had remarked about all the souls that went to hell, where there were so many Moors and Turks. Jabalera had expressed his doubts and said that not all Moors went to hell. Other witnesses claimed that in general he was a bad Catholic, eating meat on prohibited days, avoiding attendance at Mass, and even keeping his wife from attending. His questioning by inquisitors was revealing. Jabalera admitted that a young Frenchman had lived in his father's house and had taught him about Lutheran beliefs. This boarder had laughed at women who kissed a papal bull and had ridiculed a certain sermon about the Passion. Jabalera was no fool. He deflected the investigation by "almost" admitting to less theological sins. He said that on a couple of occasions he had been tempted to have sex with a donkey, but, recognizing it was a sin, he had stopped. He had also desired to have sex with his stepmother and had kissed and caressed her, but for lack of a place to do it, he had desisted. As for telling people about Lutheran ideas, he claimed he did so in order to show how bad that young Frenchman had been and not because he believed such things. On the matter of the Jews and Moors going to heaven, he claimed what he had said was that they and heretics could do so if they returned to the law of Christ, received baptism, and did Christian works. This was a glib and intelligent defense, but the Inquisitors were not convinced. He was subjected to torture but held firm. Since he could show that one of the witnesses was an enemy and since the matter of keeping his wife from Mass could not be established, his punishment was relatively light: appearance in an auto de fe and one hundred lashes.[15]

Ideas similar to those expressed by Jabalera probably circulated widely and were often discussed among acquaintances without leading to denunciations. Strangers and foreigners expressing the same ideas were always at much greater risk of denunciation, and they were a particular concern of the Inquisition.[16]

Attitudes toward Other Religions

Relativistic or universalistic ideas among the Old Christian population can best be approached in relation to groups that were perceived and described as being hostile to the true faith. The definition of non-Catholics or false Catholics as not only theologically damned, but also politically dangerous was a constant preoccupation of both the Church and the state throughout much of this period. The effect of such definitions was to create a broadly based suspicion, rejection, and sometimes fanatical loathing of such groups. Such hatreds were long lasting. The *refraneros,* collections of common expressions and proverbs, are filled with negative wisdom about Jews, Muslims, Gypsies, and, to some extent, Protestants. The author James Michener, when he asked an Andalusian farmer in the 1960s why the irrigation ditches did not work, was told that the Jews had damaged them, and this in a place where there had been no practicing Jews since 1492. Against Jews and Muslims the state had eventually imposed expulsion decrees, a policy that was later extended to Moriscos. Suggestions for the same action were also made about Gypsies but never fully enforced, although there was considerable judicial repression of Gypsies at various times. In the face of such effective efforts by Church and state, evidence of individuals who did not accept such definitions and had the courage or the poor judgment to say so is not lacking. In the Basque country María de Guniz, a sailor's wife who had lost a relative to pirates while he was on a voyage selling arms in North Africa, reacted to the local gossip that he had died in sin. She responded it was no sin to sell arms to Moors no matter what the pope said; one has to live. Moreover, the Moors respected their holy book, and they are better than many bad Christians, she told her neighbors — who then denounced her.[17] Her statement expressed a combination of self-interest and fair play. It is not surprising she was denounced. The whole weight of social and religious pressure demonized the Moors and Moriscos, but her willingness to speak well of them in 1580 echoed the sentiments of a century before, when that Sorian farmer had said in 1480 it was wrong for the king to take the homes of the Moors from them when they had not done him any harm.[18] These were expressions of a sense of justice and fairness that ran against state policy and religious teaching. The existence of such statements and such people lies at the heart of the issue about the individual and the power of institutions.

The contradictory tendencies of condemnation and admiration or fear and attraction had long run beneath the relations among the followers of the three laws. Centuries of contact had also led to architectural, linguistic, poetic, and other cultural fusions and crossovers, to translations, incorporations, and emulations.[19] Nevertheless, as the political and religious conflicts between the three cultures intensified after the fourteenth century, so too did the negative image of the cultures and people of the other faiths.

Literature offers some insight in this regard. While the image of Jews in Christian Hispanic literature after 1492 was, with a few exceptions, almost invariably negative, the vision of Muslims was more complex and varied. The Moorish kingdom of Granada and the heritage of learning, crafts, and especially architecture associated with Muslim Spain came to represent an exotic and sometimes romantic cultural past, appealing on an esthetic and a cultural level. The frontier wars of Granada had provided a context for the development of literary traditions of chivalry and heroism that were only enhanced by making the enemy worthy and ultimately tragic. The battles between Moors and Christians were celebrated and recalled in public folk performances that even today are enacted in many towns across Spain and in Latin America. In these festival performances, the image of the Moorish leader or hero, who is usually converted to Christianity in the climax of the performance, is a positive one. In more formal Spanish literature, the Muslims of Granada, especially under the last rulers of the Nasrid dynasty, represented a brilliant civilization on the verge of decline, admirable in its accomplishments but flawed by its false religion and thus destined be replaced. Granada itself took on the image of exotic luxury, and the fall of its ruling dynasty was perceived in the mold of tragedy.[20]

The themes of admiration for the Moor but unrelenting opposition to his false religion became central aspects of Spanish literature. Despite the medieval prohibitions against sexual contacts and the long history of political and religious conflict and hostility, Muslims were sometimes presented as attractive, admirable characters in the literature of the sixteenth and seventeenth centuries. The classic (and earliest) text of this tradition was *El Abencerraje* (c. 1561), a frontier story of military chivalry and romantic love. Ginés Pérez de Hita's *Guerras civiles de Granada* (vol. 1, 1595) was a prose work that also made use of these themes as they related to both the wars for Granada and the subsequent Morisco rebellion in the Alpujarras in the 1560s.

During the Golden Age of Spanish literature (c. 1550–1660) many of the principal authors took up these themes of the contact with the Muslims or included *moros* as characters in their works. The playwright Félix Lope de Vega Carpio used them extensively, often as secondary characters in works that were purely fictional or that drew on historical events related to the wars of Granada or to encounters with the Turks in the Mediterranean. Moorish garb and dialect became common elements in Golden Age drama, intended to amuse and provide a simultaneous sense of familiarity and the exotic.[21]

But the relationship of the literary image to attitudes and to the practical reality of everyday life was complex. Noble Moors of a doomed Granada or Turkish pirates were easier to represent positively than restive, rebellious Moriscos, at least for most authors. Lope de Vega, closely associated with the court, remained ambivalent about Moriscos and supported their expulsion as well as the *limpieza de sangre* laws, although he could still present Muslim individuals in a positive light. In one historical play, Lope has the hero respond to a Moorish proposal of a marriage union with this reply: "With the Moors one should not mix, for in the end they are all dogs." Literary "morophilia" had its limits.[22]

In this regard and perhaps most relevant to my topic are the writings of Miguel de Cervantes, author of *Don Quixote*. Cervantes knew the Islamic world. He had spent some five years as a captive in Algiers, and he knew some Arabic as well as Turkish.[23] He wrote four plays on the theme of Christian captivity and incorporated a tale of captivity and return of a renegade to Christianity within the structure of *Don Quixote*. Like other Spanish authors of his age, he made no positive concessions to Islam, yet he did write positively about Muslim individuals. In fact, he even used as a literary device the discovery of the original account of the adventures of Don Quixote in an old Arabic manuscript as the supposed source for the exploits of the Man of La Mancha.[24]

Perhaps most important is Cervantes's treatment of the story of Ricote told in *Don Quixote*.[25] Ricote was a Morisco shopkeeper who was expelled with the Moriscos from Spain but who returned in disguise as a pilgrim, and when he is recognized by his old neighbor Sancho Panza, the archetypical Old Christian commoner, their reunion is one of long-lost friends. Even though Cervantes was careful to make Ricote a true convert to the Church and has him justify the expulsion of the Moriscos as a necessary step against potential domestic enemies, the pain of Morisco exile is also sympathetically made clear: "Wherever we are we weep for Spain; for after all we were born here, and this is our native country." Expulsion had divided his family. His wife and daughter had gone into exile in Muslim Algiers, but Ricote had gone to Germany, "where," Cervantes has him note, "everyone lives as he pleases, and over the greatest part of the country there is liberty of conscience." Ricote had returned to Spain to recover a treasure he had buried before the expulsion — another Christian trope about the Moriscos — and although he offers to share it, Sancho refuses to help. He cannot aid the Morisco enemies of his king, but neither will he betray his old Morisco friend. Later, however, Sancho helps reunite Ricote with his beautiful and virtuous daughter.[26] Sancho's ambivalence and the story of Ricote itself are used by Cervantes, within the constraints imposed by his society, to open the conflicting paths about the relations between the Muslims and Moriscos and Christian Spain and about their image in that society. But the extent to which Cervantes's sympathies and ambivalences reflected his social milieu remains at question.

Extracting social reality from literary images is always complicated, even when, as in the case of the Moors in Spain, the sources are rich. I want to explore for a moment other kinds of sources in order to examine the attitudes toward two groups perceived as enemies by the sixteenth century: one old, the Jews, and one more recent, the so-called Lutherans. The campaign of opprobrium and denigration carried out against Judaism and by extension against New Christians became a central motif of Spanish and Portuguese cultural life in the sixteenth century.[27] In the face of considerable danger that anything but complete rejection of Judaism or Jewish practice might cause someone who demonstrated sympathy toward Jews or their descendants, there remained a powerful attraction for some Old Christians. Why should that have been so?

Don Diego Sarmiento, a native of Murcia and a member of its municipal guild organization, had an interest in mysticism and in esoteric knowledge, or at least he knew enough about it to use it as an excuse before the Inquisition. Sarmiento had traveled to Oran in North Africa, and there he had been in contact with Jews. The Spanish North African outpost at Oran had been occupied in 1509. It played a special role as a place where the three religions continued to be practiced legally long after 1492 and remained so until the expulsion of the Jews in 1669.[28] Upon occupation, the Spaniards had imposed a strict policy of control on the Jewish residents, seizing their synagogues and instituting various restrictions. The community remained, however, often serving as intermediaries and translators between the Spanish administrators and the local Muslim population. Closely tied by trade to Murcia and having a resident commissioner of the Inquisition of Murcia, Oran nevertheless was one of the few places where Spaniards could still interact with practicing Jews.[29]

In Oran, Sarmiento had entered the Jewish quarter and had conversed with Jews about the *Zohar*, the medieval Jewish text considered to be the best compendium of kabbalistic knowledge. The Jews had led him to believe it contained powerful knowledge and was a key to understanding the world. He had also inquired about the *Kabbalah* and its mysterious contents and had asked to learn the names of God and other of its secrets. Sarmiento had gone with them to visit the synagogue and had inquired about other aspects of the law of Moses. He had broken bread with the Jews of Oran and apparently had been welcomed in their homes. What could have caused such behavior and the flaunting of convention? Sarmiento was clearly fascinated by the possibility of esoteric and forbidden knowledge and by a chance to experience an exotic other, but before the Inquisitors his defense was that he had done these things "for curiosity."[30]

This theme of curiosity appears in a number of the stories told by Old Christians accused of consorting with Jews and possibly of being "infected" by their ideas. Demonization of Jews and New Christians did make them a despised other, but this policy also turned them into exotics whose culture and practices generated a certain attraction and fascination. The tale of Juan Pablo, tried in Murcia in 1584, is noteworthy in this regard. Pablo was a Converso silk weaver who had been born in Rego in the Duchy of Ferrara. He had traveled to Spain as a soldier in the galleys, and from Cartagena he had made the voyage to the Spanish North African outpost at Oran. There, he had gone into the Jewish quarter and had stayed for four days, eating with the local Jews and entering the synagogue. Witnesses claimed they had seen him in the *judería* teaching little Jewish boys to read Hebrew. Pablo explained his behavior as a scheme for extracting money from the Jews. He claimed he had told them he was a galley slave and asked for money to buy his freedom. Upon examination, the inquisitors discovered that Pablo knew his Christian prayers well, and they took note of the fact that while in the quarter he had been accompanied by a Christian companion. His punishment was light: he was released with an admonishment. What Pablo's real motives were and how he identified himself are matters of conjecture now beyond our ability to know, but the case raises another issue. How to explain the four witnesses who saw him in the *judería?* What were they doing there? They were Old Christians, honorable enough to be considered legitimate witnesses by the inquisitors. Why had they gone to see the Jews? Their explanation was simple: they had been moved "by their curiosity."[31]

What did the word *curiosity* imply in this context and at this historical moment? Individuals were willing to observe the ideas and practices of other faiths and cultures and offered *curiosity* as their justification of contact with nonbelievers. This was exactly the case of Baltasar André, a Portuguese living in Brazil, who had been captured at sea by the English and taken to Southampton. He admitted in 1592 while living in England that he and his companions had sometimes visited the Lutheran churches out of curiosity. Curiosity was held responsible or credited for the actions of those involved in these contacts. In truth, curiosity was emerging by the end of the sixteenth century as a neutral or sometimes positive human characteristic, but it had not always been so, and there had been a long classical and medieval theological tradition which condemned humankind's unbridled desire to know things and to question the world as it was given to them. St. Augustine had linked curiosity with distraction from a Christian's primary responsibility in the quest for his own salvation, and a similar line of argument had characterized other patristic and, later, monastic moralists. Curiosity was seen as an aspect of cupidity or ambition and thus was to be avoided or controlled. Curiosity was transgressive. It challenged norms and standards of behavior and belief.

These critiques of curiosity often had as their targets those who wished to know the secrets of the globe through travel or who hoped to explore the mysteries of the natural world.[32] The critics saw curiosity as "the original temptation and sinne," in the words of Francis Bacon, but, as he argued, learning might better reveal God's plan, and when it was combined with contemplation it could improve morality.[33] This new thrust of curiosity was often linked to exploration and travel and might be justified as a desire to know God's plan, but travel also implied knowledge of other peoples and cultures and thus contact with other religions. That potential danger was balanced by the utility of this curiosity for the spreading of the Christian message. A semantic shift valorizing curiosity took place as a new missionary zeal and purpose emerged in the sixteenth century. The concept of curiosity itself underwent a transformation in usage and a new prominence. Whereas in the mid–sixteenth century the word *curiosity* appeared in the title of fewer than 50 books per decade in the major European languages, by the 1690s that figure had risen to almost 350 titles.[34]

This was a cultural curiosity that was growing, and by the seventeenth century, stimulated by economic considerations, political motivations of *raison d'état,* and religious considerations of reformist and apocalyptic Christian thought, it had produced a philo-Semitic movement among European elites. What is striking from the evidence presented here is the existence of a popular fascination with and curiosity about Jews that predated the later and often more practical or advantage-seeking approximation to Jews and Jewish culture of the seventeenth-century philo-Semites. Figures like Queen Christina of Sweden, the Portuguese Jesuit writer and preacher Padre António Vieira, and pragmatists like the Count Duke of Olivares and the French minister Colbert, all of whom saw economic or political advantage to be had in a more tolerant attitude toward the Jews, represented the pragmatism of the *politiques* combined, in some of them at least, with curiosity and tolerance. That combination, however, was not limited to rulers and statesmen.

Practicing Jews were, after all, strange and exotic in early modern Iberia;

Conversos were not. Conversos were a part of everyday life and objects of common opprobrium, but they also sometimes made a positive impression on Old Christians. One way they did so was by the nature of their constancy to the old law and their refusal when faced with death to surrender their beliefs. In 1595 or so, Fernando de Ludena was a thirty-six-year-old public scribe (*escribano*) in the town of Mahón who had been discussing the actions of the Inquisition of Toledo. Ludena had told his companions that "the good Moor should die as a Moor and the Jew as a Jew and the Christian as a Christian." Ludena had said that those who had not abandoned their faith at the last moment, that is, who had not accepted the cross and thus the favor of being garroted before being burned rather than being burned alive had "died like good soldiers, never taking a backward step."[35] Such attitudes were not exceptional. Catalina Crespo, a *beata,* or religious woman, from Baeza in Andalusia had a reputation as a woman who was a particular friend of the Conversos and a person who refused to speak ill of them. She warned her neighbors of the possible apocalyptic cost of injustice and that "many were punished or died without fault and some clear day will come when all will be revealed."[36] The idea that those who died in the Inquisition's flames were martyrs for their faith and died unjustly was expressed not only by Conversos but by Old Christians as well, people like Jerónima de Campos, wife of a wool carder from Ubeda denounced in the 1570s for saying that a particular Converso had died "a guiltless martyr."[37]

If the attitudes toward Jews and their descendants grew from the ancient enmity and coexistence of the Iberian Middle Ages, the feelings toward Protestantism were, by definition, something much newer. Reform Christianity had made some inroads in Spain in the early sixteenth century, and despite Erasmus's famous "Hispania non placet" (Spain does not please me) response to an invitation to go to Spain, his ideas and more radical ones did penetrate the peninsula. Whether growing from northern pietism, Italian apocalypticism, or indigenous Spanish mysticism, mendicant zeal, and illuminism, ideas at odds with those of Church authority flourished in limited circles in Spain. This fact and the growing restiveness and rebellion in the Low Countries, which was partly fueled by religious dissidences, troubled both the crown and the Church. In the 1520s a group of *alumbrados,* or illuminists, who practiced a kind of passive inner mysticism were prosecuted in Toledo. The Inquisition also prosecuted the followers of Erasmus's brand of spiritual reform. As the historian John Elliott has noted, the more open Spain of the Renaissance was giving way to the closed Spain of the Counter-Reformation, as the tolerant humanism of the Erasmians was suppressed.[38]

Denunciations of relativist or universalist beliefs regarding Lutherans fell on two categories of people: Old Christian Spaniards and foreigners. Foreigners included German artisans, English merchants and mariners, other Europeans, and, most of all, the large number of French who were found in Catalonia, Aragon, the Basque provinces, and major ports and cities. The very fact of foreign origins or, especially, French nationality or birth was reason enough for suspicion, and the statements of French residents and itinerants in Spain were carefully scrutinized for their potentially heretical content. Often the statements were like that of Juan Falcó, a native of Narbonne (Langueduc), who had gotten into a conversation about religion while in Mallorca. When asked how many types of people there were in the world, Falcó had answered, "Christians, Hugenots, Lutherans, and Jews, and all believe in one God." When told that those who were unbaptized and did not believe in Holy Mother Church could not be saved, he responded, "Neither you nor I can say that." Falcó's rationalization of his position grew out of common sense, decency, and biblical foundations. First, he argued that if all these people were going to hell, the devils would have too much to do.[39] As for the fact that the Jews had scourged and crucified Christ, Falcó remembered Christ's words, "Father forgive them for they know not what they do," which he took to be a sign of their ability to be saved. Christ's words, he said, were always of great power. Falcó was sentenced to public penitence, reclusion, and religious instruction, and his speech was judged to be "suspicious of heresy," but by offering Christ's own words and example he was able to make his point, and the inquisitors were inclined to be lenient.[40]

The statements by various Frenchmen arrested by Spanish tribunals often displayed both a strong sense of national pride and a certain willingness to accept the validity of Protestant ideas. The Frenchman Luis Trabalon, a native of St. Martin, was a peddler. He was only twenty-one when arrested in 1615. He had been at a Valencian inn when he began to discuss the wedding of a prince of Spain to a French princess. Someone had said the marriage was ill-advised because the French were without honor and they were Lutherans. Trabalon had risen to the challenge. The French were as good Christians, he said, as the Spaniards. They too believed in God, and those that were Protestants followed the precepts of their sect better than did the Spaniards — although he admitted they were in error. Finally, Pedro Govion, a young laborer native of Vañol (Bañul) but residing in Orihuela, had responded to a remark that France was a land of Lutherans who were all going to hell by saying that "the Lutherans go to heaven if God wills it," and witnesses said he had added that the Moors could also go to heaven with God's aid.[41]

It is difficult to separate their cultural pride as Frenchmen from their feelings about religion, but many of these French expressions of the relative validity of

Lutheran beliefs seem to reflect some experience with that religion and its believers. Juan Viñas, a thirty-five-year-old rural worker from Toulouse, could simply not believe in the damnation of so many persons of quality in France. He asked, "How was it possible that with so many [illustrious] men, dukes, counts, doctors, and so many Lutheran ladies that all were going to hell? And when told that all who separated themselves from the law of Christ were so condemned, he responded, 'How do you know who will be saved and who will be lost? Only God knows.' "[42]

Within the context of French political and religious life these relativist statements or those expressing admiration or sympathy for Protestants make some sense, but there were also people in Spain who found the prosecution of the Protestants a misdirected policy and who believed, like the followers of the three traditional laws, that the Protestants too could be saved. Francisco de Amores had attended an auto de fe in Valladolid at which a number of Protestants had been executed and a condemnatory sermon had been preached. Amores believed that the punishments meted out and the sermon given had been against the principles of Christian faith. Amores held that "each person can be saved in his own law, the Moor in his, the Jew in his, the Christian in his, and the Lutheran in his."[43] Sometimes, the criticism was self-serving. William Keith, a Scot resident in Madrid, told the inquisitors that there was no precedent in the primitive Church for burning heretics and that they should be left to God's mercy. His attitude toward the inquisitors was so confrontational that they deemed him mad.

One line of interpretation of the expressions of toleration holds that they were primarily the natural outgrowth of Iberia's peculiar medieval experience of coexistence and contact between the three religions. This position, perhaps most forcefully argued by Henry Kamen, tends to see Spain as a distinctive place, and the argument seems reasonable given Spain's long multireligious experience, although there is also much evidence of hostility as well both before and after the anti-Jewish riots of 1391. Evidence, however, indicates that when they were in Spain and Portugal or their colonies, foreigners from other parts of Europe also expressed ideas of toleration and criticism of the discrimination suffered by the descendants of Jews and Muslims. For that offense they were brought before the Inquisition. Giraldo de Goz, a soldier from Artois, was a member of the contingent of Flemish archers in the king's guard. In 1585, he had been in some rooms near the Carmelite monastery in Madrid with some other guardsmen when the fact that the descendants of Jews and Muslims were not admitted to positions in some churches had been discussed. Goz had said this was wrong because the Church "should be equal for all."[44] His position provoked a response that it was just that "the children and grandchildren and descendants of those who had won the land and defended the holy Catholic faith and spilled their blood should be favored," but Goz remained unconvinced.[45]

Doubters

The number of prosecutions for the proposition that there were many valid ways to God was probably never statistically significant and, in fact, seems to have declined in the mid–seventeenth century. This apparent reduction parallels the decline in prosecutions for other crimes against morality as well as other propositions, and it has led some observers to argue that this trend reflects the success of the Inquisition in imposing a more consistent and orthodox brand of Catholicism among the population. The decline, of course, could have come for other reasons; people may have simply learned to be more circumspect in the expression of their beliefs, or the Inquisition may have simply given up trying to impose uniformity of belief on certain topics not felt to be threatening after the major Protestant scare had passed. But I doubt that the inquisitors were turning a blind eye toward relativism or universalism because such ideas had strong theological implications.

For this reason I wish to close this discussion with three cases which are chronologically rather late and which represent different types or expressions of religious indifference, confusion, or toleration. The first case is that of Fray Fernando Ramírez de Arellano, who was tried by the Inquisition in 1682.[46] Ramírez at that time was a Franciscan about forty years old who had been born in Oran. In 1677 he had turned up in Seville, where before the Inquisition he claimed that at the age of five he had been taken by a (presumably Muslim) family as a slave to Algiers and from there to Constantinople, where he had been circumcised. He then served on Turkish corsair ships, but in Sardinia he had escaped and gone to the Inquisition, where he had been absolved of his conversion because of his youth and ignorance. He eventually went to Seville. where he took orders as a Franciscan.

Thus far Ramírez's story sounds rather typical of that of many of the renegades, but further investigation produced strange and conflicting details. Ramírez admitted that while in Cádiz he had dealings with Jews (probably meaning Conversos) and that with them he had read the Bible in observance of the law of Moses. He admitted in later questioning that while in Cádiz he had begun to doubt his Christian faith and that "he much desired to be a Jew and deal with Jews and to reduce Catholics to do the same and to believe in the law of Moses, which he studied with great pleasure." He later claimed that among the Jews of Alicante he had discussed the Cabala and that he had come to believe that Christ was not the real Messiah, "but having been the servant of a prophet and blessed with the gift of making miracles, they said he was the Messiah." The inquisitors pushed hard in various hearings. He admitted that he had lived with his parents until age fifteen and that he had gone to Algiers and had lived there "as a Turk" for nine years. Upon returning to Christendom, he had gone for awhile to America. In conflicting stories, Ramírez told the inquisitors first that he had fled to the Indies to escape arrest, but later that in fact he had convinced the Inquisition of Seville that he had a brother still a captive in Algiers so that he was allowed to go to raise money for his brother's ransom. In four sessions, the inquisitors tried to get his story straight. Ramírez admitted he was an atheist "in his heart." But in reality, he seems to have been a man unsatisfied with all the faiths and desperately looking for some satisfaction in each, or perhaps all, of them. Franciscan friar, Turk, and would-be Jew, Ramírez had sought a life in each. But he was not willing to die for his search for certainty. In the second session he had recanted his error and said that he now hated the Jews so much that he would leap into the flames himself rather than see them.[47] Public auto de fe, perpetual imprisonment, and use of a penitential robe, or *sanbenito,* were his punishments. But what should we make of the Old Christian friar — seeker after truth? or believer in none? Was he a man open to many ways of life? or a scoundrel with no scruples? Whatever he was, he had moved between the three laws with relative ease and seemingly little hesitation, living out in practice the relativist ideas expressed by others.

Remarkable similarities between Ramírez de Arellano's odyssey and the story of the Portuguese Simeão de Oliveira e Sousa, have been revealed by the Brazilian historian Adriana Romero.[48] Oliveira e Sousa, born in Lisbon in 1678, was partially educated by the Jesuits; he sailed for Rio de Janeiro about 1695 to join his physician father. He then began to travel into the provinces of the Río de la Plata, traveling to Córdoba, Salta, Potosí, and Chuquisaca and while doing so, dressing successively in the habits of a member of the Franciscans, the Dominicans, and as a secular priest. While at university in Chuquisaca (probably San Francisco Xavier, founded in 1624) he became a discalced Franciscan and remained there for some six years before fleeing to Lima, where he was arrested but released, at which point he returned to Portugal and for awhile dressed as an Augustinian friar, only to leave that calling in order to marry. The travels continued and while sailing to Cape Verde he was captured by Barbary corsairs who carried him to Algiers. There he practiced Islam, only to reconvert to Catholicism at the urging of a Franciscan whom he encountered and who convinced him to take up the habit of Saint Francis once again. Still spiritually unquiet, however, he had contact with both Jews and English Protestants and flirted with their faiths as well.

Eventually, he returned to Portugal, where as a Franciscan he said Mass and performed other priestly functions until he was finally denounced after confessing to an illicit relationship he was maintaining with a woman. He had used over sixteen aliases during his career as a Franciscan, Dominican, Augustinian, secular priest, layman, Jew, Muslim, and Protestant.[49]

The inquisitors of Évora were somewhat befuddled by Oliveira e Sousa, but questioning revealed that he had picked up Lutheran ideas of salvation through grace alone. He was sentenced to ten years of penal exile in India, but once there he soon fell afoul of the Goa Inquisition because of a series of statements that smacked of heresy and reflected his passage through the cultural and religious middle grounds of the Iberian empires. Among his statements was his belief in the possibility of salvation outside the Church: "Our Lord God was very merciful that he had to save those who lived good lives like those who lived bad ones, especially gentiles, Moors, and Jews." He was eventually tried again in Lisbon in 1725, and he lived out his life there as a Latin tutor, still collecting materials about religion, still writing, and still on the narrow border of heterodoxy and heresy. Known as a liar and con man to some, Oliveira lived a life that was a testimony to the possibility of cultural crossings and the challenges of belief they presented.

If Ramírez de Arellano and Oliveira are examples of the permeable lines in early modern religious identities and of the way in which individuals might be willing to concede the possibility of alternate ways to salvation, there were others whose outlook seemed to be truly tolerant and who seemed to have no immediate self-interest underlying their attitude. Although in the late eighteenth century prosecutions in Spain for universalist statements or for the idea that each person might be saved in his own law rose dramatically as a seeming impact of the Enlightenment, by the end of the seventeenth century such prosecutions had slowed considerably. The arrest of Inocencio de Aldama in November 1701 was, therefore, extraordinary. Even more exceptional is the fact that the report of his case is detailed enough to permit one to get beneath the surface of his statements and beliefs.[50] Aldama was a tall, twenty-eight-year-old man, of light complexion with short brown hair and an aquiline nose. He was of Old Christian stock and was a native of Oquendo (Alava) in the Basque country. In November 1701 he had been admitted to a hospital in Villarobles (Murcia) and there had entered into conversations with a holy man about the life he was living. Aldama had apparently wanted at some point to be a priest, but, as he said, God had not willed it to be, so he was living the life of a vagabond with no fixed residence and no profession despite the fact he could read and write. He was, he said, a man whom God had destined to be a vagabond and to suffer tribulations. The holy man was critical and told him it was God's will that he apply himself to an honest trade "proportionate to his salvation." The conversation touched on a number of theological points, such as the value of baptism, about which Aldama had some dissident ideas which upset his questioner. The conversation then turned to salvation, and Aldama had made this statement: "that any person can save themselves in the law that they may profess so long as they keep it, be they Moor, infidel, or heretic and that we all come from the same stock from which different roots appear which [all] give fruit, and so too are all the laws and sects and that all are saved in that which they wish to hold so long as they keep it responsibly."

The hermit found such ideas to be schismatic, and he reported the conversation to the local commissary of the Inquisition, and this had led to Aldama's arrest. Information was gathered and the inquisitors voted to place him in the secret prison and to seize his property. Arrested on January 4, he was first questioned on January 9, 1702. Corroborating witnesses were called to testify, and Aldama's remarks were submitted to three churchmen to be evaluated. All three found his statements to be formal heresies.[51] Further sessions followed, in which Aldama claimed God had taken from him his free will for not continuing his studies, and on the issue of salvation the best the inquisitors could do was to have Aldama say that he did not know if those who were not Christians could be saved.

Aldama was assigned a court lawyer for his defense and under his advice, the defendant swore that he believed in all the Church taught, but the nature of his statements now began to become cloudy and unclear. For example, he told the inquisitors that life was like the rope of San Francisco with many knots in it, and it depended on the principal Spirit, and if he could unite with all, he would do it but for this he had instituted the Holy Sacrament. He said this, the inquisitors reported, and "many other foolishnesses." By February, the tribunal's staff was becoming convinced Aldama was mad and getting worse. A physician brought in by the court came to the same conclusion, and by April his lawyer was asking that the case be dismissed and Aldama released. But the madness was problematic. When asked if he knew what an oath was, Aldama had responded, "That is bringing God as a witness to affirm or deny something and to all testimonies." He was responding "in a disorderly manner." The responses were convoluted and confused but among them were perceptive observations. Try as they might, the inquisitors could not dissuade him of some things. He told them, "Each person has his orientation, and from this position not even the theologians of Salamanca could convince him."

How to deal with this case and how to explain these strange ideas? The investigation continued. Aldama had apparently lived with his maternal grandmother and his uncle, a priest. At some point he had been disrespectful, and, fearing his uncle, he had fled to Madrid and there was pressed into service as a soldier. He had campaigned in Catalonia, Sicily, and Naples before he returned to Madrid. Relatives had sought to send him back to his homeland, but he had refused, and they came to see him as melancholy and often speaking to himself. His discussion with the inquisitors led to further confusion and consultation, and the result was a vote to place him for observation in a hospital for the mad in Valencia.[52]

How should Aldama be viewed? Was his melancholy like that of Hamlet, feigned and real at the same time; a strategy for survival and a mask? The historian Juan Blázquez Miguel has argued that rather than being mad, Aldama was a man of "great culture, brilliant intelligence, and sharp reasoning" who tried to convince the inquisitors of his position.[53] He seems to have been in many ways a man who had been battered by life and had withdrawn into himself, but also a man who had traveled widely and lived abroad. Mixed in with his strange ideas about the Holy Spirit and chrism was a truth he held that was shared by others, that each person could save themselves in their own faith, that all the religions were part of the same plant, and that all bore fruit, and that each person had a destiny. On these points, he held, not even the doctors of Salamanca could dissuade him.

These three exemplary lives are, of course, constructions, self-representations made under threat as well as the products of testimony created by the inquisitors themselves, but despite artifice and obfuscation, there are patterns that suggest some commonalities. Many of those like Aldama who expressed religious tolerance or relativism were people who had seen the world or who were open to ideas through their access to books. Undoubtedly, travel broadened, and it is tempting to see them as part of a subculture of difference, people often marginal in occupation or status, prone to change, more mobile than their peers, and more open to ideas than their peers. But such a reading is too facile and implies a contrast with an immobile Iberian rural society that is no longer easy to sustain. Tens of thousands of rural people moved along the highways and roads each year as part of the harvest cycle, thousands of others marched off to Flanders, France, Italy, Catalonia, and Portugal in the king's armies, thousands of others made their way from villages and towns to the seaports to serve in the fleets or merchant vessels, and a constant stream of immigrants moved from places like Trujillo and Brihuega to cross the Atlantic to live in Puebla or Potosí, many of them maintaining contact with relatives and friends in their old communities.[54] What impact this mobility had on rural society is open to debate. It may have allowed traditional attitudes and practices to continue by drawing off the sources of demographic and social pressure. It may also be that dissidents and innovators were more prone to travel, but through their correspondence and the eventual return home of some, the patterns of migration may have also introduced change into the rural communities. For those who left, undoubtedly travel and experience had the potential to open minds to new ideas, but not necessarily. Many a sojourner was denounced by his traveling companions or shipmates. There seems to be no set of social characteristics that placed those who developed the ideas of tolerance or relativism apart from their more orthodox peers. Every person was a potential traveler, each traveler a potential heterodox thinker, but many who took to the road or the sea remained entirely orthodox in their beliefs. Individual decisions and convictions rather than social characteristics seem to determine what path of belief they took.

4

Portugal: Old Christians and New Christians

*If God did not want the New Christians to be Christians, why did the
Lord Inquisitors wish to make them Christians by force?*
                                    —Domingos Gomes (Évora, 1623)

In 1578, Dom Sebastião, the young and reckless king of Portugal, after
involving himself in the dynastic politics of Morocco, led a military expedition under the guise of a crusade across the Strait of Gibraltar. The results
were disastrous. On the sands of Alcazarquivir, the expeditionary army was
routed; the flower of the Portuguese nobility was killed or held for ransom;
and in the midst of battle the king disappeared, never to be seen again. His
vacant throne was soon claimed and occupied by his distant uncle, Philip II of
Castile. But even before the battle, there had been those in Portugal who had
raised doubts not only about the need for such an adventure, but about its
justice as well. During an inquisitorial visit to the Portuguese Alentejo in
1578–79, for example, Manuel Rodrigues, an Old Christian, called into question the justification of Portugal's campaigns in North Africa. He warned that
"only God knew if this war was just or unjust because the Muslims were also
his creatures," and when told that all the Muslims were condemned to hell, he
answered that "only God knew if they went there or not." In that same inquest, a certain Lianor Martins, a New Christian, descendant of converted

Jews, complained that Dom Sebastião's campaigns in Morocco had unmade many marriages and caused many people to be lost because he had not allowed each person to live in his or her law, the Jews in theirs, the Muslims in theirs, and the Old Christians in theirs.[1] Here was the old Iberian refrain, spoken with a Portuguese inflection by both Old Christians and New and advocating, in simple language, the ancient idea of freedom of conscience.

Throughout the previous chapters I have noted cases involving the Portuguese, and it would seem that the elements of both a profound religiosity and of occasional religious dissent or heterodoxy were as characteristic of Portuguese society as they were of the various kingdoms and provinces that composed Spain and its empire.[2] Both countries had a deeply rooted Catholic identity, both felt threatened by Erasmian reform and the Protestant Reformation, and both sought through repression and internal reform to fortify the faith and reinvigorate the Church. Nor can one ignore the fact that beginning in the fifteenth century, Portugal was embarked on a course of overseas maritime expansion to North Africa, Africa, Brazil, and in the Indian Ocean and beyond to China and Japan. This experience of trade and exploration and of contact and conflict produced an impact on the mental framework of Portuguese society. From the literature and chronicles of the age of discovery a picture emerges of a series of cultural encounters that brought the accepted beliefs of late medieval Catholicism into confrontation with other faiths and other peoples. These contacts generated a sense of mission in Portugal that eventually produced a providential vision of the country's role in history and within the divine order as a bearer of the cross to new lands and peoples; a vision appropriated and used to advantage by the crown and by the missionary orders. At the same time, the imperial thrust of overseas expansion created some unexpected attitudes. Like the existence of cultural or religious minorities in Portugal itself, overseas cultural encounters had the potential to promote violent intolerance and confrontation, but also to suggest the possibilities of coexistence with peoples of differing customs and ways and may have made some Portuguese particularly prone to the kind of religious relativism or universalism we have seen thus far in the Hispanic world.

Such sentiments were often mixed with the same range of heretical propositions found elsewhere in the Iberian peninsula: doubts about the Eucharist, the efficacy of the saints, the virginity of Mary, the sinfulness of sex, and the existence of purgatory, heaven, and hell.[3] The teachings of the Church on the issue of sexuality were much in dispute.[4] An example is Francisco Pegado, a bachelor who lived in the district of Torres Vedras. Pegado lived *amancebado* with a woman and was in the habit of saying that sex between an unmarried man and woman was no sin. When warned in 1651 that St. Paul had said that fornicators would not go to heaven, Pegado had responded that if St. Paul was correct, then no one would be saved. He added that many inquisitors also had such relationships and that if the New Christians they arrested were rich, the inquisitors never returned their property to them. In other words, he had joined his heterodoxy about sex to a critique of the Inquisition's treatment of the descendants of the converted Jews. The men called to give witness against him, Francisco Lourenço, a farmer, and Gaspar de Colonia, a black former slave, refused to do so, claiming they had not heard these statements. Although they were admonished to hide nothing, they refused to testify against him. The charges against Pegado were dismissed.[5] Like many of those who uttered heretical propositions, Pegado expressed a questioning or nonconformity that reached outward from the most mundane and carnal aspects of life to more spiritual ones and extended to a dissidence and critique of authority.

The Portuguese Preoccupations: New Christians and Superstitions

Here a word about moderns' ability to penetrate the mental universe that opinions like Pegado's suggest. One's knowledge is affected, not by a lack of documentation, but by its nature and origin. While the Portuguese Inquisition functioned after 1547, and its principles and objectives were quite similar to those of the Spanish tribunals, its structure and its preferences or fixations differed considerably from the Spanish Holy Office. The Spanish tribunals, after an early preoccupation with Judaizers between 1480 and 1520, greatly expanded the scope of their interests, and by the later sixteenth century they gave considerable attention to a broad range of crimes from bigamy to blasphemy, from sexual deviation to heretical propositions. Between 1540 and 1700, prosecutions for Judaizers made up only about 10 percent of the activity of the Spanish tribunals.

The four Portuguese inquisitorial courts did prosecute the same range of offenses as the Spanish tribunals, but they remained far more concentrated on the question of crypto-Judaism. Although the records from the Goa tribunal have been lost, of the circa forty thousand remaining trials of the three continental Portuguese courts, between 70 and 80 percent were of people accused as Judaizers, and in those cases prior to the 1770s, when the official designation of New Christian or descendant of Jews was abolished, that figure is even higher. Thus, while there is an abundant inquisitorial documentation, the fixation of the Portuguese inquisitors on crypto-Judaism has produced a historical image of society and of the variety and frequency of heterodoxy within it that cannot be taken as representative of its reality since so many of the so-called lesser crimes were left to episcopal investigation and courts or to secular authority. These courts tended to be more interested in customs — that is, issues of family life, sexuality, putative public offenses like disrespect of the clergy or failure to attend Mass, and other deviant behavior — than in issues that implied heresy. The two systems of religious authority functioned together and overlapped (sorcery, for example, was punished by both), but they tended to be directed toward different elements of the population, the Inquisition for New Christians and foreigners, the episcopal visits and courts for Old Christians. A blasphemous statement, if uttered by a New Christian, would most likely be prosecuted by the Inquisition and the offender prosecuted as a secret Jew, while an Old Christian speaking the same words would probably be admonished and corrected by episcopal authority. It was not the offense but the origin of the accused that determined how and with what severity punishment was carried out. The Inquisition, moreover, was far more likely to confiscate the property of New Christians than that of Old Christians.[6] Crimes of speech or thought might be prosecuted in either system, but if their content was defined or suspected to be heretical, then the Inquisition examined them. The problem was that the Portuguese Inquisition remained relatively uninterested in this crime unless it involved suspected Jews or Protestants. Various quantitative studies of the Portuguese tribunals make this clear. Whereas propositions and blasphemy made up 27 percent of the Spanish Inquisition's activity from 1540 to 1700, in the Portuguese Inquisition of Évora prior to 1668 it was only 3.3 percent and in Coimbra in the sixteenth century only 6.7 percent. During inquisitorial visits to the Portuguese colony of Brazil in 1591–93 and 1618–19, prosecutions for propositions were 6.6 percent of the total.[7] These figures do not necessarily suggest a more orthodox attitude among the Portuguese population, but rather an institutional policy difference between the Spanish and Portuguese religious authority.

Along with a fervent orthodox faith and occasional nonconformity, Portuguese religiosity also included a broad range of beliefs about the supernatural that could be defined as superstitions and that lay on or beyond the margins of what the Church found acceptable. As in the rest of Europe, these beliefs involved practices ranging from palmistry and alchemy to divination, astrology, and sympathetic medicine, but also included what was defined as magic, witchcraft, and sorcery. They constituted an attempt to influence human affairs, heal the body, or affect the sentiments by reaching for elements of the supernatural. Rather than being seen as an alternative to organized religion, these beliefs and practices were commonly viewed as a parallel and often complementary system, so that those who practiced these arts or who sought out others who had such knowledge did not necessarily think they were acting against the precepts of the Church.[8] In fact, while learned opinion in Portugal reflected the early modern trend to find in such beliefs the work of the devil, there was also a tendency to see in these ideas not implicit heresy, but the superstition of rustics in need of instruction.[9]

In fact, the relationship between the occult and the Church was complicated, and it varied over time. The Church, for example, accepted astrology in the sense of using the movements of the heavenly bodies to interpret human events and character, but judicial astrology, that is, the ability to predict events, implied powers that were those of God alone. It was cause for prosecution.[10] Witchcraft was another case in point. There was a broad popular belief in witchcraft and acceptance of its reality by theologians, but the Inquisition and the ecclesiastical courts tended to be skeptical of charges and relatively lenient in punishments in comparison with northern Europe. The Portuguese tribunals received over seven thousand denunciations of such practices, but only about a thousand cases were actually tried. Although the idea of a witches' sabbat and pacts with the devil were not unknown and sometimes prosecuted actively by individual inquisitors, Portuguese religious authorities were skeptical in most cases, at least in Portugal itself. In the words of the historian José Pedro Paiva, Portugal was a country that prosecuted witchcraft but "never was caught up in the frenzy and fear of a 'witch hunt.'"[11] Still, the idea of a devil who acted in human affairs was real enough, and sometimes resulted in confessions that fit the classic mold of diabolic unions and demonic pacts. For most people, the supernatural world was a real and attainable sphere for good or evil purposes. Individuals sought ways of influencing the actions of people, the flow of events, or natural phenomena outside the regular channels of Catholicism in ways that closely paralleled and sometimes intersected with a fervent orthodoxy that involved miracles, revelations, and divine intercessions in response to prayer, processions, and pilgrimages.

To counter the tendencies toward "superstition," to eliminate the unorthodox and heterodox, to guard against heresy, and to establish the authority, presence, and effectiveness of the Inquisition, a network of agents and affiliates of the Holy Office developed across the country beginning in the late sixteenth century. These *familiares* were laymen who supported the activities of the Inquisition by helping to arrest prisoners and participating in the autos de fe, and who in return were given a series of privileges like exemption from certain taxes and from military service as well as the right to bear arms. Only persons of proven Old Christian origins were theoretically eligible to serve. That fact eventually added to the prestige of the position. There were never very many familiares at any one time. Until the last decade of the seventeenth century, they did not total over one thousand individuals, the numbers rising, however, thereafter, especially after 1750. Each town might have a few and the cities more. Often they were drawn from the rural aristocracy or from the mercantile class in the cities. The Inquisition could look to them as supports for its authority, and they drew social prestige and distinction from their office. The real work of the tribunal in ferreting out heresy and unorthodoxy at the local level fell to the commissaries and their notaries. The commissary was usually a priest who took his role as a guardian of orthodoxy seriously. Many of the denunciations originated with them. Like the familiares, the numbers of commissaries expanded after the late seventeenth century. While both these offices brought prestige and privileges, the commissaries were a key element in extending the reach and inculcating the fear of the Inquisition into every community.

Portugal, like the other Iberian kingdoms, had been home to significant populations of Jews and Muslims in the Middle Ages, but there were important differences with Spain here as well. The Muslims had been expelled from Lisbon in 1147, and Muslim political control in Portugal had ended in the thirteenth century. Muslim communities continued to exist in many major cities until the fifteenth century, but by the time the final order of expulsion took place in 1496, there were few Muslims remaining. While the Portuguese tribunals occasionally accused people of seeking to return to Islam, the vast majority of them were North African Berbers and Arabs, Moriscos crossing the border from Castile, and West African Muslims who had come to Portugal as slaves. These servants, slaves, or mariners who ran afoul of the Inquisition over matters of religious practice or faith presented no great threat to the Portuguese body politic.

The converts from Judaism were another matter. Unlike Castile and Aragon, where in 1492, after a century of building pressure, the remaining Jews were offered a choice of conversion or exile, in Portugal, where many Castilian Jews had fled in 1492, no choice was really offered. There, the king, Dom Manoel, unwilling to lose a valuable population and over the objections of some at court, enforced compulsory baptism on virtually all Jews in 1497 by limiting their ability to leave the country, enslaving those who remained Jews, and seizing the children of those who failed to convert. Faced with such choices, the vast majority accepted conversion, and in a stroke these people became New Christians. Given the nature and conditions of their conversion, they were suspected of being less than fervent in their new faith. Conversion was one thing, acceptance another. A major urban riot born of popular antagonism and resentment of the use of Jews as royal tax collectors, but also instigated and encouraged by rabid pulpit preachers, principally two Dominicans, erupted in Lisbon in 1506. In a few days, some three thousand people were murdered before the crown intervened to stop the killing and looting.[12] The leaders and some forty participants were executed for their part in the riot. Royal policy granted the converts a period of adjustment to the new religion by not imposing overly zealous religious scrutiny, but after 1512 also deterring or limiting the ability of New Christians to leave the country for Flanders or North Africa with their goods or property. After extensive negotiations with Rome, an Inquisition was established in Portugal in 1531, but it was not operational until 1536 or fully functioning until 1547, and even then ten-year exemptions from confiscation of property were granted in 1548 and 1558 to New Christians accused of Judaizing. Thus, at exactly the moment of the height of the Spanish Inquisition's campaign against Judaizers in the early sixteenth century, Portuguese New Christians were relatively free from that kind of religious harassment because of this period of grace. It was also exactly in that half century after 1500, of course, that Portugal's outpost in the Americas, the Brazilian colony, was established and its society took form. Little wonder then that New Christians went there in significant numbers, seeking opportunities and a refuge from increasing surveillance and control in Portugal. By the late sixteenth century, the Brazilian colony was considered by contemporaries to be a place dominated by New Christians.

Although in its origins the Portuguese Inquisition had been created as an extension of royal authority and interests, it eventually developed as a stable, bureaucratic institution with interests of its own.[13] Eventually, to ensure the orthodoxy of the faithful, four Inquisition tribunals operated within Portugal and its empire. These were located in major cities so that they could draw on the support and expertise of their considerable ecclesiastical establishments. The Inquisition of Coimbra, the seat of the leading university in the country, kept watch over the north, while Évora heard cases from the south, the provinces of Alemtejo and Algarve, and the tribunal in Lisbon, the capital and the largest port, heard cases not only from the capital city, its hinterland, and the central region of Portugal, but also all those that came from the Atlantic islands, West Africa, and Brazil; finally, in the Portuguese city of Goa, on the western coast of India, an Inquisition tribunal looked to the orthodoxy of the inhabitants of the Portuguese Estado da India, that vast network of colonies, trade posts, fortresses, and routes that extended from Mozambique to Macao.

Although the records of the Goa tribunal have been lost, there are over forty thousand trial records of the remaining three tribunals, and while these reveal that the same issues of heterodoxy, heresy, and deviance preoccupied Portuguese Inquisitors like their Spanish counterparts, the most significant aspect of these records is that between 70 and 80 percent of the people charged were accused of being secret Jews. This concentration reflected popular opprobrium, but this situation was also orchestrated and advocated by ecclesiastical authorities and by the Inquisition itself, which after 1568 was able to confiscate the property of those accused. This peculiar fixation of the Portuguese Inquisition has become a battleground on which historians have bitterly argued about the character of the Inquisition in Portugal and about the reality or falsehood of the accusations of Judaizing among the Portuguese New Christians.[14] Some scholars have accepted the essential validity of the Inquisition's charges and the truthfulness of the voluntary and forced confessions of the New Christians as evidence of their adherence to Judaism. The New Christians, therefore, were martyrs for the law of Moses, and the inquisitors were engaged in what, by their standards, was a legitimate religious campaign to extirpate apostasy. Other scholars have viewed such charges of New Christian Judaism as essentially false and simply a justification either for a policy of racial exclusion and discrimination under the guise of religious orthodoxy or for the appropriation of New Christian wealth for the economic benefit of the Inquisition and its social allies; a campaign to destroy the economic power of an emerging mercantile class. Certainly, there were many critics from the sixteenth to the eighteenth centuries in Portugal and its empire who believed that the Inquisition's charges were exaggerated and that many people were forced to admit to Jewish practices and beliefs when none existed. Fernando Morales Penso, exiled to Brazil in 1683 after confessing to being a Jew and denouncing others, wrote from the ship in order to clear his conscience. His fate was already sealed and the sentence had been carried out, yet he still wished to set the record straight. He wrote to the Holy Office, "Since the day I was baptized until today I have never ceased being a true Catholic, never did a single thought allow me to stray from the Laws of Our Lord Jesus Christ under which I was well instructed, and therefore I declare to your Excellencies that everything I claimed in my confessions . . . concerning me and against those close to me was false, and I confessed what I did not do for fear of death and to save my life."[15] Penso, like others, knew that those who refused to confess their "Judaizing" were the most severely punished and the most likely to be executed. They were condemned as recalcitrant, obstinate, and impenitent because they insisted in their claim to be good Catholics. Penso, and many like him, became martyrs for their Christian faith.

The Portuguese preoccupation with New Christians created odd contradictions. The levels of opprobrium and hatred expressed especially by popular classes and stimulated by a prejudicial and anti-Semitic literature of sermons and religious tracts were eventually codified into prohibitions and exclusions of New Christians from government offices, military orders, certain professions, liberal arts, ecclesiastical positions, entry into the university, and the contracting of marriages with the nobility. But these restrictions were continually circumvented, avoided, or ignored, leading to recurring complaints about the presence of New Christians in ecclesiastical positions, the religious orders, as knights in the military orders, at the university, and in government offices.[16] Then, too, there were considerable numbers of marriages and associations that brought New and Old Christians together despite the considerable social and governmental sanctions against such conviviality. New and Old Christians were intimately linked in Portuguese society, and despite a long campaign to separate and denigrate the New Christians, whether for social, economic, religious, or "racial" considerations, there was too much that bound them together.

Finally, the role of political considerations in the policy toward the New Christians was not inconsiderable. From the very moment of the forced conversions of 1497, the treatment of the Jews and New Christians had been political and economic as well as religious.[17] Such issues as the ability to emigrate or confiscation of the property of those accused had varied over time, often as a result of negotiations, a euphemism for extortion which always implied large payments. The prohibition of emigration imposed by King Dom João III from 1513 to 1577 was reversed by Dom Sebastião, who was anxious to finance his adventure in North Africa and who looked to the New Christian payment as a way to do this. After his disaster, the policy was changed again in 1580, and the prohibition continued under the Spanish Hapsburg rulers of Portugal (1581–1640) until 1601, when once again an enormous payment to King Philip III produced relief for the New Christians, allowing many to emigrate from the kingdom. The interests of the king, however, were not necessarily those of the Inquisition. Both the Holy Office and the crown looked at the New Christians as a source of income, and periods of royal negotiations with New Christians over emigration laws or confiscations of property were often periods of heightened repression and activity by the Holy Office. A general pardon granted in 1605 was followed by intensification of inquisitorial activity, and the failed negotiations for another pardon in the 1610s was accompanied by a series of "visits" to the colonies and an increase in the number of autos de fe in Portugal itself. The Inquisition opposed the Bragança restoration in 1640 and resisted policies designed to bring the new monarch, Dom João IV, the support of both New Christians in Portugal and their relatives in Holland, France, and Germany. Eventually, statesmen like the extraordinary missionary, pulpit preacher, and diplomat the Jesuit Father António Vieira, confessor to Dom João IV, viewed the position of the Inquisition as destructive to the kingdom both socially and economically. Vieira was an outspoken critic of the Inquisition and its policy toward New Christians. Protected at court until a palace revolution in 1662, Vieira became a target for a variety of reasons. The Holy Office responded by prosecuting Vieira for his prophetic writings (1663–67) rather than for his position on the New Christians, but his trial was a warning to him and to others. Vieira's opposition to the Inquisition did not end, and he was able to influence Rome's decision to actually suspend the Portuguese Inquisition in 1674–81. His efforts and the Inquisition's ability to survive and deflect the pressures of both the crown and the papacy underline the various divisions, conflicts, and interests that the situation of the New Christians represented in Portuguese society and make the relations with them a suitable focus for an examination of tolerance in that society.

Souls to Be Saved

The same theological issues of grace versus merit and the central question of salvation and the true path to heaven that occupied the attention of the Spaniards also fascinated the Portuguese.[18] It was a matter of common discussion and strong opinion, a core concern of theology, and a matter of popular interest. When foreigners in Portugal asked to become Catholics, they usually stated their reason for conversion was "to be sure of their salvation" or to "save their soul."[19] Which law was best? and which would lead to salvation? The answer that only God knew for sure, or that there might be more than one path also found expression in Portugal despite its heretical implications in the face of the dogma of no salvation outside the Church. Of course, members of the ethnic minorities were prone to believe otherwise. Madanella de Segueira, a *Mourisca* in Setúbal, had wished to go to the lands of the Moors. She told Inquisitors in 1556 that "the Christians say their law is better, the Moors say theirs is better, but only God knows." Her defense for clinging to Islam was that she never really understood her Christian instruction and that sometimes she felt herself a Christian and sometimes a Muslim.[20] The New Christians, or "People of the Hebrew Nation," were also given to a certain relativism in the question of salvation. In Covilã in 1648 during the War of the Restoration as Portugal sought to gain its independence from Castile, a conversation took place in the home of the widow Clara Enriques. Antonio Montes, a cloth maker working in her house, had lamented the war since both Portuguese and Castilians were Catholics. It would be better, he said, to fight the Muslims. She answered sharply, "Why fight with them, each person saves himself in his own law." Montes answered that only in the law of Christ can one be saved, to which she answered that "she took care of herself." Montes was scandalized and denounced the widow, especially because she was a New Christian, even though her daughter, recognizing the theological thin ice on which she was treading, had corrected her mother immediately.[21]

But while the religious and ethnic minorities might be given to such relativism, and despite the fact that New Christians were sometimes thought to be particularly prone to religious indifference or dissimulation, this proposition was found among Old Christians as well. The Church insisted on its exclusive validity and on membership within it as the only road to salvation, but there were many people who were not fully convinced. Some based their opinions on the old theological debates about good works, natural law, and perfect ignorance; others simply drew their opinion from a belief in a merciful God who could not condemn the innocent; still others arrived at their conclusions on the basis of observation or on what seemed to them common sense. Antonio Duro, who resided in Porto Calvo, Brazil, probably represented many people for whom heterodox opinions about salvation were joined with a variety of heterodox propositions.[22] In 1699, Duro, described as a man of "a bad life and habits," told the Inquisition's representative that he did not believe in hell, and if it existed it was not for souls to suffer eternally because God only wanted to save everyone, and that God surely had a special place for these souls from which he would take them after a certain limited time.[23] This idea, that God intended to save everyone, circulated widely.[24] André Fernandes, an artisan from a town in the Alentejo, after hearing sermons about God's greatness and realizing that there were so many Turks, Moors, and gentiles in the world simply came to the conclusion that all would be saved because God would not want so many people condemned. He discussed his doubts with priests of his acquaintance, but he could not shake his doubt that baptism was not necessary for salvation. His theology was simple: How could God create Adam and allow him to sin? God created sin, and he knew when he created Adam that man would sin, but God created Adam and the world. All would be saved.[25]

Such doubts were not limited to the laity. Even ecclesiastics sometimes offered alternative interpretations of the path to salvation. The issue of salvation was surely crucial, but it was theologically complicated, and those in religious authority feared the confusion that the issue might cause among the faithful. In 1689, some theologians at the Jesuit Church of São Roque in Lisbon were queried on the possibility that a Lutheran or Calvinist having been baptized in his own religion might also be saved. Their answer was yes, if he or she was ignorant of the truth and had not committed a mortal sin or if they had sinned and then had done an act of contrition or expressed the love of God. What concerned the theologians almost as much as the question, however, was the delicacy of answering it in front of uneducated common people. As they said, "The answer should not be given before less prudent folk that may be scandalized or suffer some spiritual harm" from the discussion.[26] But despite such concerns and reticence, the issue of salvation remained a matter of popular concern and opinion as well.[27]

The concept of a struggle between true and false paths to salvation and the Church's desire to save souls by baptism lay behind the missionary impulse and had justified the imperial thrust of both Portugal and Castile. It was a matter of utmost importance to the Church but one that opened up the possibility of manipulation and deception. Many of those arrested by the Inquisition ultimately pleaded with the tribunals to be reconciled to the Church for the salvation of their souls, knowing that the language of salvation resonated with their judges.

The discussion of salvation sometimes opened strange paths and opportunities. In seventeenth-century Portugal under the rule of the Spanish Hapsburgs, the discourse of salvation could have a protonationalist purpose. Antonio Manso from the village of Sea in the bishopric of Coimbra, who made his living as a teacher, caused a scandal in a church in Alcázar de Consuegra in Castile when he knelt before a crucifix and prayed out loud, "Lord, you must save and pardon me because you died for us Portuguese and not for the Castilians, because we are very noble." Those who heard him retorted that the Portuguese were all Jews, to which he replied that if so, then they were the relatives of our Lord, who when he wished to be born chose a Jew, not a Castilian, to be his mother.[28] Here the question of salvation, the possible validity of the old law, and the insult of religious epithet were mixed together. An English visitor to Lisbon in 1633 was told at the hospital of São Bartolomeu that all peoples could be treated there, heretics, Turks, Moriscos, even Castilians. He was told, "The Portuguese love the English better than any other nation and hate the Castilians more than they hate the devil."[29]

While discussion of salvation could provide a discourse for politics, the subject remained an issue of primary concern to both lay and clergy. A strange case involved Andrea Marquies, from the county of Nice in Savoy. He had come to Spain in the company of a Genoese gentleman and then had gone to Portugal. In Coimbra, at the college of São Pedro of the Third Order of São Francisco, he had witnessed a Turkish convert baptized with great pomp and honor. Marquies saw an opportunity for himself. He told the rector of the college that he too was a Turk and wished to be converted. The rector questioned him for three days and was amazed at his knowledge of Christian doctrine. Marquies explained he was so anxious to be converted that he had devoted himself to study. He embellished the story, claiming he was born in

Jerusalem and even created names for his Turkish parents: Muley Xeque his father and Alimice his mother. The prior of the Santa Justa parish, António de Caceres, baptized him on Christmas day, 1608, as Francisco de Oliveira Castelobranco. The bishop of Coimbra was so pleased at the conversion of this Turk that he gave Marquies ten ducats to start his new life. Only later, when he was picked up as a vagrant and fake healer, did the story of his deception, his true origins, and his two baptisms come to light. He was punished "in private" so as to avoid further embarrassment to the Church.[30]

The crucial issue in Portuguese society, however, was not the salvation and role of small numbers of converted Muslims, but the status of the New Christians as members of the Church. Theoretically and theologically their salvation was possible because they were members of the Church, but doubts about their orthodoxy and loyalty to the Church remained and were united to social and ethnic prejudices. The weight of the Church and state was directed at the suppression of crypto-Judaism and the construction of a culture of religious and racial discrimination toward the New Christians. This culture had penetrated all levels of society, and so evidence of nonconformity or resistance to it is particularly useful as examples of ideas of religious relativism or of tolerance. There were considerable penalties for anyone who harbored, protected, or aided heretics or who was critical of the work of the Inquisition or of the inquisitors themselves. The Holy Office used all of its authority and power to suppress such resistance. Nevertheless, voices were raised to object.

Naturally, New Christians had their own reading of the Inquisition campaign against them, and many felt it was born of greed for their property, not from a desire to save their souls. Under considerable social, religious, and economic pressure, New Christians found themselves in an untenable situation. Some, like others in their society, simply dreamed of freedom to make their own decision about their belief. In 1603, Manuel Rodrigues de Oliveira told a ship captain who was taking him to Brazil that the Inquisition was trying to make the "people of the nation" Christians by force, and he wished to live "in his law as he desired." It was wrong, he said, to believe that "all who had the name of New Christian were Jews in Portugal."[31] Manuel Alvares Calcaterra was a New Christian but thought himself a good Catholic. He had been born in Vila Viçosa in Portugal but was residing in Madrid when in 1594, at the age of thirty, he was denounced. His trial revealed a certain heterodoxy, including a belief that Muslims went only to limbo after death because they believed God to be great, but he was eventually forced to confess and then was sentenced to appear at an auto de fe in Toledo as a Judaizer and to four years in the king's galleys. Alvares Calcaterra believed that the Inquisition was a dishonest institution and that there had even been a moment before Philip II of

Spain had acquired the crown of Portugal that the tribunal might have been eliminated. He subsequently stated that "the inquisitors of Évora are low persons who live badly and are *amancebados,* and that the blacks [slaves] of his parents are better than them, and that he had been arrested for four thousand ducats' worth of property he had, and that the New Christians of Portugal wished to rise up because of their imprisonment by the Inquisition, and that if Dom António had become king there would have been no Inquisition." Later he repented his confession, claiming "he had entered in the Inquisition as a good Christian, and now he was the biggest Jew in the World."[32] These two claims, that the Inquisition was motivated by profit and that it often turned good Christians into Jews by forcing false confessions, were repeated by many of the critics of the institution. Pero Lopes Lucena, a New Christian, told a group of people in Castelbranco in 1617 that "the Inquisition tortures according to how much money each person has, and at times they make people confess to what they have not done nor should do. And with torture they make a man who has ninety thousand cruzados confess what he should not, and they steal his money from him."[33]

The priest who denounced Lopes Lucena reported that all who heard him were scandalized, but there is considerable evidence that Old Christians also believed that the inquisitors had ulterior motives and that not all those accused were really Jews. In 1683, the Évora tribunal convicted Luís Rodrigues, a simple weaver, for saying that the inquisitors were thieves who forced the New Christians to admit to crimes they had not committed.[34] Perhaps somewhat more complicated was the case of Father Luís de Macedo Freire, a priest in Moura in the Alemtejo. He was accused in 1648 of being too friendly with New Christians, and when he was told they were all Jews, he responded that "the Inquisition makes them confess to things they did not do because they are squeezed by torture." Father Luís was a native of Estremoz and an Old Christian. He later complained that the many priests who gave testimony against him did so out of personal spite. He was also accused, however, of protecting New Christian property from confiscation and of warning New Christians about impending arrests. Father Luís was also in the habit of saying that the Inquisition acted to appropriate the possessions of the New Christians, and when he was reprimanded for such statements he responded that he was only speaking the truth.[35] A more humble example is that of the denunciation of a certain Pero Lopes, an Old Christian from Guarda who was a skeptic about the images of the saints or about miracles. His skepticism was matched by action. He hid New Christians and guided them across the border into Castile.[36]

The problem of sympathy for New Christians or disagreement with the policy of the Inquisition was important enough for a separate register to be created where the names of those who provided comfort to or hid New Christians could be entered. Many of the defenders of the New Christians were clergymen, priests, and friars who criticized the persecution of the New Christians or who, like Belchior de Macedo, abbot of São Martinho de Enguera in Mogadouro, smuggled whole families across the border into Castile. Their fight was within the Church, and they were often moved by a belief that the disadvantages suffered by the New Christians and the laws of purity of blood that excluded them from many areas of life only worked against the full integration of these people into the body of the Church.[37] But laypersons too sometimes disregarded the penalties and the prejudices to help their New Christian neighbors. Ana Luís, who had been born in Castile but lived in Arranhados, sought in 1618 to warn her New Christian neighbor and friend Isabel Lopes that the Inquisition was arresting the people of the "nation" that night. She felt it was her duty, and she wished to say good-bye to her friend.[38]

Old Christian Tolerance of New Christians

In the Portuguese context the issue of religious tolerance or relativism is most clearly displayed in actions and attitudes of defense of the New Christians. The power and authority of the Inquisition and usually of the state and of various sectors of society were firmly committed to the denigration and extermination of Judaism, and by extension to the exploitation of and discrimination against the New Christians. In the regulations of restriction and exclusion depending on blood and origins, from church pulpits and in a literature of invective and condemnation, a consistently negative message was conveyed to the population as a whole. In the face of this campaign and despite the serious potential risks of opposing the Inquisition or criticizing its policies and practices, people from various levels of society were willing to rise to the defense and support of the New Christians.

Certainly the most famous example of tolerance toward the New Christians is the Jesuit António Vieira, a master of both pen and pulpit whose long life and remarkable career bridged the Atlantic world of Portugal. Vieira was born in Portugal but went to Brazil as a child and there entered the Jesuit order, serving as a missionary to native Amerindian peoples and to African slaves. He returned to Portugal during the Bragança restoration (1640–68) and served as a statesman, confessor, diplomat, and political advisor. Of all the many dimensions of Vieira's multifaceted career none seems so modern and so out of keeping with the general tenor of his times and society than his ardent defense of the New Christians, his attack on the authority of the Inquisition, especially on its policies toward the New Christians, and his seeming attitudes of toleration in an age of intolerance. The usual image painted of Vieira is one of a singular voice in a wilderness of prejudice, but, as we have seen, his was simply the most public and most cogent expression of a more widely held opinion.[39]

Vieira's positions did not please many of his contemporaries, nor have they pleased all his later biographers. Vieira's tolerance toward the New Christians was, in fact, not at all singular in the context of west European statecraft of the mid–seventeenth century and was very much part of a growing attitude of philo-Semitism and tolerance in general that could be seen elsewhere in Europe in the mid–seventeenth century. Like many of his European contemporaries, Vieira based his attitudes toward the Jews on a combination of mercantilist ideology, political convenience, and messianic expectation. Second, Vieira's tolerance, in fact, was more limited and more instrumental than that of some of his Portuguese contemporaries and predecessors, for Vieira's hope was always for the integration of the New Christians and Jews within the project of a universal Church of which Portugal would be the spearhead.

The question of philo-Semitism in the mid–seventeenth century can be quickly discussed.[40] The increasing tide of Jewish expulsions between 1200 and 1500 in western Europe had accompanied the centralization of states and the growth of powerful national mercantile classes intolerant of Jewish competitors. This was a situation quite the reverse of that in eastern Europe, where both monarchs and local merchants were weaker and where agricultural elites preferred Jewish merchants to the local bourgeoisie.[41] By the end of the sixteenth century, this process had begun to change, and by the mid–seventeenth century a series of political figures, usually practitioners of the new *raison d'état,* had begun to make political, social, and religious moves that favored more open and more permissive societies that included the presence of Jews and various degrees of toleration. While Amsterdam perhaps led the way in this regard, to a greater or lesser degree similar policies could be found in the actions of statesmen like Oliver Cromwell in England and Jules Mazarin in France, figures who either protected resident Jewish and New Christian communities or stimulated the arrival of immigrants into those communities.[42] During the Portuguese restoration, under Vieira's urging, a move in that direction was also made in Portugal. In all these cases, including Vieira's, the basis of policy was twofold. First, there were the considerations of a practical statecraft that saw considerable benefit to be derived from the commercial network provided by Jewish and New Christian traders. Second, millenarian ideas that drew on a Jewish prophetic tradition and that viewed the conversion of the Jews as a necessary step toward the coming of a new age also supported a new opening to Jewish settlement and residence in various countries.

In this context, Vieira seems in no way strange or radical. His pro-Bragança

Father António Vieira.
Jesuit priest, missionary, prophet, diplomat, preacher, and writer of extraordinary ability,
Vieira became an ardent advocate of a policy of tolerance toward the New Christians as a
practical matter and a bitter opponent of the Inquisition. From an engraving by Arnold
Westerhout (1651–1725). Courtesy of the Biblioteca Nacional of Lisbon.

statecraft after the Portuguese restoration in 1640 made the protection and instrumental use of the New Christians essential. If, as he said to the new king, Dom João IV, in his proposal of 1643, "the Castilian wishes to reduce Portugal to a province and break its forces by taking merchants from it and calling them to the cities of Castile, Your Majesty should call them back and restore Portugal."[43] Vieira's advocacy of the Brazil Company in 1647 funded with capital from New Christians protected from seizure by the Inquisition and much of his pro–New Christian and anti-Inquisition rhetoric of the 1660s and 1670s stemmed from a mercantilist practicality not unlike that of Count-Duke of Olivares or later of Colbert.[44] In this sense Vieira was very much a *politique*. At the same time, Vieira's attachment to the prophetic tradition of the sixteenth-century shoemaker and popular prophet Gonçalo Annes Bandarra and his millenarian expectations expressed in the *Clavis prophetarum* and his *Historia do futuro* is also in keeping with a strongly philo-Semitic Christian millenarian tradition which found expression elsewhere in Europe in places as widely separated as the pseudocourt of Christina of Sweden in Rome to Cromwell's Protestant England. This Christian messianic interest coincided and intersected with contemporary Jewish messianic beliefs.[45] Vieira's meetings in Amsterdam with Rabbi Menasseh ben Israel in 1647 and his later service as Queen Christina's confessor in Rome brought him into contact with figures who held similar, millenarian beliefs.[46] Finally, the Jesuit belief that the missions to the heathen were themselves a fulfillment of biblical prophecy, a belief later suppressed by the Church, contributed to Vieira's fervor.[47] In a European context, then, Vieira seems not at all out of step with his times, but even within Portugal itself, as we have seen, he cannot be presented as an admirable anomaly. Father Vieira saw the problem of Portugal's survival primarily in economic terms, and he thought the culprit in Portugal's weakness was not the New Christians but their principal persecutor, the Inquisition. For him, the destruction of the New Christian mercantile class in Portugal had opened the door to the exploitation of the empire by foreigners. The king, he said, "within his court sustains a citadel so powerful and invincible against himself . . . , it is the business of the monarchy that, for the same reason, the kingdom and the conquests are so weakened and exhausted and so wasted by foreign merchants who are all in their manner enemies, or at least thieves who rob us."[48]

In response to the critics of the New Christians and the claims of their treason, Vieira wasted no patience.[49] While Vieira's principal motive was primarily practical, he had avoided much of the prejudice toward Jews in general that had become part of a popular mythology sponsored by the Inquisition and at times by the crown. For example, after the fall of Salvador, the capital of Brazil, to the Dutch in 1624, when a number of the official chronicles of events claimed the city had been taken because of a "stab in the back" by New Christian or Jewish collaborators (a charge given considerable diffusion in a lackluster play by Lope de Vega), Vieira, an eyewitness to the events, in his first writing, the Jesuit annual letter of that year, made no mention whatever of New Christian cooperation with the invaders.[50] In 1671, the sacrilege of a church in Odivelas, outside of Lisbon, in which a number of objects, including the Eucharist, were stolen produced an upsurge of anti-Semitic tracts and popular demonstrations by those who believed that only a New Christian or Jew could have committed these acts. Vieira would have none of it. He wrote to the king insisting that New Christians were not involved in the incident, bore no guilt, and should not suffer for it. The culprit turned out to be an uneducated youth of Old Christian background who had stolen the objects to sell them, although many people continued to insist on his New Christian background despite the Inquisition's own evidence to the contrary.[51] During Vieira's service as a diplomat in Holland, he had no compunctions about visiting a synagogue and even arguing biblical matters with the rabbi. Vieira's strong messianic beliefs and his attachment to the prophecies of the New Christian cobbler Bandarra and to a Jewish prophetic tradition led him to a cultural and theological acceptance of Jews and of New Christians. Although more eloquent than most, he was not alone.[52]

Vieira's toleration, as one might expect of a fervent Jesuit, was limited within the constraints of Catholic dogma. He did not believe that each person can be saved in his own faith. His life as a missionary, dedicated to the conversion of African slaves and pagan Indians, was a demonstration of his belief in the singular validity of the Catholic faith. So, too, his tolerance did not extend to Protestants. His sermons of 1638 and the 1640s directed against the depredations of the Dutch in Brazil denounced the actions of heretics against a Catholic people and its Church, and in a remarkable sermon he asked God directly why he had let the Portuguese shed so much blood to win these lands, only to have the heretic Dutch take them away and to leave the pulpits empty of priests, so that the errors of Luther and Calvin could be preached from them.[53]

But what marks Vieira in his treatment of the heretic Dutch, as with the Jews, was his ability to avoid an essentializing vision in which the Dutch and their religious error become one and the same. Thus Vieira, always the practical statesman, was able to turn to the Dutch as a model and potential ally when Portugal needed both after its separation from Hapsburg Spain in 1640. In his defense before the Inquisition, Vieira saw the Dutch as an example to be followed when he remarked that "basing their survival on commerce and having fewer resources for it than Portugal, they not only had the strength to resist the whole might of Spain, but made themselves masters of the world."[54]

With the Dutch as with the New Christians — and by extension the Jews — Vieira placed reasons of state and practical considerations before all else. Some of his statements made clear the predominance of utility over those of admiration or tolerance. This was made obvious in his correspondence with Ambassador D. Rodrigo de Meneses, in a letter of 1671 in which Vieira wrote directly and openly about his sense that Jews were less dangerous than heretics and that whatever their multiple sins and disadvantages, it served Portugal to maintain them in Portugal. As Vieira put it, "Saint Augustine says manure in the wrong place dirties the house but in the right place, it fertilizes the fields." So too with the Jews, he argued, who abroad helped the heretics, but who at home could provide capital to maintain the empire. And, he added, "Judaism is not contagious and heresy very contagious, as has been seen in all the nations of Europe where many have become heretics and no one a Jew."[55] Why, he asked, turn "useful vassals into powerful enemies"?[56] We may, of course, interpret such statements as Vieira's attempt to make his radical social program more palatable and acceptable to those in authority, and the circles in which he moved perhaps demanded such strategies.[57] Throughout his life he demonstrated a willingness to avoid the stereotypes of Jews and the denigration of New Christians, and Vieira represented a Portuguese dimension to the changing attitude toward Jews that could be seen elsewhere in contemporary Europe.

Other currents, born of experience and interest, carried the attitudes of tolerance of the New Christians in Portugal, sometimes among people of far less distinction and social status. In December of 1623, the Inquisition of Évora arrested André Lopes, known as "The Harp" (O arpa). Lopes was an Old Christian, a wool merchant (some called him a peddler, or *tropeiro*) seventy years of age who lived in Évora and who often played the harp at Church festivals.[58] He was married to a New Christian woman who had been sentenced by the Inquisition (apparently for Judaizing). He sometimes criticized the Inquisition and spoke favorably about the New Christians. Friends who had found Lopes's attitude toward New Christians overly sympathetic had denounced him. They considered his remarks about the Holy Office's persecution of New Christians scandalous and his general attitude toward the Holy Office and its members calumnious. Lopes had gone to visit a sick friend, and during their discussion he remarked that the Inquisition was forcing people to confess what was not true and thus making them into Jews. As he said, "Some persons enter the Holy Office innocent and leave from here as Jews."[59] Sometime later, shortly after an auto da fe, Lopes had told his friend that the people who had been sentenced were martyrs and saints, and when admonished for his offensive words he responded, "There is no reason to fear, for there are those who are born to burn and those born to be pardoned."[60] Lopes, in fact, had not gone to witness the auto because he claimed that since these peoples were martyrs, there might have been lightning bolts from the heavens, as there had been at the martyrdom of Santa Barbara. There had been a storm during the auto that Lopes claimed was a sign of the innocence of those condemned. Such attitudes had led his friend's wife to say that Lopes was "more a Jew than his wife." For whatever reason, Lopes avoided witnessing the public executions staged by the Inquisition.[61]

What seemed to bother his acquaintances even more than his often expressed sympathy toward the New Christians was his criticism of the practices and procedures of the Inquisition itself. Lopes had remarked that when the town fool, Rodrigo, had heard of the Inquisition's preparations for an auto and the erection of a platform, or *cadalfaso*, for punishments, he had punned, "Cadafalso e bem falso" (a *cadafalso* and really false), and Lopes had remarked, "Often the mad speak truths." He told his friend, "There is no inquisitor who will not end badly and . . . one had died recently in Madrid trying to prevent the general pardon" of New Christians that was at that moment being negotiated. "As in ancient times there were martyrs," he went on, "so now God also wanted martyrs," meaning those accused by the Inquisition. Lopes denounced the motives of the inquisitors, their forcing of women prisoners to testify in "knickers and shirtsleeves," and that all the Inquisition's actions were done in order to "eat and spend the property of those arrested."

In Lopes's formulation one sees a critique of the Inquisition's actions as arbitrary and self-interested as well as the suggestion, later emphasized by Vieira and, in the eighteenth century, by many others, that by forcing confessions the Inquisition made Jews out of Christians.[62] These criticisms paralleled and predated some of Vieira's denunciations, and they represent a line of objection not limited to New Christians or even to those who, like Lopes, were married to them. One witness forced to testify against Lopes, his friend the Old Christian tailor Domingos Gomes, remembered Lopes's hypothetical question: if God did not want the New Christians to be Christians, why did the *Senhores Inquisidores* wish to make them Christians by force?"[63]

Imprisoned, Lopes finally admitted his errors. He was sentenced to pecuniary fines, public whipping (commuted because his father had been a town councilman in Thomar), and exile.[64] But lest one see him as a curious and marginal figure perhaps moved only by love and sympathy for his New Christian wife, the fact is he came from an established family of the urban patriciate, and among his brother's children, his nephews, was the priest confessor at the monastery of Nossa Senhora da Graça of Lisbon and another who was a knight in the Order of Santiago. Most of the testimony against him came from friends and acquaintances who were Old Christians, mostly artisans, and most of it was the result of nonvoluntary depositions, the witnesses having been called to testify. Their testimonies indicate that Lopes's remarks were made repeatedly and that the topic of the Inquisition and the New Christians was commonly discussed. Criticisms like those of Lopes may have been offensive to the ears of his friends but most had not been moved to denounce him. When asked why they had not done so by the inquisitors, they presented the usual excuses of ill health, lack of opportunity, or having already told their parish priests. One has the impression that a level of popular criticism of the Inquisition may have been far more common than students of the period have been led to believe.

Odysseys Across Empires

The questioning of the Inquisition and of the policy of intolerance could flourish in the maritime world of the Iberian empires, where authority was limited, anonymity great, and imperial and religious-ethnic identities and boundaries permeable. Vicente Gomes Coelho had been born in Lisbon in 1659 but was arrested in Havana, Cuba, in 1688 because he had been heard to say that "King Sebastião was on an island and would return to Portugal, 'robbing hearts,' and that prophets and holy men had said this was so." He was, in other words, a Sebastianist, a believer that the king who had died over one hundred years before on the sands of Africa would return to restore Portugal to greatness. This was the story of the Ilha Encoberta, the hidden island of messianic expectation, that circulated widely in the seventeenth century.[65] Moreover, Gomes Coelho mentioned to people that he himself had been on some island where he had lived with Jews and that he had attended a synagogue. The commissary of the Inquisition in Havana found these statements suspicious enough to order Gomes Coelho's arrest, and he was sent as a prisoner to the tribunal at Cartagena de Indias.

During examination a picaresque tale began to emerge. In his first session before the tribunal, Gomes stated that he had lived in Lisbon with his parents until his early twenties and then had sailed for the Portuguese state of India, where he soldiered in Macao and in Goa. He returned to Portugal, and in Lisbon, he told the inquisitors, he had been sentenced to death for counterfeiting, but the sentence had been commuted to perpetual exile in Angola. In Africa, however, he had convinced an English captain, probably of a slaver, to carry him to Jamaica, but the captain had required a promissory note of fifty pesos. Gomes then convinced some Portuguese Jews that he was a coreligionist and received their help.[66] From Jamaica, he eventually sailed to Cuba and was making his living as a surgeon despite the fact that he had only scant experience and a few books on the subject, never having studied medicine. Like many people who ran afoul of the Holy Office for heresy, he could read and write, although he had not been to university. He insisted that all his relatives were Old Christians but that one had married a New Christian.

There was much that troubled the inquisitors both about his contact with Jews in Jamaica and about his Sebastianism, which they found to be offensive and schismatic. He was interviewed again in May 1689, now under considerable suspicion, and his story began to change. An examination showed he had not been circumcised, and he denied the charges, arguing that he had lived as a Christian, and as proof of his sentiments, like a good Christian he had always called the Jews dogs. Further interviews explored both his purported Judaism and his Sebastianism, which he had acquired by reading Father António Vieira and accepting his idea of an *encoberto,* a hidden king.[67] Still, there were over fourteen witnesses who had heard his statements. As to being a Jew, he argued that if that were the case, he never would have left Jamaica, where his credit was good, and gone to Spanish Cuba, where he might be apprehended.

The story continued to change, Gomes Coelho admitting he had been accepted by the Jews and instructed in their beliefs even though he did this only for material ends. He created stories about Jewish beliefs, but he was soon changing the story again and perhaps getting closer to the truth when he admitted that "in Jamaica he had been a Jew with the Jews and a Christian with the Christians." Eventually, he admitted being a secret Jew, initiated into that religion by his cousins in Goa, and of having followed the law of Moses in Lisbon and Angola, but he was soon disclaiming that admission. Tortured, his story became no clearer or consistent. At the end, he was claiming he had practiced Judaism in India, had begun to doubt it in Jamaica, and now wanted only reintegration within the Church. He was, of course, punished in an auto de fe, but both then and now separating truth from fictions in his story is virtually impossible. Gomes Coelho lived socially and geographically on the margins, between empires, between faiths, and between loyalties. Whatever his true feelings, he moved easily between religions, and his life demonstrated the difficulty of separating the population into easily defined categories of Old and New Christians.

The final story touches almost all parts of the worldwide empire Portugal created. To set the scene, I will take account of the settlement of Brazil. By the close of the sixteenth century it had become a thriving plantation colony in which the Portuguese settlers, after trading with and later enslaving the native Indian population, had begun to import African slaves. Over time a society based on considerable cultural and racial fusion developed, a society in which the New Christian element was strong since the colony, because of its distance from authority in Portugal and its economic opportunities, had attracted a flow of immigrants. Crown and Church sought to impose the religious standards of Portugal on the Brazilian settlements, and inquisitorial visits were sent to the major areas of settlement, Bahia and Pernambuco, in 1591–93 and again in 1618.[68] The visits handled a broad range of crimes, from blasphemy to heterodox ideas about fornication with Indians, but a major target of the investigations was, in fact, the New Christians. The visit of 1618 had resulted in a large number of denunciations, and the prisoners had been sent back to the Inquisition of Lisbon, where they would be examined and punished. It was in the Estaus, the prison of the Lisbon tribunal, that in 1620 one of the strangest examples of tolerance took place, one that has escaped the notice of historians until now.

On September 25, 1620, the jailer of the inquisitorial prison sought an audience with the tribunal in order to report a strange happening of the previous night. He reported that during the night shots had been fired in the city and that these had actually been signals to the prisoners that a general pardon of the New Christians had been signed in Madrid and that one of the inquisitors had died suddenly. In other words, these were communications designed to give heart to the prisoners and to strengthen their resolve not to confess.

The question of a new general pardon was very much alive in Lisbon at the moment. In 1605 the New Christians had, after considerable wrangling and in the face of violent opposition from elements of the population and from the Inquisition of Portugal, concluded an agreement with the pope and the king that granted them a general amnesty, excusing them for past religious faults and allowing them to emigrate and take their property. The total amount paid for this pardon had exceeded two million *cruzados,* an enormous sum that included not only the official figure but also bribes and "contributions" to a number of officials, including the Duke of Lerma, Philip III's chief advisor. Discontent with the policy of such pardons festered in Portugal, stimulated to some extent by the Inquisition deprived of a source of revenue and by some of the more rabid clergy, and when payments could not be made on time, the pardon was revoked in 1610. The next decade had been one of new restrictions and worsening conditions for the New Christians. They actively made a new attempt to conclude an arrangement with the crown. It was also an era of intense lobbying by the Inquisition in which ideas such as the expulsion of all New Christians and the creation of walled resettlement camps for them in Morocco, to be paid for out of their own pockets, were put forward. The crown did not expel them, but by March 1619 the last exemptions of the pardon of 1605 were abrogated.[69]

The prisoners caught up in the inquisitorial visit to Brazil of 1618 had thus arrived at a moment of great tension in Lisbon. No wonder that rumors of another pardon were circulating within the community. But what the bailiff had told the inquisitors was even more troublesome.

The man who was interpreting these signals and who was organizing the resistance of the New Christian prisoners to the tribunal was a Catholic priest, Father Fernando Pereira de Castro.

Pereira de Castro had already earned a negative reputation in the prison for speaking out loudly in favor of New Christians, arguing that they were unjustly imprisoned and that the inquisitors had exceeded their authority. If the New Christians remained firm, he promised, all would be released with "great honor." These urgings were especially important for one young girl in the prison whose mother and sister had already confessed.[70] Pereira de Castro had counseled her to be strong, for God would free her. The bailiff reported that Pereira de Castro, by his denigration of the tribunal and its judges, had defamed the Inquisition and convinced the Brazilian prisoners to resist. In this he had been aided by a New Christian prisoner nicknamed Fleur de Lys. One might have expected that Pereira de Castro was himself a New Christian, but that was not the case. He had been arrested in 1613 for sexual improprieties with young men, but there may have been much more to the story than sodomy.

Fernando Pereira de Castro had been born in Goa, and he was by his appearance and speech identified as a *mestiço*, that is, the child of a Portuguese and an Indian woman. Judicial descriptions referred to him as a mulatto, or *cabra*, that is, a person of swarthy complexion and mixed origins. His father had come from Oporto, and Pereira de Castro claimed status as a gentleman (*fidalgo*), implying that his grandfather had actually been a viceroy of India, but the inquistors doubted the claim. Pereira de Castro had grown up in the Estado da India, and like many of the young men of the Portuguese colony he had become a soldier. He had participated in the famous siege of Chaul in 1571, but he had a taste for reading and had eventually entered the priesthood, a somewhat exceptional situation since *mestiço* priests, although not unknown, were relatively rare. Pereira de Castro eventually traveled to Lisbon, studied at Coimbra, and then traveled to Brazil and Spain as well as visiting Milan and Rome. He returned to Brazil probably in the retinue of Francisco de Sousa in 1608 when that *fidalgo* was sent as governor of the mines of southern Brazil, but there Pereira de Castro got into trouble and was arrested by the ecclesiastical administrator in Rio de Janeiro, supposedly for sexual contacts with young men.[71]

There are, however, some anomalies in his case. Arrested in 1613, he was still in prison in 1620, when he was reported to have been urging the Brazilian

New Christians to resist the Inquisition. In his trial for sodomy, he had been subjected to torture, but he had remained *negativo,* that is, he had denied all the charges. What he claimed instead was that he had been imprisoned "because he knew of the tyrannies done here to the New Christians and prisoners, and that he had been arrested not for being either a Jew or a sodomite, but because he knew the truth about the business of the New Christians." Eventually, despite his claims of innocence and despite the fact that the testimony against him for sodomy was unspecific and vague, he was suspended from the priesthood and sent to six years of penal exile to the furthest corner of the Portuguese empire, a rock in the Atlantic, the Ilha do Principe.

Whether Pereira de Castro was a homosexual or not is impossible to know, but he had taken on the cause of the New Christians, and he was sure that this stance was the cause of his troubles. Soldier and priest, like many of the *tolerantes* we have examined, he had lived in other lands and knew other cultures. He was broadly traveled, had visited the Spanish court in Madrid and the Vatican as well as coasts and towns of southern Brazil, and was perhaps better educated than many of his contemporaries. His attitudes toward the New Christians had come at an importune moment in the midst of the struggle over the pardons. But he perceived the situation of the New Christians as unjust and had been willing not only to speak against it, but to stimulate or organize resistance in the prison. There was no new pardon in 1620. His was a futile, if noble, effort against the regime of intolerance.

PART **II**

American Liberties

5

American Propositions:
Body and Soul in the Indies

After the East and West Indies and Guinea were discovered, the nations
have become mixed and they have not conformed or united with each other
as [the Prophet] Daniel had called for, as can be seen because they call each
other "Indian dog," "mulatto dog," "mestizo dog," and so they remain in
discord among themselves, and we await that which must come.
— Juan Plata (Puebla, 1601)

In 1511, on the fourth Sunday of Advent, the last before Christmas, in
the principal church on the island of Española, capital of Spain's most important colony in the New World at that time, a Dominican friar, Antonio de
Montesinos, preached a remarkable sermon to the conquerors, settlers, and
royal officers. Montesinos thundered from the pulpit that the mistreatment of
the native peoples and the seizing of their lands and property were mortal sins,
and that all Spaniards involved in this wretched business were damned. He
and the other Dominican friars would deny them the sacraments so long as
their misbehavior continued. Uproar followed. The leaders on the island were
scandalized. The governor quickly sought and obtained the priest's recall, the
Dominicans were admonished to be less intransigent, and matters returned to
the status quo for the most part. Still, the incident underlined the fact that the
opening of the New World and the creation of the Spanish Indies had raised a

series of political, theological, and moral issues which needed to be resolved: What was the basis of Spanish sovereignty? What was the role of Christianity to be in the new lands, and how was Spanish authority linked to its missionary obligations? What was the nature of the peoples of the new lands, and how should they be converted, and then integrated into Spain's political and social systems?

These questions have generated extensive study and scholarship since the sixteenth century, when they were first raised, and there is no need to review in detail here the debates that lay behind the policies of the crown and the Church that grew from them.[1] Instead my purpose is to examine dissident or heterodox opinions that developed from the same encounter of previous assumptions and implicit understandings with the perceptions and realities of the New World. These were opinions transferred in the process of conquest and colonization that did not receive the support of the crown or the blessings of the Church. I want to inquire how the Indies and their inhabitants may have transformed and expanded those attitudes by providing a human and political geography quite unlike that of Iberia. Spaniards and Portuguese came from societies that for centuries had been multireligious and which at the time of the opening of the Indies after 1492 were becoming religiously exclusionary. In contemporary Europe itself the political context of religious belief was changing, and a series of reforms associated with Erasmus, or with Luther and Calvin, was altering the way in which Christian universalism could be conceived. Europe was entering the great age of conflict of the Wars of Religion. Meanwhile, the voyage of Columbus had revealed whole continents filled with peoples of different ways and beliefs whose very existence challenged certain theological assumptions about the universality of Christ's message, but also offered a tremendous opportunity to the Church's missionary impulse. No wonder some contemporaries viewed the trajectory of events as part of an apocalyptic plan. Franciscan missionaries in New Spain liked to point out that Hernán Cortés, the conqueror of Mexico, and Martin Luther were born in the same year, 1485.[2] This was no coincidence. Surely, what the devil had taken from the Church in Europe, God would restore across the Atlantic.

The story of the imposition of Spanish rule and the conversion of the native peoples of the Americas has been told many times. I need only outline it here. Ferdinand and Isabella sought papal authority for Spain's exploration and sovereignty in the Indies almost immediately after Columbus's return, but they also negotiated diplomatically with Portugal in 1494 to assure and define spheres of interest. For about a decade, the occupation of the new lands proceeded without much concern for legal and theological issues, but after Montesinos's sermon, the question of sovereignty and the legitimacy of Spanish actions in regard to Indian rights and claims could not be avoided.[3] Theologians and canonists set to the task of explaining and justifying policy. One line of interpretation, held by Juan de Palacios Rubios, argued that the pope had universal dominion as Christ's representative both temporally and spiritually and thus could assign the new lands to Spain. The Indians, he believed, lived according to natural law and thus might be saved within it up to the time Christianity was preached to them, but after that moment, only through the Church could they find salvation, and it was the king's duty to sponsor the conversion of the gentiles. Despite the fact that Palacios Rubios argued against forced conversion, enslavement, and undue dispossession of the Indians, his line of argument placed absolute power in the pope and through him in the king of Spain. Other theologians and canonists followed this line of argument and expanded on the necessity of using force and causing bodily injury to facilitate the greater good of conversion and spiritual salvation. Some, like the humanist scholar Juan Ginés de Sepúlveda, even turned to Aristotelian categories and used the perceived barbarism, unnatural customs, and practices of the Indians and their resistance to Christian preaching as evidence of their natural inferiority and as a justification for their subservience.[4] The Indians, he argued, were *homunculi,* "little men," who fell into Aristotle's category of natural slaves, lesser folk, born to serve others.

Opponents to the idea of papal authority in the secular world were not lacking. The Dominican Francisco de Vitoria, in his *De Indis,* offered arguments that limited papal authority to Christian lands and thus undercut Spain's claims over the Indies and the right to conduct "just wars" against infidels on the basis of the papal bulls.[5] Vitoria made the connection between the pagan inhabitants of the New World and the unbelievers of Europe. Unbelief did not abrogate rightful ownership or rule. Just as it was robbery to take the possessions of Jews, Muslims, and heretics in Spain, it was equally wrong to do so with Indians. Only a law that applied to all parties, not just Spanish law, should regulate their interaction. Thus the titles for occupation of the Indies had to conform to natural law, which came from God's grace and was thus universal, immutable, and indispensable. It allowed all peoples regardless of their beliefs to understand God's wishes inherently. In natural law, of course, all people were free, and all sought proper moral conduct. The *ius gentium,* the law of nations, should be man's rational attempt to understand and enact natural law. In that sense, Vitoria was more a spokesman for internationalism than for Christian universalism.[6] But Vitoria's treatise did not deny Spain's right to be in the Indies. Vitoria, despite his emphasis that conversion had to be voluntary, found reasons that prohibited the Indians from denying or limiting the presence of the Spaniards and of the missionaries in particular. Moreover, based on what little he knew of them, he seemed to have slight respect for Indian capacities, calling them cowardly and simple. Others would use these purported limitations as justification for rule.

As the pace of conquest continued, and as the fullness and variety of Indian cultures became known following the European discovery of the great civilizations of Central Mexico, the Yucatán, and the Andean highlands, a contrary line of argumentation also developed that, while never doubting the justice of Spain's mission and the need to preach the Catholic faith, nevertheless recognized preexisting indigenous sovereignty and, to varying degrees, looked upon Indian cultures in a positive light. To some extent, recognition of the Indians' freedom of conscience and their right to adhere to their former religions was theologically necessary if their conversion and baptism were to be voluntary. But theory and practice were often far apart. Debates developed among theologians and missionaries about when the use of force was justified, since even when conversion had to be voluntary, the use of force to prohibit idolatry or to make reluctant heathens listen to the gospel was arguably necessary. One of the more radical exponents of peaceful conversion, the Dominican Bartolomé de Las Casas (1474–1566), held that the faith could not be forced under any conditions and that only peaceful means should be used to bring it about. The infidelity or non-Christian belief of the Indians did not abrogate either natural law or the law of nations.[7] The king of Spain could rule over native princes, amending only bad laws and exercising jurisdiction much as kings ruled over dukes and counts in medieval Europe. Las Casas, while never denying that such customs as human sacrifice had existed among the native inhabitants of the Americas, nevertheless emphasized their cultural accomplishments, religiosity, and abilities and thus their potential as members of the universal Church. Above all, Spanish exploitation, especially the grants of Indian labor, or *encomiendas,* and the general abuse of native peoples had to cease if the gospel was to be heard. The famous exchange between Las Casas and Sepúlveda before a royal council in Valladolid in the late summer of 1550 brought these two lines of interpretation into direct confrontation, but the debate, although conducted as it was in theological and legalistic terms, was never isolated from political and economic contexts and considerations. The crown, the various missionary orders, the pope, the colonists, especially those who held encomiendas, and the Indian peoples themselves all had an interest at stake. The debate continued well into the following century, taken up by jurists, missionaries, and theologians, defenders of papal authority and opponents to it, and eventually by Protestants as well as Catholics and, of course, by ordinary Spaniards and Native Americans.

While in the lecture halls of Salamanca and the antechambers of the court these debates over the nature of the peoples of the Indies and Spain's claims to sovereignty raged, a parallel, sometimes intersecting, but quite different process was taking place as Spaniards and other Europeans who joined them, men and women, laypeople and clerics, crossed the Atlantic and through conquest and colonization began to construct a new society. In the face of considerable pressures for conformity, these people brought with them the beliefs and doubts that often resulted in thought and behavior at variance with what was expected of them, and then American realities created a peculiar venue where existing European beliefs and practices needed to be adapted, resolved, and articulated.[8]

In this chapter it is not the prevailing institutions of state and Church or of predominant ideology and dogma that concern us, but rather the heterodox thoughts, popular dissidence, and doubt that confronted those universalistic and potentially hegemonic ideas.[9] The process of creating the early modern Spanish monarchy and post-Tridentine Catholicism was uneven and messy, and although Spain is sometimes projected as a classic example of the absolutist state, of baroque conformity, and of the "persecuting society," I will present here evidence of a vibrant culture at odds with the dominant ideologies of Church and state.[10] It was in many ways, as the historian Henry Kamen has called it, a "society of dissidence."[11] For this task, the records of the Inquisition, a biased source to be sure, but one which allows at least some approximation to popular attitudes and culture, provide the best guide.[12]

American Inquisitions

In terms of establishing religious orthodoxy and norms of morality, the Americas presented to Spain a challenge of enormous proportions. Whereas in Spain itself, eventually some sixteen tribunals of the Inquisition functioned to cover an area of five hundred thousand square kilometers, in Mexico alone a single tribunal exercised control over three million square kilometers, to say nothing of its additional jurisdiction over the Philippines, Central America, and the New Mexico frontier.[13] The two other American tribunals of Lima and Cartagena faced similar problems. The Lima Inquisition heard cases from all of the viceroyalty of Peru, including far-off Paraguay, Chile, the Río de La Plata, and, until 1610, from northern South America and Panama as well. After that date, the tribunal created at Cartagena de Indias on the coast of modern Colombia exercised jurisdiction over Colombia, Venezuela, Panama, and the Caribbean islands. The network of bureaucratic control, therefore, was stretched to the maximum by the geographical extent of the area covered, eventually by the size of the population, and by the possibilities for deviance, despite the fact that the American Inquisitions eventually reproduced the infrastructure of commissaries or local agents and of *familiares,* that is, laymen who served the tribunals in various capacities. Structures and intentions were similar, but American realities intervened. Control was stretched to the limit. A petition from the Jesuits in the Río de la Plata in the eighteenth century spoke of the need for a tribunal in the region, or perhaps even two or three tribunals, such was the excessive level of liberty. Control was essential, the Jesuits argued, "if Spain did not want in its dominions that each person live in the law that they wanted."[14]

The Catholic monarchs, Ferdinand and Isabella, did not immediately impose the Inquisition in the New World after Columbus's first voyages. The first steps to grant inquisitorial powers in the Indies were taken between 1517 and 1519.[15] At first, local clerics or bishops exercised control in matters of the faith through episcopal courts. In New Spain, after the conquest by Cortés in 1523, for example, early Franciscan missionaries exercised inquisitorial functions until the first bishop, Juan de Zumárraga, assumed them. Between 1536 and Zumárraga's departure in 1543, about 130 cases were tried, the vast majority involving Spaniards. This apostolic Inquisition functioned as a precursor to the formal Inquisition tribunal that was created in 1569, although it did not begin to operate regularly until 1571.[16] The Mexican and Lima tribunals were part of a political decision made by Philip II to strengthen royal power in the Indies by using the Inquisition as a means of ideological control.[17]

The early versions of the inquisitorial tribunals in the colonies had sometimes pursued, persecuted, and even executed Indians who rejected conversion or who questioned matters of faith. A number of spectacular trials and executions of Nahua and other indigenous nobles and leaders in New Spain were used to demonstrate the power of the Church and the costs of rejecting its message. The potential for dissidence even among those indigenous people who had received intense Christian instruction was great. In 1539 don Carlos Ometochtzin, the *cacique* of Texcoco, a leader of the highest lineage and authority, was tried for blasphemy, concubinage, and heresy. His most serious crime seems to have been that of developing cultural resistance and relativism parallel to that expressed by some of the Spanish dissidents. He was accused of having said that the Franciscans, Dominicans, and Augustinians each had their own habit and their own way of teaching and each was good, so why then could the indigenous way of life not also be valid? That was an argument that could not be permitted by the bishop or the viceroy, and don Carlos was executed at the stake.[18] But the execution raised serious questions about this policy and its possible effects on driving Indians away from the Church. Eventually, the native peoples, as recent converts to the faith, were exempted from

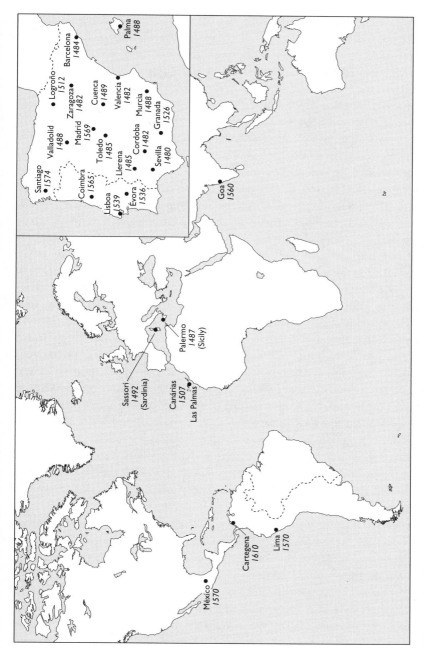

The tribunals of the Inquisitions of Spain and Portugal with their dates of foundation.

Santiago 1574
Logroño 1512
Barcelona 1484
Palma 1488
Valladolid 1488
Zaragoza 1482
Cuenca 1489
Valencia 1482
Madrid 1569
Murcia 1488
Granada 1526
Toledo 1485
Cordoba 1482
Coimbra 1565
Llerena 1485
Sevilla 1480
Lisboa 1539
Évora 1536
Goa 1560
Palermo 1487 (Sicily)
Sassori 1492 (Sardinia)
Canárias 1507
Las Palmas
Cartegena 1610
Lima 1570
México 1570

the Inquisition's authority.[19] Thus, the Mexican tribunal concentrated on Spanish colonists and soldiers and their "Spanish" and mestizo descendants as well as on blacks and mulattos. This was also true of the Lima and Cartagena tribunals. The records of these courts reveal a great deal about orthodoxy and deviance in the Indies, but unfortunately their rather late establishment and the loose organization of the American Inquisitions prior to 1570 prohibit one from using the records to gain a deeper insight into Spaniards' first perceptions of the new peoples and the alternate worlds they confronted. Moreover, it is often forgotten in histories of religion in colonial Latin America that the original contact and settlement took place prior to the Council of Trent and that tremendous effort had to be exerted not only to convert the Indians, but also to impose the Tridentine decisions on the European faithful. In fact, no American bishop had been invited to attend the Council of Trent.[20] While it is true that both the crown and the Church sought to keep America free of the contagion of groups or ideas thought dangerous, the task proved impossible.

While the religious origins of Columbus and some of his mariners remain in debate, the crown quickly moved to assure religious orthodoxy among those people immigrating to the Indies. Legislation prohibiting the immigration of Conversos and foreigners to the Indies began as early as 1510, and this was followed by prohibitions directed against slaves from particular West African groups known to be Muslims.[21] Immigrants often found ways to circumvent this legislation, and the crown itself sometimes broke with its own policy. Morisco silk makers, for example, were sent to New Spain to initiate that industry despite the restrictions against their presence in the Indies. It was the presence of the traditionally suspect groups, Conversos and Moriscos, and of foreigners who might be Protestants — as well as a fear about the dissident opinions and immoral behavior of the Spanish colonists themselves — that placed the orthodoxy of the American colonies at risk. It was such concerns that moved Father Las Casas in 1516 to call for the establishment of the Inquisition in the Indies.

The level of intensity and activity of the American tribunals differed from that of their peninsular counterparts. Prior to 1700, the three American tribunals handled fewer than three thousand cases, and although, as in the peninsular tribunals, all the standard crimes were prosecuted, only a small percentage involved formal accusations of heresy, not the case in Spain. In the American tribunals there were trials of foreign pirates and freebooters as Protestants beginning in the mid–sixteenth century. Then, in the mid–seventeenth century, there was a flurry of activity against supposedly Judaizing Conversos, especially those of Portuguese origin. It diminished when the combination of religious, political, and economic factors that caused this activity subsided by the end of the century, although individual cases against Judaizers continued. Prosecutions of Islamic practices were relatively few because of early prohibitions against Morisco emigration, and thus such charges were limited to occasional West African slaves of Muslim origin or to Christian renegades. Far more important were matters of heterodoxy and social control, and thus the higher percentages of people charged with blasphemy, propositions, and sexual improprieties. The Indies, with their mixed populations, their great distances, the presence of allegedly superstitious beliefs of Africans and Native Americans, and a relatively loose structure of inquisitorial control, offered tremendous opportunities for freedom of expression, for unrestrained sexual appetites of laity and clergy, and for the liberty to think skeptically. For example, whereas in Spain sexual transgressions of the laity made up only about 6 percent of the total cases heard, in New Spain the figure was closer to 25 percent. The same could be said about sexual improprieties of the clergy committed with their "daughters of confession." The level of incidence of this abuse in New Spain was about three times that in the Spanish tribunals.[22] Propositions of all kinds made up about a quarter of all cases heard in the American tribunals between 1540 and 1700. Heterodoxy and dissent, it would seem, flourished in the New World. The inquisitors' task was overwhelming, but one must remember that for the most part, even in Spain itself, denunciations were usually commonly made by other members of the community, not by the commissaries or agents of the Holy Office.[23] Of course, in the hierarchical, multiethnic world of the Indies people might use denunciations as part of a class struggle or to settle personal scores. The many instances of blacks or mulattos accused of witchcraft and sorcery and the many denunciations by them against owners or employers demonstrate the ways in which institutions like the Inquisition could be appropriated as weapons in other battles. Rather than the Inquisition's activity representing an increasing regimentation of society against which individuals and interest groups were virtually powerless, as has been suggested by the works of Michel Foucault, people in the Hispanic world found innumerable ways to turn the tendency toward regimentation to their own purposes, subverting the state's designs for institutional control.

In all of this process and despite their relatively small numbers, Spaniards and other European foreigners were by far the most often charged. In Lima, in the sixteenth century, for example, Spaniards and their descendants made up almost 80 percent of all those charged by the court, while blacks, mestizos, and mulattos were less than 5 percent of the total.[24] The content of the propositions in the Indies closely resembled that of Spain. Here, as in Spain, however, I will concentrate on those propositions and attitudes that contested the Church's position on carnal sin and on salvation, on body and soul, and especially as these attitudes may have related to the perception of people of other religions and ways of life.

The Indies: A Sexual Revolution

In the world of the putative *convivencia* between Muslims, Christians, and Jews in Spain during the late Middle Ages, sexual contact was one of the frontiers that had been most important in establishing the limits of their inter-action. Prohibitions against sexual contact between the three faiths were strict and sometimes brutally enforced. The *Siete Partidas,* the basic medieval law code, had prohibited Christians even from eating or drinking with Muslims and Jews. By the fifteenth century accusations of crossing the religious bound-aries sexually became one of the most common charges because they were so effective in setting the judicial machinery into motion.[25] Even contact with prostitutes was prohibited across religious lines. Interreligious or interethnic sexuality became a danger zone and a place where distinction was defined.

In the Americas, these prohibitions were broken continually and on a level that exceeded anything previously known in Iberia. Sexual exploitation by rape and concubinage was common in all the conquests, as many of the chron-iclers made abundantly clear, but it was also true that as new areas were conquered, leaders sometimes fostered marriages with local, often highlyborn women as a means of stabilizing the area and appropriating land and author-ity. To this end, conversion served as a prerequisite to sexual gratification and to reaching political and material goals. But the conquerors and settlers were confused on the issue. The tradition in Spain had prohibited sexual relations with unbelievers, so there was some question in the Americas whether sleeping with a baptized or unbaptized gentile was the worse offense.[26] Francisco de Aguirre, a powerful commander on the Chilean frontier and conqueror of Tucumán, ran afoul of religious authorities for a number of scandalous propo-sitions, among them his statement that making mestizo children who would become Christians by having sex with Indian women was more a service to the Church than a sin. His services had been considerable. He admitted to having fathered some fifty illegitimate children. In the same way many of the de-fenders of simple fornication had defended their action, he pointed to God's admonition to multiply and fill the land.[27]

Here, then, were deeply ingrained beliefs and practices at odds with the teach-ings of the Church. In the reality of America, these ideas found a new context in which to flourish in the shadow of Iberian concepts of family, sexuality, and appropriate relations between men and women as well as in terms of ideas about race and social hierarchy. These ideas prospered in the New World for a number of reasons. First, the Church and Inquisition in Spain did not begin to prosecute ideas of simple fornication with any regularity during the first half of the sixteenth century, exactly the period of first contact, settlement, and occupation of the continents. These attitudes were relatively uncontested at exactly the moment of conquest. The fact that much of the conquest took place prior to Trent needs to be kept in mind not only in terms of sexual attitudes but in regard to religious practice in general. Moreover, in the context of unequal power and exploitation, the old belief that sex was not a sin if consented to or if paid for was easily adapted to situations of cultural contact in which concepts of consent and of compensation were easily reformulated to serve the interests and libido of the Europeans. While the Church seemed particularly concerned about the laity's sexual behavior, it also confronted a continual problem of controlling the libido of the clergy. This was a problem in Spain itself, but the opportunities for exploitation in the Indies were seemingly limitless.[28]

Finally, the American context itself created conditions that reinforced these opinions and practices. Great distances and difficulties of communication made bigamy a common offense, and the availability of Indian women taken by force, barter, or alliance made *amancebamiento* a common practice.[29] Whereas concubinage was eventually controlled in Spain, in the Indies it flourished. "Public sins" were a matter of local government, but their control encountered continual resistance or disdain. As a measure of the difference between Spain and the Indies, rates of illegitimacy in southern Spain slightly exceeded those of northwest Europe, but those of America were on another scale altogether, reaching 40 percent of all births in some places.[30]

Not much consideration was given to (non-Christian) Indian marriage as a limiting factor that would have excluded married women or placed them in a separate category.[31] Sex with an Indian woman or a slave was not a sin.[32] The opportunities for sexual gratification seemed endless. Take Pedro de Herrera, seventy years old, a native of Castile. He had lived in concubinage with an Indian woman for twenty years, "as holy as the angels," he said, and he had told his son to do likewise. "Why go around with a rosary? As a young man you should have a girlfriend or two." When reprimanded he pleaded ignorance and the fact that "it is such a common thing."[33] These attitudes of sexual license were not limited to Spaniards. Many mestizos were prosecuted for expressing similar ideas, and they were often just as exploitative of indigenous women.

The levels of restraint were low. Despite the efforts of early missionaries, especially against concubinage, popular sexual ideas were rarely contested or controlled. In the context of colonial power, it is not surprising that sexual exploitation accompanied other forms of control or that Indians were, as pagans or barbarians, thought to be lesser beings, but this behavior was not simply the result of ideas about racial or cultural superiority. They reflected instead an old set of traditions and beliefs about the sexual relations between men and women, justifying to some extent free male access to women but recognizing certain restrictions depending on marital status, consanguinity, and ritual relationships. These attitudes also recognized as legitimate, if not without some sin, long-term sexual contacts through concubinage and paid sex. Indian women, lacking marital attachments and protections recognized by Europeans, easily fell into the status of free women, especially when the equation of force also favored Europeans.

Popular ideas about premarital and illicit sex conflicted directly with Church dogma.[34] The prosecutions for simple fornication in the American colonies and in Spain diminished in the eighteenth century, but the lower numbers did not necessarily attest to a change of behavior or signal the triumph of the theologians of Trent. High rates of illegitimacy attest to the continuing strength of practice, at least among the lower classes, but it was never the fornication that the Inquisition sought to control, only the idea that it was not a sin. It is probably fair to say that the Church was to some extent effective in instilling a sense of guilt that led to the denunciations of immoral behavior.[35] Over time these ideas went increasingly unprosecuted because fewer people were willing to state them in public and perhaps because the Inquisition became less threatened by the heresies with which simple fornication had been associated in the sixteenth century.

The great American historian of the Spanish Inquisition, Henry Charles Lea, believed that the Inquisition's assertion that these ideas about sexuality suggested heresy and thus fell under its jurisdiction had been an obvious arbitrary abuse of its authority.[36] Surely it was, but what the inquisitors perhaps understood better than Lea was that the attitude of people who held these heterodox propositions about sexuality inclined them to other doubts about matters of dogma, even on something as essential as the best path to the soul's salvation or the exclusive validity of the Church. Time after time, an investigation opened because of sexual peccadilloes or because of expressions of doubt about the sinfulness of sexuality revealed that the culprit held a variety of beliefs that questioned dogma and that often indicated more serious heresies, including a tolerance or openness to other ways of thought and belief.

Religious and Cultural Tolerance

In 1594, a young Spanish rural laborer named Juan Fernández de Las Heras fell afoul of the Inquisition in Lima, Peru. His statements had made it clear that he believed that sex between unmarried people was not a sin. The arrest was no surprise for, as we have seen, the Inquisition since the 1560s had been prosecuting many people for holding this belief, which it held to be a negation of the Sixth Commandment. As the investigation proceeded, upon further and more intensive questioning, it became clear that as in many other cases, Las Heras's attitudes toward sex were not an isolated aberration, but in fact were part of a broader ideology of dissidence. Las Heras held many other scandalous and heretical ideas ranging from doubts about the Eucharist to praise for Henry VIII of England, who had defied the Church of Rome. Among these propositions was that other, far less common but also widely held belief: that "each person being good can save themselves in their own law." Las Heras believed that the Church's position that only its members would be saved was simply arrogance, for surely God would save all the good people of the word in their own law. Las Heras's heterodoxy and dissidence went even further. The world was not right, he said, and he spoke out against the way things were, and when the inquisitors questioned him about the relations existing between the Church and the Protestants, he responded, "Both sides are wrong for they have torn the Faith asunder, and in Asia there are places where they know God better than in the Church." Where had he learned these heresies? The inquisitors were suspicious of foreign influences, but Las Heras was from Old Christian stock, born in Castile, and had never left Spain except to travel to Peru. Under investigation he was obstinate and uncooperative. He refused to swear an oath on the cross. He refused legal counsel. Thought to be mad by some of his interrogators, obstinate by others, he continually refused to retract these "truths." He could not believe in the goodness of a God who would condemn men to perpetual punishment just because they were weak and imperfect. For these ideas, and even more for his pertinacious refusal to recant them, he was burned alive.[37]

The proposition that each could be saved in his own law traversed the Atlantic along with other dissident opinions. The situations of its expression and the characteristics of those who spoke it did not vary greatly from the patterns we have observed in the peninsula. Many prosecutions for this proposition dated from the last three decades of the sixteenth century, when the Mexico and Lima tribunals were just beginning to function and when, in the shadow of the Protestant threat, the principal campaign against deviant belief among the general population was at its height, but they continued into the seventeenth century and then beyond. As in Spain, these statements of religious relativism or deism could be encountered in various categories of the population, Old Christian commoners, ecclesiastics (especially Franciscans), Conversos, former renegades and Barbary captives, and foreigners. The incidence of these cases over time seems to reflect the overall activity of the tribunals rather than a change in the popularity or frequency of the ideas.[38]

People from all walks of life and of all the social and ethnic-religious categories expressed the relativist position as they sought to escape the constraints of medieval doctrine that condemned so many souls.[39] Since salvation continued to be the principal religious concern, people knew that the Church considered the proposition of the possible validity of other faiths to be heretical in its implications. Still, there were enough contradictions within Catholic doctrine to leave the issue in some doubt and open to question. Laypeople with no training in theology were, of course, prone to fall into error on the issue, but learned men were also confused. In 1558, the bishop of Mexico, exercising inquisitorial powers, charged the Portuguese merchant Simón Falcón for holding that Islam and Judaism offered a path to salvation as valid as that of the Church. Falcón was an Old Christian, and he claimed that the charges had been made by his enemies and debtors, so his punishment was relatively mild, but if his defense was accurate, it demonstrated that people understood quite well the seriousness of the charge.[40]

An example of this reality and of society's preoccupation with the question can be seen in two other incidents from New Spain. In 1569, Juan de Aramua, a Fleming, got into an argument with Luis de Castro, who denounced him to the local priest. Castro had said he had captured many Huachichiles (a people from the region of San Luis Potosí), women and children, in a military expedition, and Aramua had commented that they were innocent and that the children could also be saved because "they had done no wrong in their law like the Christians in our law." Castro said that was impossible because only through baptism was salvation possible, and Aramua told him to shut up. Aramua admitted that he had said that the children and Huachichiles could be saved in their own law, but he claimed he said this out of ignorance and not with heretical intent.[41] Such attitudes were not limited to the uninformed, however.

The early chroniclers of Mexico, especially the Franciscans, in their enthusiasm to demonstrate the Christian potential of the indigenous peoples, had found evidence of Indians who had been illumined by the light of natural law before the arrival of the Spaniards. Fray Toribio de Benavente, "Motolinia," believed that Quetzalcoatl, the lawgiver of ancient Mexico whom the Indians had later deified, had actually preached the natural law. He also recounted the story of a simple man who had lived without offense to God or his fellowman and who was about to be sacrificed in the barrio of Tlatelolco. Calling on God in his heart, the man was visited by a messenger of God, who told him that soon the bloodshed would end and that new lords were coming to take control of the land. This he conveyed to the people. Motolinia implied his salvation within natural law.[42] The chronicler Mendieta developed a similar argument, that a merciful God had enlightened some Indians to see beyond "the errors of their gentile state and the blindness of their vices" to give them a foreknowledge of the salvation that was to come with the missionaries. He noted that Nezahualpilli, the king of Texcoco, had doubted that his gods were really true and had abhorred and punished the sin of sodomy and that Nezahualcoyotl, the poet king of that city, as well as others were inspired "to live conforming with natural law and the rule of reason."[43] The Franciscans seemed particularly given to this emphasis on the possibility of salvation through natural law for the meek and humble and to their emphasis on the innocence and simplicity of the common folk who did as they were ordered and harmed no one.

Fifty years after the fall of Aztec rule, this was still an issue. On Holy Thursday in 1573, Fray Pedro de Azuaga, a Franciscan friar, a man schooled in theology at Salamanca, was preaching in the principal church of Guadalajara. All the people of importance attended this solemn event, including the judges of the *audiencia*, or high court, the bishop, and various officers of Church and government.[44] Fray Pedro was a man of humble origins, but his education was sound, and, having served in Andalusia and in other places in Mexico, he had extensive experience. He was also something of a theoretician and had written a tract defending Spain's right to use force to guarantee peace and to punish evil, a position applauded by the Mexico City town council, anxious to find an intellectual champion to justify the exploitation of Indians by the Spanish settlers.[45] Later, he was to win the bishop's seat in Santiago de Chile.

The sermon caused a scandal in the church. From the pulpit, Fray Pedro had stated that "each person can save himself in his own law, the Moor in his, the Jew in his." Franciscan witnesses who were there reported that there was an immediate uproar in the church. Two of the *oidores*, or high court judges, attending the ceremony immediately called for one of the senior Franciscans to approach the pulpit and get Azuaga to correct himself. His colleague Fray Pedro de Zamora tugged on Azuaga's cassock, trying to get his attention, but in the heat and passion of the sermon it was hard to stop him. He would not change his statement and claimed that it was correct and that he would preach another sermon in the future explaining why. That explanation was found to be unsatisfactory, and Azuaga was denounced to the Inquisition. The issue of salvation outside the Church had been raised in the midst of the Mass to the dismay of the most powerful members of the colonial elite.

But Pedro de Azuaga understood what was at stake in his statement, and, once denounced, he mounted an able defense. First of all, he claimed that the statement had been simply "a slip of the tongue," a *lapsus linguae,* but what he argued was that infidels could not save themselves in their law but only in natural law, which is reason; thus one could explain how those who had been raised as infidels could become saints, citing Job and Saint Gregory. Finally, he recognized that the Catholic faith was necessary for salvation. Azuaga had defended himself with the old shield of natural law, and this buckler and his contrition stood in his favor. The inquisitors forced him to abjure, ordered that he stop preaching, and deprived him of any vote in his order's activities for two years. The inquisitors required Fray Pedro to retract his original statement formally, and in the retraction one can clearly see the accepted position of the Church. He confessed, "It is proper to observe natural law and to separate from the wrong ways taught and permitted in the [other] law, and in this way God will bring the light of knowledge of the Catholic faith of Our Lord Jesus Christ so that one can be saved in it, for no one can be saved without faith in Our Lord Jesus Christ; and that which I stated absolutely that men can be saved in all the laws is false and heretical and as such I detest it and abjure it by order of the Honorable Inquisitors of these provinces."[46] Azuaga had recanted and saved his career, but the theological questions remained, and the idea that perhaps not only Catholic Christians might find salvation continued to be expressed.

More extreme deviations from orthodoxy were also possible. In 1601, Juan Plata, chaplain of the convent of Santa Catalina de Sena in Puebla, Mexico, was denounced for a number of irregularities of both a spiritual and carnal nature. Plata was in fact part of a group of *alumbrados,* or illuminists, a mystical sect seeking a purer kind of religious inspiration outside of the usual structures of worship. Such groups had been suppressed in Spain in the 1520s because they seemed to mix Erasmian heterodoxies with other unorthodox beliefs, including for some a belief in the divine nature of carnality and thus their tendency toward the "erotization of religiosity."[47] Plata had admonished families not to place their daughters in convents, and despite his knowledge of theology he had denied the sinful nature of the violation of the Sixth Commandment. But in his defense before the Mexican Inquisition, Plata had also revealed a utopian vision of an expanding world and a critique of the society of New Spain. The biblical call for unity and to love one's neighbor had been ignored, and Plata warned of an apocalyptic future: "After the East and West Indies and Guinea were discovered, the nations have become mixed and they have not conformed or united with each other as [the Prophet] Daniel had called for, as can be seen because they call each other 'Indian dog,' 'mulatto dog,' 'mestizo dog,' and so they remain in discord among themselves, and we await that which must come."[48]

The Council of Trent had recognized the importance of both free will and grace, but it had avoided clarifying their relationship. The old controversy that had caused Augustine to denounce as heretical Pelagius's emphasis of free will in the fifth century, that had plagued the conflict with the Protestants in the sixteenth century, and that would reemerge within the Church in the seventeenth century in the form of Jansenism, with its emphasis on grace, remained unsettled and open to wide interpretation.[49] By emphasizing humankind's capacity to do good and thus individuals' ability to influence their own salvation, a space was created for even non-Christians to benefit from God's salvific power.

The matter smoldered in the monasteries, especially among the Franciscans but not exclusively so. Fray Francisco Martínez, who preached in the Franciscan convent of Seville, was denounced by nine of his Franciscan brothers in 1604 because he had argued that not all the infidels were damned and that if they were it was for original sin and not for a failure to accept the true faith. The *calificadores,* or theologians, brought in to evaluate his propositions found his problem to be an "error of understanding" and unfamiliarity with the terms of theology. In Mexico City in 1616, the stonemasons denounced a man who lived among the building stones being used to construct the cathedral and who seemed crazy. Among the things he said was that "among the Moors and other non-Christian nations were some who were saved."[50] In Upper Peru (Bolivia), Hernando Palacios Alvarado, archdeacon of the city of La Plata, was denounced in 1581 for saying that those who had lived in the old Mosaic law had found salvation, as had those who lived in the law of nature. When asked what he meant by "law of nature," he responded with a Latin quotation: "*quod tibi non vis alteri neferens*" (Do unto others as you would have them do unto you), but the theological evaluators remained unsure if his statement implied error or heresy concerning salvation.[51] In both these cases, however, the accused, the accusers, and the *calificadores* all shared the same cultural understanding. Their dispute was a matter of interpretation. As we shall see, there were many people for whom the theological distinctions were far less important than their own sense of justice and morality.

While those with theological training usually justified their expressions of religious tolerance and universalism by turning to the possibility of natural law as a path to salvation, people with less education or those more secular in their approach to life justified themselves in other ways. First, there were those people who just wished to be left alone to believe what they thought best. This was often the position of persons with nonorthodox ideas. Mariano Gordon, an Englishman living in Guatemala, in an argument about the validity of papal indulgences, said, "You believe in your law and I'll believe in mine, and on judgment day, we shall see."[52] Then there were those whom we might call skeptical believers. They believed man was incapable of knowing God's will and only God could know which religion was best. A certain Tomé de Medina, a pastry chef in Potosí, was denounced in 1582 for saying that only God knows whether the Muslims could be saved. These were God's secrets.[53] Since we could not know with any security which path to follow, then we must be what we are. Medina said, "The Muslim, the Jew, or the Lutheran, keeping their law, can save themselves better than any Christian. In those laws God created them, and in those laws they will be saved and go to glory, and in this there is no doubt. And if I had been raised in one of those laws, I would find salvation there, for all of them are good." This belief that God's will is beyond our knowledge and the recognition that we each have a destiny that can be fulfilled according to God's will went to the heart of the matter. Medina's position was, in fact, quite like that of the Friulian miller Menocchio, who at roughly the same time had made a similar argument to the inquisitors in his country.[54] It was a testament to a faith in God's benign nature and in man's essential goodness. Even when arrested, Medina told the inquisitors he had only meant to say that the innocent among the Moors were not damned. He could simply not conceive of a God who would do that.

The origins of these ideas remain obscure. Many people seem to have believed in the validity of all religions as a matter of common sense. Others learned about it through reading. Manuel Muñoz de Acuña told the inquisitors in Lima that he had read in some book that any infidel gentile could be saved without baptism.[55] The Mexican inquisitors in 1600 wanted to know exactly how Diego Enríquez, a Dutch barber, had gotten this same idea, and he was subjected to torture to extract the information, but he revealed nothing else.

It was not strange that a Dutch barber had been arrested. Foreigners are overrepresented in my sample simply because as outsiders they were automatically suspect and because, as was often the case in denunciations to the Inquisition, persons who lacked a local infrastructure or network of kinship and friends were more likely to be accused. But the denunciation of foreigners is also noteworthy because it tends to negate the claim that this sort of religious relativism was a peculiarly Hispanic phenomenon that had taken root during the *convivencia* of the Middle Ages and had continued to flourish. In New Spain alone, Savoyards, Flemings, and Frenchmen were all accused of religious relativism. The cases of two Flemish speakers arrested in Mexico City in 1601 offer some insight. These were humble men. Andrian Sisler was a craftsman from Antwerp who worked on churches and had lived in New Spain for twenty-five years when he was denounced for stating that "all the nations can be saved by keeping the law they profess without the water of baptism." His reputation as a Christian was good, and he had been imprisoned for almost a year, so the inquisitors had sentenced him only to abjure in a private Mass. He had been so poor that the tribunal imposed no fine or loss of property.[56] His son-in-law, the barber Diego Enríquez, was not as fortunate. Also denounced for religious relativism, the investigation revealed that he had doubts about the images of the saints, the power of the famous cross of Burgos, and other heretical opinions. Ten witnesses made statements about him, and although he admitted that he had said that "Turks, Moors and other infidels can be saved, each in his law," his confession contained too many contradictions. Enríquez was subjected to torture, but they could not break him. He would admit to nothing else, and he was sentenced to abjure *de vehementi* in a public auto de fe and to pay a hundred-peso fine.[57]

Personal contacts with peoples of other religions also had their effects. Take, for example, Antón de Niza, from Nice, who lived and worked in Mexico City. He had been denounced in the 1570s for saying that it was "better to be a good Lutheran than a bad Christian. It was rumored he had been among Protestants in La Rochelle and Geneva.[58] When reproached, he snapped his fingers and cocked his head to show his disagreement. Once arrested, in prison his feelings about Spain and its Inquisition had come out. The Spaniards, he said, were a bunch of buggers for allowing the Inquisition to function, and the Neapolitans were far better for trying to keep out the tribunal. In his country there were none of these *bonetes* (caps), meaning the inquisitors, but just plain folks, "each person living as he wanted." He had no patience with papal bulls or inquisitors, nor did he believe that anything he had said required absolution. The inquisitors sentenced him to two hundred lashes, but they could have been much harsher. They saw him as a poor man without much capacity to think who had uttered these challenges to the Church without really meaning them, more or less the way soldiers utter blasphemies. But in truth, Antón de Niza's words implied a utopia of freedom of thought and action, a rejection of order and control, and a world of common folk free from the direction of learned men in authority. No philosopher kings here, just plain folks. Here was Plato's republic turned inside out.

Conversos in the New World, as in Europe, caught between the two faiths and constantly asked to believe in one, or question both, or believe in none, were always liable to become relativists even though their faith might be firm. The historian Nathan Wachtel has traced in detail a number of revealing cases like that of Francisco Botello, who died at the stake in Mexico in 1659 as an impenitent Jew, but who said, "Whatever one is, one must die as one is. Let each man be what he is. Whomever I follow, I follow." Botello had a sense of identity and loyalty to his heritage and a desire to honor and maintain it, but he believed that all the laws were valid. His wife, Maria de Zárate, after all, was an Old Christian, and while Botello was sorry she did not follow his law, he believed she lived a holy life. With love and considerable religious confusion, he said, "If everything she did in her law she did in our own, she would be a saint and canonized."[59] Botello and his wife had made an arrangement to live together, each following the law of the community into which they had been born.

The relativism or universalism of Conversos or those who lived with them was understandable enough given the ambivalence of their position in society, but others in society also expressed such attitudes of tolerance or esteem about them. In spite of the efforts to demonize Jews and Conversos, there is continual evidence that some people insisted on their own interpretation of the matter. In 1575, in Santiago de Chile, when in a conversation a friend had criticized the Portuguese king Dom Manuel for allowing the Castilian Jews into his country and then converting them, Pedro de Morales had come to the defense of the king and the Jews: "Nowadays all the best faith is in the converts."[60]

Sometimes the expressions of religious relativism and tolerance came from unexpected directions. Take, for example, the case of Diego de Mesa, a *vecino,* or citizen, of the town of Tolú in New Granada. Mesa was only in his mid-twenties, but he was a man of some importance, an *encomendero* and the owner of cattle herds on his *hatos,* or rural properties. One day in 1608, while talking with some men, Mesa had said that "in the days that they had lived in the law of Moses, it was as good as the law we follow now, and men could be saved in it." The three witnesses differed to some extent on what they heard and whether Mesa had meant to say that the old law was just as good as the new, but when they argued with him about it, Mesa had held his position and said that "he would put it in writing."[61]

Mesa had apparently given the matter some thought. He argued that many of the ceremonies practiced by the Church came from the Mosaic law. He implied that many aspects of the old law were still valid. Such talk was enough to set rumors in motion. One witness claimed he had heard that Mesa's father was a Jew. Fearing a denunciation, Mesa voluntarily came to confess to the Inquisition, insisting that he had only said that the law of Moses had been good in its time and that men had saved themselves in it. Whoever said it was bad should be punished, he felt.

Mesa was arrested, his goods seized, and an investigation begun, but, in fact, he had raised a thorny issue since the Church's position was that the old law had been valid before it had been superseded by the evangelical law. Much hinged on what exactly he had said and how he had spoken. Five theologians were called in to evaluate his statement, and they agreed that for him to say that the Mosaic law was as good for its time as the present [Catholic] religion was heretical.

Mesa was now on the defensive, and in his interviews before the inquisitors he tried to explain his error away. He said he could not remember whether he had used the preterit (*fue*) or the imperfect (*era*) when he described the old law as valid, the former implying a completed action in the past, the latter, a continuing action. More important, Mesa said he had heard this idea from learned men like the Dominican Fray Andrés de San Pedro and that he had discussed it with other important men, an Augustinian, a Franciscan, a certain Captain Ceballos, and with Fray Esteban del Valle. During the proceedings Mesa realized where the danger in his statements lay. He insisted that he had never said the old law was just as good as the law of Christ, and he recognized that the old law had been supplanted. But there was too much at stake here, and his statements had raised the contradictions in the Church's position about the validity of the Mosaic code. The punishment he received was stiff: public auto de fe, a hundred lashes, three years in the galleys, and then perpetual exile from the Indies. Not even the colonial elite, in this case an *encomendero*, was free from doctrinal error or from its suppression. Nothing about Jewish origins was found; otherwise Mesa surely would have been charged as a Judaizer. Finally, the case is interesting also from the viewpoint of the relation between learned and popular culture. Mesa provided evidence that he had heard this idea from those with theological training, and he cited them as authority for his position. He had apparently interpreted their statements in a way that was logical to him, but he had failed to note the theological nuances that made his statements border on heresy.

As in Spain, so in the Americas the prosecution of Judaizers who held firmly to their faith in the face of cruel punishment sometimes elicited admiration, not the repulsion the inquisitors sought. In Lima, Francisco Maldonado da Silva, a Portuguese of partly New Christian origins but born in Tucumán and resident in Concepción in Chile, played out a similar drama. He had converted himself to Judaism by reading against its intended message a book by a Jewish apostate designed to convince Jews of the truth of Catholicism. He had then circumcised himself. Denounced by a sister and arrested in 1626, this thirty-five-year-old surgeon claimed adherence to the faith of his father, but he eventually challenged and induced the inquisitors to debate with him by seeming to be willing to be convinced of his error.[62] Some fifteen meetings took place before they realized that his scholastic skills were being used to undercut their arguments, not to help Maldonado to see the light. His short escape, his preaching to other prisoners, and his attempt to contact the Jews of Rome all contributed to his condemnation to the stake in 1639 and to his reputation in the Jewish communities across Europe. The attitude or the defiance of victims like Diego Díaz, who at the moment of his execution in Mexico in 1659 was offered a cross to kiss as the "instrument of his salvation" and who, had he accepted it, would have been spared the horror of being burned alive, but who retorted, "Take it away, Padre, a stick will save no one," caught people's attention.[63] Such steadfastness impressed those who heard of it or who witnessed the executions. Not surprisingly, Jews in Amsterdam and Italy celebrated these martyrdoms, but even Christian observers were impressed.[64] In New Spain, for example, the exemplary death of the Converso merchant Tomas Treviño de Sobremonte in an auto de fe in Mexico City in 1649 in which he remained steadfast in his Judaism to the end made an indelible impression. A mulatto slave who saw it used to say defiantly when he was drinking, "I'm not a Christian, I'm Treviño."[65]

Similar cases can be found in Peru. Antonio Leal was a simple pastry maker in Lima who expressed his admiration for a young man who had been burned in Lisbon and had never denied his faith in the God of Israel. Such talk got him arrested as a suspected Jew, a doubtful charge. In 1618 he was punished with a year in prison and loss of his property. An even more striking Peruvian example involved the execution in 1736 of a well-known, respected Lima matron, Maria Francisca Ana de Castro, known as "a madama Castro," the last person burned by the Lima tribunal.[66] Accused as a Judaizer, she had gone to the pyre with singular calm and had even straightened her hair and placed the garrote around her own neck. Juan Ferrera, an old soldier who had seen something of the world and had been to Brazil, Buenos Aires, and Chile, was greatly impressed. "What kind of land is this? Witches walk about loose, and la madama Castro is burned. With Christ, without Christ: Wasn't Christ a Jew?" This opinion cost him his possessions and two hundred lashes, but he was not alone in his sense of injustice. A priest, Nicholas Flores, in the *doctrina* of San Pedro near Lima also found the execution unjust and said so, along with other criticisms of the Inquisition. He was forced to pay a fine and to publicly state that "everyone is obliged to believe that the decisions of the Holy Office are correct and just."[67]

Protestants, Lutherans, and Heretics

Attitudes toward Protestants in the Indies had a firm religious basis but could not be separated easily from national or political sentiments and interests. The trials of English, French, and Dutch corsairs as heretics continually drove home the point of the political and religious danger these interlopers posed to the religious security of society when in reality their danger was also political and commercial. Corsairs, however, were one thing, immigrants were another. Despite prohibitions, thousands of foreigners traveled to the Indies and resided there, many of them from lands that had been touched by the Protestant heresies. Moreover, many of the Spaniards resident in the Indies had in their experience as soldiers, merchants, pilgrims, and travelers observed life in foreign lands or come into contact with Protestants. Finally, the people read, debated, and discussed continually the political and religious geography of their world.

Often in conversations when someone would mention the Lutherans or Protestants in a negative light, someone else would respond that they might not be so bad after all. Genaro Monte, a Milanese merchant, had spoken in these terms in 1580 while in Soconusco, Guatemala, saying that the Lutherans were not as bad as they were said to be. For this he was denounced as a promoter of heretics, in the midst of a civil suit. Charges were dismissed for lack of evidence, but a decade later, while residing in the mines of San Andrés in Nueva Galicia in Mexico, he was in trouble again for speaking in the same way.[68] A continent away, Domingos Hernández had been chatting with friends about the sexual appetites of the women of Valdivia, Chile, in 1581 or 1582 when someone mentioned the Lutherans with disdain. Hernández said that he had sailed with them and that there were good Christians among them who did Christian works. Luis Briceño de Araya, governor of Panama in 1591, had fought in Flanders and was married to a Flemish woman. He called the Lutherans charitable and said that they lived the life of the apostles. In debates about religion, said Briceño, they shut the Catholics up and make them look as dumb as slaves just off the boat.[69] Briceño's positive opinions of the Lutherans were mixed with Spanish antipapal attitudes. When told by a priest that he had to pray for the pope, he snapped back that he had only to pray for the king: "Here we don't know the pope, who is a foreigner and who is always at odds with us and wishes us ill."

There were plenty of reasons to fear and hate the Protestants, but certain of their criticisms of the papacy and of Catholic practice resonated with people, and there were those who wished to know more about them or who thought that perhaps war was not the best way to deal with religious dissent. These ideas penetrated to the very heart of the Indies. Juan de Salas, a forty-four-year-old rope maker from Paris, was traveling with some companions from Tucumán up to the silver-mining city of Potosí in 1600. Salas was a good Catholic and had married a Spanish woman before he had gone off to campaign as a soldier against the English at San Sebastián and in Portugal and then for the king in Flanders. He had with him a book about King Henry IV of France printed in French that he had borrowed from a Basque youth, and, at the urging of his companions, he read it aloud to them, translating the French into Spanish. The book contained the text of the edict of Nantes of 1598, which had established freedom of worship and peace between Protestants and Catholics in France, and it dealt with liberty of conscience, about which he expressed his approval. When questioned by the Inquisition of Lima on this point, Salas's defense was supple. He claimed he had not approved of freedom of conscience, only that given the time and the necessity in which the king of France found himself, he could do nothing other than order that there be peace. Since the king was a Catholic, Salas argued that the book must also be Catholic as well. His case was dismissed. Neither the book nor what he said was found to be against the faith. What his companions had thought of the content one can only wonder, but the fact that they urged him to read to them about the edict indicates their curiosity in the possibilities of religious peace.[70]

Books and Readers

Reading and books were a problem on both sides of the Atlantic. Whatever the intentions of authors, books were always read creatively, and readers understood their message in their own way and saw the contents within their own realities. As the case of Salas demonstrates, readers could always draw their own conclusions, and those who could read shared their reading with those who could not. As the new scholarship on readership has emphasized, early modern oral and written culture were not really separated, and books and their contents circulated broadly in various forms.[71] The revolution of print had made ideas widely accessible to a growing segment of the population. As the Spanish political writer Diego Saavedra Fajardo put it, doubts and questioning were growing, "and much of the blame can be given to print, whose clear and pleasant form invites one to read; not like before when manuscript books were more difficult and less numerous."[72] Of course, in Spain and Portugal illiteracy was common among country folk, but it was not as pervasive as one might think. Almost all nobles, clerics, university graduates, and merchants could read and write, as could many artisans and tradesmen. People acquired first letters, that is, rudimentary skills of reading and writing, from family members, parish priests, and, most of all, teachers in informal schools. While it is true that literacy was more common in urban than rural areas and that men had markedly higher rates of literacy than women, studies in various places in Spain and Portugal reveal that by the mid–seventeenth century over 50 percent of the male population were at least marginally literate.[73] In the Americas, given the large indigenous and slave populations, that percentage was much lower, although it may have been roughly similar for those of European background. In any case, the ability to read coupled with a desire to know created both opportunities and dangers for authority and orthodoxy. Inexpensive primers, or *cartillas,* for reading and for catechesis were prepared in the tens of thousands by the Church. In addition, during the sixteenth century alone 232 catechisms were published in Spain and 137 in the Americas, to say nothing of the translation of foreign ones. But, at the same time, reading opened the door to curiosity. In the art of Golden Age Spain, artists often placed books next to the symbols of death to warn of vanitas and the transience of this life, and Cervantes could warn that "books carry men to the stake [as heretics]."[74] The written word was dangerous, and both the Church and state sought to control the threat to order and orthodoxy that it represented. As the great Spanish poet and playwright Francisco de Quevedo, usually a defender of orthodoxy, put it, "Princes fear those who have nothing to do but imagine and write."[75] After 1520 governments established censorship everywhere in western Europe as part of the wars of religion, and in Spain various technologies of control were established. The crown, through the Council of Castile, asserted the right to censor and license books before their publication, while the Inquisition exercised control over books once published by banning or expurgating them. Between 1559 and 1805 the Holy Office published eleven catalogs of prohibited books, their principal targets being writings that dealt with religion and astrology, although by the eighteenth century liberalism, egalitarianism, pornography, and anticlericalism were also the censors' concern. Scholars of the history of reading argue about the effectiveness of these prohibitions and about their effects. Many Spanish and Portuguese intellectuals did face censorship and prosecution at times, but this period was also the Golden Age of Spanish letters, so opinions vary on the force and outcome of censorship. My interest, however, is how the control of reading and writing was viewed by the consumers of the written word and how they felt about literacy and the freedom of thought it represented. Those with doubts about dogma often found reading was a path to truth, and they were jealous of their access to books. Silvestre Pinelo was arrested in Murcia in 1585 for his soteriology. He held that all would be saved since Christ had died to offer salvation to everyone. Questioning revealed he read a lot; too much and the wrong kind of things, the inquisitors believed, but Pinelo told the inquisitors that he did not think reading books on the magical arts would condemn him, and as for the books of chivalry that he liked, they only confirmed the word of God.[76]

One kind of text that was in great demand was the Holy Scriptures. In Spain, as early as 1554 the Inquisition moved against the publication of the Bible and all holy scriptures in vernacular languages. This was a measure aimed at eliminating erroneous interpretations by rustics, mystics, street prophets, and the uninformed; "little ladies and idiots [*mujercillas e idiotas*]," as they were called by the Salamancan Dominican theologian Melchor Cano.[77] But the control of Holy Scripture by inquisitors alone was contested by the humanists and philologists, who now found their intellectual freedom constrained and at times punished. Even more striking was the reaction of those who simply wished to have personal access to God's word and wished to directly confront God's word even though they could not read Latin.

Legislation prohibited the publication of the Bible in vernacular language and also interpretations of the gospels and even books with extracts from scripture. The beautifully illuminated "books of hours" of the medieval nobility had generated by the sixteenth century popular, cheaply printed volumes for a general public often illustrated with simple woodcuts. These and other devotional books were very popular, even among the illiterate, who used them as talismans or as objects of a magical nature whose images and text pressed on an injured extremity or the stomach of a woman in delivery could protect and heal. Church authorities sought to eliminate these books from private hands and to end such "superstitious" uses, but not without resistance. In Toledo in 1581, a field hand (*labrador*) named Alonso de Cubas, when admonished by his friends to give up his book of hours in Spanish because these volumes had been banned, answered that the book had cost him fourteen *reales* and that he would not burn his book even if the pope objected. He argued that such prohibitions had been issued in the past, but these books were still circulating. The inquisitors admonished him to obey the edicts, but his reluctance demonstrated a deep attachment to such books.[78] Shipping lists suggest that this kind of literature was popular in the Indies despite prohibitions. In 1621 a blind itinerant merchant in Mexico who was selling books of the gospels whose pages could be used as talismans was arrested, and while there were eight witnesses to his activities, none of them thought there was anything amiss in such sales.[79] Books of hours became a point of reference and of argument. Francisco Gómez de Triguillos in Mexico was a materialist in many ways. He said he preferred to live under a Moorish king who would feed his subjects and that the Eucharist was no consolation. He also said he had read in a book of hours that Saint Augustine had said that if you attended Mass you would not lose your soul, but that since his own enemy, the mayor of his town, attended mass regularly, and since Judas had received communion, Saint Augustine must be a liar. The inquisitors failed to see the humor in his ironical reference to his reading.[80] Whether for humanist intellectuals, itinerant merchants, or simple laborers, books and the ability to read them, use them, and think about them were closely associated with the idea of liberty of conscience.

In the mental and physical spaces of America the problem of the book and the dangers it represented may have been exacerbated. As early as 1531 and then again in 1543 the crown prohibited the importation of books of chivalric romance because of their possible negative effect on the Indian peoples, but the repetition of such laws indicates that they were ineffective. Not only was enforcement lax, but the Inquisition was also not very interested in many types of writing of a literary nature. Moreover, many people continued to read books despite prohibitions. An active book trade to America flourished, and ship manifests and bookseller inventories reveal that the colonists had a penchant for religious texts and for fiction.[81] Fray Luis de León's *Libro de oración y meditación (Book of prayer and meditation)* and Cervantes's *El Quijote* topped the list of books imported to the Indies.[82] As the new scholarship on the history of books and reading has emphasized, the question was not a matter of what was read, but how. How did readers interpret the written word, selecting, editing, and incorporating it into their own understanding of the world? This was the concern of authority, which had begun to impose restrictions on the importation of books to the New World and censorship.

The passion for reading and writing among those who had the skill was strong. In books, or in what individuals heard of their contents from those who could read, they found solace, inspiration, and spiritual satisfaction. They found ways to read "against the grain." Conversos are a useful example here. The teaching of the Church was that the old Mosaic law had been surpassed and replaced by the New Testament. Books of the Judaic tradition were strictly limited, but the Old Testament circulated in various forms. There are numerous examples of Conversos like Duarte Enríquez, a young Portuguese arrested in Peru as a Judaizer, who knew his Old Testament well enough to believe that it proved that God had done the Jews many mercies, or Manuel de Fonseca, a surgeon arrested in 1608 in Cartagena de Indias, who could recite all the psalms of David by heart and who even in prison found a way to copy a medical treatise, stopping in his transcribing only on Saturdays so as not to violate the Sabbath.[83] In a famous case from New Spain, Luis de Carvajal, of Converso origin but relatively ignorant of Judaism, was sentenced as a Judaizer to penitential work in a school in 1589. He used his access to the school's library of religious works to learn about that faith, and in essence to convert himself. "God filled my hands with treasures," Luis later explained.[84] But the practice of interpreting texts against the grain was not limited to Conversos, and it could lead anyone to an independence of mind even on issues as clearly defined as who merited salvation.

The passion for the written word was sometimes reflected in individual stories. Juan de Castillo was a street peddler and a troubadour who knew something of the world.[85] He sang and played his guitar and sometimes read palms to make his living, but he was also a man with a taste for reading and a feeling for Catholic theology. He was not reluctant to discuss his ideas with those who would listen. Someone had told him that there were no longer any saints in the world, and Castillo had disagreed. He responded that "he who is good is a saint," and he had even praised the Roman philosopher Seneca as a saintly man. His companion disagreed. Seneca was a gentile and unbaptized, but Castillo was adamant. In matters of faith, he said, the pillars of the Church, Saints Jerome, Augustine, Gregory, and Ambrose were as valid as the scriptures, and Saint Jerome had placed Seneca among the saints. That led to an argument in which his listener told Castillo to "shut up and don't speak of things of which you know nothing." But Castillo was adamant. He claimed he had this from a good source because he had read it in the book of Fray Domingo de Valtanás.

The reference was important. The Dominican friar Domingo de Valtanás (1488–1565), from Jaén, was one of the reformist Spanish clerics who wrote during the Council of Trent. Although not as distinguished as his contemporaries Juan de Avila and Luis de León, he was widely read as an author of books of moral and spiritual guidance aimed principally at lay readers.[86] These were often small, inexpensive, octavo volumes that easily fit the hand and could be slipped into a pocket. They were very popular, and since most were published in Seville they were perhaps taken as shipboard reading by passengers to the Indies. In any case, they appear regularly among the shipments of books to the New World. Perhaps Castillo had confused Socrates with Seneca. He might have read Valtanás's *Compendio de sentencias morales (Compendium of moral sentences)* (Seville, 1555), which had celebrated the virtues of Socrates and had insisted that the philosopher had found salvation. Or maybe the book Castillo had referred to was Valtanás's *Concordancias (Concordances)* (1555), a little volume designed to resolve seeming disagreements or inconsistencies within the scriptures and writings of the fathers of the Church, and whose title page bore the image of the four sainted pillars of doctrine.[87] The volume carried a number of messages that pointed in the direction of a salvation available to all. Valtanás emphasized that "it is works that make or unmake a man" (clxxxix) and that "in my father's house are many dwelling places"(xxx verso). He also pointed out that many serious scholars believed that those who lived in the law of nature or in the old (Mosaic) law as well as those children who had died before baptism were offered salvation by their "intention and faith" (*voto y fe*), and thus it would be unthinkable that God would treat with less sympathy those who lived in grace within the Church.

Castillo had clearly thought about the issue, and he had tried to follow the teachings of the Church. His reference to the Dominican underlines the dialogue between learned and popular culture, between author and readers, that made the circulation of ideas so important. Perhaps Valtanás had not been the best guide to orthodoxy. The Dominican had been one of those theologians who had opposed the injustice of the purity of blood restrictions imposed on New Christians, and he had eventually been tried and sentenced by the Inquisition for Erasmian ideas.[88] His works were full of a Christian humanism, and he had applauded those gentiles who had done Christian works and had criticized those Christians whose faith had not resulted in positive actions.

Castillo's confrontation had given him pause, or at least he was worried that he might be denounced, so he decided to act on his own. He had some other books as well, and he also kept a notebook in which he wrote verses (*coplas*), and now he thought perhaps he should seek a license to have them. He brought them to the Inquisition of Lima and asked that they be reviewed and their content approved. The result could not have been worse. The inquisitors were unsympathetic to a common man with a penchant for theology and an inclination for poetry. They found much of his writing profane and filled with the "ignorance and looseness of a man of little knowledge ("as in effect is the said Castillo, a man who goes about singing and playing a guitar"). The inquisitors simply tore out many offending pages and then returned the notebook to him with an admonition and a stern warning.

Castillo's reaction reveals the deep value that common people placed on their ability to read and write and on their own creativity. He left the Inquisition building in a fury and threw the notebook to the ground in front of a number of people gathered on the street. Lifting his eyes to heaven, he shouted repeatedly, "Damn whoever gave me birth, I deny who gave me birth. There has never been done to anyone a greater injury or cruelty." They had destroyed his writings. The crowd tried to silence him, they said the inquisitor had not offended anyone, but Castillo persisted. If there was a ship going to Castile, he would take it to report the injustice of the inquisitor because, he said, in Peru there was no judge who would do anything. Of course he was arrested and extraordinarily, without trial, exiled to New Granada for six years.[89]

6

American Adjustments

Faith is a dead thing without charity, and both virtues are the same thing. — Pedro Ramírez, Chiloé, Chile (1573)

Worship of God and obedience to Him consist solely in justice and charity toward one's neighbor.
— Baruch Spinoza, *Tractatus Theologico-Politicus* (1670)

The ancient conflicts with the Muslims and Jews and the more recent ones with the Protestants generated theological and political interest and concern in the Indies, but in terms of social organization and the challenges of daily life, except for brief periods, they were a relatively minor concern when compared with the colonial reality of an enormous subjected indigenous population. While the theologians and canon lawyers debated the sovereignty of the Indies, the nature and rights of their indigenous inhabitants, and the best means to bring them to the Church, ordinary Spaniards who crossed the Atlantic acted on the basis of a mixture of preconceptions, practical understandings, self-interest, and their own interpretation of dogma. The transition from a tradition that recognized the possibility of salvation within the monotheistic religions of the Mediterranean world or within the Protestant sects to a consideration of that possibility among the peoples of the New World was not easy. Reasons of state, of personal interest, and of theology militated against it, but enough evidence exists to indicate that in various ways, on various levels, and to various degrees it did take place. Spaniards may have expressed such feelings of cultural or religious relativism more commonly when dealing with the peoples of the old Native American empires of Peru and Mexico, who, whatever their faults, lived in *policía,* or an ordered society, rather than those peoples of the forests and plains, who did not.[1] Still, because the record of the first half century of the conquest is so spotty, it is difficult to get a clear picture of the process and attitudes, especially among the laity. The recognition of the separate laws of non-Christians was extended from medieval Iberia to the New World. Prior to their conversion, Native Americans testifying before Spanish courts were allowed to swear according to their own "law," and as late as the early nineteenth century, African slaves who gave testimony in court cases in Cuba were permitted to take an oath in their law as well.[2] But legal practices do not reveal the variety of responses to the cultural and religious differences encountered.

Indian Salvation

The missionary orders conveyed the importance of salvation to the New World. Scenes of the final judgment became a regular decorative feature of early convents and churches in Mexico and Peru, but even as the European representation of that eschatological moment declined and few final judgment scenes were painted after 1630, in the Americas these scenes continued to flourish.[3] They were especially popular in areas with large indigenous populations. The indigenous chronicler Felipe Guaman Poma de Ayala thought that each church should have such a scene displayed so that "heaven, earth, and the pains of hell" could be clearly seen. In principal churches like the cathedral of Lima and in more humble temples like the church at Carabuco on the shores of Lake Titicaca, artists painted versions of the final judgment, sometimes integrating indigenous elements or figures, which could be easily read, and in which Christ, the apostles, the Archangel St. Michael, and the separation of the saved and the condemned were always present. The occasional representation of church and civil authorities among the damned underlined the equality of sin and salvation. In the Andes, despite the medieval conceptualization of these scenes, they were painted well into the nineteenth century.[4] They highlighted the importance of salvation, but not everyone was persuaded by the idea of exclusivity through the Church that they conveyed.

If all peoples could be saved in their own law, then it was logical to ask why not the Native Americans as well? Ysabel de Porras was a Spanish woman

Final Judgment by José López de los Ríos (1684).
Scenes like this were placed in churches throughout the Americas, often incorporating local and indigenous elements and directed toward the indigenous populations. Courtesy of Carlos Rua Landa, Director, Patrimonio Cultural del Viceministerio de Cultura, Bolivia.

who had been born in Cuzco, the ancient capital of the Inca empire, a city in which interaction with Indians was continual. In 1572, she was fifty years old, living as a widow in Lima when in a conversation she told some friends that "before the Spaniards came to these lands, the Indians who died went to Heaven." Her argument seemed to be based on an understanding of natural law and a belief that the native Andeans were capable of living a good life according to it. Her friends disagreed and told her she should report her error to the Inquisition. Ysabel de Porras apparently realized that her statement went against dogma, and she sought to use purgatory or limbo to her advantage. When pressed by her friends and later by the inquisitors, she said she had only meant that they went to "some good place." Some of the Inquisition's theologians found her statements heretical, others, only in error and superstitious, but she was clearly voicing a kind of cultural and religious relativism in conflict with the mission and position of the Church.[5] These ideas and her reputation as a woman who could recite one of the folk incantations, the "prayer of the stars," and who used other superstitious practices led to her punishment by the Lima tribunal. The association of the possibility of salvation for gentiles and magical or allegedly superstitious practices suggests we are dealing here with a universe of belief in which religion was not limited to the orthodoxy of the Church and in which natural and supernatural forces merged. The occult certainly had its place in local religion in Iberia, but the possibilities for its expansion in the cultural milieu of the Indies were infinite.

Ysabel de Porras's relations with the native Andeans of her world are unknown, but certainly her attitude about the possible salvation of those who had lived prior to the arrival of the Spaniards must have resonated positively among them. In ancestor-oriented societies like that of the Andes, Christian missionaries often found one of the greatest stumbling blocks to conversion to be their insistence on the damnation of the ancestors of the potential converts. In Mexico, China, and Japan, as previously in Europe itself, missionaries had found that people preferred to join their forebears in hell rather than find salvation with the Christian God.[6] Purgatory, in a way, had been a theological response to the problem, and Ysabel de Porras's belief, with no clear theological argument, seems to be a practical, commonsense equivalent that would have allayed a major Andean objection to the new faith. But it also trod closely to one of the theological paradoxes about the salvation of those who had lived before Christ's coming or who were unaware of his message. The fifteenth-century theologian Alonso Fernández de Madrigal, "El Tostado," had sought to resolve the issue by explaining that before Christ's sacrifice, the Jews had been saved in their law and the gentiles only in the law of nature. If they died repenting their sins but had not atoned for them, they went to purgatory. But after the message of Christ was made available through the Gospels, Moors, Jews, and pagans did not go to purgatory but went by necessity to hell, "like all those who die in original sin and in present mortal sin; the children not having been baptized and adults not wishing to accept it."[7] This position seemed to run contrary to a more generous understanding of Christianity's message as people like Ysabel de Porras understood it.

For others, it was not theology but cultural practicalities that determined relations to native culture. Take, for example, the curious tale of a renegade priest in Upper Peru.[8] Sebastián de Herrera was a native of Toledo who when arrested in 1579 was a priest in an Indian parish, or *doctrina*. His story, often told and elaborated for his listeners, however, was that of a typical *renegado*. As a young man he had lived in North Africa as a paid mercenary in the service of Muslim lords against both Christians and Muslim enemies. As a captive, he had fallen in love with a Moorish woman, and she had convinced him to convert. He also had told listeners that he had fallen in love with a Jewish woman who loved him very much. Some witnesses implied that his own family may have been Conversos and that his father had been called the Jew of Ganso, but that seems not to have been true. He was of Old Christian stock on both sides of his family.

What brought him to the attention of the Inquisition, however, was the way in which he carried out his religious duties among the Indians of his *doctrina*. He celebrated the Mass with them and blessed the "Inca Indians, their dead, infidel ancestors," and, it was said, he asked the Indians to pay him for doing this. Once arrested, Herrera claimed he was falsely accused by the dean of the cathedral in La Plata, whom Herrera had publicly denounced, but he did admit to having lived in North Africa, where he had been the slave of a Jewish master who had treated him well. Perhaps Herrera was simply exploiting his parishioners, but one may wonder whether his experience with other cultures and religions as a captive and a convert in North Africa had made him willing to attend to the Indians' concern for their ancestors, or if he realized that blessing those ancestors made it easier to assure the adherence of his parishioners to the Church.

Like Herrera, other European immigrants drew on past understandings and expanded them to incorporate American realities. In the 1580s in Panama, the Inquisition acted against a certain Master Andrea, a Neapolitan carpenter. Andrea had apparently said that "the Turks and Moors believed in God and that each can save himself in his own law, and the Moors without the water of baptism."[9] His interlocutors had denied his proposition and insisted that neither the Moors nor Jews or Lutherans could be saved, to which he had responded with the old refrain, "Each can be saved in his own faith." The incident was serious enough to make Master Andrea denounce himself in 1583 to the local Inquisition representative, before whom he tried to place his statements in a positive light and to deny any intention to speak against the Church's position on the matter. His testimony revealed that his opinions were formed from experience. For many years, he had lived as a captive among the Turks and Muslims, probably in North Africa, and he knew of their religiosity. He tried to claim he had said that if the Moors accepted baptism they could be saved, but the testimony of witnesses contradicted him. The theological experts qualified his remarks as impious rather than heretical, but he was, nevertheless, arrested.

In many ways, Master Andrea's story, like that of Herrera, seems to be that of a typical renegado, who, having lived among the Muslims, had come to believe that they were religious and could seek salvation in their own way. Curiously, however, in his defense, Master Andrea had broadened the category of non-Christians. He told the inquisitors "he did not believe in the law of the Turks, Moors, and Indians, but that if the Turks, Moors, and Indians believed in Our Lord Jesus Christ and that he had been born of a virgin mother that in their law they could be saved." In other words, he tried to convince the inquisitors that he had argued that these other faiths were valid, but only so long as they accepted Christ. The inquisitors remained unmoved. He was arrested, his possessions seized, and he was finally punished in 1587 when he was forced to renounce his sins publicly and then to suffer six years of exile.

Master Andrea's thinking on the issue seems to have been born of his Mediterranean background, and his story presents little evidence of direct contact with Indian peoples, but there were other cases where such interaction was clear. Francisco de Escobar was a Peruvian mestizo of the first generation after the conquest.[10] Born in Lima about 1543, and apparently recognized by his conquistador father, he had grown up in the valley of Acari (Arequipa) on his father's sugar hacienda, surrounded by Indians and black slaves. He was educated to read and write Spanish (but not Latin), and it was said he would sometimes stand on an oxcart and preach to the assembled workers. The scene is reminiscent of a famous and much debated chapter in Cervantes's classic in which, at an inn, Don Quixote and Sancho Panza encounter a collection of books of chivalry that the innkeeper says he kept in order to read to and entertain the workers at harvest time.[11] Scholars have long debated the accuracy of this tale and its significance in the history of reading, but Escobar's case seems to resolve the matter once and for all. Testimony revealed that he would mount the oxcart and read to the slaves "the things of Amadis and from the books of chivalry," in a scene seemingly drawn right from *Don Quixote*. But his relationship with Indian and African workers was not limited to recitations. Escobar eventually held lands and Indian dependents. He was apparently completely unrestrained in his sexual appetites. He danced and drank with the Indians, lived in concubinage (*amancebado*) for many years, slept with many Indian women, even mothers and their daughters, and was accused of telling other mestizos and Indians to take the women they desired. He used the common biblical justification of those who held that fornication was not sin: God had said, "crescite et multiplicamini et replete terram."

What brought him to the attention of the Inquisition, however, was neither his reading nor his libido, but rather an argument with his neighbors. They had complained that his Indians did not attend Mass and that if he only cared more for their salvation, his fields would be more fertile. He responded, "Shut up and leave the Indians alone. There are many in Lima before the altars [of the Church] that have the Devil in their hearts while there are others in the mountains that have their hearts with God. . . . Do you think it is everything to have beads [a rosary] around your neck or go around praying? This is hypocrisy."[12]

Eventually, his excesses, his other propositions such as doubting Mary's virginity, and certain violent crimes caused him to be arrested and sentenced to death by civil authorities before he was transferred to the prisons of the Holy Office.

Escobar's testimony reveals that doubts about the body and the soul, about sex and salvation flourished in the context of the Indies. His attitudes seem not to have been born of theological or moral considerations, but rather out of experience, self-interest, and a skeptical libertinism that allowed him to redefine basic cultural and religious understandings. Self-serving to be sure, his defense, nevertheless, affirmed that Indians were capable of finding God in their own way.

But the issue of salvation of the Indians was also a matter of grave theological and therefore political concern since the legal basis of Spain's presence in the Indies rested on the papal concession based on Castile's missionary effort. In Peru, that mix produced a strange and potentially dangerous situation when in the 1570s the Inquisition arrested a self-proclaimed street prophetess named María Pizarro who had begun to develop a following, including some clerics. The Inquisition called upon a well-educated, Salamanca-trained, Dominican theologian named Francisco de la Cruz to assess the heretical content of her statements, but he became convinced that she was, in fact, a true prophet.[13] He became her advocate and began to articulate a strange theology. Influenced by the ideas of Las Casas and perhaps of Erasmus, upset by the prosecution of Archbishop Carranza of Toledo and other "Lutherans" in Spain, and moved by the idea that Spain would be punished for destroying the Indies, he argued that a new Church would be raised in Peru and that Lima would supplant Rome as a new Jerusalem. He was a man who, his critics said, was often given to "that which the flesh demands." He fathered a child with María Pizarro and expected that his son, Gabrielico, would become a new messiah. Perhaps unsurprisingly his new utopia would have a clergy that could marry, and, in fact, polygamy would be permitted. He believed that the conquest of Peru had been just and thus the position and demands of the conquerors were legitimate. In the political context of late sixteenth-century Peru, where four civil wars had been fought and the conquerors and their heirs always felt unrewarded, this made his predictions very dangerous, and the viceroy feared that his ideas might support further rebellion. Like other early clerics in the Indies, de la Cruz had come to the conclusion that the native peoples were the descendants of the lost tribes of Israel and that Hebrew and Quechua were, in fact, related languages, although he spoke neither. The Indians, he believed, had fallen into idolatry, but they were like children so their sin was not mortal. The brutal extirpation of idolatry that clerics carried out in Peru would never succeed. What was needed, he argued, was the integration of Christian concepts and indigenous rites, a slow syncretization and conversion. Perhaps most shocking to other priests was the idea that he had preached from the pulpit in the town of Pomata near Lake Titicaca, where he had served as resident priest after his arrival in 1561, that it was enough for Indians to have "implicit faith in Christian truths" for them to achieve salvation. This was a heretical position for its time, although by the twentieth century it was to approximate some interpretations of the Church's position at Vatican II.

The story of de la Cruz and María Pizarro and their New World Christian utopia was extraordinary, but the projected salvation of the Indians he envisioned showed that the step from Las Casas's universalism and his argument that "all mankind was one" and thus acceptable within the Church to a belief that the salvation of Indians within the Church was implicit, even for those not fully instructed in the faith, was not difficult. Others like Escobar and Ysabel de Porras had gone even further to suggest that perhaps it was not even necessary.

The fact that Francisco de la Cruz's soteriology was also mixed with his ideas on sexuality was also not exceptional. It is curious how heterodox opinions concerning both sexuality and salvation remained linked in the minds of Europeans who came to the Indies and how these affected their perceptions and dealing with the native peoples. Here the focus shifts from Peru to New Spain, where the case of Father Miguel de Bolonia is instructive in this regard. He was already in his late seventies when the constable of Suchipilla, in Michoacán, where Bolonia lived and worked in the Franciscan monastery, denounced him to the Inquisition. Born near Bologna in Italy during the 1490s, Fray Miguel had become a Franciscan in the 1530s and had formed his opinions of dogma and practice in the years preceding the Council of Trent. He had apparently come to Mexico in the second wave of missionaries who were arriving at the end of the decade of the 1530s. His activities had generated the respect of the indigenous leadership in the region, at least to the extent that they were willing to write a letter in Nahuatl to the inquisitors, "crying before you on behalf of our beloved father Fray Miguel."[14] In a written deposition, Cristóbal de Barrios, the *alcalde mayor,* or senior magistrate, accused Bolonia of a number of propositions, reflecting a certain leniency toward the sexual habits of his Indian parishioners. The magistrate had apparently tried to arrest an Indian who was cohabiting with a woman thought to be his niece. The Indian had fled to the Franciscan monastery and Bolonia had refused to turn him over to the civil authorities. He denied the alcalde's claim that the man and the woman were related or that the crime was very serious. Fray Miguel had apparently said on a number of occasions that simple fornication was not a sin, and that of all sins of the flesh, fornication was the least serious. He went so far as to suggest that if an Indian couple cohabited with the intention of marrying, the first time they had sex it was a sin but not thereafter, and some witnesses claimed he had implied that sexual relations of a Spaniard with an Indian woman were less of a sin than sex with a European.

Fray Miguel claimed that the whole matter was due to the bad intentions of Barrios and his brother, who had been exploiting the Indians, and that when he, Bolonia, had interceded, this charge was trumped up to get him replaced by a more compliant priest. In his defense, he noted that he did not have "much notice of the Tridentino," and he also argued that he was misunderstood since his Spanish was not good.[15] Supporters argued he was an aged, simple man. Nevertheless, he was forced to abjure his errors and was suspended from his priestly duties for a period of a few months.

This might have been the end of the matter, but the case had grown more complicated once the investigation was opened because Bolonia's propositions about Indian sexuality were clearly linked to other heterodox ideas. One complaint was that he was reluctant to confess Spaniards. One man had asked him to give confession, and Bolonia had begged off. This was a serious matter. The near north of Mexico was still a war zone because of resistance from the nomadic Chichimeca tribes, and death cast a constant shadow. The Spaniard pleaded with Bolonia that since he had not been confessed for years his soul was in peril, but the priest told him to go to Guadalajara, and if there was an emergency he could always confess directly to God, as the Lutherans did. As the inquest into Fray Miguel's ideas continued, the inquisitors discovered through denunciations by other Franciscans that he and some other members of his convent had also stated that "all people can be saved in their law by the absolute power of God." This was an understanding of divine power that undercut the necessity of baptism and of the Church itself. But one must remember, as Fray Miguel himself pointed out, that his theology had been learned before the Church at Trent had ruled the doctrine of salvation by faith alone heretical. In some ways, Fray Miguel seemed to share a theological understanding and universalist hopes with the reformist Italian evangelicals whose movement was suppressed after Trent.[16]

This accusation was more serious than the comments about simple fornication, and the prosecutor of the Inquisition claimed it was a heretical proposition and that Fray Miguel should be tortured to extract the truth and surrendered to the secular authorities to be burned. But Fray Miguel was no fool and not so simple as some people believed. When he had made the original statement and was challenged by some of his Franciscan listeners about its heretical content, he had added the gloss, "by the absolute power of God."

This complicated matters. Three evaluators (*calificadores*), a Dominican, a Franciscan, and a Jesuit, were called in by the Inquisition to give opinions about the content of the proposition. They were forced to admit that the gloss could not be denied and that even though the statement implied a contradiction, the necessity of the Church for salvation and the absolute power of God, Fray Miguel had neutralized the implication of heresy. A defender of the Indians with a pre-Tridentine understanding of sexuality and a belief in the absolute power of God to save any who lived according to God's commandments, Fray Miguel represented both continuity with the past and its transformation in the Indies.

Finally, not all instances of the acceptance of indigenous practices or concepts were accompanied by the dangerous statements that might provoke the interest and repression of religious authorities. Across the Indies there were innumerable instances when Spaniards and mestizos and those who lived within the Hispanic cultural world adopted or permitted indigenous practices and at times the beliefs of the indigenous populations with whom they lived and whom they often commanded.[17] In far frontiers or in isolated regions like the eastern foothills of the Ecuadorian Andes and the northern frontier of New Mexico pockets of Europeans and their descendants "went native" or became accepting of Indian ways.[18] Then too there were regions like the Argentine pampa and the Chilean frontier, where there were innumerable Spanish and mestizo prisoners, many of whom chose to remain with their captors, and others who sometimes returned from their captivity with sympathy and comprehension of Indian culture, much like those Mediterranean renegades who had returned from the lands of Islam with a respect and appreciation for the ways of their captors.[19] Those who truly passed the frontiers of identity and culture and crossed from civility to barbarism and from salvation within the Church to perdition outside it presented political as well as cultural challenges.[20]

Less colorful and dramatic than such cases but far more common for colonial society was the extensive syncretism of indigenous and European beliefs and usages at many levels. American plants were adopted to traditional European medical practices and Indian folk healers were sought out and employed by Europeans, mestizos, and Africans as well as by Indians, a process that suggested widespread belief in their efficacy. Such belief was not limited to those at the bottom of colonial society. The governor of Chile, Martin Ruíz de Gamboa, captured an important *cacique* on the frontier. He had allowed an Indian woman to cure the ailing chief using traditional medicine and, as some witnesses reported, by calling upon devils. The governor defended his actions by saying he did this because "the life of that *cacique* was important for the pacification of the land."[21] Political considerations had outweighed his cultural preferences.

Africans, the Slave Trade, and Popular Tolerance

The attitudes of religious relativism that broadened in the New World to encompass Indian peoples and their religions could be extended even further. Slavery as an institution had existed in Iberia since Roman times and had been reinforced by the tradition of slavery in Muslim Spain as well as by the custom of both Christians and Muslims of enslaving prisoners taken in the wars of the reconquest. While slavery as an institution had disappeared in much of northern Europe during the Middle Ages, in the Mediterranean, and especially in those areas which formed contested cultural and military borders like the Balkans and Iberia, it continued to flourish. Christian captives in Algiers or Fez and Muslim or Morisco slaves in Cordoba or Seville were a regular part of the human landscape of those cities. Black slaves had also been long known on the peninsula, and by the end of the fifteenth century they were growing in numbers. By 1565, Seville had a mostly African slave population of over five thousand. Lisbon, main terminal of the Portuguese African trade, by 1630 had some fifteen thousand slaves and two thousand freedmen of African descent.[22]

By the early sixteenth century, with the depletion of the Indian population on the major Caribbean islands, African slaves began to arrive in the Americas. While some came as household slaves, and even some free blacks who had been resident in Spain or in the Canary Islands also arrived, the majority were Africans brought to do labor in the mines and fields. Black slavery accompanied the European movement to the mainland as the Spanish conquered

Mexico and then South America. Meanwhile, the Portuguese, Europe's principal sources of African slaves since the fifteenth century, had followed a similar
course in their Brazilian colony, where the development of a sugar plantation
economy and the demise or resistance of the Indian population had created a
demand for laborers. This demand became easier to fill during the period
1580–1640, when the Hapsburg rulers of Spain also ruled Portugal, thus
making commerce between the two empires far easier. By the close of that
period, Portuguese slave traders were delivering some five thousand to eight
thousand Africans a year to the Americas, unloading them at the major slaving
ports of Vera Cruz in Mexico and Cartagena de Indias on the coast of modern-
day Colombia. Numbers are difficult to establish for these early years, but by
1650 there were probably some forty thousand black slaves in the viceroyalty
of Peru alone, about half of them in Lima and the others spread over the cities,
mines, and agricultural zones. Brazil had perhaps another eight thousand to
ten thousand by the mid–seventeenth century.

The enslavement of Africans presented a moral and theological problem to
the Europeans. How could it be justified? and how were Africans to be incorporated into the community of the Church? At the same time, the presence of
thousands of Africans, speaking in a variety of tongues and adhering to religious beliefs and practices far from Christian norms, challenged the limits of
theology and of tolerance. As early as 1462, Pope Pius II, in the bull *Pastor
bonus,* had prohibited the enslavement of those natives of the Canary Islands
and of West Africa who had already been baptized, but the question of slavery
in general had not been resolved.[23] The purchasing of captives on the African
coast and their baptism either before the voyage or shortly thereafter raised a
number of theoretical issues. Did it matter to the purchasers that the slaves
had been captured in just wars? Were baptisms valid even if instruction had
been scant? How could Africans be best incorporated into the Church? Over
the course of three centuries, these issues and others were addressed mostly by
theologians, and their answers formed an intellectual platform that supported
the institution of slavery and the continuation of the slave trade.[24] The reasoning behind the enslavement of Africans, although crafted by theologians, was
appropriated by royal officials as well. A good example of it comes from
Francisco de Auncibay, a high court judge in Quito, who in 1592 defended the
use of African slaves because "it is very helpful to these wretches to save them
from Guinea's fire and tyranny and barbarism and brutality, where without
law or God, they live like savage beasts. Brought to a healthier land, they
should be very content, the more so as they will be kept and live in good order
and religion from which they will derive many temporal, and which I value
most, spiritual advantages."[25]

Such arguments formed the spine of an ideological defense of slavery that met with general acceptance, at least by those not enslaved.[26] They drew on an Aristotelian view that some people were born to be masters and others to be servants in the natural order of the world, and on St. Thomas Aquinas's reworking of this idea in a way that justified society's needs over individual rights. While occasionally certain observers, usually voices within the Church, advocated good treatment of slaves, the Church fully supported both the institution and the slave trade. Not only was slavery beneficial to the crown and to the Spanish colonists, and thus to the commonweal, but it could also be justified because it brought heathens into contact with Christian society, and through conversion would eventually lead to the salvation of the Africans.

Occasional protests were raised, such as that of the Dominican Tomás de Mercado, whose treatise on commerce advocated halting the slave trade, and that of Bartolomé Frias de Albornoz, professor at the University of Mexico, whose book *Arte de los contratos* (1556) attacked the legality of the slave trade and questioned as well the idea of just war in Africa and the morality of saving souls through enslavement. Even Bartolomé de Las Casas, the great defender of the Indians, eventually adopted the cause of the Africans and in 1547 also wrote in defense of their liberty and of the injustice of the slave trade. Such voices of dissent, however, were few. One of the most notable and curious of them was the Portuguese cleric and humanist Fernão Oliveira. A man of considerable learning and talent, Oliveira was the author of the first grammar of the Portuguese language (1536), but he was also an unquiet and questioning mind. He had been a Dominican priest and had served for awhile as a tutor to the famous Portuguese chronicler João de Barros. He had also seen the world, having served at the courts of Henry VIII in England and Francis I in France as well as a stretch as a captive in Muslim North Africa. Erudite and cosmopolitan, he developed a series of unorthodox ideas that ran him afoul of the Inquisition, among them a profoundly critical stance toward expansion by military means and of any Christian justification of forced conversion. In his book on maritime matters *Arte de guerra no mar* (1555), he took the position that those who had never been Christians, "like Moors, Jews, and gentiles," were outside the authority of the pope and thus war against them was unjustified.[27] "To take their lands, impede their free use of them, or enslave those who never blasphemed against Jesus Christ nor resisted the preaching of his faith when it was done modestly, is manifest tyranny." Oliveira denounced the buying and selling of people like animals. He also had no patience for the argument that in return for the eternal salvation of the Africans, it was justified to require their service. Oliveira pointed out that without profit Christians would never go to the African coast. As for the slave owners, their failure to treat slaves well or to allow them access to the sacraments demonstrated that they had no claim on compensation for the benefit they had brought their slaves. To bring someone salvation by injustice was not an apostolic doctrine, and to call it so was a blasphemy. He offered an apocalyptic and prophetic warning: "He who enslaves will become a slave. No one should have confidence in the present prosperity that through injustice that some men do to others, God changes kingdoms from some lands to others. As the prophet Jeremiah warned, 'The slaves will become our masters, and [then] there will be nobody to free us.' "[28]

Oliveira's denunciation of slavery was a rare exception among learned authors. Far more common was literature not condemning slavery as an institution — there were too many biblical and classical precedents to do that — but rather advocating good physical treatment of slaves and attention to their moral and spiritual needs. Here, the work *De Instauranda Aethiopium Salute* (1627) by the Jesuit Alonso de Sandoval is surely the most important example. Sandoval, who was born in Spain in 1573 but raised in America, joined the Jesuits at a young age, served as a missionary among the Indians, and then dedicated his missionary activities to the slaves arriving at Cartagena de Indias, the major terminal of the Spanish American slave trade. Sandoval was in Cartagena at the height of the slave trade in the first decade of the seventeenth century, when Portuguese contractors were delivering thousands of captives, mostly from Angola. Sandoval solicited ethnographic information from Jesuit coreligionists in Angola, drew on classical authorities, and conducted extensive interviews in Cartagena with men involved in the slave trade. His main objective was to determine the slaves' preparation for baptism and thus the quality of the baptism they received, the justice of their capture according to canon law, and the best ways to improve their conditions while bringing them to the Church. To do this, he not only collected a vast amount of ethnographic material about the slaves' African origins and cultures, but also inquired into the conditions and justice of their enslavement.[29]

Sandoval's condemnation of the slave trade and its abuses and his comments on the injustice of the African wars that produced the captives make clear where his sympathies lay, but his book is also interesting from two other standpoints. First, his position in regard to the religion and culture of the various peoples of Africa, South and South East Asia, and the Pacific was strictly orthodox, with few traces of relativism. These peoples lived in ignorant darkness that only the true faith could dispel. At the same time, he too raised serious questions about the justice of slavery, and in the method of his questioning he revealed that some of his contemporaries shared these concerns. As part of the research for his book, Sandoval had interviewed many people in Cartagena about aspects of slavery that impinged on their world. He reported that a number of ship captains doubted the legality and the humanity of the slave trade. One captain phrased the question to him in these terms: "Father, I go for blacks to Angola; on the trip I undergo great trials, costs, and many dangers. At last, I get my cargo, be they captured justly or not. Here's my question: Have I justified this enslavement by the trials, dangers, and expenses so that they can be sold in Christian lands where they will become so rather than to leave them as gentiles for all their life."

These were doubts raised not by canonists and moralists concerned with abstract issues of religion and state policy, but by those who directly participated in the enterprise of the Americas. One might ask if Sandoval had placed such questions in the mouths of common people as a literary device in order to raise the legal and moral issues of slavery and the slave trade that canonists, theologians, and missionaries usually made. That is certainly a possibility, but other evidence, some from Cartagena itself, indicates that not only churchmen were concerned with these issues.

Among the propositions of various dissidents who appeared before the American tribunals of the Inquisition, the question of slavery and its morality sometimes appeared. Perhaps the most interesting case in this regard comes from Cartagena de Indias, the very heart of the slave trade. There, in 1628, the Inquisition arrested Andrés de Cuevas, a man of fiercely independent mind. This was not Cuevas's first scrape with the religious authorities. He had been publicly punished in an auto de fe in 1614 for heretical propositions he had refused to retract even under torture.[30] Cuevas was a craftsman, a carpenter from Jaén in Andalusia who had settled in Cartagena, where he had been successful and had accumulated a considerable sum of over thirty thousand pesos. His case is particularly interesting because his attitudes about slavery were part of a broad worldview at odds with the political and religious norms of his society, as was the case with so many other of the dissidents prosecuted by the Inquisition.

Cuevas had originally been denounced for a series of blasphemies and heretical propositions that had scandalized his neighbors, but when confronted by the inquisitors, he had denied everything. Tortured, he remained firm in his denial and unrepentant and so was sentenced to appear in an auto de fe and to receive two hundred lashes and then be sent into perpetual exile from the Indies and to serve a two-year sentence in Seville. He was also required to pay three thousand pesos as a fine. On review, however, the *Suprema* in Madrid, that is, the Inquisition's governing board, felt that the torture, seizure of property, and exile had been excessive, and Cuevas was exonerated and his property returned. Why this happened is unclear. Perhaps he had contacts in the right places, but for whatever reason, the sentence was not carried out. Perhaps overconfident at his release, at this point he began to denounce the Inquisition and its members, repeating some of his more outrageous propositions. One of them was that thoughts, even if accepted, if they were not put into action were no sin. In other words, he defended freedom to think as he chose.[31]

Eventually over forty witnesses were called to testify against Cuevas, who was clearly a man not hesitant to share his opinions. He continually complained that God had done nothing for him and that all he had came from the sweat of his brow. To those who repeated to him the common refrain "God will repay you," Cuevas usually responded that he was still waiting and that the angel carrying the repayment must have gone to the wrong house. When friends pointed out that one should thank God for what one had gained and achieved, he responded that it would be better to confide in ten thousand devils. What use to put one's faith in God or in San Jose, the patron of carpenters? What had they ever done for him? When recovering from an illness, a friend had told Cuevas that God would give him health. "What God gives me," he responded, "is a lot of shit." Cuevas had little use for the saints (he had no images or a crucifix in his home) or the teachings of the Church. Various witnesses noted that appeals to him for charity usually provoked sarcasm. "Go ask the king, or the bishop, or the Church, or God," was his usual reply. Once he refused alms to a beggar and told a friend, "If God wants this fellow to be poor, let him be so, if I give him charity it will be against God's will; he will get rid of his poverty and give it to me." When asked for alms for the Franciscans, he told his interlocutor that he wouldn't give any even if Saint Francis himself came down from heaven to ask. This was a self-made man, at war with life and authority of all kinds, the king, the Church, the inquisitors, and God himself. The king, Cuevas believed, ruled poorly. What purpose did it serve to give so much to the bishops, inquisitors, governors, and the rich, who were a group of thieves who only sought to exploit the poor? The inquisitors, he said, were a bunch of drunks, and he had a singular dislike for the inquisitor Juan de Mañozca, who had conducted his first trial. At one point when someone defended the Inquisition as the most serious of tribunals, Cuevas pointed out that he, a good Christian and a Cuevas, had been punished on the false testimony of four scoundrels who had all died badly, that his fines had been returned, and that the inquisitors had been reprimanded by the archbishop of Toledo for this injustice. This was something he mentioned to many listeners. But Cuevas's complaints were not limited to the Inquisition or to his personal trials. All of those in authority in the Indies, he believed, "sought only to eat, drink, fornicate, and take it easy. They took no care in governing the Indies, and those who came to govern were no Christians, buying their posts for twenty or thirty thousand ducats, and then robbing the land. The inquisitors, bishops, and canons were of the same type; they came to do nothing in the Church of God except to rob the world and fornicate with as many women as possible." "This government of Christians is a government of drunks. The heretics and those in other lands are governed better."

Mixed with his personal bitterness, his religious skepticism, and his dissident attitude was a perception of the social injustices around him, and in Cartagena that meant slavery. At one point when asked to provide alms for an orphan's dowry, Cuevas refused. When his friend complained that doing so would be a charitable act, Cuevas shot back that if the friend wanted to act charitably he could give his slaves something to eat. Another witness complained that Cuevas had even told one of his slaves that he would have been better off as a gentile in Guinea, suggesting even missionary activities were a waste of time. Since God had created them pagans, if he wanted to take them to heaven, he would make them Christians as well.

Here was the crux of the matter and the reason Cuevas is important to my discussion. In the midst of his heterodox and dissident opinions Cuevas had applied a moderated version of the old relativist argument about religion to the situation of the Africans, and he had also raised the old question of the use of force in conversion. He also went to the extreme of suggesting that perhaps Africans might be better off living in their own land in their own way. The slave trade was wrong, and the king was to blame for allowing it to continue. Cuevas questioned the whole moral and political basis of slavery itself when he stated many times that "the king of Spain acts badly to allow blacks to be brought to his kingdoms. Why must they be made Christians by force? Rather they should be allowed to live in their [own] law and in their own lands where they were raised. The king does this for his own self-interest and for no other good intention."

Here was a direct affront to both the crown's and the Church's justification of slavery and the slave trade and the whole theological edifice on which it had been built. Like the learned Sandoval, Cuevas advocated better physical treatment for the slaves, but, unlike the Jesuit, Cuevas viewed the whole project of catechism and conversion as doubtful and thus in no way a justification for capture and enslavement. This was a position far more radical than that of Sandoval, but it grew from the same social milieu shared by these two contemporaries. It demonstrates that antislavery sentiments were by no means limited to theologians, but it raises, once again, the intractable question of the direction of influences between learned and popular thinking.

One thing was certain, however. Cuevas's brand of dissidence could not be left unchecked. Returned to the prison of the Inquisition, he expressed contrition for his sins and claimed he had spoken while out of his head with anger or had not realized the implications of what he was saying. It was to no avail. He was convicted to appear at a public auto as a blasphemer, be exiled from the bishopric for five years, and pay a fine of three thousand pesos. It might have been much worse, and many in the city felt he had escaped lightly. Perhaps he continued to have some influence with someone in high places.[32]

Men and women like Cuevas had sought to draw their own conclusions about right and wrong, about God and humans, about men and women. Often their thinking had led them to question not one aspect of their world, but many. If outspoken enough, neighbors might think them outrageous, heretical, or even mad.

I end here with the paradigmatic case of Mateo Salado, a foreigner in origin but long resident in the Indies. Salado or Saladé was a forty-five-year-old Frenchman from Beauce, between Paris and Orléans, who lived near Lima when he was arrested in 1571. He was a *huaquero,* a man who searched for treasure at Indian burial sites, and he had worked alone in one between Lima and the coast for so long that people thought him deranged.[33] Salado had been denounced to the Inquisition for religious attitudes of a suspect nature, asking why one should adore a cross that was simply an object made by a silversmith with a hammer, or stating that there were many worse things in the world than being a Lutheran. At first the inquisitors were reluctant to arrest him given his reputation as a disturbed individual, but witnesses began to reveal a wide range of heretical, anticlerical, iconoclastic, antipapal, anti-inquisitorial, and pro-Lutheran opinions that Salado had spoken. Outrageous opinions: there should be no monks and nuns; priests ate up the rents of the Church or gave them to women. They took the sweat of the poor and sold Christ each day for a peso, giving water instead of wine in the communion. He wanted the mythical world of plenty, Cockaigne. It should be like Germany, he said, where communion was with baskets of bread and jugs of wine. The pope wasted the income of the Church and spent it on the public women of Rome, and he was just like the rest of us. Within twenty years the Germans and French will make sure there is no more pope, and the wars in Italy and Germany will remove the cardinals and bishops and their evil ways of living, and we will all be Christians. God had illumined Erasmus and Luther. The sacrifice of the Mass is blindness. Where there is true Catholic faith, there are no ornaments or chalices. He ridiculed papal bulls and dispensations, said that pilgrimages were unnecessary and that many who had died at the stake in Spain, burned by the Inquisition, had died as martyrs for the faith and law of Martin Luther. His theology was his own. The trinity was only two people, Father and son, since the Holy Spirit was not a person but the love of the two and the spirit of God. Christ was not God, but only the Son of God, and thus the Virgin was the mother only of Christ, not of God. The souls of the dead went directly to heaven or hell. There was no such thing as purgatory. Where did he get these ideas? He told the inquisitors that some twenty years ago in Seville, a Frenchman had given him a "new testament," and he cited it often as his source of authority.

But on many matters, it was not authority but his own observation that led to Salado's dissidence and his sense of injustice. His dislike of the rich and the life of the ecclesiastical hierarchy, his sympathy for the poor made him angry and heretical. On slavery and the slave trade he said "that any man who sells blacks and mulattos cannot go to heaven, but are condemned to hell, and that the pope that permitted this trade was a drunk." Like Cuevas and, one may suspect, others in their world, the justifications of Church and state and the benefits that many derived from the injustice of the slave trade were not enough to convince them.

Salado was subjected to torture but would reveal no accomplices. He was poor; there was no property to confiscate. He held his opinions to the end. The inquisitors stated the matter in this way: "He went about speaking these heresies so clearly and digging in that *huaca* by himself that the people who heard him attributed it to madness, but he is not crazy, rather he is a convinced heretic." So many of the dissidents mentioned in these pages, Bartolomé Sánchez in Cuenca, Inocencio de Aldama in Murcia, Juan de Las Heras and Mateo Salado in Lima, were thought by many to be mad, and true enough, some had been, or became unbalanced during their ordeals and long imprisonments, but there are also remarkable continuities and similarities in their opinions about the givens of their world and their desire to change them for the better. This was a challenge that could not be allowed, and madness became an effective way of defining and dismissing their claims; repression was another.[34] Impenitent to the end, Salado was released to secular authorities in a public auto de fe and burned at the stake in Lima in November 1573.

His ashes were scattered, but his name was not forgotten. Today in Lima, encroached upon by the urban sprawl of the city, the remnants of the site of his digging remain. The pre-Incaic area he had excavated or, perhaps better said, looted in silence for ten years, as he dwelled upon the wrongs of this world and his hopes for the world to come, is still called, some four centuries later, the *huaca* of Mateo Salado.[35]

Popular Piety, Syncretism, and Salvation

The dissidence and criticism of men like Cuevas and Salado and so many others mentioned in these pages should not be seen as extraneous to the general patterns of the practice of Catholicism in the Hispanic world. Scholars now often avoid speaking of popular culture because it is so hard to define the exact meaning of *popular* and because often ideas or concepts held by common folk were also expressed by the wealthy and the learned.[36] Certainly, more than one friar or parish priest has crossed these pages because he too had become convinced that God had intended salvation for all peoples, even if they lived outside the Church. This was a belief held not only by the unlettered, although those accused often used their rusticity as a defense.[37]

The anthropologist William Christian has suggested that while popular religiosity emphasized practice and the problems of dealing with the immediate realities and insecurities of life like drought, plague, and war, it is more useful to think about its features as "local religion": a view of the world that emphasized the importance of local shrines and saints, festivals, vows, chapels, and lay confraternities.[38] This was a fervent religiosity that was developed and sustained by the laity with the help of sympathetic clergy, and it was constantly under scrutiny by the bishops or by Rome itself, both of which sought to impose centralized control of liturgy, dogma, and practice. In fact, much of the history of the Catholic Reformation has centered on the efforts of inquisitors, missionaries, and bishops, who often worked in concert, to bring local belief and uses into line with dogma and to eliminate its excesses.[39] Success in this project varied widely from region to region across Europe. Missionaries sent to southern Italy spoke of that region as "the Indies of Europe" because of the backwardness and supposed superstitions of the local populace, whom they perceived as being barely Christian, but such opinions were not limited to that region.[40] "The Indies of Europe" was a phrase that more than one frustrated cleric used to describe the pastoral challenges he faced.[41]

The pervasiveness and fervor of this local religiosity did not preclude the kind of skepticism and disbelief we have seen expressed in these pages. As Christian himself recognized, "Not all the hermits are holy, all pilgrims devout, or all villagers credulous."[42] The simultaneous existence of religious credulity and incredulity among people drawn from the same social backgrounds and who shared the same cultural understandings speaks to the potential independence of mind and thought that was always possible to individuals, even if they did not have a systematic understanding of the implications of their beliefs.

The overlapping systems of belief in natural and supernatural forces provided a certain parallel between the power of the Church and the power of magical or occult forces. One person's magic was another's religion. The Church, through prayer, relics, images, blessings, pilgrimage, and especially through the intervention of the saints, could achieve miraculous results, and it elicited devotion because it mediated between divine and supernatural forces and society; but it also sought to discourage what it considered popular or lay excesses and superstitions. Catholicism, moreover, provided a liturgy, a doctrine, a system, and a moral compass while magic remained pragmatic and problem oriented, geared to the immediate challenges of life.[43] Still, in the sixteenth and seventeenth centuries the power of the Church through miracles and the Mass and that of magical or demonic forces were often conflated in the thinking of many. The laity, the historian John Butler has argued, was ecumenical regarding religion and the occult.[44] Theologians at the time complained of this as superstition and looked upon magic and the occult as both a competitor with orthodoxy and as evidence of the devil's work. Modern historians have sometimes complained that the populace of Europe in that period was barely Christian at all since so much of its understanding and practice drew on ancient pagan or pre-Christian beliefs, but perhaps it is more useful to emphasize the conjuncture of Christianity and a world that included magic, witches, the devil, astrology, divination, and other ways to influence supernatural forces, some of them not entirely discouraged by ecclesiastical authority.

This collective culture, with its fervor, fears, hopes, and doubts, crossed the Atlantic in the minds and ways of the immigrants. The Iberian colonization of the Americas revealed that the borders of the magical universe could always be expanded. In a process of cultural fusion and recombination, Native American, African, and Hispanic beliefs were constantly redeployed in ways quite unintended by those who had hoped to find parallels of practice and belief that could lead Indians and Africans to Christianity.[45] Although Indians were generally outside the jurisdiction of the Inquisition, they appear regularly in the trials as the purveyors, teachers, and intermediaries of witchcraft, healing, and cures. Spaniards did not need indigenous people to teach them about the occult or about ways of manipulating natural and supernatural forces, but there were always the possibilities that there might be local potions, prayers, or spirits that could be effective. Indians were juridically and theoretically separated into their own "republic," but there was undoubtedly a continual social and cultural interaction between Spaniards and Indians resulting in the intended Catholic religiosity of the Indians as well as in the unintended fusion of ideas and practices related to the occult or to heterodox, if not heretical, beliefs among Europeans, Indians, and their mixed descendants. Indians often entered this world by selling their magical skills and knowledge and their pharmacopoeia and, in doing so, finding a niche in the market economy of the colonial world.[46]

In terms of credence and efficacy it would be misleading to believe that the world of magic was separated from that of orthodox belief. The anthropologist Laura Lewis discusses a case from Michoacán in 1624, when the local curate, after punishing an Indian of his parish for concubinage and forcing him to admit he was a witch, then fell ill. The priest was diagnosed by his Indian parishioners as having been bewitched, and he then sought out an Indian woman to rid him of the effects. He later felt uneasy enough about the incident to report it to the Inquisition and to emphasize that he was sure no pact with the devil had been involved; but the very fact that this cleric had sought indigenous remedies to indigenous magic shows how intertwined the worlds of orthodoxy and heterodoxy were in the Indies.[47] The devil seemed to thrive on the cultural frontiers. While Spanish and Portuguese theologians were often skeptical about witchcraft, the presence and actions of the devil were broadly accepted at all levels of society. Europeans easily transformed the newly encountered deities of America and Africa into manifestations of the ancient enemy. Indians were no less ready to incorporate the European devil into their pantheon of supernatural forces, and Africans, mulattos, mestizos, and other groups contributed to and drew upon the mix of religious traditions, employing them to subvert and invert the relations of power and authority in colonial society.[48]

Christianity and Native American religion were not "mutually exclusive alternatives" from which Indians or Europeans chose, but rather elements that coexisted to a greater or lesser degree in colonial society.[49] The Americas became the center of a new syncretism on an enormous scale. It was a multi-directional process of absorption, adaptation, and incorporation, but one always unbalanced by the unequal power that underlay the traditions involved and the ability of Hispanic culture through the state and the Church to limit, extirpate, censor, and repress anything which contested its cosmography.

If America, with its great expanses and its myriad and previously unknown populations, opened the possibility of utopian and millenarian projects for a newly invigorated Church as well as the opportunities for the expansion and integration of new elements into the fabric of popular beliefs, it also provided a rich environment for the growth of doubt and a questioning of the sureties of dogma. As in Spain and Portugal, in the New World examples of a dissident soteriology could be found across the social spectrum. Pastry chefs, cobblers, mestizo encomenderos, governors, and occasionally clerics voiced sentiments of tolerance and religious relativism. These expressions sometimes grew from an openness to alternate means of affecting the supernatural, sometimes were based on a simple materialism, and at times sprang from the soil of an inclusive, universalistic Christianity that emphasized peace and charity. And sometimes they were the result of incredulity and doubt about all religion. But they were not only the result of some kind of peculiar peasant skepticism and limited to common folk. Giordano Bruno, the heretic Italian philosopher, told his cellmates in 1593 that there was no hell, for in the end all would be saved and God's wrath was not eternal.[50]

These advocates of salvation for all (or for none) could be found in Iberia and across the Indies. Their origins were varied: Spaniards, mestizos, Flemings, French, Neapolitans, and Portuguese. Mostly men but occasionally women made these statements, as far as we can tell, but that male predominance may be a result of the Inquisition's lack of interest in prosecuting female opinion. Many were cosmopolitan in the sense that they were mobile and had seen other lands and other ways. All of the European-born, of course, had traveled, they had voyaged to the Indies, but many of them had also journeyed before, and some, as captives and renegades, had lived in the world of Islam.

Where did they get their ideas? The American examples of religious relativism or indifference, like the Iberian ones, raise the question about the interaction of popular or local and elite or learned culture. There has been endless speculation about the relation of "high and low" cultures or between the "little and great" traditions.[51] Perhaps it is more useful to emphasize the cultural unities across social classes or groups and to recognize that it was more in the interpretation and sometimes "performance" of culture that the distinctions were created. Local culture or, in this case, local religion was not so much a set of specific traits as it was a certain interpretation of elements that were shared with elite or learned culture. Ideas circulated from high to low and low to high, and while common people might not have the education or background to write a play or a sermon or to formulate dogma, they had their own understanding of right and wrong, good and bad. As it was noted in 1686 in a preface to a published sermon dedicated to an inquisitor of Mexico, the laity could discern a good sermon even when it did not fully understand its theology.[52]

In the discussions of the relationship between high and low cultural norms and understandings and the circulation of ideas it may be useful to move from the theoretical to the practical and to look at the crucial role of people who were socially and culturally in an intermediate position. Many of those who made expressions of a dissident soteriology were in fact not peasants or laborers but persons in the trades or from the middling sectors of society. With the exception of the occasional clerics and friars, who seemed to be drawing on earlier theological debates about salvation, most of them had not been to university and had no theological training, but they were literate, and they used that skill to open their horizons and think for themselves. Their tastes were eclectic, and while occasionally they mentioned religious works like those of Fray Luis de Granada or Domingo de Baltanás, more often they seemed to be reading popular books like the romances of chivalry. Above all, they used this skill to access learned culture, but also to bring to it their own reading and interpretation. Together they perhaps represented a subculture of people more open, more traveled, better read, and more independent-minded than the majority of their contemporaries, but always mixed among them were individuals who did not fit the pattern of mobility and doubt and who still had come to believe that each soul must find its own path.

Nepantla: A New People between Faiths

Because of the structure of inquisitional authority and its preoccupation with the Hispanic population, it is difficult to know if relativist ideas about religion also arose among the majority population, composed as it was of the indigenous masses, who for the most part were excluded from inquisitorial jurisdiction. In many places Indians remained under episcopal authority in matters of orthodoxy.[53] In New Spain a tribunal, the *Provisorato,* acted somewhat like an Inquisition for Indians, and in Peru there were major campaigns to extirpate Indian superstitions well into the seventeenth century, but the preoccupation of these tribunals was always the elimination of idolatry, that is, pre-Christian belief and practice, rather than other kinds of heterodox or heretical opinions. Even in the seventeenth century, when more lenient churchmen preferred to define adherence to indigenous rites and practices as superstition rather than idolatry or heresy, the claim of religious relativism among the Indian population was rarely made.[54]

The transformation of indigenous religions in the process of evangelization, however, had made the Indians into a people in between faiths, the condition of what the Nahua-speakers of central Mexico called *nepantla,* a status in-between. It would be interesting to know the extent to which religious relativism and expressions of tolerance emerged among Christianized native peoples, who lived between their old beliefs and their new faith, as they sometimes did among Moriscos and Conversos and as they occasionally did among Africans and their descendants in the Americas, whose own traditions and beliefs presented another field of challenge to orthodoxy and an opportunity for syncretism.[55]

The great theme of religious history of the Iberian Americas is found in the story of encounter between Iberian Catholicism and the religions of the indigenous peoples of the Americas and those of the imported Africans. Various

Auto-de-fe in the town of Otzolotepec (Mexico).
This is actually a depiction of a ceremony performed in 1716 by the Provisorato, not the Inquisition. The indigenous penitents are similarly attired in penitential gowns and conical caps, while churchmen and Indian parishioners sit in attendance. Courtesy of the Museo Nacional de Arte, Mexico City.

authors have conceptualized this process of encounter as either the slow penetration of Christian belief and thus the destruction of indigenous religion, or, conversely, the considerable success of indigenous peoples in maintaining their belief system in fact while seeming to accede to the demands for conversion and the acceptance of the new religion. A third alternative has been to emphasize "absorption, adoption, and assimilation," that is, to focus on the process of syncretism and the resulting creation of hybrid religiosities which combined indigenous and Catholic belief and practice.[56] In that process, there was, of course, change over time. The early campaigns to eliminate indigenous religions were met with stiff resistance in places like Yucatán and the Andes, and only slowly did a synthesis of the two traditions emerge in the later seventeenth century, or, as some historians prefer to describe the result, the indigenous tradition submerged itself within the Christian one.[57] In fringe areas like the middle reaches of the Orinoco River, indigenous peoples who had developed less complex religious systems than those of the civilizations of Mesoamerica and the Andes proved no less able to contest and evade the acceptance of Christian doctrine, as the complaints of the missionaries against the persistent inconstancy and disloyalty of their Indian neophytes attest.[58] In the Andes and in central Mexico indigenous peoples, under severe pressures, maintained their cosmology within a fervent Christian context, so that the two systems of belief became intertwined in ways that even the practitioners could not separate.[59] In the Andes, for example, the ancient cult of the *huacas,* honoring the sacredness of particular places and objects, was replaced or overlaid with the devotion to the Christian saints.[60] In New Spain, both the initiatives of the mendicant friars to replace preexisting beliefs and the religious imagination of the converted Indians resulted in the fervent devotions of the Virgin of Guadalupe and other cults.[61] The Church's teaching on salvation through Christ and the representation of hell and of the final judgment were made visible through murals designed to convince indigenous parishioners that their behavior in this world would determine the fate of their souls.[62]

Modern scholarship has emphasized that the old model of a clash between the orthodox Catholicism of the missionaries and the putative superstitions of ancient indigenous religions is inadequate to explain the nature of the religious encounter in the Americas. The Spaniards who crossed the Atlantic, especially those who arrived prior to the Council of Trent, brought with them the full range of beliefs, including the nonconformities, deviations, superstitions, local practices, and propositions that comprised lay religiosity. The first generation of friars often lamented that the task of conversion of the native peoples was slowed by contact with lay Spaniards, because of their abuses of Indians, but also because of their bad example to the neophytes and the contagion of their ideas and beliefs. In part, that bad example included the heterodoxies and doubts as well as deviant or superstitious practices.

Indians certainly shared with Moriscos and Conversos a status as people pulled between faiths. Some of the early indigenous arguments for the validity of the old religion, like that of the *cacique* don Carlos of Texcoco, bear the stamp of self-justification and defense of an old law in the face of pressure and thus seem to be better understood as defensive strategies rather than as statements of tolerance or relativism, just as it had been among many of the Moriscos of the first generation after conversion.[63] Certainly a number of indigenous religious systems were pantheistic and historically had, before the arrival of the Spaniards, allowed other cults to be maintained or had allowed subject peoples the equivalent of freedom of conscience so there was at least a theoretical basis for toleration, but the question of power must also be considered.

There was, of course, a major difference between the Native Americans and the Moriscos and Conversos, who as minorities in Iberia were never in a position to argue for or grant religious toleration, even if they had desired to do so, because they did not have the power to enforce such a policy. Conversely, Native Americans formed the vast majority of the population in Spanish America, but colonial policies continually sought to reduce their culture and social organization to a minority status, so that the ultimate powerlessness of Indians matched that of the Iberian ethnic minorities despite their demographic weight.[64] By the eighteenth century, policies promoting syncretism as well as Indian strategies of survival and dissimulation had produced a fervent Catholicism that often incorporated varying degrees of local practice and belief.[65] Its orientation was either intensely local or at times enthusiastically millennial. For the most part, the question of tolerance for other religions was not a concern. Indifference rather than intolerance was the best way to describe their attitude.[66] The demands of a reformist Church and a newly activist state in the eighteenth century had created new pressures on many Indian communities. By the close of that century, the question of how these new, indigenous Christians would respond to the pressures for freedom of conscience and the other programs of reform and secularization would become an essential issue in the creation of the nation-states that rose on the ruins of the Spanish empire.

7

Brazil: Salvation in a Slave Society

The customs of the Portuguese settlers that are found in these towns are almost those of the Indians because although Christians, they live the life of gentiles. — Father Manoel da Nóbrega (1558)

As the Portuguese began to cross the seas in the fifteenth century, their encounter with other lands and other peoples sharpened both confidence in their own religious obligations and mission and their conviction in the superiority of their own culture. But overseas voyaging had also raised questions about the nature of non-Christian peoples and about the validity and value of other faiths. By the mid–sixteenth century, the Portuguese had created a far-flung empire of ports and maritime outposts down the coast of West Africa and across the Indian Ocean,

In the Atlantic, after settling the uninhabited islands of the Azores and Madeira in the fifteenth century, the Portuguese made a landfall on the coast of South America in 1500, and in the next years, a colony began to slowly take form. After decades of relative neglect and desultory settlement, sometimes using penal exiles, this Brazilian colony began to flourish, first in the 1530s, when minor nobles were made donatary captains and allowed to develop their territories, then when a large expedition in 1549 established a royal capital under a governor-general at Salvador, but especially after 1560 as fields of sugarcane were planted and began to spread along the streams that flowed to the sea in the captaincies of Bahia and Pernambuco.

The early infamy of Brazil as a colony settled by New Christians and convicts from civil and religious courts (the expedition of 1549 had included hundreds) began to fade somewhat as the colony became profitable and the origins of the first settlers were forgotten.[1] The real key to the colony's progress, however, was the relationship between the growth of the sugar economy and the exploitation and elimination of the indigenous Amerindian peoples and then the introduction of African slaves. This process changed the human face of the colony in terms of its population. It also brought together elements of the cultural and religious systems of three continents while at the same time creating a series of overlapping inequalities based on religion, race, and origin that favored the Europeans, even the poor among them.

But in truth, the distance of the colony from civil and religious authority, the absence of strong religious or administrative controls, and the seemingly endless opportunities of a material or carnal nature had drawn all kinds of religious dissidents and people from the margins of Portuguese society as well as simply those people seeking to better their lives. Early accounts of Brazil swung from edenic descriptions of its geography and celebration of its potential to turn poor men into rich ones to demonizing descriptions of its native peoples, who were presented as naked, pagan cannibals lacking any sense of modesty or sexual morality. Many of these attributes also made the colony attractive, albeit to different groups for different reasons. Moreover, the constraints of formal religion were few. The presence and influence of the clergy in the first half century was minimal, and only in 1551 was a bishopric established at Salvador. Thus the first fifty years of settlement and the formation of society as well as the early contact between the colonists and the indigenous peoples took place before there was a strong ecclesiastical establishment and also prior to the Council of Trent and its attempt to reform and regularize Catholic practice and to establish the centrality of the priesthood and the sacraments in the everyday life of the faithful.[2]

In Brazil, the principal agents of the Tridentine reforms when they were introduced were the members of the Society of Jesus, a newly formed religious order, itself closely linked to the Catholic Reformation. Six Jesuits had accompanied the expedition of the first governor general in 1549, and they quickly began an intense missionary effort to Christianize the indigenous populations. The Jesuits in Portugal viewed the new colony and its indigenous inhabitants as their particular enterprise, and they were willing to suffer discomforts and dangers in order to convert the pagan inhabitants of Brazil, whose barbarism and ignorance of the gospel, most felt at first, could be conquered by missionary zeal. While the Jesuits became an integral part of Portuguese society in the colony and a primary influence on the educational, spiritual, and economic life of the colonists, their principal impulse was directed toward the missionary effort. They believed that the major obstacle standing in their path was the violent immorality of the Portuguese settlers, who enslaved Indians, took their women, and lived in complete disregard or ignorance of the precepts of the Church.

More than morality was involved in this struggle. The colonists viewed the Jesuit mission villages as competitors for the control of Indian workers, who were increasingly necessary on the growing sugar plantations, especially as disease and resistance made Indian labor even scarcer. Both colonists and Jesuits sought the support of the crown in this struggle. Meanwhile, there was also a dispute with ecclesiastical authority. The Jesuits argued against the first bishop of Bahia, who felt that the principal business of the Church should be the Portuguese laity, not the heathen Indians. The bishop's death at the hands of Amerindians cut short the dispute, and the Jesuit approach emphasizing the conversion of the Indians predominated until the decades of the 1580s, when the other religious orders began to establish houses in the colony and religious life was regularized under episcopal control.

As part of this process of regularization, two visits of the Inquisition were sent to the colony, one in 1591–93 and a second in 1618. Almost a thousand individuals were denounced and many arrested in an attempt to impose ortho-doxy in the colony. While Judaizing New Christians were the single most accused group, the net of the tribunal in Brazil was cast widely, and in percent-age terms there was more interest in the deviations, errors, and blasphemy of Old Christians than was usually the case in the Portuguese continental tri-bunals.[3] The Jesuits fully collaborated with the Inquisition, and, in fact, the sessions of the visits were conducted in the Jesuit establishments of Salvador and Olinda. Only later in the seventeenth century, as we have seen in the discussion of Father António Vieira, did the interests and politics of the Jesuits and the Holy Office diverge.

It was ironic, then, that the two groups most attracted to the new colony in the sixteenth century were New Christians who hoped to find in the colony eco-nomic opportunities and some respite from their disadvantages in Portugal and the Jesuits, who first viewed the colony as a kind of purgatory but hoped to create in Brazil a Christian utopia among the heathen. Their goal was to establish a land of orthodox Catholic practice guided by the Tridentine re-forms.[4] A New Christian merchant, Diogo Lopes Ulhoa, so powerful that some had called him the Count Duke of Brazil, said at one point that "this land was made for us and our ancestors." In a similar fashion, the Jesuit leader, Father Manoel da Nóbrega, had written from Brazil with identical conviction, "This land is our enterprise." But the Jesuit program was threatened and frustrated by the avarice, licentiousness, and ignorance of the settlers, by the presence of potential heresy represented by the New Christians, by the recalcitrance and superstition of the laity, and by the difficulties presented by the process of converting the Indians. For all these reasons, the Jesuits at first viewed the Inquisition as an ally in their project.

Conversely, the New Christians certainly did not welcome the arrival of the inquisitorial visitor, and a number of them referred to the agents of the tribunal as devils. In 1622, the inquisitor general of Portugal had argued that given the growth of the population and the nature of its people the colony needed a permanent tribunal, but the plan was never realized, owing perhaps to New Christian opposition.[5] But in their fear and dislike of the Holy Office, they were not alone, and some of the Old Christians in Brazil also resented the imposition of orthodoxy and the limitation on freedom of conscience that the tribunal and the reforms of Trent implied.[6]

Early Heretics

If the plan of the Jesuits and the Inquisition was to isolate Brazil from the heterodox and heretical currents that were rising in Europe, their hope was stillborn. The Portuguese colonists brought with them the full range of superstitions and beliefs, doubts, critiques, and ironies that had been expressed in Europe. They had a deeply Catholic belief and a profound religious sensibility often demonstrated in external elements of the cult.[7] The population venerated the saints and adhered to the rites of the Church, but they were also attracted to alchemy and astronomy, to a belief in good and bad witchcraft and sorcery, and to the occult arts. On many positions of dogma there was dissent. In the minds and mouths of the colonists it is easy to find all the usually condemned propositions about the Trinity, the virgin birth, fornication, and the others. The two visits of the Inquisition for which detailed records have survived reveal the full range of the dissidence, irreverence, and questioning that was seen in Portugal itself. In addition, as we will soon see, the reality of Brazil, peopled as well by pagan and Christianized Amerindians, African slaves, and the mixed race offspring born of the contact between them and the Europeans created new situations of interaction that produced new kinds of propositions or intensified the beliefs in the old ones.[8]

Then too there were dissidents of more educated background who were able to meet and debate with the churchmen and especially the Jesuits on a more or less equal intellectual level, or who exercised authority of a secular nature that contested that of the Church. These men introduced ideas that were alternatives to the Jesuit theology of the Catholic Reformation, and at times their blasphemies and heresies resonated with the ideas of the general populace and sometimes with those of the Protestant heretics, or, at least, so their accusers claimed. In fact, however, much of what they said or thought sprang from the same roots of dissidence and heterodoxy from which emanated the critiques and doubts of the settlers and their mixed-race offspring.

These individuals appear relatively early in Brazilian history. The classic case is that of Pero de Campos Tourinho, the first lord proprietor of the captaincy of Porto Seguro. Tourinho was not an intellectual, but a man with a colonizing mission. A nobleman from Viana do Castelo, he began to settle his area in 1535 with a group of settlers he led out from Portugal. He was a man who often spoke freely and who did not hesitate in his irony and sarcasm to criticize the local clerics and the ecclesiastical establishment or to argue with them. The clergy was not amused. In June 1546, a coup led by a French priest took place. Tourinho was imprisoned and charged with blasphemy and sent back to Portugal in chains. The Inquisition, still in its earliest stages, held an inquiry in 1547. Although he denied most of the accusations, the charges themselves perhaps reveal the nature of his thoughts, or at least seem to be the kind of heresies that were common enough to be credible: a critique of the Mass, disrespect for the saints, criticism of the clergy for living with female companions and above all of the bishops, whom he called buggers and tyrants for being both venial and dissolute.

Mixed among such irreverence, not surprisingly, one finds an implicit religious relativism. The first charge leveled against Campos Tourinho was that when he did some task, he would say "that if God would not help him, then the faith of the Moors was better than that of the Christians, and that he would become a Moor." The possibility of admitting the value of another religion was a serious charge, but the Inquisition apparently treated him leniently. Although he never returned to Brazil, his offspring and descendants suffered no particular infamy. If he was a heretic, "he was only an intermittent and dilettante one."[9] The Inquisition in Portugal was after bigger game.

Why had he been accused? Campos Tourinho claimed that his enemies objected to his rule because he had punished those who had refused to work or who were doing evil to the Indians by "sleeping with their wives and daughters, and doing other things they should not do."[10] In that, at least, his criticisms paralleled those of the Jesuits. How to treat the Indians and how best to lead them to salvation remained a crucial issue.

Other early dissidents were closer to more formal heresies. João de Bolés, a

Frenchman, had abandoned the French outpost at Guanabara Bay over religious differences with its leaders. He arrived in São Paulo in 1559, where his talents as an orator and his knowledge of classical languages and Hebrew impressed both the local colonists and the resident Jesuits. So too did his criticism of the pope, his disbelief in the saints, his condemnation of the venality of the clergy, and his defense of the freedom of his homeland, which, unlike Portugal and its colonies, allowed one to read whatever one wished. Eventually arrested and tried, this French humanist provoked the suspicion of his Jesuit opponents in Brazil, who believed he was planting the seeds of the Protestant heresies which, given his eloquence and knowledge, endangered the spiritual health of the colonists. This was a weed the Jesuits would not allow to grow in a colony already awash in sin. Eventually, Bolés was forced to recant his errors and reconcile himself to the Church.[11]

The defenders of orthodoxy had similar fears about another foreign humanist who resided in the sparsely settled captaincy of Ilhéus, which lay to the south of Bahia. It had been developed as an extension of the sugar economy in the 1540s. The Company of Jesus had played an active role in the region since its arrival in Brazil in 1549 and had established missions among the coastal peoples, a residence in São Jorge, and various sugar plantations. Other *engenhos*, or sugar mills, were established with financing by Lucas Giraldes, a Florentine merchant financier resident in Lisbon who had bought the captaincy and sought to develop its sugar economy using other Florentines to manage his affairs there. The growth of Ilhéus, however, had been constrained because of the constant pressure from the native peoples, first the coastal Tupinikins and then in the 1560s the indomitable and hostile Aimoré Indians, who continually raided the Portuguese settlements and farms of the region. Even by 1600, there were probably fewer than one hundred householders at São Jorge, its capital.[12]

It was in this context that a Florentine humanist named Rafael Olivi had settled in the captaincy. He may have been originally connected to the Giraldes sugar operations. Olivi resided on *fazenda* São João, a farm in the district of São Jorge. He was well known to his Jesuit neighbors, who considered him educated and a good Latinist who knew his Plato well. But Olivi was also something of a free thinker and talker, and given his Italian background he naturally fell under suspicion of adhering to the Protestant heresy. He had sometimes said that religion was invented to subjugate people because with arms or with empire that subjugation can never be completed.[13] He was critical of the pope and of high churchmen who sinned. In addition, he sometimes referred to the sultan as a "Great Lord," and he was heard to say that "the life of the Turks is good," because they were not required to attend Mass or listen to the preachers. Such statements led to his denunciation and arrest as a possible heretic in 1584.

The Inquisition's representative arrested Olivi and seized his books. There, at Fazenda São João, he had built up an extensive library in Latin and Italian. His tastes were broad. He owned Josephus, *The Jewish War,* and a commentary on matters in Turkey. In the latter case the inventory referred only to a "commentari de las cosas de Turquia" so it is difficult to know exactly what he was reading. It may have been Andrés de Laguna's *Viaje a Turquía* (1559), a work that was circulating in manuscript that used a description of the life and religion of the Turks as a way to criticize the ills of Spanish society, or perhaps it was Giovan Antonio Menavino's *Trattato de' costume et vita de Turchi* (Florence, 1549), but in any case, Olivi had developed a positive view of aspects of life among the Turks.[14] He also owned a copy of Machiavelli's *Discourses,* a work condemned in Spain and Portugal for its advocacy of a politics divested of moral considerations. His Florentine and Italian connections were strong. He had a copy (probably a manuscript copy) of Domenico de Giovanni's "sonetti di Burchiello," a widely circulated collection of comic poetry. He also owned a copy of the *Nova scientia de Niccolò Tartaglia* (1550), the widely known Italian mathematician who had also written on the mathematics of artillery. He may have also owned a copy of Dante's *Divine Comedy,* although the list of his books is not always clear and the actual titles of the listed books are at times difficult to determine. Of course, he had a taste for classical authors like Aristotle, and he even had some of the erotic poetry of Catullus. Charges against him stated that he was well read in Plato. The library also included works on nobility, horsemanship, morality, and religion.[15] But whatever the nature of his taste in reading, unlike João de Bolés, Olivi's humanism and his library had not directly threatened the local clergy. Even though he seems to have been something of a free thinker whose reading included books of suspect themes and interpretations, the charges were eventually dropped, apparently because his Jesuit neighbors came to his defense. Still, his presence and his library demonstrated that even the remote spaces of the colony were not beyond the reach of alternative ideas.

To the north, in the more populous and wealthy captaincy of Pernambuco, yet another famous threat of humanism and heresy emerged, this time in the person of a New Christian poet named Bento Teixeira. Teixeira had been born in Oporto around 1560 but had come to Brazil as a child and had been educated by the Jesuits.[16] He was apparently a good student because he had gained the sponsorship of highly placed people in the colony. He lived for a while in Ilhéus and had married there before moving to the thriving captaincy of Pernambuco, where he lived as a teacher of Latin, arithmetic, reading, and writing to children, but Teixeira's intellectual reach went far beyond elementary instruction. He had a broad education and a questioning mind. He knew the works of Fray Luis de Granada, Jerónimo de Osorio, and other theologians. He put his own hand to authorship and composed an epic poem, *Prosopopéia,* on the conquest and colonization of Pernambuco, the first literary work produced in Brazil. He knew his Latin well, and he enjoyed discussing theology with the Benedictines when he had the opportunity. In fact, he turned to them when he most needed help. His wife's adulteries had earned him local ridicule as a cuckold, and, exasperated, he had killed her and then sought asylum at the Benedictine monastery in 1594. It was not that act that caused his arrest, however, but rather a denunciation to the Inquisition. He had been in the habit of suspending classes on Saturdays instead of the usual Wednesdays, and this was enough to provoke suspicion that he was a Judaizer. Eventually sent to Lisbon, he confessed and was reconciled to the Church. He died in obscurity in 1600, still wearing his penitential robe.

But what was the real danger Teixeira presented to the colony? The denunciations and testimony make clear that he was a well-known figure, thought by many to be the most cultured man in Pernambuco. True, he read prohibited books and sometimes swore by the private parts of Our Lady, but his real threat lay in his theology, which he seemed willing to discuss with laymen and clerics alike. He had argued that there was no pain in hell, the pain was that of our own conscience; hell and purgatory were not real places, but more a state of being. This was a direct negation of the Thomistic accounts and of a whole literature that had described in excruciating detail the torments that awaited sinners in hell and that had turned purgatory from a waiting room in heaven to an antechamber of eternal punishment.[17] It was a position that smacked of Erasmus or Pico della Mirandola. He had debated with the Benedictines the question of Adam's sin and its relation to the existence of death in the world. Teixeira believed that even without eating the apple, mankind would know death. In this, there seemed to be a tendency toward a concept of predestination. That was the charge of the Jesuit António da Rocha, who reported that Teixeira had written to the Jesuits in Ilhéus suggesting in a thinly veiled way that once God had decided one's destiny good works could not alter that course.[18] As the Brazilian historian Adriana Romero has aptly pointed out, Teixeira's view that man was made in God's image and that he was composed of the four basic elements touched on a number of crucial theological issues and also displayed a familiarity with the rediscovery of ancient philosophy characteristic of the sixteenth century. Because Teixeira was a New Christian, his threat was perceived as that of a relapsed Judaizer, for that was the prism through which the Inquisitors viewed his beliefs, but like those of Bolés or Olivi, his questions and interpretations implied doubts that went far beyond the limits of ethnic or religious origins, and while these were all men of a humanist education, much of what they believed and the nature of their questioning were shared by a far larger and much less well educated population.

Savages, Sex, and Salvation

The colonial setting presented a context for individual choice and free will. This above all made Brazil a place of considerable moral and theological danger. The bishops and the Inquisition struggled to eliminate or control this freedom, while the colonists, or *moradores,* although usually claiming to adhere to the precepts of the Church and the practices of "a good Christian," sought to enjoy the liberty that the colony seemed to present. Many held that the ability to live and to think, and, for some, to read as one chose was a precious goal whose value increased as the control of everyday life intensified. In 1606, Frei Diogo de Paixão, while on an English ship, met a Portuguese from Oporto who had married in England and who served on the ship as second in command. He seemed like an honest man. Frei Diogo asked him why he lived in a land among this heretical people, to which the man responded simply, "There, he lived in freedom of conscience."[19] Similarly, Brazil seemed to offer endless space and unlimited opportunities for such freedom and for other liberties as well. The ability to get rich by exploiting Indian labor and to live without sexual constraint with access to Indian women was a great attraction. The Jesuits thundered from their pulpits against these abuses, condemning licentiousness and liberty, not only because of their effect on the program of conversion, but also because of the peril that such sins caused for the souls of the Portuguese. God, they feared, would vent his ire on the whole colony. In the 1620s, Matheus de Sousa Coelho, vicar of Nossa Senhora da Vera Cruz in São Luís de Maranhão, observed in a case involving the sexual exploitation of the Indians of that region that his efforts and actions were intended to "avoid those offenses to God from which generally are born the punishments of America caused by the liberty of conscience with which people live in this conquest."[20]

The Portuguese colonists brought to Brazil during much of its first century the full range of beliefs and practices of European popular Catholicism. They mixed their understanding of theology and dogma with their ideas of witchcraft, sorcery, astrology, and magic and their understanding of sin, sexuality, and salvation. This was as true for New Christians as for Old Christians.[21] After 1570, the reforms of Trent began to be instituted in the colony, and episcopal control extended over the life of the colonists, but the transformation was slow and made more difficult by the carnal opportunities and spiritual challenges created by the process of colonization and the growth of a regime of slavery with its inequalities based on origin, culture status, and eventually color.

In terms of cultural relativism, the early contact between Europeans and Indians produced a series of contradictory and challenging opinions. The Jesuits, in the face of their frustrations and sometimes their doubts, believed that the Indians had souls and could be integrated into the Christian community. The colonists were often unconvinced. In Pernambuco, Bernardo Velho had told companions that unbaptized Indians had no souls. Francisco Luís, in speaking about the cruelty of the hostile Potiguares, claimed they had "no more soul than a pig."[22] The colonists sometimes turned this belief to the advantage of their sexual gratification. Many transferred to the colonial context the old proposition that sleeping with unmarried women or prostitutes was no sin, so that now they held that sleeping with a *negra,* that is, an Indian, was permitted, or that at least sex with an unbaptized Indian was no sin. The Portuguese or their mixed-race descendants, called in Brazil *mamelucos,* who went into the interior and lived among the unreduced tribes sometimes admitted, as did Pedro Bastardo in 1594, that they did so because they could have as many women as they wished.[23]

If contact with Amerindian peoples could lead the Portuguese to self-serving opinions that questioned the humanity of the Indians and facilitated their availability as workers or sexual partners, such contact could also lead to cultural and religious exchanges that were less exploitative. Many settlers, Portuguese and people of mixed background, penetrated into the interior and lived among the native peoples for extended periods of time. Often their intention was to trade with or to bring back Indians as workers or slaves, but while in the *sertão,* they lived as Indians, speaking Tupi, tattooing their bodies (which implied killing enemies and perhaps eating them), living in polygamous relationships, and generally ignoring the precepts of the Church. Like the Mediterranean renegades, they knew that to be reconciled with the Church, they had to insist that their actions and behavior had only been a strategy for survival. Their testimonies, then, give us only a fleeting glimpse of the true motivations and their real sentiments, but they reveal that some actually fought against the Portuguese, sold arms and horses to Indians, and convinced Indians not to live with the Jesuits, where they would have to surrender their way of life and forgo the honor of slaying a captive and taking a new name or the prestige of having many wives. These men found in the culture of the *gentio* a freedom that appealed to them, not because Amerindian cultures had no social constraints —

of course, they did—but because as men in a cultural middle ground, these transfrontiersmen found a space between cultures where the expectations on their compliance to rules were loosened.[24] Such cultural sojourning was, in fact, a tradition of Portuguese expansion around the globe. The chronicler Manuel Faria e Sousa in his *Asia portuguesa* wrote that in Portuguese India each person lived for himself, and that to make their way "they forgot their fatherland and even their faith, dispersing themselves among our very enemies, serving them against their own nature in the hopes of getting rich."[25] The lives of these people raise serious questions about the fixity of religious identities, and they open the issues of religious hybridity.

Here I can mention the strange Brazilian syncretic religious movement of *Santidade* among the Tupi-speakers that flourished in Jaguaripe in southern Bahia in the 1580s. Such *santidades* had sprung up among the coastal peoples since the 1550s. They often drew on Tupi traditions of messianic leadership by the shamans and on a belief in a "land without evil." In Jaguaripe, the movement had been influenced by the Christian concepts absorbed by Indians who had been under Jesuit care, but the movement attracted Indian slaves, those in the missions, and *gentio* still not converted. It combined aspects of Catholic religious practice such as a rite of baptism with indigenous ones. Its followers burned farms and sugar estates and began to carry out a war against the whites and the colonial regime. Raids and pockets of resistance continued well into the late 1620s.

That this kind of religious syncretism might develop among an Indian population that had been exposed to Jesuit attempts at conversion is no surprise, but what is perhaps stranger is the way in which the Portuguese and the mamelucos in Bahia dealt with the "heresy of the pagans." A sugar planter, Fernao Cabral, sent an expedition into the interior under the command of a mameluco, Domingos Nobre, known as Tomacauna. He and his mameluco and Indian allies lived for months among the rebels; drank, smoked, and ate with them, and finally brought them to the *engenho* of Cabral, where they were allowed to settle. He apparently used them as workers, but it became public knowledge that Cabral allowed them to practice their religion and even paid respect to their leaders. Cabral was a man with an already bad reputation as a blasphemer and cruel slave master, but his dealings with the Santidade created a scandal in the region. Cabral claimed that he allowed the sect to operate for convenience, with no real belief in it, and that he visited its ceremonies out of curiosity, but many mamelucos and even some Portuguese became convinced it was a real religion and true path. This was especially the case of those born in Brazil who were more familiar with and perhaps more open to indigenous ways. Luiza Rodrigues, a white girl, admitted that, in speaking with Christian and pagan Indians, they had convinced her that "the Santidade was holy and good, and that the law of the Christians was not." She later blamed her error on her youth. In all, twenty whites, forty-six mamelucos, sixteen Indians, and seven blacks and mulattos were eventually incriminated to the Inquisition for collaborating with the Santidade movement.[26] Included among them were not only marginal mamelucos, but other sugar planters and people of substance, including Cabral's own wife.

The inquisitorial investigation of 1591–93 in Bahia dealt rather leniently with those implicated, accepting, for the most part, the renegade-style explanations of outward collaboration without spiritual commitment. Perhaps the inquisitor was unable to accept the idea that these pagan "abuses" truly constituted an attack on the validity of the Church in the minds of the colonists in same way that Islam or Protestantism did. But in the forests and cane fields of Brazil the opportunities for the old ideas of religious relativism could flourish and could lead to real deviations. The mameluco Lázaro Aranha told a companion that "there is a God of the Christians, a God of the Moors, and a God of the *gentio*." He was a man who had lived for long periods among the Indians as an Indian and had developed a sense of relativism out of that experience, but the framework in which he was able to place his thought was the traditional one of implied equality of the monotheistic religions, to which he added the beliefs of the Indians. Aranha's friends were soldiers and sugar technicians and other mamelucos, and with them he gambled, swore, called on the saints, and blasphemed against them. His doubts about dogma were profound, so deep in fact that at one point he questioned even the whole concept of immortality of the soul when he stated, "The only thing in this world that is immortal is the coal beneath the ground."[27] A half-breed Epicurean or a tropical materialist, Aranha joined the ranks of the Spanish and Portuguese doubters who appeared before the Iberian tribunals accused of saying that there is only birth and death, and all the rest is false. There was no evidence here of Converso rationalism or the influence of Averroës, as has sometimes been suggested as the source of such ideas. Instead, Aranha seems to have been an irreverent man able to question the nature of the soul and even the singularity of the Christian God.[28]

The Santidade movement in southern Bahia demonstrated that the contact of cultures could lead to new variations of old doubts and syncretism that moved in various directions. It was simply the most extreme example of cultural fusions and adaptations that led to the use of indigenous techniques of divination to African pharmacopeia and healing rituals. This was a society with enormous opportunities to transgress frontiers and to realize that union of licentiousness and liberty so feared by those who wished to protect the moral and political order.

The idea that religious exclusivity made for a more moral and a more holy society underlay the Church's claim for singular adherence. But the idea that an individual's freedom of conscience in matters of religion might not weaken society continued to appeal to some people. In 1612, Paulo Sonio left his native Antwerp to work in the shop of a man in the Brazilian sugar trade in Viana do Castelo. There he came into contact with New Christians who were Judaizers, and he felt compelled to confess this to the Inquisition. Nevertheless, he insisted that all men could save themselves in their own law, and he reasoned that in the absence of an Inquisition in his native Flanders, there was just as much "santidade" there as in Spain, perhaps remembering the brutal repression of the Inquisition that had operated in the Spanish Netherlands in the time of Charles V and Philip II.[29] Another Fleming, Alberto, long resident in Bahia as a merchant, expressed the same idea in the 1590s when he was denounced for arguing that God had created the Jews, the Turks, and the Moors in their law, and thus God intended for them to be saved in that law. As in Spanish America, eventually individuals appeared in Brazil who extended the possibility of salvation even to unbaptized Indians. In Maranhão in 1696, for example, a young Carmelite novice named Florentino, who was dismissed from the order, argued that no pagan or gentile was condemned, all could be saved. All of the urgings and arguments of learned theologians and of his Carmelite mentor could not dissuade him of a truth evident to him that God had not condemned the Indians.[30]

The theological importance of salvation as a measure of orthodoxy was not lost on the laity. People clearly understood the implications of not believing that the path to salvation lay exclusively through the Church. In June 1708, for example, Josepha da Silva Lopes denounced her husband, Paulo de Almeida Botelho, to the commissary of the Inquisition in Salvador for saying that "of all the laws that exist, God knows which is good and true." Of course, we do not know if he actually said this, or if his wife for other reasons found the Holy Office to be an effective way to carry out her domestic argument in another sphere, but the fact that she chose this often-spoken expression to condemn him indicated her correct perception that its theological content was serious enough to cause her husband trouble, and the phrase itself common enough to be believed by the commissary.[31]

People knew what was at stake in this matter. Take, for example, the argument that transpired between Father Manuel Americo da Costa and Captain Cosme da Silveira about 1713 in the latter's home in Olinda. Silveira was from Paraiba and was probably a New Christian. He had come to Olinda to prevent the wedding of a daughter of his whom he had placed in the Olinda convent of Nossa Senhora da Conceição. Both men apparently liked to read. Father Costa had lent Silveira a copy of Fernão Mendes Pinto's *Peregrination,* that widely popular if perhaps fanciful account of travels in China and Japan that may have been a disguised critique of Portuguese imperialism.[32] In discussing a brutal attack of the Portuguese on one particular people, Silveira had taken the position of religious relativism. He stated that surely these people had thought their law was true and valid, and that only God really knew for sure. Father Costa later claimed to have been shocked. He told Silveira that "only our law is firm, solid, and true, propagated by our Redeemer Jesus Christ to the Holy Apostles and Evangelists to be spread to all the world." Here was an orthodox defense of the Church's position. Silveira's relativism could not be left unchallenged. Curiously, however, Father Costa only brought this incident to the attention of the Inquisition some nine years after the exchange had originally taken place.[33] The Old Christian priest and the New Christian Silveira had been close enough to share books, and Silveira had felt comfortable enough to state the old refrain that each could be saved in his or her own law to his clerical friend.

New Christians, Old Christians, and Inquisition

The New Christians had from the inception of the colony played an active role in its development, and far from the immediate gaze of the Inquisition they had taken a prominent place in Brazilian society. Despite increasing disabilities and discrimination in the form of restrictions on their mobility, professional activities, and educational opportunities as well as the financial penalties suffered by the payments for the general pardons, the New Christians in Brazil had flourished as sugar planters, cane farmers, artisans, merchants, and clerics, some even attaining positions of municipal office or other governmental positions. Their presence cast a shadow over the colony as a whole in the minds of many observers. As late as the 1620s even the governors of Portugal during the Hapsburg period felt that the New Christians still dominated the colony and that little help could be expected from the colony's residents.

In the face of growing hostility and of a campaign of vilification, the relations between Old and New Christians in Brazil on a daily basis were often close and amiable.[34] One need go no further than the considerable evidence of intermarriage between the two groups. In the visit of 1591–93, the marriage partners of 158 New Christian men and 75 women were recorded. For both men and women, over half of the unions were with Old Christians (59 percent of the men and 56 percent of the women).[35] These unions often involved sugar planters, the local aristocracy, and "men of governance," those entitled to hold municipal office, with the daughters of well-known New Christians. Surely, there were various reasons for these matches, such as economic considerations and family strategies, and these marriages do not necessarily imply religious toleration, but the rate of New Christian exogamy suggests a constant interaction and relatively common social contact between the two groups. One must imagine the courtships, the meetings, and the interaction of families at the weddings to grasp the level of interaction that these figures imply. Then, too, one must keep in mind that in the multiracial slave society that had formed in the colony Old and New Christians were, despite their putative differences, drawn together by the fact that both groups were white and both Portuguese, and that counted for a great deal in a colonial world of racial distinctions. New Christians had used success and whiteness to overcome the social barriers set in their path. Marriages with Old Christians could bring advantages as well, but there was always the risk that familiarity and contact with a spouse's family might also lead to denunciations for Judaic habits or practices.[36] That was also the situation in relation to free and slave Afro-Brazilians. Slaves knew quite well what went on behind closed doors, and some used denunciation of their New Christian masters as a strategy in their own struggle against slavery. At the same time, crypto-Jewish slave owners sometimes tried to instruct slaves and servants in Judaism and promised good treatment for keeping their secrets. The reality seems to have been that every group in society devised strategies for appropriating the power of the Inquisition to their own situation.[37]

Certainly, the matter of religious origins was a topic of general knowledge and concern. People had a relatively clear idea of their neighbors' and acquaintances' religious origins, and when opportunities to use that knowledge to settle old scores or to fulfill one's obligations to orthodoxy arose, it was used, as the denunciations to the Inquisition make clear. Nevertheless, interactions and contacts between Old and New Christians were relatively easy.

Some impression of these relationships can be gained from testimony given during the inquisitorial visits. In 1618, António Mendes, an Old Christian sugar merchant, was in his shop in Bahia talking to clients and friends when one suggested that he take a loan from another man because he was an Old Christian, implying that he could be trusted. Mendes spoke out, "In the matter of business we should leave aside whether one is an Old or a New Christian, at times what is more important is to be a good Christian and a New Christian than to be a disreputable Old Christian."[38] It was a variation of the old saying, "Better a good Moor than a bad Christian." On another occasion, Mendes had spoken in favor of the New Christians and later explained to the Inquisition that he did so not because they followed the law of Moses, but because some were rich and successful, they had treated him fairly, and "because they help each other, something the Old Christians do not do, because many of them lack charity with their neighbors, whom they call infamous."[39]

One sees in these conversations and interactions a conviviality and indifference to religious origins and even expressions of admiration and respect despite an awareness of those differences of origins at the same time. Even in many of the denunciations made of New Christians for Judaic practices it is clear that the knowledge of peoples' habits and practices was often derived from close personal contacts. Sometimes such contacts led to resentment, enmity, and hostility, but they could also produce friendship, attraction, and even respect. Old Christian and New Christian merchants did business together on a regular basis and formed various kinds of temporary and long-term partnerships.

Both groups also proved that at times personal advantage and conviction outweighed national identity or religious associations. There were accusations of New Christian complicity and perfidy in the Dutch attack on Bahia in 1624, and then during the Dutch occupation of northeastern Brazil from 1630 to 1654. During the era of Dutch control, in fact, a number of New Christians actually openly professed Judaism during the period in which freedom of conscience was permitted. But episcopal and inquisitorial investigations revealed that both Old and New Christians had collaborated with the Dutch, for individuals of both groups had found advantages in doing so.

Portuguese Response to Freedom of Conscience in Dutch Brazil

The occupation of northeastern Brazil by the Dutch West India Company, and especially the period of the government of Count Maurits of Nassau (1637–44), is sometimes presented as a kind of Camelot on the Capiberibe River, a moment when under the protection of a humanist governor, an enlightened Renaissance prince, Catholics, Protestants, and Jews were able to live in relative peace and tranquility, a peace and harmony that in its concessions to freedom of conscience and of worship exceeded even that of Amsterdam itself.[40]

Toleration, or the multiconfessional state, was viewed by most governments at the time as a prescription for internal dissent and disloyalty. Count Maurits did not have an easy time in enforcing such a policy. He had to struggle continually against the intransigence of most of the local Calvinist ministry as well as the pressures for a less tolerant policy in the colony demanded of him by the directors of the Dutch West India Company. Moreover, he faced the steadfast opposition to his government and the presence of the Dutch by many of the resident Catholic clergy, directed in their opposition by the bishop of Salvador, the capital of Portuguese Brazil.[41]

This doctrinal opposition to Maurits's pragmatism in matters of religion was accompanied by the use of a rhetoric of religious conflict that became increasingly a reality after Count Maurits was recalled by the West India Company and an uprising of the Portuguese residents (the War of Divine Liberation, 1645–54) broke out. The ties of political interest and religious affiliation, long present but stimulated by wartime rhetoric and propaganda after 1645, hardened along national and religious lines, and the bellicose discourse of both sides emphasized the heretical nature of their opponents, disguising to some extent a period of political and social collaboration, or at least relativism and indifference, that had preceded it.

Most studies of Dutch Brazil have explained the ideological and practical reasons for a policy of toleration as an extension of Dutch practice and interests without much explanation of why and how the Luso-Brazilian residents as well as the free Indian population participated and cooperated, at least for awhile, in this experiment in tolerance. The Dutch occupation makes it possible to examine the forces among the inhabitants on the other side that led, for a time at least, to a period of collaboration and even conviviality between the Dutch and the Portuguese and to a lesser extent of the Jews, who also enjoyed a modicum of religious toleration in Dutch Brazil. In short, Dutch Brazil and the period of Maurits of Nassau offer a limited opportunity to imagine what possibilities for tolerance might have existed in Portuguese society when the authority and power of the Church and especially of the Inquisition had been diminished.

Even before the arrival of Count Maurits in 1637, the West India Company had sought to neutralize Portuguese resistance by promising the Luso-Brazilian inhabitants, the *moradores,* the security of their property and positive economic benefits as well as freedom of conscience and belief. This was made clear in the general outline for rule of the colony set out in 1629. The West India Company had been founded to carry out war against the king of Spain and his possessions, and although Spain and Portugal were under the same monarch, the company had targeted Brazil to some extent because it hoped the inhabitants might be less inclined to resist, given the traditional enmity between Portuguese and Castilians. Of course, Portugal was a Catholic kingdom, but Holland had been a major trading partner with Portugal since the Middle Ages and, in fact, had carried much of the early Brazilian sugar trade. Religious differences were not seen as an insurmountable obstacle to renewed collaboration. Moreover, there were various groups in the Brazilian colony who might find advantage or benefit in cooperating with the Dutch.

After the Dutch seized Pernambuco in 1630 they immediately found that some kind of religious toleration had to be extended if the colony and its sugar economy were to function at all. Sometimes the pressures came from surprising directions. Dutch and other foreigners who acquired Brazilian sugar mills quickly learned that the slaves simply refused to work if, at the beginning of the sugar harvest, the mill and the workers were not blessed and sprinkled with holy water and an appropriate prayer said by a priest. Despite complaints by members of the Reformed Church about such idolatry, the practice was generally allowed. Portuguese sugar planters were, of course, encouraged to stay by the Dutch and urged to abandon their estates by the Portuguese because both sides knew that without sugar the colony would fail. Nassau realized that the old Portuguese planter class was a powerful and potentially dangerous element, and he hoped that eventually they might be supplanted, but he also realized that without the Portuguese cane farmers and sugar technicians, the colony could not succeed, and so he sought to keep them in place.[42] On the other hand, despite a tradition that insisted that the Dutch had little skill or interest in sugar making, it is interesting to examine a report of the sugar mills in Dutch Brazil made in 1639. A number of the mills had been acquired by Dutch merchants or employees of the West India Company, and while some of them were absentee owners, there were others like the physician Servaes Carpentier, who became a resident *senhor de engenho* and remained so for the rest of his life. The 1639 report also revealed that many of the mills depended on sugarcane grown by dependent cane farmers, as was the Brazilian custom, but that Dutch and other foreigners, including merchants and men in administration of the colony, often supplied cane alongside Portuguese cane farmers.[43] Whether the mill owners were Portuguese or Dutch, a mixed group of cane suppliers could be found on many of the sugar estates. Little is known of their relations with each other, but they certainly shared the same interests and must have seen and interacted with each other regularly. Sugar created its own logic of identity and interest between the Dutch and the Portuguese.

One gets some inkling of what that contact and possible collaboration and perhaps tolerance might have looked like from a Portuguese episcopal investigation that was carried out in 1635–37 by Dom Pedro da Silva, bishop of Salvador. Rumors of a certain degree of collaboration with the Dutch by members of the Catholic clergy in Paraíba had moved the bishop to conduct this inquiry, and as a result some eighty individuals were denounced, eight of them clergymen, twenty-four New Christians, and forty-eight Old Christians.

The New Christians, of course, were no surprise, and some of them took the opportunity offered by the Dutch invasion and the extension of religious liberty to the Jews to openly return to the Judaism of their ancestors and join their coreligionists from Europe who came to the colony. What was more surprising were the Portuguese Old Christians, both lay and cleric, who for personal or religious reasons were willing either to accept Dutch rule, were indifferent in matters of religion, or converted to the reformed religion of the Protestants.[44]

Some of the cases were scandalous, like that of the priest Frei Manoel "dos Oculos" Calado do Salvador, who dined and drank with the Dutch, urged his flock to accommodate to their rule, invited Calvinist ministers to his home, and became a confidant of Count Maurits. He was a man who changed sides with ease and skill, and his later account from a pro-Portuguese perspective is still invaluable.[45] There was also the case of the infamous former Jesuit missionary Manuel de Moraes, who fully went over to the Dutch, using his linguistic skills in Tupi to turn the indigenous peoples under his care to the Dutch side.[46] Many local Portuguese claimed he had given the invaders considerable help with a sword in his hand, giving up the cloth and later marrying in Holland. The kind of daily interchange that emerges from the denunciations reveals many reasons for collaboration or a willingness to get along. Perhaps most famous of all was João Fernandes Vieira, the later hero of the Portuguese restoration of Brazil. Vieira, a man of humble origins from Madeira, had arrived in Brazil with few prospects. He had originally resisted the Dutch invasion, but he provided self-interested help to the high councillor, Jacob Stachouwer, who then used Vieira as his agent and clerk. Together, based on their "tight friendship," they made a fortune. Vieira eventually owned fifteen sugar mills and by 1637 was joining with other Portuguese, both New and Old Christians, to complain to the West India Company that any plan for a monopoly of trade would be a violation of the promises they had received of "greater liberties not only in justice and religion, but also in the development of our business and capital." Vieira became a confidant of Count Maurits and one of the colony's wealthiest men. His collaboration and success earned him the enmity and jealousy of many, but eventually his decision to side with the rebellion seems to have been made when the West India Company began to demand that the Portuguese planters pay their loans to the company. Vieira held the largest debt, and he had good financial reasons to resist payment even though he eventually couched his resistance in terms of loyalty to Portugal and detestation of heresy.[47]

Despite all of the efforts of the Catholic clergy, there were many marriages between the Portuguese and Dutch. Domingos Ribeiro had married three of his daughters to Dutchmen, apparently in Protestant marriages, and when someone questioned him about it, he was reported to have said that the Dutch were better Christians than the Portuguese. In another instance in Igarassú, two girls, called the Pimentinhas, the nieces of a man called Pimenta had married Dutchmen, their elders defending the match by saying that "a Fleming is worth more than many Portuguese," a paraphrase of the old Iberian saying, "Better a good Moor than a bad Christian."

These unions were frequent not only in Pernambuco, but elsewhere in Dutch Brazil. In Rio Grande do Norte, many Dutchmen married Portuguese widows, and Father António Vieira reported from Maranhão in 1642 that not only were there marriages, but also that Portuguese men and women were accepting "the customs and even the rituals of the Dutch."[48] Some of the Dutch, like Gaspar van der Ley, who married Portuguese women became Catholics while others, like Jan Wijnants of Haarlem, a *senhor de engenho* who married a planter's daughter from Goiana, remained Calvinist. One of the daughters of Mateus da Costa of Ipojuca married a New Christian who became a Jew, while another married a Dutch Protestant.[49] But the number of these unions was enough to cause the concern of both the Protestant and the Catholic clergy, for such marriages always implied a certain insecurity of national and religious identities. After the outbreak of hostilities in 1645, a number of locally married Hollanders joined the rebel cause, and some enlisted in the eight companies of former employees of the West India Company (most of them French and other Catholics) who joined the Luso-Brazilian forces.

Marriages between Portuguese women and Dutch soldiers, New Christians consorting with openly practicing Jews in Recife, the circulation of prohibited books, friendships, business contacts, attendance at Calvinist churches. All of these actions were denounced and reported in the Portuguese episcopal investigation of behavior in occupied Brazil prior to the arrival of Maurits of Nassau, but with his arrival in 1637, despite his personal reservations about Catholics and Jews, the policy of toleration was vigorously enforced and the opportunities for contact increased.[50] There continued to be tensions and sometimes scuffles over the use of churches, religious processions, and the other moments of public contact between Catholics, Protestants, and Jews. Despite considerable opposition, however, Nassau extended the guarantees of freedom of conscience to all and sought to incorporate local Portuguese, even clerics, into his confidence.[51]

An excellent opportunity to do so came after the Portuguese restoration of 1640 made Holland and Portugal allies against Philip IV of Spain. To celebrate the new situation in April 1641, Count Maurits organized a great spectacle in

Recife with horse races and equestrian competitions in which Portuguese and Dutch gentlemen paraded together and competed for the cheers and favors of the ladies as well as for various prizes.[52] The era of goodwill did not last long. Dutch refusal to abandon the Brazilian colony, the Dutch attack on Luanda in 1641, the withdrawal of Count Maurits, and new demands on the West India Company's debtors, all contributed to increasing hostility between the Portuguese and the Dutch which grew from primarily political and economic considerations. Maurits, however, remained an example of what was possible to achieve by toleration, and because of that a danger. A multiconfessional society was a threat. Doña Margarida, the vicereine of Portugal, warned in 1639 that the faith of the settlers and converted Indians of Brazil was imperiled by contact with the Dutch enemy and that "carried by private interests and relations they might leave (God forbid) the Holy Faith and separate from the purity of the Christian religion."[53]

In fact, even after 1641, while relations improved, the number of conversions was small, but Portuguese appreciation for Nassau's religious and commercial policies was great. *Moradores,* Indians, and blacks cried at his departure. Portuguese settlers still referred to him as "our Saint Anthony," and years later, in 1647, after Maurits had gone back to Europe, the very possibility of his returning to Brazil was enough to make Portuguese policy makers afraid that he might undercut the rebellion by attracting the inhabitants of Brazil to his side once again.[54] The joint inducements of liberty of trade and liberty of conscience posed a real threat. The Portuguese ambassador in Amsterdam even floated the idea of sending Nassau back as governor of Portuguese Brazil (despite the problem of his Calvinism), such was the depth of his popularity in the colony.

Once the War of Divine Liberation had begun, the rhetoric of confessional animosity and national loyalties set the parameters of behavior again and were later adopted in a nationalist historiography.[55] Under ecclesiastical urgings from pulpits and on the battlefield, Luso-Brazilian forces and leaders meted out particularly harsh punishments to Catholic converts, black or Native American allies of the Dutch, and especially to New Christians, who were looked upon as heretics and turncoats. The terminology of orthodoxy and heresy became the mold into which the war was poured, and so it becomes virtually impossible to separate the strands of economic, political, and religious motivation and justification in the struggle.

But the use of the language and concepts of religious intolerance was not uncontested. When Recife fell on 28 January 1654, the Portuguese commander, Francisco Barreto, treated the vanquished Dutch with all the courtesies of war, abiding by the surrender agreement and enforcing strict control of his troops to prevent abuses. Even more impressive was his treatment of the remaining Jewish community. Despite the objections of the Inquisition, he allowed them to depart unharmed and to sell their property, and he even helped to provide adequate shipping for their voyage. Surely, said the Jewish chronicler Saul Levy Mortara, God had saved his people by influencing the "heart of Governor Barreto."[56]

While the experiment in tolerance had taken place in Dutch Brazil, the forces of orthodoxy in Portuguese Brazil had felt highly threatened by the shadows of apostasy and heresy. In 1645, the Inquisition ordered a major investigation in Bahia, choosing as its agent for the task a special investigator, the Jesuit Manoel Fernandes. It also depended on the bishop of Salvador, dom Pedro da Silva, and above all on the governor-general, António Teles da Silva, both of whom were closely tied to the Inquisition, the latter being, in fact, the principal architect of this new tightening of the reins.[57] They hoped that a large-scale investigation, "the Great Inquiry [Grande Inquirição]," would bring under control the disorder of spiritual life in the colony, a place where "scandalous license" reigned. The historian Anita Novinsky has written an excellent analysis of this inquest, in which 118 people were denounced for various sins from sodomy to blasphemy, but 73 percent of those accused were New Christians, many of them from prominent Bahian families of merchants and sugar planters. In that sense, the inquest followed the traditional pattern of the Portuguese Inquisition.

Certainly the vast majority of people in Bahia had no admiration for Judaism and had absorbed the discourse of denigration that had demonized Jews for a century. Then, too, there was a war in Brazil in which Jews were allied with the Protestant Dutch invaders, but many of those people called to testify offered imprecise, secondhand information filled with rumor and imagined practices, often dating from years before. All of the traditional affronts of Judaizing New Christians were reported, the whipping of crucifixes, the disrespect of the saints, the secret meetings. But even more important, many Old Christians refused to come forward to denounce New Christians and sought to be excused from deposing. The governor had to take serious measures to force their participation.

Syncretism and Dissidence in a Slave Society

The divisions between Old and New Christians remained an element of important social distinction in colonial Brazil, but they eventually became secondary in the face of the growing presence of large numbers of African slaves and their descendants. Africans brought with them elements of culture and religions, and these combined with the beliefs and practices that the Portuguese had transferred, including many folk practices or devotions that the clergy held to be superstitious, unseemly, or heterodox. That African beliefs and practices were widely distributed among the population, both black and white, is borne out by a variety of sources and by various denunciations before the Portuguese Inquisition. The diffusion of these beliefs had taken place since the arrival of Africans in Portugal in the fifteenth century, but in the context of Brazilian slave society various aspects of African practices had become common, not only among the slaves and their descendants, but among the society as a whole. The result was a considerable social and religious ambiguity and fluidity.[58]

African practices took a number of forms but most popular, or at least the most challenging to Portuguese cultural hegemony, seem to have been the *calundus,* or religious ceremonies accompanied by African religious practices of spirit possession.[59] These gatherings included drumming and dancing that brought the participants into a state of trance. Orthodox thinking associated these dances with demonic possession. The first literary mention of them is made by Nuno Marques Pereira in his *Peregrino da America* (1722), in which he saw them as hellish rites accompanied by the sound of African instruments.[60] But if the slaves sought respite from their burdens and the healing of illness in these dances, it was not their fault. Marques Pereira placed the onus of slavery's legacy on the masters, not the slaves. As he said, "It is certain that the master makes the slave, not the slave, the master." And went on, "O State of Brazil, how I fear the great punishment that will come because of the bad government that many of your inhabitants practice with their slaves and families."[61]

While Marques Pereira was the first to publish about the calundus, the phenomenon was already well known in the colony and already a concern to the Church by the time he wrote. Traces of these practices had been suggested in the early seventeenth-century inquisitorial visit, but by the last decades of that century references to them were common. In a text of 1702, Father Francisco de Lima, who worked as a missionary in the Bahian Recôncavo, reported that in the parish of São Gonçalo a black woman named Magdalena was in the habit of publicly dancing the calundu. Father Lima was upset because he considered these to be diabolical dances in that they led to trances and visions among the participants, who at times were left speechless and almost moribund by the dance. These meetings and dances were, in his mind, work of the devil, who had been able to penetrate the community because of other spiritual failures. Father Lima complained that it was widely held that the local priest of the parish was rumored to be a New Christian and was not living up to his responsibilities. Lima was scandalized that during the feast of Our Lady of the Assumption celebrated by a mulatto brotherhood, its *juiza*, or leader, was a colored woman named Rosa, who also happened to be the mistress of the New Christian priest's brother. She was apparently responsible for a number of heretical propositions as well, but despite that fact, both the priest and his brother protected her from prosecution. Father Lima was convinced the devil was in the heads of these *pardos (mulattos)* and blacks and that the danger and the calundus were spreading.[62]

While the Portuguese white colonists viewed the calundus as an African practice, the attractions these ritual dances seemed to offer proved appealing to them as well. At first, slave owners had turned to calundus as a way to heal their bondsmen, and even some clerics supported them in this, apparently taking these practices to be a form of natural magic and therefore permissible, but over time, as the appeal of these rites began to grow among the white population as well, they were condemned as superstitious or demonic. António Fernandes da Cruz, a bachelor who lived near the docks of Salvador in the parish of Nossa Senhora da Conceição, told the commissary of the Inquisition that he had been lead astray to participate in these rites quite by chance. On his way to visit the farm of a friend the previous Christmas he happened to pass by the home in Itapagipe of Lucrecia Vicenza, a free black woman from Angola. Hearing the drumming and the dancing, he had entered the house, "carried there by curiosity."[63] Asking what was happening, he was told by the black men and women that were there that "they danced *lundus,* which was the custom in their land, and that they were able to cure illnesses and spells." He was told that if he paid and participated he might be cured of any ills that afflicted him. His participation in the calundu, despite his lame defense, revealed that these African practices were known and that the rest of the population also took part in them. Priests complained of the popularity of calundus for whites as well as blacks. Despite the efforts of crown and clergy, this syncretism proliferated over time. By the eighteenth century, as the Brazilian colony and slavery expanded into the gold mining regions of Minas Gerais and as the city of Rio de Janeiro grew in size and importance, the practice of calundus and related rites and activities also spread, favored to some extent by slave owners who saw these practices as a way of satisfying slaves' spiritual needs, but also supported perhaps by an implicit acceptance of their possible efficacy.[64]

The spread of African practices may have been based on a perception of their effectiveness, but they undoubtedly were also attractive because they paralleled the group of beliefs in sympathetic magic and the occult that were widely held in Portugal itself. Inquisitors imposed the framework of sorcery, witchcraft, and superstition on these references available to them, but the existence of a belief in alternate channels to the supernatural outside of the institutional Church or parallel to it was already well established in the colonial population, and it made the adherence to new forms of African and Amerindian origin that much easier. The occult offered a series of alternative beliefs and possibly effective means to achieve beneficial ends that seemed to many people equal or similar to the power of relics, the utility of prayer, the intervention of the saints, or the benefit of clerical blessing. People sought out and gave respect to those who mastered the techniques and knowledge of either orthodox Catholicism or of these alternative systems of belief.[65] In this world of the occult, of astrology, love potions, calundus, and prognostication by dream interpretation, the casting of cowrie shells and the finding of objects by the "trick of the basket" Catholic authorities saw either superstition or the devil, but many people remained convinced of their effectiveness and at least unsure that they were, in fact, evil or wrong.[66]

That insecurity created an atmosphere of tolerance in the sense that these alternate approaches might be joined to, or even replace, the orthodoxy of the Church, and people resisted attempts by Church authorities to impose orthodoxy. The colony was rife with heterodox opinion, supposed superstitions, and critiques of religious authority, especially of the Inquisition. Some clerics believed that the New Christian attitudes that had been in the colony since its beginnings prepared the religious soil for the weeds of heresy.

By the beginning of the eighteenth century, Bahia, with its layer of New Christian elites and its sea of free and enslaved Africans and their descendants, seemed to be a locale of great spiritual danger, or, as the commissioner of the Inquisition, Fray Rodrigo de São Pedro, put it, a place where witchcraft, sorcery, and superstition went from height to height.[67] He noted, for example, the popularity of a slave sorceress called Mother Catherina, who had a great following of people and who was allowed to live outside her owners' control, a situation not that uncommon in urban Salvador. She was said to invoke the devil during her dances, called, he said, in the language of Angola, calundus. She had so bewitched her master that his wife and daughter lived in a promiscuous manner, and the master himself sometimes fell so deeply asleep in a chair that only shaking and moving him could make him awake. These were all symptoms of social disorder and the inversion of accepted practices and thus almost prima facie evidence of demonic presence.[68]

In the mind of Fray Rodrigo, the presence of these African practices and of superstition in general was linked to a widespread climate of disrespect for orthodoxy and the Holy Office, a direct result of the "multitude of New Christians that live in this land." To document this disrespect, he reported an incident that had taken place during Lent in 1704. In Salvador's Benedictine

A black sorcerer, or *feiticeiro*.
Magic and sorcery in Brazil combined elements from Portuguese, African, and Native American traditions, so that boundaries of culture, race, and belief were often crossed. Watercolor by Jean Baptiste Debret. Courtesy of Biblioteca Nacional, Rio de Janeiro.

monastery, Frei Ruperto, a serious Benedictine friar and an advisor to the Inquisition, had been preaching on the Sundays of Lent on the theme of the Vanities of Brazil or, more specifically, of Bahia. His message of "vanitas vanitatum et omnia vanitas" (vanity of vanities and all is vanity) (Ecclesiastes 1.2) had so offended the listeners that they had begun to compose satirical doggerel against his sermons and against his person, accusing him of being a drunk. From the pulpit he warned that he knew exactly who was sending him the offensive verses but with apparently little effect in promoting any respect for him or his office. When Frei Rodrigo denounced supposed revelations by a street healer's superstitious inventions, her defenders told his companion Frei Alberto that Frei Rodrigo must be drunk to say such things. Frei Alberto defended his colleague and told the critics to be careful of what they said, for Frei Rodrigo did not drink and he was a commissioner of the Holy Office of the Inquisition. His critics seemed unimpressed by the gravity of his office. "A commissioner of shit," was the answer thrown back in Frei Alberto's face.[69]

Frei Rodrigo's letter reveals a situation in which the status of unbelief in Bahia and by extension Brazil reflected the social composition of the colony as well as its religious origins. There were disrespectful New Christians who scoffed at the teachings of the Church and denounced its attempt to instill orthodoxy.[70] It was the kind of criticism certainly not limited to New Christians. Even more troubling for the defenders of orthodoxy was the defiance inherent in alternative practices. African rites or beliefs, perhaps most common in the form of calundus, indigenous practices, and pharmacopeias, and the Portuguese traditions of faith healing, divination, sorcery, magic, and dream interpretation combined to create what learned men perceived as a superstitious society, but also one that was profoundly religious. The Church's own emphasis on the power of prayer or of the saints to combat evil or the devil reinforced belief in the effectiveness of these inversions of true belief.

If alternate and effective ways to influence the supernatural existed, then the possibility of alternate or parallel paths to the divine was also possible. In such an environment the traditional arguments that a merciful God could save whomever he chose, or that those who lived according to natural law even if unbaptized could be saved, or that God had given each person his or her own destiny to fulfill could flourish. And there were always doubts. In 1699, António Duro, who lived with his wife and children in Porto Calvo in southern Pernambuco, a man, it was said, of "bad habits," argued that he did not believe in hell, where souls were eternally damned, for God's purpose was to save everyone, and if there was some place for souls to go, then the time there would be limited and "God would take them from there by his good will."[71] This was an idea similar to that held by Pedro de Rates Hennequim, who was sentenced in 1744 for a series of heretical ideas and strange propositions.[72] Hennequim had lived in the mining zones of Minas Gerais and had become convinced that Brazil was the location of an earthly paradise and of messianic expectation. He liked to read the Bible himself and to interpret it as God had revealed it to him. When others spoke ill of the Jews, Hennequim had said, "What harm have they ever done me?" He predicted that in a few years the whole world would be united into "one flock beneath one shepherd" and that the ten lost tribes of Israel would be gathered from all over the Americas, where they had gone into exile. But the principal reason for his denunciation was that he had often said that all those who went to hell would ultimately be saved, "for God had not created any soul in order for it to be lost."[73] When questioned then why purgatory existed, he had responded that God had many houses, drawing as his text of justification John 14:2, "In domo patris mei mansiones multae sunt" (In my Father's house are many mansions). Hennequim wished to read his Bible in his own way and to link its message to a millenarian perception of Brazil and to a sense of toleration in which all souls would eventually find salvation in the hands of a benevolent God.

People like Hennequim who mixed orthodox and heterodox or heretical theology or who were able to accept the Church's teachings while still deeply involved in a universe of spells, magic, and incantations were common. The case of an itinerant Brazilian, Sebastião Damil e Sotomaior, demonstrates this clearly. He had been born and raised, as he told the Inquisitors, in Rio de Janeiro "of Portugal" about 1665 to Old Christian parents. Baptized, confirmed, and a regular participant in the sacraments of the Church, he knew his prayers and Christian obligations well. He was literate, having received his first letters in Brazil, and had lived on his father's rural estate, probably a sugar plantation, until at age thirty-two he had sailed to Angola. From there he had gone in an English vessel to Jamaica, where he remained for three months before arriving in Cartagena de Indias on a slave ship. He settled there, working as an estate manager (*mayordomo de estancias*), a job for which apparently his rural experience in Brazil served him well. But he was a man who did not keep his opinions to himself, and because he was a foreigner, his listeners were unwilling to turn a deaf ear to his deviations from dogma. Eight people gave witness against him, noting his bad habits, his avoidance of church attendance, and his strange ideas. Denounced, Damil e Sotomaior was arrested for expressing a number of suspicious opinions, but he refused to admit anything; after three audiences with the inquisitors, however, he began to discuss the propositions that had caused his arrest.

The trouble had started in April 1699, when, in a conversation about a recent earthquake in Lima, someone had said that such events had divine causes since not a leaf on a tree moved without God's will. Damil disagreed.

He stated that God had no power over the elements, and when, for example, the sea swallowed a ship it was not God's will but simply the force of the elements. After the creation of the world, Damil told the inquisitors, God had conceded his power to the elements, the sun, the planets, and the stars, and these things and each person operated through their own will. Someone else in the conversation had complained of his unhappy married life and said that his miserable marriage had been God's will, to which Damil had said their union was not God's will but that of the unhappy man himself since we all have free will in all we do. God had ceded much to nature. God did not create the plants and animals. The plants were created by the sun, and animals, just like mosquitoes and frogs, were created from the putrefaction of the earth. Here he was advocating the ancient idea of spontaneous generation, the creation of living things from inanimate objects, a belief that could be traced back to Aristotle and Lucretius and that had remained part of the understanding of the physical world of many, although exactly in this period that belief was under scrutiny.[74] Where had he learned these things? In this case, unlike so many others, he was able to inform the inquisitors, he had not read them in a book but had learned them from a Jesuit in Rio de Janeiro named Simão de Vasconcelos.[75] This was not just any informant. Vasconcelos was a prominent, well-read Jesuit who wrote about his order in Brazil and who represented in many ways the Jesuit attempt to reconcile scholasticism with observation and doubt.[76] He was also a man with some curious ideas about the edenic character of Brazil, and if we can believe Damil, some unorthodox interpretations of dogma.

But if Damil e Sotomaior emphasized individual freedom of will and seemed to be a protodeist in some ways, he was also clearly mixing these seemingly secularizing or "modern" ideas with a bundle of folk superstitions and practices and an understanding of dogma at variance with the Church's teachings. He believed, for example, that Christ had not been carried in Mary's womb for nine months, for he could not believe that in those "nauseous entrails [*bascosidades*] God would be incarnated. Mary had remained a virgin after the birth because God was all-powerful, and Christ had been conceived when Saint Gabriel had placed three drops of blood in the heart of the Virgin. He also did not believe in devils or in hell. Devils, he claimed, were simply Christians who had died. The inquisitors wished to know more. Had he really questioned the existence of hell? Damil was too smart to admit that. He explained that when in a conversation about St. Patrick's visit to hell someone had argued that the souls there were being punished with razors and chains, he had said that it only appeared so because the souls were only spirit and had no body to suffer such torments.

As his defense before the inquisitors developed, Damil was not reluctant to admit that he knew certain prayers (*salmos*) that could kill snakes, iguanas, and worms or that could cure people.[77] He was what the Portuguese called a *benzedeiro* or a *saludador,* a popular healer. He had learned his craft from various sources. He knew a prayer to cure fevers; another to stop bleeding. He recited in Latin a prayer against the plague that he had been taught by a Portuguese priest named Mota in Rio de Janeiro. One had been taught to him in Rio de Janeiro by an old woman, another by a black man. Another he admitted having read in a book entitled *Thesouro de prudentes (The Treasure of the Prudent).* This was a very popular almanac filled with information on the tides, the stages of the moon, eclipses, and other curiosities and natural phenomena. First published in 1612, it went through at least eight editions over the course of the next century.[78]

By word of mouth and from popular sources Damil had enriched his repertoire of prayers, mixing orthodox devotion and magic. The prayers themselves were filled with references to the saints, to Jesus, and to the Virgin, but their intention was to affect the world through natural magic. Deism and magical spells: his cosmology had contradictions, but he seemed comfortable with them. In the end, neither his explanations nor his plea for pardon helped him. The Inquisition seized all his property in 1699, and he was sentenced to perpetual prison at the king's oars.

Here at the dawn of a new century Damil was mixing orthodox theology with heterodox and heretical beliefs and with folk practices of the occult. Like many of these folk practitioners, he was a man who had traveled and seen the world and who had developed his own cosmology. He saw no conflict in his mixture of Catholic belief and natural magic. By the eighteenth century such ideas were under attack by a new rationalism even within the Inquisition that emphasized a more scientific approach to healing.[79] Some men and women went even further than Damil's deviations. They were skeptical of all religion and willing to build the basis of community on other criteria. In Brazil, as elsewhere in the Atlantic world, their numbers were growing by the eighteenth century.

PART III

Toward Toleration

8

From Tolerance to Toleration in the Eighteenth-Century Iberian Atlantic World

Not only is it extremely cruel to persecute in this brief life those who do not think the way we do, but I do not know if it might be too presumptuous to declare their eternal damnation. It seems to me that it does not pertain to the atoms of the moment, such as we are, to anticipate the decrees of the Creator. —Voltaire, A Treatise on Toleration (1763)

Intolerance is a fundamental law of the Spanish nation, it was not established by the common people, and it is not they who should abolish it. —Inquisition Proclamation (Madrid, 1789)

In 1774, the Inquisition arrested one of the most well known and admired figures in the Spain of his time. The incident had all the trappings of a show trial, the exemplary punishment of a prominent representative of reform who seemed to some to embody modernity and progress, but who, for that same reason, represented to the forces of tradition all the dangers of foreign ideas, secularism, amorality, and change that threatened the very basis of religion and society. The accused, the Peruvian Pablo de Olavide y Jáuregui, was a fitting symbol in many ways; a man of the Iberian world, a traveler between continents, intelligent, vain, imperfect, and a man who, as a self-identified believer, found it difficult to reconcile the Church's teachings and politics with his perception of the needs of society.[1]

Born in Lima to a distinguished colonial bureaucratic family, Olavide had demonstrated intellectual talent at an early age and had received a doctorate in canon law in Lima in 1742. Still in his early twenties, he was, through his talents as well as the money and influence of his family, appointed as a judge of the *audiencia,* or high court, of Peru. His performance there was irregular and led to difficulties that resulted in his suspension from office, and in 1750 he sailed for Madrid. During his journey he stopped in Dutch-controlled Cura-çao to conduct some illegal trading, an incident that caused his arrest on arrival in Spain. Although his punishment was light, his career as a judge was essentially over, but his rise was just beginning. In 1755 he married a wealthy Spanish widow and now became a figure at the court in Madrid, where his bright intelligence, affability, connections, and lack of personal inhibitions helped to further his career. Troubles at court moved him to travel to France, where he became friendly with François-Marie Arouet Voltaire and others of the French philosophes, and his home in Paris became a salon where he received some of the leading figures of the Enlightenment. He amassed a remarkable library that he shipped back to Spain, much of it composed of French authors like Jean-Jacques Rousseau, Charles-Louis de Secondat, Baron de La Brède et de Montesquieu, and the abbé Guillaume-Thomas-François de Raynal, many of whom were on the Inquisition's list of prohibited authors and books; like other court intellectuals of his day, however, he had been able to get a license to read those works. He thought of himself as "the Christian philosophe" who would introduce the ideas of Montesquieu, Denis Diderot, John Locke, and Pierre Bayle to Spain, and on his return to Madrid he turned his home into an active center for the diffusion of Enlightenment culture. There, in friendship and collaboration with the count of Campomanes and count of Aranda he became a leading figure in the project for the renovation of Spain. In 1766, he was denounced to the Inquisition as a libertine for having "pornographic" paintings in his home, but this did not slow his career, and with Aranda's support the following year he was appointed intendant of Seville and superintendent of the new agricultural colonies being created in the Sierra Morena of Andalusia. For the next ten years he designed or carried out a series of reforms of education, commerce, industry, landholding, and religious practices that increasingly defined him as an opponent of various entrenched interests, especially those of the Church, and a symbol of the attack on tradition.[2] Many of the reformers, or *ilustrados,* as they were called, men like the counts of Campomanes or Aranda, were simply too well placed and powerful at court to present suitable targets for the Church's defense of its perceived interest, but the creole Olavide, a figure of the Iberian Atlantic world far from home, lacked the position or the connections that made others immune from prosecution. He was denounced and arrested again in 1776, and in 1778, in a private ceremony in which leading notables of Church and state were required to attend, he was sentenced for a wide variety of sins of the age: irreligion, atheism, libertinism, formal heresy, and being an *afrancescado* influenced by the godless philosophes. The lesson was not lost on others that even for those well placed in the court and government the Inquisition could cause considerable trouble if they wished to change and secularize society.

Olavide subsequently escaped from confinement and fled to France, where he was celebrated as a hero of conscience by the leading French intellectuals of the day. That episode as well as his later abject reconciliation with the Church, when in 1798, in order to return to Spain, he recanted his religious and ideological errors, is outside the scope of this story. But what is notable is the nature of some of the things of which he was formally accused. In his new agricultural communities he had made religion a secondary matter and had tried to limit the role of priests and the number of churches, altars, masses, and religious celebrations. He had doubted the existence of heaven and hell, and he had suggested that the Bible might not be entirely accurate since "the Chinese were older than Adam." In general, he had placed matters of this world before those of the next. He had said that "tending a piece of earth, planting a tree, and fathering a son are the most glorious things of this life." Most important for my analysis, Olavide had questioned the exclusive validity of the Church. He was reported to have said that Socrates was a philosopher who had been saved, implying that baptism was unnecessary. He had also taken up the ancient refrain of salvation for all and had added to it the new concerns of government and morality, arguing that "each person can save himself in any law that he may follow. . . . Each person who complies with the obligations of the State and his position and observes with precision moral virtues in whatever sect he may belong will be saved."[3] One sees in this statement the growing influence of Locke: the individual and the state have become the rationale of toleration.[4]

The Sources of Tolerance

The case of Olavide makes clear that in eighteenth-century Iberia and its American colonies two intellectual traditions concerning the acceptance of other religions became intertwined and braided together into a complex strand of religious tolerance that formed part of a fabric of liberal and reformist ideas that attacked and undermined the traditional institutions of social and political life, or at least so it seemed to many in authority. As we have seen, despite consistent pressure and the definition of tolerance as both theologically hereti-

cal and politically disastrous, there was an ancient heritage of freedom of conscience and religious relativism that drew its strength from different sources:
Catholic ideas about charity and natural law as well as religious indifference
that grew from the doubts inherent in materialist and skeptical views. Although
occasionally expressed by clerics with some theological training, usually these
views were popular in the sense that they were held by laypeople of often
modest social origins. Moreover, these ideas were uncodified and unsystema-
tized and were thus often expressed in terms of practical considerations or
rationalizations, or as religious interpretations that were considered by those in
authority as theologically uninformed and simplistic. Typically their advocates
were people without letters or those who could read and write, but who lacked a
formal university education. These ideas, however, while not fully developed,
were no less important and no less entrenched because of their popular character.

   Parallel to these popular ideas there was in the eighteenth century another
strain of thought whose origins lay in the intellectual ferment that had been
sweeping Europe since the time of Spinoza and that could be found increasingly in Spain and Portugal as well. Drawing on rationalist arguments and on
those of economic and political pragmatism, first Montesquieu and Voltaire
and then the subsequent generation of Diderot, David Hume, Rousseau, and
Jean Le Rond d'Alembert advocated a concept of religion that was either a
pragmatic support for civil society or a guide for a moral existence, but which
was far less concerned with ultimate or absolute truth. Montesquieu argued
that religion inculcated useful ethical values, and even the deist Voltaire, with
all his doubts about the ecclesiastical establishment and the existence of an
afterlife, still believed in a beneficent deity and recognized the social utility of a
popular belief in hell that could keep society in order.[5] Many of the philosophes came to believe in a "natural religion" and had little preference for
any particular confession. Most were certainly advocates of freedom in the
matter of conscience so long as belief was not disruptive to civil society. In
Iberia advocates of such ideas often drew their inspiration from these French
and other foreign sources. They made the defense of freedom of conscience an
integral aspect of their growing advocacy of religious toleration. As the Hispanic world was pulled into the process of philosophical, political, and religious change that has come to be associated with the Enlightenment, tolerance in matters of conscience became a fundamental tenet of many persons
committed to various kinds of reform, some of them in prominent policy
positions at the Iberian courts. For Spaniards and Portuguese these changes
came slowly, and some of the principal exponents of intellectual change were
in fact found among the clergy who sought to reconcile rationalism and empiricism with authority and orthodox religion. But even this "moderate En-

lightenment" was opposed by the Church hierarchy and the Inquisition, which found in this attack on scholasticism the roots of irreligion and heresy.[6] Nevertheless, by the middle of the century, it was clear that new ways of thinking about society, religion, and individual rights were being broadly discussed at many levels in Spanish and Portuguese society. Increasingly, the impact of foreign writings and ideas were felt in these discussions, and the question of religious toleration and the acceptance of cultural and religious difference was seen both by proponents and by those who wished to preserve traditional society as an integral element of the new thinking and the project of change. Elsewhere in Europe, Spain and Portugal continued to carry the reputation of official fanaticism, but, in fact, the concept of natural religion and the idea of freedom of conscience were spreading in salons, in the periodical press, and at various levels of society despite the efforts by defenders of tradition to define such ideas as subversive and heretical.[7] They were spreading even among liberal elements in the government, who saw religious exclusivity detrimental to Spain's commercial and diplomatic interests and who wished to promote freedom of conscience as a way of making such ties easier.

The Spanish eighteenth century was seen at the time, and has been since, especially in the twentieth century, as a cultural battleground where the contending forces of two opposing visions of the Spanish past have disputed its effects on the nation's trajectory and character.[8] For those nostalgic for Spain's greatness, the Enlightenment, with its profound debt to foreign influences, was held responsible for the weakening of those unions of monarchy and faith and of mysticism and military might that had once made Spain a dominant world power. For them, the scientific revolution, rationalism, and the secularization of the state had been accompanied by irreligion and "the arrogant spirit of the New philosophy" that weakened and destroyed what was uniquely Spanish. Spain could not be France, and the more it tried to be, the weaker it would become. Herein lay the explanation of the nation's ills. But other Spaniards saw the matter differently. For them, the eighteenth century was the time when the inherent weaknesses of a closed and controlled religious and intellectual climate symbolized by the Inquisition and by a repressive political system turned the country into a second-rate power. Spain's problem for these liberal critics was not that it had accepted the new scientific thought and rationalism of the age, but that it did so in a limited and incomplete way because of the continual opposition and obscurantism of a still-powerful Church and an ecclesiastical hierarchy in control of national intellectual life and its social order.[9] Of course, these positions lacked nuance. The Enlightenment in southern Europe owed much to progressive thinkers within the clergy, some of whom represented an intellectual cutting edge in the country and others of whom became ardent critics of the obscurantism of the Inquisition. The ideological lines were not between secularists and clergymen, but instead represented a division between alternate views of social stability that crossed that division.

A similar if less virulent debate has also taken place in Portugal where it has been less organized around questions of national decadence and more concerned with the role of the enlightened despotism of the marquis of Pombal, who guided the country from 1755 to 1778, the relation of the state to traditional society, and the relative impact of European ideas and political trends in Portugal and its colonies.[10]

Throughout the eighteenth century the old relativist doubts continued to be expressed in the Iberian world. In some ways it is more difficult to document their presence than in the previous centuries because the nature of the Inquisition's activities and the target of its concern shifted markedly as the century progressed. Studies from a number of Spanish tribunals indicate a similar pattern. The repression of vocal sins and of questioning of dogma had been intensive in the period of the late sixteenth century after the first wave of prosecutions for Judaizing had crested. Even in the seventeenth century, when a new surge of major heresy trials was initiated against supposed Lutherans, Jews, and Muslims, prosecutions for these crimes of word and thought still made up between 17 and 20 percent of all the trials in the tribunals of Toledo, Granada, and Galicia.[11] As was always the case, the persons accused of these crimes were overwhelmingly males. Overall, from 1540 to 1700 prosecutions for propositions and blasphemy made up over 27 percent of all the cases heard by the tribunals of Spain itself and a quarter of all the cases in the three American tribunals. Equivalent statistics have not been gathered for the next century. The early eighteenth century began with a new concern with supposed backsliders to Judaism and Islam as the newly installed Bourbon regime consolidated its support with the ecclesiastical hierarchy. As a result, prosecutions for blasphemy and heretical propositions dropped off in the first decades, but after 1750, propositions again became a target of inquisitorial interest as concern grew that these ideas might be tied to foreign influences. By the 1750s the Spanish Inquisition was also placing far more emphasis on the censorship of books and their importation from abroad than on the traditional crimes of sorcery and heretical propositions. But cases for these latter crimes appear in all the inquisitional tribunals with enough frequency to make it clear that the ideas behind them had certainly not disappeared. There were still the defenders of fornication, no less convinced that unmarried sex was not a sin but now increasingly defined as libertines and suspected of bearing pernicious philosophical influences from France. The doubters were still present, judged in every tribunal of the Holy Office, but now they were often referred to as atheists.[12] Joseph Hario Amaral, denounced in Murcia in 1735, held that there was no purgatory, the pope had no power over the destiny of souls, and dispensations were an invention designed only to make money for priests.[13] The naval gunner Enrique García told his shipmates in 1781 that there was no afterlife and the soul of a man died like that of an animal. They could not believe their ears "since he was a Spaniard" and thought he must be out of his head to speak in his way, but when he reaffirmed the fact that he was an atheist, he was denounced to the Inquisition agent in Cádiz."[14] These ideas and doubts could be found throughout the Iberian world. In 1758 Joseph Castaños, a thirty-nine-year-old Spaniard living in Mexico, in a dispute with his lover told her that a merciful God would not create a hell and that no one would be damned.[15] Such arguments were everywhere. Increasingly, so too was the questioning of the exclusive validity of the Church as the only path to salvation. As Manuel Pereda argued in Seville with logic and a quantitative sensibility, "Since the vast majority of people are infidels and the followers of sects and the Catholics are so few, if the former are condemned for their religion, then God is a tyrant who must enjoy condemning them."[16]

As the kind of thinking that such propositions seemed to represent became increasingly prevalent, the forces of tradition sought to eliminate the channels by which these ideas came to Spain and Portugal. The government in Spain continued to control the publication and importation of books through prior censorship by the Council of Castile, which had exercised that right since the sixteenth century, and the Inquisition maintained its index of books to be censored or expurgated, with penalties for those who ignored it. Theoretically designed to cover matters of religion, the index in its new versions of 1747 and 1790 increased with the addition of books whose content was lascivious or political.[17] In Portugal, similar censorship had been carried out by the Desembargo do Paço (a Council of Justice) and by the Inquisition, but in 1768 a Royal Board of Censorship assumed these duties as part of the project of increasing state authority.[18] Despite these efforts, the relatively easy acquisition of licenses to read prohibited books, the Inquisition's inability to really distinguish between questions of politics, morality, and theology in the prohibited writings, and the general spirit of indifference to the Inquisition's attempts kept the channels of such ideas open. Licenses were easy to obtain, and by the last decades of the century even in the interior of Brazil there were private libraries liberally stocked with prohibited books.[19] Control of reading was difficult to enforce. By the eighteenth century the Inquisition itself had become a less active institution, given to political positioning in the struggles between Church and state, and increasingly under control of royal authority, which mobilized it after the French Revolution for the defense of monarchy. It was still able to wreak havoc on some lives but was less a force than it had been in previous centuries. Still, it continued to symbolize the traditional order and the primacy of the Church and as such became the rallying point for all its defenders. These protectors of the old order knew who their enemies were: the rationalists, the importers of foreign ideas, and above all the dangerous "false philosophers," the foreign, and especially French authors of the Enlightenment, who threatened the country with atheism, deism, immorality, and false critiques of Spain and Portugal themselves.

To meet the challenge, the Inquisition began to specifically target the new threats: "encyclopedists," libertines, and freethinkers.[20] The Freemasons, for example, fell into this category. Rome and the Spanish and Portuguese Inquisitions at first were befuddled by them and what they stood for. Dating from the seventeenth century in England, Masonic lodges were founded in 1727 in Portugal and in 1728 in Spain, but the earliest prohibitions and prosecutions of the Masons began in 1740 as the secrecy and liturgy of the order seemed to challenge or detract from the Church's prerogatives. In Portugal prosecutions were few in the period of rule by the dictatorial marquis of Pombal until 1777, but thereafter the patterns became similar between the two countries. As the Inquisition became more familiar with Masonry's philosophy, its liberalism, free thinking, and association with English and French ideas and with sojourners to Iberia, these became the major justifications for its suppression. Moreover, one of the Inquisition's major charges against the Freemasons was that they were indifferent to religion and would allow Protestants, Jews, atheists, materialists, and Spinozists to fully participate within the association.[21] Such an attitude, what the Church increasingly called indifferentism, essentially made religion irrelevant, and thus it struck at a fundamental precept of the Church. It also linked Masonry to the idea that religion in itself did not define the quality of a person's character.

By the 1790s, after the beginnings of the French Revolution, these various perceived threats to traditional society became confused into a litany of actors that seem to menace both Catholicism and the civil order: "the Freemasons, Indifferentists, Deists, Materialists, Pantheists, Egoists, Tolerationists, and Humanists," and others whose beliefs presented the "poisonous doctrines of liberty, independence, and toleration."[22] The Inquisition made a concerted effort to control the flow of these ideas. Between 1780 and 1820, the tribunals of Spain heard 6,569 cases, of which 3,026 were for propositions. Most of the propositions had an ancient genealogy, but those persons prosecuted were increasingly members of the educated and professional classes, lawyers, merchants, clerics, military men, city officials, and the like.[23] The Inquisition also shifted its focus to censorship and increasingly merged its concern over moral and theological issues with political ones.[24]

During the second half of the eighteenth century, as the ideas of the Enlightenment took hold in Iberia, the question of religious indifference and tolerance was increasingly perceived as a core concept in the challenge to orthodoxy. The Inquisition and its supporters developed a word for it, *tolerationism,* a caustic term that implied a sometimes naïve but still heretical disregard for revealed truth and therefore a philosophical position that directly contradicted the teachings and dogma of the Church. Tolerationism was thus a direct attack on revealed religion because it assumed there was no difference in the relative quality or truth of various beliefs.

In Spain and Portugal, where the unity of religion had been enforced, no philosophical theory of toleration had developed nor had toleration been instituted as state policy for pragmatic political and economic reasons, as it had in Holland, France, and the German states. But the Iberian nations were not unaware that there might be limited reasons to grant it. Both Spain and Portugal had granted a restricted freedom of conscience in the seventeenth century to Protestant merchants and mariners from nations involved in diplomatic or commercial alliances with them.[25] Portuguese treaties with England in 1640 and 1654 and later with the United Provinces in 1661 had specifically recognized the exemption of their allies from inquisitorial inquiry and the right to exercise their religion in private, although the Inquisition was at times reluctant to honor such agreements.[26]

Jews were another matter altogether. The attempts by the count-duke of Olivares in Spain in the 1630s and Padre Vieira in Portugal in the 1660s to make use of New Christians and even practicing Jews in important financial and commercial roles had been met with stiff opposition. In 1797, when Pedro Varela, secretary of the treasury, urged the crown to allow Jewish merchants to return to Spain "now that the ancient prejudices have disappeared," the Inquisition once again opposed the idea.[27] In that year the crown authorized the arrival of foreign craftsmen to work in factories, granting them freedom of conscience and exemption from inquisitorial control so long as they were not Jews.

Despite these restrictions, Spaniards and Portuguese knew that elsewhere the tide of toleration was turning in Europe.[28] The examples of freedom of conscience established by the Quakers in Pennsylvania and Roger Williams in Rhode Island, as they became known through works critical of the Spanish and Portuguese like Raynal's *Histoire philosophique des Deux Indes,* seemed to those anxious for change to support their belief that freedom of conscience presented no danger to the order of civil life.[29] The defenders of the traditional order remained unmoved, but, even more important in the context of regalism, the Iberian rulers emphasized that any concessions in this area were the prerogative of the state. A project for an "enlightened" reform of the Inquisition of Portugal during the reign of Queen Maria (1777–99) noted, "Today no one can doubt that civil tolerationism is a right of Majesty that is of a higher order that belongs to princes, and that our kings put it into practice when they allowed Muslims and Jews to have mosques and synagogues."[30]

For the critics of the Church in the last decades of the century, *intolerance* was the term that characterized its most negative features, while for the defenders of traditional religion *tolerationism* had become a catchword that described the worst aspects of secularism. Catholic defenders of intolerance emphasized that unity of religion had historically eliminated social division and had promoted peace and prosperity. Moreover, to find equality in religions was to turn away from the fact that the Church bore witness to a revealed truth. If there was only one path to salvation and thus one true religion, then society or the ruler was wrong to permit the worship of another faith. Error could be given no rights as a doctrine, but compassion called for charity toward those individuals deprived of truth or who had become lost. Toleration, then, was always to suffer what is bad. Good needs no toleration. As one defender of the Church's position later put it, "To tolerate good, to tolerate truth, to tolerate virtue would be absurd monstrosities."[31] The union of the "perverse" ideas of liberty and equality with natural law set theologians and jurists in Spain and Portugal and in the American colonies into a defensive stance justifying the utility and moral imperative of intolerance.[32]

The reformers contradicted this position on practical and theoretical grounds. Manuel de Aguirre, an officer in a cavalry regiment and a contributor to the periodical press under the pseudonym of "the Ingenuous Soldier," penned in the 1780s a number of letters that criticized the tradition of religious intolerance and exclusion, what he called "the terrible monster of intolerance disguised beneath the respectable cover of religion." In the *Correo de Madrid* of May 7, 1788, he argued that the expulsion of the Jews and then of the Moriscos had only benefited other nations and deprived Spain of their industry and energy. The presence of competing beliefs would force those who held or preached the true faith to make their arguments even stronger. Denouncing superstition and intolerance, he argued that "civil tolerance has made happy and populous all the possessions of Catholic, ecclesiastic, and Protestant princes of Germany; the hereditary states of the great Catholic Emperor; rich and powerful England; admired France; industrious Holland; the enviable country of the Swiss; and the nascent but already powerful American republic and other kingdoms whose genius, order, peace, wealth and simple and honest customs we admire."[33] Opponents responded that such ideas would lead to the "total freedom of conscience and independence from Supreme Powers." Aguirre was seen as a purveyor of the poison of Voltaire and Rousseau, and his arguments naturally led to prohibition of these issues of the periodical and charges against the author. The Inquisition's sentence is revealing both in its recalcitrance toward change in this matter and in its recognition that this policy originated with those in authority: "Intolerance is a fundamental law of the Spanish nation, it was not established by the common people, and it is not they who should abolish it."[34]

Tolerance in the Portuguese Enlightenment

Despite variations owing to national differences and the specificity of its situation, the Portuguese case followed a similar trajectory in regard to tolerance and the emergence of sentiments in favor of freedom of conscience. On the parallel between Castile and Portugal, the archconservative Spanish historian Marcelino Menéndez Pelayo wrote disapprovingly, "How could it be otherwise, if at the same time we had [both] bathed in the troubled streams of encyclopedism, laughing at one of the quips of Voltaire, and enraptured ourselves in Rousseau's apotheosis of the savage life."[35] The winds of the Enlightenment had blown across Portugal, which, during the first half of the century, the reign of Dom João V (1706–50), had enjoyed substantial prosperity as Brazilian gold flowed into—and out of—the country. The New Science, rationalism, and the works of authors like Descartes, Locke, and Voltaire began to circulate, especially among those who had contact with the foreign commercial and diplomatic establishment in the country or who themselves had traveled or lived abroad. The term *estrangeirados* (the foreignized) was sometimes applied to them, but modern scholarship has become wary of the concept and its tendency to separate the men intellectually from the context of national life.[36] In any case, these men, both lay and clergy, began to suggest and initiate reforms in science, education, commercial policies, and political organization that kept Portugal current with the general intellectual trends of Europe. Among them should be counted the marquis of Pombal, who had represented Portugal in Vienna and London and who eventually became the virtual dictator of Portugal, where he instituted a series of mercantilist and centralizing governmental reforms, including a reorganization of commerce, university, and other educational reforms, the expulsion of the Jesuits, an attack on branches of the nobility, and in 1773 the abolition of distinctions between Old and New Christians.

For both pragmatic and ethical considerations some of these innovators had also confronted the issue of intolerance as state policy. In Portugal and its colonies, the question of the New Christians continued to plague the national conscience and the preoccupations of the Inquisition into the eighteenth century. Tolerance in Portugal and its colonies always implied an attitude toward this internal minority more than it did in Spain, and that situation continued until Pombal ended the distinction between Old and New Christians and prosecutions for Judaism in the Portuguese tribunals ceased entirely.[37]

By the first decades of the eighteenth century, although the Inquisition was very active in prosecuting supposed Judaizers in Brazil and Portugal, important voices began to be raised against the Inquisition and against intolerance. Dom Luís da Cunha, Portugal's most outstanding diplomat, a man with experience in Holland, Spain, France, and England, had become a convinced opponent of the Inquisition and the policy of intolerance. He had many occasions to seek the help or advice of Jews and Portuguese New Christians in his various posts, and, like Padre Vieira before him, he perceived that their persecution had been a disaster for Portugal.[38] In his *Political Testament* (1736), da Cunha, a firm Catholic, identified three "bleedings" that were weakening the country: an excess of monasteries and nunneries; the pernicious effect of these and thus of celibacy on Brazil, where so many people were needed to work in mines and plantations; and the Inquisition itself, which had driven men and their capital from Portugal to the benefit of other countries. He advocated the return of the Jews to Portugal and argued that in Portuguese India freedom of conscience should be extended to pagans and in Brazil to Jews in order to make those colonies productive.[39] Finally, with a poignant detail the ambassador suggested that intolerance had been the ruination of Portugal. He pointed out that whereas in Spain the French-born Philip V preferred to avoid attendance at the autos de fe, in Portugal the education of the Portuguese ruler Dom João V by the inquisitor-general had made that monarch eager to watch the executions, "as if those miserable unfortunates were not his vassals." Da Cunha added with wistful irony, "Such is the power of upbringing that it makes us lose the sentiments of humanity, and so too were the ideas (although more glorious) that they gave to Dom Sebastião in regard to the Muslims, and with this he lost himself and all [the rest] of us as well."[40]

Another example of such thinking, although by a man of less weight and importance, was the Portuguese writer and diplomat Francisco Xavier de Oliveira (1702–83), usually called the Knight of Oliveira because of his membership in an honorific military order. Oliveira was a free thinker of liberal ideas, and his writings, mostly in French, brought about his condemnation by the Inquisition, an institution he considered retrograde, its theologians, ignorant and stupid. After his conversion to Anglicanism while he was in London, his works and ideas and his conversion caused him to be sentenced to be burned in effigy by the Lisbon tribunal in 1761. His response to the sentence, published as *Chevalier d'Oliveyra brulé en effigie comme Hérétique. Comment et Pourquoi?* (London, 1762), was an impassioned plea for tolerance, particularly of the Jews, and a no less impassioned condemnation of the Holy Office, which he called "an affront to all laws, divine and human."[41] Portugal, he said, will never be happy until the complete abolition of the Inquisition, and he suggested, one suspects with a desire for retribution, that the interests of the kingdom required that the king allow the Jews to have a synagogue in the Estaus of Lisbon, the very palace where the Inquisition presently sat.

While these ideas could be dismissed as the excesses of an apostate *estrangeirado,* they nevertheless represented a change in attitudes that began to circulate among some of the elite and the upper bourgeoisie. Pombal himself was not averse to using the Inquisition for his own purposes as an extension of state power and political control, even appointing his brother as inquisitor-general. But his goals were not those of the Holy Office. His ending of the official discrimination against New Christians was not a singular episode, although in his case it responded more to economic considerations than to moral or philosophical ones. The Portuguese Inquisition itself was "enlightened" under Pombal's direction. A new *regimento,* or set of bylaws, was issued for it in 1774 that did away with the former "cruel use of torture" and other abuses, but the essential thread of the new *regimento* was to emphasize the subordination of the tribunal to the state. As in Spain, the Inquisition's traditional independence of royal authority had always been disliked by the rulers, but at the same time Pombal recognized its utility as a social and political support. Still, there was a new spirit toward religion critical of the excesses of baroque piety, which detracted the people from industry and led to practices unseemly in the age of enlightenment. In Brazil this new spirit was sometimes applied to old problems. In Pernambuco in the 1780s and 1790s, a series of royal governors, under the urging of metropolitan officials and sometimes Inquisition officials as well, imposed increasing restrictions on the celebrations and practices of black and mulatto lay brotherhoods, whose devotions and processions seemed to combine African superstitions with Catholic practices in ways contrary to "the light of Reason."[42] As the shadows of Paris and the slave revolt of Haiti spread over the Atlantic world, the concern with these excesses turned from morality to political stability.

But superstition and popular practice were old targets of control. With state encouragement the Inquisition had turned its interest elsewhere as the currents of foreign thought seemed to be threatening belief.[43] But despite inquisitorial efforts the ideas and books and attitudes continued not only to spread in Portugal, but also to be carried to the colonies as well by returning students, royal officials, merchants, foreigners, seamen, and immigrants. Parallel to this diffusion was a change in the nature and image of the Inquisition itself, which was losing status as a proof of religious orthodoxy, and of family honor, as a sharply declining number of requests to be listed among its officers indicated.[44] By 1821, when the Portuguese Holy Office was finally abolished, there were few willing to defend it, but during most of the eighteenth century it had still represented the orthodoxy and legitimacy of the traditional order.

Utopias of Conscience

Thus despite the restrictions created by religious and sometimes civil authority, at least in certain learned and elite circles the ideas of toleration as outlined by authors like Locke, Bayle, and Voltaire and the example of the benefits that freedom of conscience seemed to bring to England and the Dutch republic were debated and advocated. But did these attitudes penetrate the life of common people? and what might their conceptions of freedom of conscience include?

For many people, to be left alone, to be able to think and read and believe what you wanted without the interference of others, seemed like a dream. It was beyond the reach of most people in the early modern world, and those in authority until the end of the seventeenth century, whatever their religious belief, would have generally agreed that such thinking was profoundly dangerous. Prohibiting the development of such ideas was deemed to be a necessary and legitimate task of the Church. But for many people, the exercise of free will as taught by the Church and of freedom of conscience as a general concept was a desire that the presence of a vigilant Church and state only sharpened. People of different beliefs voiced it. In 1656, the New Christian prisoner Juan de León, who had left his home in Livorno and had traveled to New Spain, where he was imprisoned by the Inquisition as a Jew, lamented out loud in his cell, "What made me come to this infamous land? What was I lacking there, in my homeland where I was born? There, [there were] houses in which each person lives as he wishes and nobody bothers anyone else; not like these houses here where there are the kind of men who treat honorable men worse than blacks."[45]

The idea of a land where each person could live as he wished moved the imagination. Freedom from the constraints of society and the limitations placed on individual behavior was a distant hope in the minds of many. Men like Julio Martínez of Murcia, who boasted that if the Inquisition seized his property he would become a Moor, were voicing a threat that was often, but not always, more a daydream than a reality. Still the idea of becoming a "Turk" expressed a utopian vision for Christians of a world in which morality and constraint were inverted.

That Mohammed's paradise included a promise of sexual liberty was not lost on Christian observers, and for some dissidents, sexuality and liberty were closely associated, as the term *libertine* that began to enter the western European languages more frequently toward the close of the seventeenth century suggested. Sometimes, the desire to live in a land of freedom had more to do with the body than the intellect or the soul. There were always those given to excess and extravagance, men like don Sancho Matamoros, a Spaniard arrested in Lisbon in 1704. Matamoros ate meat on Fridays, blasphemed continually, and said that for him glory was having plenty of food and women. He said, in fact, that he liked women so much that if "Saint Catherine should appear, he would sleep with her too." He was a Salamanca graduate, he said, so he could defend his statements. Freedom for Matamoros was freedom to satiate himself.[46] But in most of the declarations about this desired land of liberty, the visions of unrestrained sex and the land of Cockaigne are absent. The utopia sought here, or at least the one that fascinated and threatened the inquisitors, was usually one of conscience or of thought, not of appetites.[47]

Although the inquisitors sometimes argued that the ideas of freedom of conscience were heretical misconceptions by those untrained in theology, occasionally the people who voiced these ideas turned to Catholic doctrine itself to make their case. The concept of free will (*libre albedrío*) was, of course, an essential tenet of Catholic doctrine that placed moral and ethical responsibility on the individual for his or her actions. The relative role of free will and divine grace had long preoccupied the great theologians, and after the Reformation it had become a matter of central importance within the Christian confessions. The idea that belief should be voluntary and that coercion was against the Church's own doctrine lingered on among the faithful. Julian de Anguieta, who lived in Una in the bishopric of Cuenca, had argued eloquently, among other errors for which he was tried in 1662, that "it is wrong to take from each person the free will to believe that which they wish and to oblige Christians to believe in the law of Jesus Christ by force, and it seems to [me] to be against that which Christian doctrine teaches us."[48]

By the eighteenth century, as social and intellectual changes began to move Europe perceptibly in new directions, religious authority in Spain and Portugal reinforced its defenses against the contagion of irreligion. The ideas of the French Enlightenment in general seemed particularly threatening to the Iberian Inquisitions, so much so that the label of *afrancesado* (frenchified) was placed on anyone who expressed doubts about dogma or gave indications of traces of deism or other dangerous social and philosophical attitudes.[49] After the war of the Spanish Succession and the establishment of the Bourbon dynasty on the Spanish throne, it was natural that French influences would be felt in court circles and political life, but the idea of France as an alternative model was already established in the Spanish world. As a pharmacist in the Canary Islands told the inquisitors in 1707, there was no poverty or subjugation in France because no one there made a point of discovering who each person was or what religion he professed: "And so, he who lives properly and is of good character may become what he wishes."[50] This was, of course, a simplification and an exaggeration of the status of toleration in France, where the Huguenots had been pragmatically tolerated under the Edict of Nantes in 1598 but where that concession had also been revoked in 1685.[51] In reality, heterodoxy tended to be prosecuted among the lower classes and allowed to some extent among the "libertines" of the upper class. But it is fair to note that authors on toleration like Bayle, who radically advocated the right of an individual to freedom of conscience and whose books, although prohibited in France as elsewhere, were widely read, became, along with Voltaire, Rousseau, and others, the creators of "the devotional literature of the new cult of humanity."[52] Many Spaniards from a variety of social strata found these ideas attractive.

But while Spanish and Portuguese reformers, thinkers, and authors, because of linguistic affinities and religious commonalities, tended to look first for Gallic inspiration, it was really England that held a special place both in learned circles and in the popular mythologies of liberty and freedom of conscience.[53] It was English empiricism and rationalism that had most attracted the Iberian intellectuals seeking to reconcile the new methods of thought with the traditional order. So too for the popular classes England seemed to present the most attractive model on the matter of freedom of conscience. The question of religious toleration had been an issue of central importance during the English Revolution, and England had passed the Act of Toleration in 1689, granting freedom of conscience and worship to dissenters and, while not extending its protections in law to Catholics and Unitarians, allowing in practice considerable private liberty to Catholics and Jews. Locke's *A Letter Concerning Toleration* was published in the same year, and although neither the act nor Locke's essay had extended full religious toleration to Catholics or atheists, still, both implied an important change in a move away from "the beautiful ideal" of the state as a Religious Society.[54] Even a most ardent anti-Catholic bishop like Gilbert Burnet could write in 1688, during the revolution that placed the Protestant William of Orange on the throne of England, that the God he loved "could never limit to any form or party of religion, and so I am none of those that damn all Papists; for I have known many good and religious men among them."[55] England was moving toward a situation in which freedom of conscience was a matter not of concession but of law, and while the English continued to be somewhat "schizophrenic" on the matter, in comparative terms and especially in practice, it seemed to be a society increasingly given to tolerance.[56]

This was the England Voltaire celebrated in his famous *Letters* of 1726, when he wrote, "An Englishman, as one to whom liberty is natural, may go to heaven his own way," and with characteristic irony he suggested, "If one religion only were allowed in England, the Government would very possibly become arbitrary; if there were but two, the people would cut one another's throats; but as there are such a multitude, they all live happily and in peace." Voltaire's popularity among Iberian dissidents in the eighteenth century is surely undeniable, but it would be an error to see only his hand in shaping attitudes toward England and its toleration. In fact, well before he wrote, many people in the Spanish and Portuguese Atlantic world held a positive image of England as a place where liberty of conscience was firmly established and looked to that country as a model for their own hopes in that regard. For example, in 1606, Father Diego de Paixão, while on an English ship, discovered that a short, dark-haired Portuguese, a native of Oporto, was serving as the second in command. When the priest questioned the mariner as to why he was living among these heretics, he was told by the man that he did so because he could live there with "freedom of conscience."[57] A century later, Pedro de León, a young man from Alicante, was arrested when in a dispute he claimed that the French and English could find salvation in their religion. He knew this from his own experience, having sailed with both as a captive and then as a corsair, having lived in Marseilles and England, and finally sailing from Guinea to Buenos Aires, where the incident took place.[58] Men like this sometimes demonstrated a keen willingness to speculate about matters of religion and theology, to choose belief for themselves, to change their minds about such things, or to grant the possibility that it was best to let each person decide individually. By the time Leandro Fernández de Moratín, the distinguished playwright of eighteenth-century Spain, wrote in 1792 that "in England there is an absolute freedom of religion; in following the civil statutes each person can follow the belief he chooses and the only one called infidel is he who does not comply with his contracts," there were many others far less distinguished who had already reached that conclusion.[59]

A Caribbean Crucible

Within the Iberian Atlantic perhaps no area was more susceptible to the penetration of foreigners and their ideas than the Caribbean. Since the sixteenth century freebooters and contrabandists of various nations had raided and traded in the area, and by the mid–seventeenth century, the Dutch, English, and French had all been able to establish their own settlements and colonies and with them their ideas and religion. From the point of view of Spain's claim to exclusive control and its desire to avoid the contagion of heresy, the foreign presence was filled with dangers.[60] The dangers of the Caribbean situation were outlined by fray Antonio de Chincilla, the commissary of the Holy Office on the island of Santo Domingo, who wrote a memorial to the king in the second half of the seventeenth century.[61] He complained that in the Caribbean region, which included twelve administrative units, or *gobiernos,* and extended for some four hundred leagues, there were hardly any qualified agents of the Inquisition because it was hard to establish the bloodlines and thus the orthodoxy of many of the Spaniards and also because many people were mestizos. The Inquisition tribunal at Cartagena de Indias did not send out visitors, and in places like Santo Domingo and Puerto Rico there were scarcely any agents of the Holy Office. They were sorely needed because of the continual landings of English, French, and Dutch ships loaded with slaves and other goods. This explained why in the time of Philip II, despite negative economic consequences, seven towns in the north of Española had been abandoned to avoid the danger of contact with the foreigners in matters of religion. Devoid of proper controls, the area had also been under the threat of Portuguese, that is, crypto-Jewish, arrivals, and Chincilla emphasized that in Puerto Rico, Caracas, and Isla Margarita many of the families that held important offices and positions were of suspect origin. The presence of heretics was all the more serious because Indians and mestizos could be infected by their contacts, and the native peoples were already easily given to magic, pacts with the devil, and the use of herbs for poisons and potions. To make matters worse, there were also constant jurisdictional squabbles between the bishops of the region and the Inquisition over who had the authority to publish the edicts of the faith that were necessary to warn people of these spiritual dangers.

By the eighteenth century contact through commerce, contraband, and warfare was creating a space of continual interchange in which ideas and books as well as goods and people were moving between imperial systems. Places like the Dutch outposts at Aruba and Curaçao, just off the Venezuelan coast, with their populations of Catholics, Protestants, and Jews, for example, became societies of continual cross-religious contact, places of conversions, intermarriages, and interchanges. So much so that the priest on Aruba could report to his bishop in Coro, Venezuela, in 1753 that local Jews had voluntarily contributed money and materials for the building of the church.[62] The Inquisition was always on guard against foreigners who might introduce heretical ideas. When someone tried to engage William Hallafan, an Englishman living in Vera Cruz, about his religion, he answered, "Let's leave this alone and find a way to eat and survive."[63] Nicolás Silverio, who resided in the Río de Sinú, was really Silverio Aterle, a native of the island of Guadalupe, the child of French parents. He had become a corsair and had passed to Curaçao and eventually to the north coast of South America, where he settled. He argued that those baptized by Protestants were not damned and neither were the Carib Indians. He also argued that his friend Henrique Dutric from Brussels, who also lived in the region, was no heretic. Raised a Catholic, Dutric had been arrested in 1709 for expressing many doubts about doctrine. He did not believe in hell or purgatory, he claimed papal bulls were just an excuse to raise money, he did not confess regularly, he had sexual relations with pagan Caribs, and he believed that good works would free a person from purgatory. He had also said that "each person is in the position that he must perform in this world," in other words, each person had his own star and his own destiny.[64]

The opportunities and openings presented by these contacts were not lost on many in the Hispanic world. People crossed imperial frontiers with relative ease and found opportunities and freedoms in their passage. I want to examine three American cases of the eighteenth century in which religious tolerance was expressed and in which a desire for freedom of thought played a central role. All these cases involved relatively unlettered, simple men, one a soldier, the others mariners, but all were literate, all set a high priority on freedom of conscience and on what they could read, and all expressed an admiration for lands where such freedom seemed to be a reality.

The first case in this trilogy is a true Caribbean odyssey. Antonio de la Abuja was a native of Candás in the principality of Asturias. Born about 1685, he had arrived in Cartagena de Indias on a small ship from Santo Domingo. In his sea chest he had carried a number of books, and he recommended them openly, especially a copy of the Holy Scriptures in Spanish. Someone noticed that these books did not have the usual licenses and warned Abuja that they might be prohibited volumes. Abuja said he had no interest in heresy, but since the books were in Spanish they seemed good to him. The friend with whom Abuja resided then took the books to the rector of the Jesuit College for an opinion of their contents, and the Jesuit recommended that they be taken to the Inquisition. The inquisitors wanted to know more. Abuja was arrested.[65]

He recounted his life story. All of his grandparents and parents were Old Christians, and he had been baptized, confirmed, and instructed as a Catholic. He knew his prayers well and gave every indication that he had been raised a Catholic. He also knew how to read and write but had never attended university. Abuja had left home at eight years old and made his way to Cádiz and from there had sailed to the Indies. From Cartagena de Indias he had made voyages as a mariner to various ports of the Caribbean, eventually reaching the Dutch island at Curaçao, where he had stayed for a few years, serving as a sailor on Dutch ships in contraband trade along the Venezuelan coast and also visiting the Virgin Islands and the islands of the French and English. He had finally returned to Cartagena, where for three years he had shipped out as a sailor on vessels involved in the slave trade to Dutch and English islands. At one point he had been captured by the English and taken to Bermuda and from there to Carolina. Abuja was a man who crossed cultural frontiers easily, and his experience demonstrated the futility of policies that sought to isolate the Spanish Indies from foreign influences. But it was his taste in reading materials that most troubled the inquisitors.

Abuja's chest had contained four books. His favorite was a folio volume in Romance (Spanish) entitled *The Holy Scripture with the Apocryphal Books.* This he had bought on the island of Barbados from a Jew named Moses Brandon, probably a Portuguese New Christian named Brandão. This was forbidden fruit. The Spanish Inquisition had prohibited the reading of scripture in Spanish or any other vulgar language since the 1550s, and the various indices of prohibited books had sought to keep this literature out of the hands of ordinary people.[66] Abuja wanted to know for himself. He brought it, he said, so that he could read the Bible. If it was written in Spanish, how could it be bad?

The other books were smaller, quarto volumes of a similar nature, including a volume in Spanish entitled *The New Testament of Our Lord Jesus Christ,* "given to him by some English friends on the island of Carolina." In these he had read little, but in the folio volume he had read often because that book seemed to him "good and beneficial." He claimed he had no idea that these volumes and the Holy Scriptures in particular might be bad since it had been printed in Amsterdam and corrected by don Sebastián de la Encina, minister of the Anglican Church! Abuja may have been sadly misinformed, extremely frank, or simply ingenuous, but his desire to know things for himself indicated an independence of mind that led him to other difficulties.

One witness reported a conversation with Abuja that I reconstruct from the trial proceedings. The witness had called the English "damned heretic dogs."

Abuja responded, "How do you know the heretics are damned?"

"Like the Moors," said the witness.

"And how do you know that the Moors are damned?"

"Because they are unbaptized; all those who are outside the community of Our Holy Religion are damned."

"How do you know? Have you seen it, has someone come to tell you so?"

"I know this by the light of faith. Why would you ask me if I know if heretics or Moors are damned?"

Abuja then answered, drawing on his understanding of scripture, perhaps from his own reading of the Bible, "St. Thomas says, 'Love God above all else and your neighbor like yourself.' Aren't the Moors and heretics our neighbors [próximos]?"

"All of Adam's descendants are."

"Then how can you wish evil for our fellowman by saying that they are damned?

Here was the proposition that others might find salvation from a merciful God, and in his testimony Abuja indicated that there were those among the English who were charitable and did good works, and while he told the inquisitors that none could be saved without faith in God, it seemed to him that some of the heretics might be saved, and that God, in an act of piety or mercy, could not allow all to be damned. If that happened, said Abuja, then "the fruit of Christ's blood would be lost."

He held other heretical propositions as well, and the inconsistencies in Abuja's testimony, such as his claim that he thought that because the books were in Spanish they must be good, revealed deception on his part. In later sessions before the judges he admitted that he had ridiculed relics and that he had doubts about the presence of Christ in the Eucharist and reservations about the existence of purgatory. He began to interpret the Bible himself. It was, for him, "the book of books, the law of God, and what God and the Prophets had said." He admitted that since the Bible had come into his possession he "had some inclination toward heresy since it seemed to him freer to live in liberty, but he had never been sure in this, and had lived undecided between the two faiths."[67]

Eventually, Abuja recanted. He sought mercy and asked to be reconciled to the Church. He admitted hiding money to keep it from being confiscated by the court. He was contrite. He asked for the Inquisition to take his life or place him in some monastery where he could serve God. A medical report indicated that he had a confused mind with a tendency toward dementia. The court was relatively lenient. He was sentenced to reconciliation in a public auto de fe with a sanbenito, various religious obligations, the confiscation of all his property, and then two years of penitence in Seville. In 1711, along with other prisoners, he boarded the flagship of the galleon fleet and sailed for Spain to serve his sentence.

To this point Abuja's tale and the disposition of his case by the religious authorities seems typical of that of many of the dissidents examined here, but his story was far from over. The galleon carrying him and the other prisoners was attacked and captured by the English three days out of port, and Abuja and the others were taken to Jamaica. He had no desire or reason to return himself to Spanish sovereignty, and so Abuja settled on the island, living with and finally marrying a Catholic woman from the island of Curaçao, having three children with her. He earned his living as a mariner on English ships, most likely in the contraband trade. For Abuja, Jamaica, the metaphorical land of liberty, had now become a reality. In 1716, while on the Spanish island of Trinidad, he was recognized and seized; after various adventures and attempts to escape, in one of which he broke out of the leg stocks and went overboard trying to swim for shore off Panama, he was eventually returned to the prison of the Cartagena Inquisition, this time as an impenitent, relapsed heretic who had remained willfully among the Protestants of Jamaica to avoid his sentence.

Abuja was able to tell the inquisitors in detail the nature of his marriage ceremony and that of the baptism of his children, all of which were done in the Anglican rite. His confusion or liminal position between his Catholic identity and Protestantism seems to have continued. So too did his desire to read. He continued to read the Bible in Spanish and the liturgy that the English called *The Book of Common Prayer.* He explained that, "having no other spiritual nourishment, he recited those prayers some days." He asked for pardon, but in the meanwhile he was trying to pry the bars of his cell from the old walls of the jail. He still clung to the old propositions: he thought that confession directly to God was best, he doubted the power of the saints, he did not wear a rosary, and he admitted that in Jamaica he had lived as a Protestant, "but he always had doubts about these things." What he tried to argue was that he had wished to live and die among the Protestants of Jamaica, but not in their religion, that is, he sought to make a distinction between their civil or political society and their religion.[68] He had married in the Protestant rite, but only to protect the legal rights of his wife and children. He had accepted the Protestant faith, but he did not attend their churches. He tried to convince the inquisitors that he had always believed that the religion his parents had taught him was best. On his beloved books, however, he was clear. He had continued to read his books because he enjoyed them so much, and that if this was heresy and apostasy, so be it.[69] This time he was sentenced to a public auto de fe, perpetual prison, and seven years at the oars in the king's galleys. He sailed for Seville as a prisoner on the *Xavier* in March of 1719.

What to make of Abuja and his story? Our tendency to see the world of faith in terms of clearly defined beliefs and confessional loyalties has come under questioning by recent scholarship. Theologians and learned men could see the differences, but for people like Abuja, the lines between the religions were not always easily defined. The possibility that a person might select different elements from them or that private practice might differ from public adherence seems to be confirmed by his story. Not only were there gray areas between confessions, there were people like Abuja who lived in those areas, accepting some beliefs, doubting others, and, in his case, trying to decide for himself about God's will.[70] Consistency, theological coherence, and allegiance did not appear to cause him much concern. Even before his residence in Jamaica, it had been this kind of thinking that had led him to believe there might be positive aspects in any or all the faiths and that even heretics or Moors might be saved, and he was not alone.

Felipe Tendeur was a Catholic. A soldier from Brabant in the Lowlands, he had entered the king's service at an early age and had served in Catalonia before being stationed in the castle of San Luis de Bocachica, which guarded the port of Cartagena de Indias. He had been taught to read and write by a Dominican friar, and he liked to read. He owned a few books — an Old and New Testament, another book in Swedish with some woodcuts of saints that he liked, and also a book in Dutch called *Prayers and devotional songs for seamen*. It was this book that was the source of his troubles. Some other member of the garrison had seen the book and had asked Tendeur about its contents. Tendeur replied that it was a heretical text, and the questioner responded that reading it might cost him dearly. Tendeur dismissed the warning with a defense based on his creative and selective reading. He claimed that he "read the good parts and left out the bad ones, and that he could read the books that he liked." His companions were not satisfied. They warned him that he would pay dearly for his reading if caught, and someone had been threatened enough by Tendeur's independence to have taken the book later and burned it. Tendeur was furious and made threats against the culprit.

Tendeur seemed to have a reputation among his companions for religious doubts and strange opinions. At one point he refused to buy papal bulls of dispensation, claiming that soldiers did not need to purchase them since the king bought the dispensations for them. His interests were materialistic. When someone had told him that he should thank God for making him a Catholic, Tendeur responded that God had done nothing for him and could have just as well made him a heretic as given him wealth. In a conversation about social hierarchy, when asked if he would consider marrying an Indian woman, he had answered that if she had wealth, it would be more important to him than if she was a heretic or an Indian, and he appears to have put his ideas into practice by maintaining a relationship with a woman of suspect lineage. His attitudes, his choice of a female companion, and his reading preferences led to warnings that the Inquisition might punish him, to which Tendeur answered with a soldier's bravado, but at the same time revealing in his answer a concept of the possibilities of liberty. If the Inquisition challenged him, he said, "he would become a pirate and burn the Inquisition and Cartagena along with it, and it would be easy for him; there was nothing like living in Jamaica where there is freedom of conscience." Another witness claimed that what Tendeur had said was that as a pirate he would become "the greatest blade against the Spaniards, especially the friars and priests." In the Indies, the Turkish dream had been transformed into a pirate fantasy, and the island of Jamaica, under English control since 1655, turned into the equivalent of Constantinople, a metaphorical land of liberty.

Arrested, Tendeur put up an able and intelligent defense. He claimed he had acquired the book in Dutch from a French ship only so that he would not forget his native language. As for the book in Swedish, he ingenuously told the inquisitors that there was little difference between that language and Dutch. In any case, he had only read these books "out of curiosity," and for no other reason. The inquisitors suspected he was a heretic and a potential danger to the faith and to the port. He was tortured with little restraint, given five turns of the rack. He became suicidal and was beaten by his jailer, but through it all he refused to admit to the charges of heresy. When urged to save his soul by confession and repentance, he answered that the Inquisition had deprived him of his honor, and now he did not care about his soul. He was sentenced to exile from the Indies and service in the king's armies.[71]

There is much in this case that merits comment, but lest one dismiss Tendeur too quickly as a foreigner despite his long residence in the Hispanic world, one should consider another case with many parallels involving a Spaniard, although one who had admittedly spent much time abroad. Juan Pablo de Echigoíen was born in San Sebastián in Guipúzcoa around 1725. He had gone to sea at the age of nine in English ships, probably as a cabin boy and then as a *grumete,* or novice seaman, and by the time he was eighteen he had become a pilot serving in the armadas of Spain and the kingdom of Naples. Echigoíen knew much of the world. He had lived in London and had sailed to Jamaica and to other Caribbean islands of the French and the Dutch. He had finally gone to New Spain, and there in the mines of Chontalpa he had raised suspicions about his origins and orthodoxy. He owned a book in English of heretical content and he could not speak Basque properly, and those facts plus his questionable opinions led to a denunciation to the Inquisition of Mexico in 1761. Someone gained his confidence, elicited his opinions, and then reported him to the Inquisition.

What were these questionable ideas? First of all, he was a Copernican. He believed that it was the earth, not the heavens and the stars, that moved. The heliocentric view of the universe was, of course, contrary to dogma and had been considered formally heretical since 1616.[72] He was also accused of being a Freemason and of having said and approved of the fact that this organization admitted members without regard to sect or religion, even allowing Jews to join, "since they only sought good men [*hombres de bien*]." He claimed that many kings and Spanish nobles, Jesuits, and the governor of Cuba were Freemasons, and that even in Madrid, at the Puerta del Sol, a Masonic lodge operated. His positive comments about the English were thought to be evidence that he was, in fact, a foreigner. When someone had spoken positively about the charity of a zealous person, Echigoíen had said that his former master, the ship captain, although a Protestant, had been even more charitable. When told that such charity was worth little because as a Protestant the captain was condemned to hell, Echigoíen had responded with the ancient argument: "Shut up, all can be saved by different roads."[73]

This was, of course, a heretical proposition, and the inquisitors at first thought that since Echigoíen had been raised among the English that perhaps he had been uninstructed in the true religion. They were interested in the religious details of his biography. It was a fascinating story. He was of old Christian stock, baptized and later confirmed by a Catholic bishop in Ireland. He had received religious instruction from an English Jesuit and could recite his prayers properly in Latin. The English master in whose service he had entered had taught him to read and write, and although a Protestant, the captain not only never deterred him from the Catholic religion, but had also insisted that the sailors on board never ridicule him or seek to make him a Protestant. On this point he was adamant and appreciative. He told the inquisitors, "Neither the said master nor any other Englishman with whom he dealt ever spoke to him about matters of religion because it is a political law among the English and in all of England not to speak with Catholics or with persons of other sects on matters of religion, and it is one of the principal maxims of their government that everyone should live in liberty."

Life in England suited Echigoíen, and he had lived there for over twenty years, but eventually pressure to marry the niece of his patron had moved him to return to Spain. Hoping to make his own fortune, and with a one-hundred-pound gift from his former master in his pocket, he sailed from Cádiz to Jamaica in hopes of using his maritime experience and his command of Spanish and English to enter the contraband trade. In two years he had amassed a fortune of seven thousand pesos, but in a storm in St. Anne's Bay off Jamaica he lost it all. He found passage to Havana and from there to Mexico.

The inquisitors remained skeptical of Echigoíen's orthodoxy. They wanted to know more about the heretical book in English reported to be in his possession. He explained that the pilot on the ship that had carried him to Havana was also a Freemason and had given him the book and asked him to translate it. On board ship, others had asked him to read it aloud, and, to satisfy their curiosity and their desire to hear English and its pronunciation, he had done so. Like Tendeur, Echigoíen claimed that the combination of the aural and visual aspects of his books was what fascinated him, not their heretical content. He too liked to hear the sound of a language familiar to him, and he very much appreciated the illustrations. He told the inquisitors that he had shown the book to others because the plates were so beautiful and because he wished to demonstrate that the English also had saints in their books.

The investigation dragged on, and Echigoíen became despondent. He seemed to go mad, but a medical examination returned the opinion that his dementia was feigned. He was finally sentenced in 1765 to abjure *de vehementi* in a public auto de fe, exiled from the Indies, and sent to serve for four years without pay in the Moroccan garrison outpost at Ceuta. Like Tendeur and Abuja, Echigoíen had not read Locke or Voltaire. Their opinions were formed by life's experiences and their own perceptions, and they held out hopes for themselves and for others.

Luso-Brazilian Libertines

The questioning of dogma and the impact of rationalism as well as the persistence of superstition were no less apparent in the Luso-Brazilian world. To some extent this was perhaps an unintended result of the centralizing policies of the marquis of Pombal, whose expulsion of the Jesuits in 1759 and attempt to restrain ultramontanism and make the Church a pliable arm of the state had weakened respect for religion. By the 1770s and 1780s, as the state imposed an end to the campaign against New Christians, the *Cadernos do Promotor,* the Inquisition's notebooks of denunciations, were filled with charges of witchcraft, bigamy, doubts about the Sixth Commandment, and a series of heretical propositions about the validity of the concepts of heaven, hell, and salvation. From Lisbon to the far corners of the empire there were prosecutions of such ideas. And of men like Manuel Joaquim, a ship captain resident in Lisbon, who believed in a God of infinite mercy and held a practical view of the question of salvation: "We cannot judge if the heretics will be saved or lost, and if they are all going to hell, a bigger hell will be needed. They also praise God as do the birds of the sky."[74]

The defenders of authority sought an explanation for what seemed to be a rising tide of irreligion on both sides of the Atlantic. In Portugal itself the impact of the Enlightenment could be seen in many ways as it penetrated from the cities and universities into the countryside. In 1779 the local priest of Vilaflor in the province of Tras-os-Montes denounced a young man for a series of heretical propositions. The man in question, Manuel Felix de Negreiros, had studied medicine at Coimbra and lived in Oporto, but his father had owned a property in Vilaflor, and the son had come out to the country to see the couple that made olive oil on the old property. He had studied theology and canon law at Coimbra, and he was thought to be very learned, so his remarks had been particularly shocking. He had said that the doctrine of transubstantiation showed that the Church could lead one to believe that that which was absent was real and that which was real was absent.[75] He also said he doubted the existence of hell because "it is incredible that a sin which is momentary would be punished eternally," and finally and most seriously, he asked why, if Christ's power was infinite, so few nations had been convinced to follow him? Negreiros was a man of quality and had lived for awhile in the home of the marquis of Marialva. The priest was certain that he was a follower of the "diabolical maxims" of Voltaire, and another witness testified that Negreiros, in fact, carried a volume of Voltaire in his coat pocket. His discourse was also flippant. He said only the English were enlightened because "they eat meat while we get *bacalao* (codfish)." Negreiros was, it was claimed, a man "full of liberty and without religion."

Such attitudes were not found exclusively in well-connected Coimbra graduates in Portugal but across the empire.[76] Take, for example, Maçal Ignacio Monteiro, former administrator of the Company of Grão Pará e Maranhão, who supposedly read not only Voltaire, but also Machiavelli's *Prince* as well as the works of the seventeenth-century Venetian theologian Paulo Sarpi, a critic of papal authority. An informant stated that Monteiro not only read these books but shared them with others.[77] He was by all accounts a "libertine in his speech," and he showed little respect or fear of the Holy Office. *Libertine* implied at the time a person who believed that reason rather than revelation was the best guide to understanding. This at least was the definition given by the Brazilian-born Antonio de Morais e Silva, author of the first dictionary of the Portuguese language and himself denounced as a libertine to the Inquisition.[78]

This spirit of dissidence and disregard for the authority of the Church was by the final decade of the eighteenth century a matter of growing concern. The Inquisition itself was increasingly questioned, an attitude that had deep roots in Brazil, where, as we have seen, since the sixteenth century New Christians and Old had often demonstrated hostility toward the Holy Office.[79] Antonio Rodrigues de Sousa, a *familiar*, or lay agent, of the Holy Office in Guarupi-tanga, Ouro Preto, brought charges in 1779 against three prospectors who had defamed him by calling him a mulatto and by implying he had acquired his office by bribes. They had tried, he said, "to stain the incorruptible spirits of the Inquisition's most noble officers." And they had done it in the way that carried real weight in colonial society, by playing the race card.[80]

People at various social levels expressed their doubts about Catholic orthodoxy. Joaquim José Gomes dos Santos was a Pernambucan who captained a corvette named the *Santissimo Sacramento*. Almost everyone on board, the chaplain, the doctor, the pilot, and the crew, denounced him in 1791 for his outrageous ideas and irreverence. He was a libertine, he ate meat on prohibited days, and he claimed that nature had created the world. He was a man, they said, "inclined to read French books and to be friendly with others who also read them," and he had no compunctions about debating his ideas with others on the voyage. In fact, Gomes dos Santos admired the English, who, he said, made their voyages without having to pray continually. His liberal ideas scandalized everyone. He shocked the chaplain by asking why Christ had waited so long to bring salvation since so many souls had already been lost by that time. He compared Mohammed to Christ not unfavorably, and said that if Christianity was the true law, then Portugal should be the most opulent and wise country, but instead it is the poorest, most ignorant, and worst governed. The Turks and Tartars, like the English and Dutch, nations that the ignorant or uninformed call barbarians, are in fact better off in their way because they had eliminated the worst abuses in the system of government. If there was a God, he had not favored the Portuguese. The use of force by Christianity to spread the gospel had been successful only against small countries and weak peoples like the blacks of Africa or the "rustic people of America" because such tactics could not be used against great empires.[81]

The fact that Gomes dos Santos was denounced demonstrates that many people still upheld orthodox belief, but the numbers of dissidents were increasing. Not surprisingly, the question of the exclusive validity of the Church also reemerged in this atmosphere of doubt.[82] In 1794, an inquest was held in Rio de Janeiro in order to question the actions and ideas of a group of young men supposedly infected with French, that is, revolutionary, ideas. These men often gathered at the shop of António Bandeira on the Rua do Ouvidor, the principal street of the city, where conversation often turned to controversial matters. Bandeira, an outspoken critic of the Church, was reported to have often stated that there was salvation outside the keys of the Church, and he had even gone further by offering this proposition: "Given the situation that the French are in, although they have done badly in regard to the obedience and death of their sovereign, nevertheless, they can be saved outside the dominion of the Roman Church."

As had long been feared, freedom of conscience was now being tied to other kinds of liberty. And why had this happened? An anonymous poet in Spain reacted in 1794 to the French Revolution and its attack on monarchy and God with the following dialogue:

And who has created a France
Without faith, force or opulence?

The freedom of conscience.

And what is the primary cause of
Cases so scandalous?

Writings so seditious.

And these writings, why have they
Created such sedition?

Because there is no Inquisition.[83]

The Long Good-bye

A profound transformation of political and religious attitude took place
in Spain and Portugal in the last decades of the eighteenth century, during
which the terms *intolerance, religious toleration, freedom of conscience,* and
Inquisition came to represent conflicting political, social, and religious views
of the world. Both sides used a rhetoric of hyperbole that expressed the depth
of feeling and the belief that the essence of the nation's soul and its future were
at stake in the resolution of the question of tolerance. The virulence of the
rhetoric employed by the liberal critics of the Inquisition in the battles that
characterized the Iberian transition to the nineteenth century disguised the
fact that the activity of the Holy Office as well as its power had declined in the
second half of the century. The auto de fe became a private rather than a public
ceremony. Madrid celebrated its last public auto in 1680 and Lisbon in 1683.
Punishment now became a more private act conducted within churches before
an audience of invited dignitaries. As the influence of the state over the tribunals grew there was an increasing reluctance to having clerics making essentially political decisions, and so spiritual matters were separated from political
ones. In Spain, only fifty-six people received public punishments in the period
1759–1788, and very few were executed. In Portugal, Pombal ended discrimination of New Christians in 1773, thereby removing the principal targets of
inquisitorial control from the tribunal's hands. The new Inquisition bylaws
issued in 1774 also made clear the state's control of the tribunal. And in the
same year, for political and commercial reasons, Pombal also abolished the
Inquisition tribunal in Goa, which in the eighteenth century had been the most
active and most repressive of all the Portuguese tribunals. Although it was
reestablished in 1778 following his fall from power, all of these events signaled
a diminishing power and respect. For example, the attraction of being part of

the Holy Office's apparatus was no longer the same. In Portugal, the number of appointments of *familiares* of the Inquisition fell precipitously after 1770, a sign of the declining prestige of the institution as a way of acquiring honor, legitimacy, and status. The activity of the Holy Office itself also declined. The three tribunals of Lisbon, Coimbra, and Évora had tried 7,204 cases between 1675 and 1750, or about ten cases a year, but from 1751 to 1767 it heard only 743 cases, or a yearly average half the previous level. Still, the ratio of executions to trials did not diminish, remaining at just about 4 percent of those tried.[84]

In many ways rather than a groundswell of popular opposition or the telling critiques of Liberal opponents, it was centralizing regalism that undercut the role of the Inquisition and the official policy of intolerance it represented. The crowns of both Portugal and Spain sought to bring their Inquisitions under control but also to redeploy ecclesiastical authority toward more political ends. Since its beginnings the crowns and the ecclesiastical establishments had sought to use the Inquisition for their own purposes, but the Inquisitions had developed distinct goals and at times operated quite independently of royal or episcopal authority. By the mid–eighteenth century there were many in state and ecclesiastical service who saw the Inquisition as an anachronism and a liability. But even in the 1790s reformers moved with caution. The Spanish minister Gaspar Melchor de Jovellanos wrote in 1794 that feelings against the Inquisition were still not general and that the best way to control it was to dismantle it piecemeal, giving its religious authority to the bishops and its censorship duties to the Council of Castile.[85]

The actual abolition of the Inquisitions of Spain and Portugal came as part of the changing political and intellectual milieu of the period. Napoleon's invasion of Spain led to abolition of the Inquisition in 1808 by the French invaders because it represented a challenge to civil authority.[86] The Cortes, or Assembly, that was convoked in Cádiz in 1810 to organize resistance to the French invasion was dominated by Liberals and Jansenists who set about drawing up a constitution, and they too abolished the Inquisition in 1813; the abolition was short-lived, however, and with the return of the monarchy in 1814 the acts of the Cortes were declared void and the Inquisition was restored in Spain and, in the following year, in the Indies as well. In 1815 the new inquisitor-general issued an edict in unrelenting rhetoric and once again defined the Inquisition as "the only means to save the precious deposit of the faith and to suffocate the evil seed planted in our land by the immoral gang of Jews and sectaries who have profaned it and also by the shameful freedom of writing, copying, and publishing."[87]

During these turbulent years two important events had taken place in rela-

tion to the tribunal. First, the abolition of 1808 had resulted in the appoint-
ment of the secretary of the inquisition, the priest Juan Antonio Llorente, to
collect and catalogue all the tribunals' papers. He did this task well and then
between 1812 and 1818 published a number of well-researched and highly
critical studies of the Inquisition that fueled the subsequent debates and criticisms of the tribunal.[88] Second, such criticism had led to a mobilization of the
defenders of the Inquisition, who now linked their insistence on the continu-
ance of the Inquisition to the popular defense of country, king, and religion.
Toleration and Inquisition became the warring symbols of two opposing visions of Spain. A liberal revolution in 1820 forced the king to accept constitutional monarchy and with it the Constitution of 1820, which abolished the
tribunal; by 1823, however, the absolutists with foreign aid had again restored
the former system and with it the Inquisition. Despite the desire by the most
conservative elements in society to restore the prosecution of heresy and to
maintain the policy of official intolerance, the Inquisition was finally abolished
in Spain in 1834, the American colonies having done away with their tribunals
as part of the movements for independence in the period from 1814 to 1825.
In Portugal, the Inquisition had kept a low profile during the Napoleonic
period and had not been a central issue. It was abolished finally in 1821 after a
liberal revolution that sought to establish constitutional monarchy in that
country.

It has become popular to find in the Enlightenment the origins of the social
ills of the modern world. Both its successes and its failures have been seen as
forerunners of the worst aspects of modernity, and to its rationalism and the
separation of religiosity from public life have been ascribed the origins of
genocide, racism, and other social ills. The Enlightenment surely had its shadows and its shortcomings. The exploration of human diversity contributed to
a belief in cultural hierarchy that contained the seeds of racialist thought.[89]
Few of the philosophes paid any attention to the rights of women, many of
them had little regard for the "vulgar classes," and the strain of anti-Semitism
in Voltaire is well known. The advocates of liberty were often blind on the
issue of slavery, and from ports like Bordeaux and Nantes merchants proud of
enlightened views and their own Masonic memberships could, without com-
punction, name their slave ships *L'Ami de la paix*, *Fraternité*, and even *Tolèr-
ance*.[90] But to apply to that age the standards of our own deforms and ob-
scures its achievements. Its failures were due not to the paths it took, but
rather to how far down those paths it traveled. Sometimes, as in the case of
slavery, it would be their spiritual heirs and godchildren in the next generation
that would carry the program forward to the abolition of the slave trade and
eventually of slavery itself. On the issue of religious tolerance, Enlightenment

The abolition of the Inquisition in Barcelona.
Popular joy and celebration as the palace of the Inquisition is ransacked. This unsigned view is
one of the very few that commemorated these events. (Archivo Oronoz)

thought had moved away from a toleration born of incapacity and exhaustion
in which religious diversity was suffered because suppression was too costly or
because no other alternative was possible. It had also moved beyond the toleration of pragmatic convenience in which foreign allies or merchants and minorities were allowed some freedom because it was advantageous or profitable
in some way. Instead, toleration was now a matter of human rights and the
equality of opportunity and freedom that all deserved. Toleration had to be
conceded because to do so was fair and proper, and in the long run, as some
argued, it was also an attitude in keeping with natural law as well as a policy
good for the state and its citizens. But in the midst of these ideas strongly
associated with the arguments of the Enlightenment, Iberians could also look
back on their own tradition. In 1813, during the heated debates and pamphlet
war about the Inquisition, a satirical poem in Castilian and Galician appeared.
Called the *Pleas of a Galician,* it found in Christian roots and in the ancient
Iberian refrain the reason to oppose intolerance:

> The law of Jesus Christ is a law of charity and love
> We should take its counsel and not betray it
>
> We should live well and have compassion for our neighbor,
> For God is who illumines us and guides our hearts

The people live in the law that they inherited from their grandparents,
The Moor in his, the Galician in his, each judges his is best.[91]

The verses were, of course, suppressed by the Inquisition. The defenders of the traditional order always tended to see these ideas and their rationale as extraneous importations, but such an interpretation simplified a far more complex reality which the Inquisition's own documentary record contradicted. The Enlightenment authors on toleration had provided a systematic view of religious toleration as part of a bundle of concepts beneficial to all societies.[92] Their ideas resonated in Spain and Portugal as elsewhere in Europe and in the Americas, but long before such ideas became a moving intellectual and social force, there had been many in the Iberian world and, I suspect, elsewhere who had already reached a similar conclusion. Without expectation of gain or advantage they had advocated tolerance because it seemed just. Some had argued that only God really knew what religion was best; some had thought that all religions might be valid; others could not believe that those who lived according to natural law and who did good works would be condemned by a merciful deity; others believed that Christ's life and message were one of patience and forgiveness. And there were those who doubted the validity of all religions and for whom personal belief and salvation were not an issue. All of these people provided the context of tolerance in which the ideas of the Enlightenment could flourish. They were as much the precursors of modernity as their more literate and eloquent contemporaries.

9

Rustic Pelagians

Historians often seek the continuities between the distant past and more recent periods, and they are trained to be sensitive to the peculiarities of each culture and each historical moment. It would be easy enough to suggest that the peculiar multireligious past of medieval Iberia, where Christians, Jews, and Muslims coexisted for so long despite their conflicts and animosities, had created attitudes of live and let live that manifested themselves as relativism in matters of religion. Similarly, it could be argued that the unification of Spain in 1492 and the forced expulsions or conversions of Jews and Muslims led to the dissimulation of their true convictions and ambiguity about the existence of any truth, and that this eventually created among them attitudes of skepticism, indifference, materialism, and doubt. But such interpretations would not be adequate to all the evidence at hand. A considerable number of those denounced to the Inquisition for relativism in matters of religion were, in fact, foreigners, not Spaniards or Portuguese. Many of those who expressed doubt or indifference were not Conversos or Moriscos, but Old Christians of unquestioned lineage. Despite the objectives of the Catholic Reformation enforced by episcopal courts and the Inquisition, such ideas and doubts were long-standing and impossible to entirely suppress. And Spaniards and Portuguese were certainly not alone in holding these attitudes. Increasingly the histories of other countries in Europe reveal their existence.

While the Iberian world with its plurireligious history, its ethnic minority populations, and its experience of empire building in faraway lands and previously unknown continents may present a special case, evidence has been growing for decades that the attitude of popular tolerance in matters of religion was a generalized phenomenon in much of Europe, but that historians commonly overlooked it because so much of early modern history has been cast in terms of religious conflicts, violence, and in the process of confessionalization; that is, in the inculcation of religious identities. To uncover the substrata of tolerance one must go beneath the histories of state policies and religious dogmas that have dominated the writing of history, and one must look not primarily in learned discourse (usually controlled) and at the policy of governments and kings, but in the actions and words of people who sought to think for themselves. What I have tried to do in this book is to demonstrate that in the Iberian world, a cultural sphere in which because of official policies of intolerance such ideas might be least expected, dissidence in matters of faith was common and an attitude of tolerance, at least among some elements of the population, had long existed. Whatever the specificities of the societies of Spain and Portugal, that attitude of tolerance was in fact shared across most of Europe, and recognition of its long-overlooked existence is the key to understanding how the formalized theories of toleration, the great texts of Bayle, Locke, Voltaire, and others, eventually became part of the general intellectual and political life of modern Europe.

In the past few decades a new generation of scholarship has moved the discussion of religious toleration away from the almost exclusive concern with the chain of great thinkers, humanists, theologians, and philosophers, who produced "the devotional literature of a new cult of humanity" that seems to form the genetic link to our own attitudes. Instead, historians have moved toward a careful study of the social and political contexts that created the conditions for toleration.[1] Rather than an inspiring story of the triumph of conviction, it is now more often a tale of pragmatism and convenience. The history of toleration had been mostly about the relationships and struggles between established churches or denominations and only secondarily about the conditions of Jews or other nonbelievers. Studies of religion in early modern Italy, Germany, the Netherlands, and central Europe have analyzed the conditions under which forms of religious toleration, freedom of worship, and freedom of conscience were accepted or rejected. Whereas the previous story of the slowly won victory of an idea achieved by a series of singular thinkers still inspires us, now much more emphasis is placed on the social and political contexts at various levels that influenced the pragmatic decisions leading to toleration.

This more generalized approach has revealed the extent of religious dissidence and the depth to which it penetrated. Work on early modern Italy, the Holy Roman Empire, Poland, and Hungary has enriched this vision. Much of it has essentially extended the story of the *politiques* into other historical contexts. Once again, however, that has meant an emphasis on state and church policies and actors, but this line of study has also, at times, uncovered attitudes of tolerance among the unlettered and laboring classes of those societies as part of the general history of religious conflict.[2] The relative weight and importance of those attitudes usually depended on the changing social, political, and ecclesiastical environment in each country. France and England can serve as useful examples for comparative purposes. The history of early modern France has long been dominated by the central theme of religious strife and the division of the country into the warring camps of Catholics and Huguenots.[3] By 1560 France had perhaps two million Protestants. Their existence could not be ignored by the Catholic majority, and it was seen by some even as a sign of impending divine judgment. Toleration was not favored by those in power, and it was usually advocated only as a temporary solution, although there were always some voices, like Michel Montaigne and Jean Bodin, who opposed the use of force in matters of religion, or like the Catholic Michel de L'Hôpital, who were willing to argue that the use of coercion could not produce true belief.[4] There were limits that the people themselves imposed. The French ambassador to Rome was informed in 1561 that he should convey to the pope that the French were subjects of their king, but "where their consciences are concerned I have always found that they are amazingly stubborn."[5] The emergence of a modus vivendi signaled by the Edict of Nantes (1598), which guaranteed Protestants the free exercise of their religion, and then its revocation in 1685 have been cast for generations in terms of political necessities and religious enmities. What the crown conceded out of weakness, it revoked a century later from a position of strength. By the 1660s, a forceful repression of the Huguenots had reduced their numbers to less than a million, and their position was increasingly precarious. There was certainly much interfaith violence in the period and considerable evidence of intolerance as state policy, but that was not the only tale to be told.

For at least a decade historians have been exploring the story of confessional coexistence rather than conflict, especially at the local level. Despite the constant effort by ideologues and propagandists on both sides to enforce separation and promote mistrust, there is much evidence of this coexistence and tolerance. In Béarn and Sedan Catholics and Protestants prayed in each other's churches; in La Rochelle, they shared a church. During the St. Bartholomew's

Day massacre, the governor of Provence refused to kill the Huguenots, and when a mob from Rouen came to Dieppe to kill Protestants, the governor locked the city gates to keep them out. In Saillons in the Dauphiné members of the two religions testified in 1599 that "they lived peaceably and as good fellow compatriots together in the free exercise of their religion." In 1664 in the Dordogne, the Catholics and Protestants of Saint-Méard shared the cost of a bell for their respective churches.[6] In Poitou, Catholics and Huguenots found ways to share adjacent cemeteries in mixed communities, at least until persecution intensified.[7] The Canadian historian Gregory Hanlon has examined the town of Layrac in Aquitaine in detail and has revealed an extensive coexistence in this mixed community where Protestants and Catholics interacted, intermarried, and interfered with each other on a continual basis to the dismay of the spiritual leaders of both. This coexistence was not a matter of toleration as a philosophical position but rather the outcome of practical considerations at the local level, and interaction tended to create ambiguities and sometimes indifference to differences of dogma.[8] The drive for coexistence, what the French historian Olivier Christin has reminded us was called "the peace of religion," grew not only from pragmatic considerations and a political need to limit violence, but also from a sense of community in some places and from a general desire for order and stability.[9] Such arrangements could be found across sixteenth-century Europe from the Swiss cantons to Poland and the Netherlands as well as in France.[10] To make these arrangements possible in a world increasingly concerned with heresy and God's imminent punishment was the challenge that rulers and theologians confronted, and often when the need to do so diminished, as it did in France in 1685, they pushed for religious conformity.[11] But the evidence of cooperation or amity across religious divides raises the question about alternatives and their origins. Christian charity, incredulity, indifference, and doubt all made their contribution to tolerance alongside the programs of the *politiques*.

The history of England offers an even better vantage point from which such attitudes might be viewed. England, after its separation from Rome and its creation of a national church, was an intolerant society, one in which nonconformists and Catholics suffered repression and restrictions, but there is also considerable evidence of reluctance to persecute neighbors and a certain flexibility or ambiguity in matters of religion.[12] The history of England suggests that a current of doubt, incredulity, and dissent had long characterized popular religious thought and that sentiments of tolerance and of religious relativism were often expressed by the common sort of people. Much of what is known of these attitudes must be gleaned from works that were composed specifically to combat and correct them. George Gifford, a Puritan preacher, published his

Brief discourse of certain points of the religion, which is among the common sort of Christians which may be termed the Country Divinity in 1581.[13] Written as a dialogue between the well-informed and religious Zelotes and the naïve and heterodox Atheos, it underlined the essentially latitudinarian or relativist thinking of the common folk that Atheos represents. He believes that God is merciful and is not so severe a deity as Zelotes argues. Atheos holds that no one really knows who is among the chosen and who is damned, and too many of those like Zelotes think only of damnation. Atheos objects to ministers who intervened in people's lives, the "busie controllers," who seek to impose religion when all that was really necessary was "good neighborhood" and the willingness to be part of the community, at times "to drink and be merrie." "It is well that God has not given you power to condemn men," Atheos tells his zealous questioner. Atheos's arguments reveal a dissent from the order and conformity that religion sought to impose. His own salvation was for him not in question: "I mean well, I hurt no man: nor I think no man any hurt: I love God above all: and I put my whole trust in him: what would you have more?" Zelotes's response was that much more than this was called for from a true Christian, but it was a message that seemed difficult to convey.[14]

Skepticism, ignorance, and doubt among the common people in the parishes was also the target of Arthur Dent's *Plaine Mans Path-way to Heaven* of 1601, another book that went through numerous editions and which sought to contradict a series of objections to orthodox Protestant thought that reflected the discourse commonly heard in response to the preachings of the "godly." As the historian Barry Reay has pointed out, Bible reading and preaching, central to Protestanism, had little meaning for the many who were illiterate and who saw the crux of their faith not in an ability to quote scripture, but in living by the golden rule. "I knowe, that soo long as I keepe his Commaundments, and live as my neighbors doo, and as a Christian man ought to doo, he will not damn my soule."[15] The emphasis on living a good life, believing in God, and doing no harm was a kind of "rustic pelagianism."[16] It could be found not only in the country parishes of England, but in the villages of France, the cities of Andalusia, in the mines and plantations of America. At the edge of the world in Chiloé in southern Chile, Pedro Ramírez was denounced in 1573 for saying that "faith was a dead thing without charity, and that they were the same thing."[17] The lesson of Matthew 22 had not been lost. Love God above all else, and love your neighbor as yourself. If Christianity was about both truth and charity, it was charity that moved many to believe they were following God's path by accepting difference and living in harmony with those who sought salvation in their own way.

In England as elsewhere the continual complaints of clergymen about immorality and the shallow nature of religion grew from their frustration with the culture of superstition, drinking, games, and dancing. Until 1650 laws required church attendance and Communion by all, but even though church courts used excommunication to enforce compliance, many people remained recalcitrant, and even those who complied with their religious obligations found that the quality of their religiosity remained in question. With the Revolution of 1640 and the removal of state controls of religion and with it the flourishing of a variety of sects, the previous tendencies toward heterodox if not heretical opinions always feared now became a reality. Religious and social radicalism seemed to combine in those groups who contested the authority of the established church and the position of its learned ministers. This was the short-lived "world turned upside down" of England in the 1640s that the historian Christopher Hill did so much to recreate.[18]

Here too there is a text that reveals the extent to which such radical ideas seemed a threat. The Presbyterian minister Thomas Edwards's *Gangraena* (1646) is a sometimes hysterical condemnation and catalogue of a variety of popular beliefs and religious deviations that threatened religion and social order. In the three volumes of his diatribe he identified over two hundred heresies. He singled out, for example, the belief that reason should be a measure in matters of faith; that coercion should not be used in questions of religion; that the soul died with the body; that God could be known directly through nature; that Christ's death provided for the salvation of all; and that men may be saved without Christ, and heathens may be saved within the knowledge that God has given them. All of these and many other deviant ideas are remarkably like the heretical salvific propositions that were commonly expressed in the Hispanic world.[19] In the England of the Puritan Revolution, however, such ideas could at least momentarily thrive among a variety of denominations or sects, all of which represented to Edwards the threat of political and theological disorder. As William Walwyn chided Edwards in an ironic tone, the real threat was that unlettered men should seek knowledge not directed by the learned and that commoners should have the liberty to examine all things.[20]

What most preoccupied Edwards, however, was the specter that toleration in matters of religion and complete freedom of conscience would become state policy and that coercion in matters of faith would end.[21] He asked, "Should any man seven years ago have said [that many soon would] be for Toleration of all Religions, poperies, Blasphemie, Atheisme it would have been said, It cannot be" (*Gangraena* 1:121). But while strict Puritans and Presbyterians like Edwards still felt that the political order, the magistrate, needed to enforce religious conformity and that the state and religion could not be separated, more radical groups were less inclined to that position so long as political loyalty was not in question. Debate on the issue was joined in political rather than theological terms.[22] Concessions on toleration were made in England but denied in Puritan New England not because of a difference in theology, but because the political realities were distinct. The 1650s had made freedom of conscience in England—except for papists—a reality and even though after 1660 the gentry and crown again imposed limitations, the issue of freedom of conscience remained alive, and a limited toleration was extended to some dissenters and in practice to Catholics as well. The Act of Toleration of 1689 was a political compromise following the Glorious Revolution of 1688 that granted limited toleration to Protestant dissenters, and while Catholics, Unitarians, and atheists were still not included in its protections, the tide of toleration could not be reversed.[23] Champions of religious pluralism had emerged, and now even men of very conservative opinions believed that "liberty of conscience was a thing of advantage to the nation."[24] Locke's famous *Letter Concerning Toleration* (1689) rode the crest of that tide. Its singular contribution was to frame the argument for toleration in terms of individual freedom of conscience, but in its denial of toleration to Catholics and atheists it still represented the political climate in which it was born. By the eighteenth century full freedom of conscience and lack of religious restraint still did not exist in England. Roman Catholics and anti-Trinitarians suffered legal restrictions, and ecclesiastical courts, although now limited, could still prosecute blasphemy and atheism, but toleration itself had taken on a positive connotation. As Daniel Defoe's Robinson Crusoe reported proudly from his island, his man Friday was a pagan cannibal, the Spaniard was a papist, and he was a Protestant, but he allowed "liberty of conscience throughout his dominions." In fact, in the colonies forms of religious toleration and freedom of conscience had been granted in Rhode Island, Maryland, New York, New Jersey, and Pennsylvania before 1750. The social context of toleration in England and its colonies was changing, and although it was still incomplete and imperfect, to some observers in Spain, Portugal, and their empires, as we have seen, as well as to Voltaire, England and its colonies seemed to present the demonstrable advantages of freedom of thought. England was, said Voltaire with a mixture of admiration and Gallic condescension, "a nation of many faiths, but only one sauce."[25]

Spain and Portugal had a different trajectory, but the attitudes that led to tolerance in England and that could be found elsewhere in Europe were by no means lacking in the Iberian world. In Catholic Spain, the ideas of Desiderius Erasmus of Rotterdam that called for the peaceful reconciliation of dissenters had great appeal in some quarters until they were stamped out. Philip II considered the possibility of making concessions to religious dissent, at least among Christians, but finally decided for unity. His return to Castile in 1559 was accompanied by a tightening religious repression, an attack on Erasmians and potential pockets of Protestant thought, and the increasing control of thought and publication by the Inquisition.[26] Still, there were voices in protest of repression. Fray Luis de Granada's *Introducción del Símbolo de Fe* (1582), a popular work that went through multiple editions and printings, argued that anyone who harmed heretics, Moors, Jews, and unbelievers was committing a worse sin than they committed. Such arguments were always tempered by events and by relative positions of power. Advocates of freedom of conscience were for the most part usually in the minority or out of power when they made their statements, and almost no one in the sixteenth century believed that religious plurality was a positive goal. To allow it was a concession in order to achieve peace; a temporary measure, a lesser evil. It was tolerated.

But that did not mean that Christian imperatives for peace and harmony were lacking. The idea of Christian charity, the admonition to love thy neighbor, the desire for peace and community, all of which the historian John Bossy called "the moral tradition," existed across denominations. The problem was finding a balance between that tradition and the drive for orthodoxy and conformity.[27] On various occasions, the Inquisition moved against people who had spoken out against coercion or who had cited Christ's admonition to love thy neighbor as thyself as a criticism of force. Bossy sought the moral tradition in Jesuits and Calvinist preachers, but he might have found more fertile soil for these thoughts in the reasoning of simple folk.

The Luso-Hispanic Advocates of Toleration

Looking back over the course of the three centuries covered in this study and seeking to find some general characteristics of those who made expressions of religious tolerance or universalism, I note some patterns that merit comment. First of all, just as they were rarely prosecuted for all propositions, women were rarely accused. I suspect this is a result of the Inquisition's tendency to be more interested in what men had to say rather than of any gendered difference in thinking. Second, whatever the reality of the *convivencia* of the Iberian Middle Ages, the idea that salvation was possible for those of other faiths was certainly not limited to Spaniards and Portuguese. I examined hundreds of cases in which expressions of tolerance, religious relativism, indifference, or criticism of the Inquisition's imposition of orthodoxy were voiced. The Belgian scholar Werner Thomas has identified 100 cases of such remarks among those accused of Protestanism, the vast majority of them foreigners. In a separate sample, I have identified another 116 instances of persons prosecuted for propositions in which people made reference to the specific phrase that "each person can be saved in his or her own faith" or its equivalent. In them, about 35 percent of those prosecuted were foreigners—Italians, Frenchmen, Savoyards, Greeks, Flemings, and others.[28] While the converts from Islam or Judaism might have a special proclivity to this argument and reasons to believe it, they, in fact, were only a small portion, about 20 percent, of the Spaniards and Portuguese accused of this proposition.[29] The majority by far were Old Christians. The idea of salvation outside the Church and relativist thinking about religions were also not limited to any one social group. It could be found among clerics and university students, but also among merchants, artisans, agricultural workers, and Morisco slaves. It is therefore difficult to characterize this idea as part of either a "popular" or a "learned" culture. It was an idea that cut across the boundaries of social class and reached all segments of the population, although various elements of the population may have reached a similar opinion by quite different paths. Out of a sample of 67 people accused of religious relativism for whom there is information about their occupation, about 15 percent were priests or friars, especially Franciscans, who would have had some familiarity with theological debates and some occasion to speak about such issues, but at the same time over 20 percent of the accused were workers or slaves. By the eighteenth century the accusations of *tolerantismo* seem to fall increasingly on artisans and on growing numbers of soldiers and sailors, whose mobility and supposedly dissolute lifestyles were a matter of concern. Literacy was, of course, another characteristic often associated with dissident thought, and at least 30 percent of those in this sample could read and write, but it should be noted that the trial records often make clear that those accused who were literate had not studied at universities.

What is remarkable about these people as a group is that in the contexts of Spain, Portugal, and the American colonies they seemed to have little to gain personally by their tolerance. Unlike France, England, and Germany, where confessional divisions had made life almost unbearable, or places like Holland and Poland, where there were political or economic advantages to be gained from tolerance, in the Hispanic world the context of a single state religion promised no immediate benefit for toleration. Conversos or Moriscos or foreigners might have their personal reasons for believing in the validity of their ancient faiths, and merchants might be looking to some gain in the distant future, but for the most part the expressions of tolerance by Old Christian Iberians seem to be born of experience and of a genuine conviction and sense of justice and not from a hope for direct advantage. It has sometimes been argued that the early modern advocates of religious tolerance were always in a minority position and this particular argument was a weapon of the weak. This seems not to have been the case in the Iberian Atlantic world. While there were certainly skeptics and the incredulous among those who spoke for religious tolerance, most seem to have had doubts about particular teachings or positions of the Church rather than about religion or their faith as a whole.[30] Sometimes in plain language and sometimes with considerable sophistication they sought to make their own interpretation of God's will, and they often spoke openly of their desire for liberty, by which they had in mind what Isaiah Berlin had called in his famous essay "negative liberty," the right to be left alone to do or to think or to read without coercion.[31] By the end of the eighteenth century the winds of Enlightenment thought had reached into the Iberian world, and in shops in Rio de Janeiro, garrisons in Cartagena de Indias, and on the streets of Seville the old tolerance could now be set into a new philosophical and political framework, as could the desire for liberty, no longer limited to conscience but extended to the political sphere as well, where all men might hope to share in power. In other places this was a major step on the road to modernity, but in Iberia religious toleration did not triumph. The institutional structures of Spain and Portugal, the continued authority and position of the Church, and the weight of social practice and political thought simply proved too strong to overcome.

An Elusive Goal

As we saw in the preceding chapter, by the mid–eighteenth century the Holy Office in Spain had lost its vigor and to some extent its former vocation as a weapon against heresy and an enforcer of conformity. Increasingly its concerns were bureaucratic and self-serving.[32] A flurry of activity in the first two decades of the century aimed principally at supposed Jews was something of a last spurt of activity. By the 1760s, as liberal and reformist ministers sought to increase royal power, the inquisitors were losing ground. The Inquisition did nothing when the Jesuits were expelled in 1766, and while it tried to limit the flow of subversive and foreign ideas and could sometimes prosecute a prominent figure like Pablo de Olavide, its power and influence were waning. The desire for more open commerce with the non-Catholic nations of Europe moved creoles in America and Spanish reformers toward a more open policy in regard to freedom of conscience. The French Revolution of 1789, however, reversed the picture dramatically. The king dismissed most of the liberal reformers at court and turned again to the Inquisition as a tool against the ideas of revolutionary France and against liberalism and secularism in general. When Napoleon's armies entered Spain in 1808, the emperor declared the Inquisition abolished, but the continuing instability and warfare in the peninsula left the matter unresolved. The question of the Inquisition was now part of a larger debate between liberals and those who wished to maintain Spain's traditional order. Defense of the Church and of the traditional order also took on a protonationalist significance. The two sides carried out a virtual war with volleys of books and pamphlets in which the Inquisition was a central and symbolic issue. In 1813 representatives met in the Cortes of Cádiz to discuss a new constitution, and they voted to abolish the Holy Office, but at the same time they legislated that Spain was a Catholic country and no other religion would be allowed. In 1814, with the return of the archconservative Fernando VII to the throne, the Inquisition was reinstituted as the best guarantee of the kingdom's morality and unity, and in 1815 Fernando VII, called by one North American contemporary "a bigoted biped," reinstated the Spanish American tribunals as well. Although the tribunal no longer had any real effect, it became a principal icon of the traditional order and was therefore the rallying point for absolutists and defenders of the Church and the principal target of the Liberals. In 1820 another Liberal movement again moved to limit absolutism and again targeted the Inquisition for abolition. A similar movement in Portugal actually did eliminate the tribunal in that country, but in Spain foreign intervention on behalf of the monarch cut short the movement for change.

In Latin America similar struggles took place. During the late Bourbon period various defenders of the traditional order rose to argue that obedience to crown and altar was the surest guarantee of social harmony. Following the Comunero Revolt in New Granada (Colombia) in 1781 the Capuchin Fray Joaquín de Finestrad wrote his *El vasallo instruido* to convince the rebels of the blessings of Religion and Throne.[33] During the turbulent years of the crisis of legitimacy following the Napoleonic invasion of Spain the ideas of freedom of religion were reported and discussed widely in various regions of the Americas and soundly denounced by the defenders of monarchy, Spain, and the Church.[34] During the 1820s, the Latin American revolutions attacked the American tribunals of the Inquisition as symbolic of Spain's despotism and abolished them as part of the movements for independence. But by the time of their demise, their function was no longer necessary because the theological and political convictions for maintaining the exclusive position of the Catholic Church as a bulwark against religious diversity remained deeply ingrained in many segments of the population, including those who favored political change. Most of the principal architects of independence, Miguel Hidalgo and José María Morelos in Mexico, Mariano Moreno, José de San Martín, and Miguel Belgrano in the Río de la Plata, all advocated the exclusivity of the

Catholic faith in the new nations. Simón Bolívar was somewhat exceptional in his desire to separate Church and state, but he too realized the advantages of a clergy loyal to the new order.[35] Almost all the newly independent nations of Latin America made Catholicism the state religion. In the creation of the early constitutions of the new governments even those men who favored religious toleration in various degrees were willing to compromise on the issue to achieve the political goal of independence. The issue, however, divided Liberals and Conservatives through much of the following decades, but not until the mid–nineteenth century and later did religious toleration become the law in most of Spanish America.[36]

In 1834, with the death of Ferdinand VII, Spain itself finally eliminated the Inquisition, but its demise was no lasting triumph for the Liberals. The bishops assumed the prosecution of heresy and freedom of religion. The Roman Catholic religion remained the only legal religion with the short-lived exception of a stillborn liberal constitution in 1869 and provisions in the constitution of 1876 that, while allowing private freedom of religion, prohibited any public celebration of a religion other than Catholicism. Throughout the nineteenth century religious toleration remained, in the words of the historian Francisco Tomás y Valiente, "the bastard child of liberty." But the underlying doubts and questions about religion and salvation continued to weigh heavily on the minds of many in the Hispanic world.

The echoes of the old refrain continued. Miguel de Unamuno, one of Spain's most brilliant and complex novelists, placed in the heart and mind of his protagonist Manuel Bueno, a saintly parish priest whose own faith had weakened, these words: "True religion? All the religions are true in that they make the peoples that profess them live spiritually, in consoling them that they have been born to die, and for each people the truest religion is theirs, the one they have made."[37] In 1931, the year Unamuno's novel was published, the Constitution of the Spanish Republic provided for the separation of Church and state and full religious freedom. Francisco Franco's victory in the Spanish Civil War in 1939 overthrew that document and once again created a tight alliance between Church and state. It was not until 1978 that the full guarantees of freedom of religion became Spanish law.

In Portugal, while the Inquisition was abolished under pressure for liberal reforms in 1821, the Church remained closely supported by the state during the monarchy until the Republican revolution of 1910. That government proved to be anticlerical and limited the Church in various ways. With the establishment of the dictatorial government of António Salazar (1932–68), however, a close relationship with the Church was reestablished by a concordat signed with Rome in 1940. That relationship was ended in 1971. In the

Portuguese constitution of 1976, article 41 established freedom of conscience, religion, and worship and separation of Church and state. In Brazil the first constitution in 1824 made Catholicism the official religion, and other religions, while permitted, were not allowed public display. The members of non-Christian faiths were not accorded the full rights of citizenship. Not until the Republican Constitution of 1891 was full freedom of religion legalized.

Finally, for the Church itself the question of its role in the salvation of all peoples and the nature of its relationship to the other world religions has remained an issue in continual debate and theological disagreement. The papal encyclical *Mystici corporis,* issued by Pope Pius XII in 1943, stated that those not really within the Church could not be part of its mystical body and were therefore excluded from supernatural life, but it also suggested that those outside the Church might be related to it by "unconscious desire and wish," even if only implicitly. This left the door to salvation ajar to non-Catholics. For the remainder of the twentieth century and until today, Catholic theologians have sought to reconcile the seeming conflict of these two statements. The pendulum of interpretative orthodoxy has swung between a restrictive and an ecumenical position. The Second Vatican Council in 1962, with its pastoral and ecumenical goals, was a major effort to clarify the issue. It accepted the concept that people might be associated with the Church *in voto,* or by desire, and could demonstrate that association by belief and deed. These people were potential Christians or, as one theologian called them, "anonymous Christians," and they might also hope for salvation. These ideas were codified in the papal document *Lumen gentium,* which went further than previous statements in affirming that other Christian churches might also have a role in salvation, albeit an imperfect one because they were separated from Rome. Some conservative Catholic thinkers found the ecumenical emphasis and the idea that because divine grace worked in the hearts of all people of good will to be treading too close to the old heresy of apocatastasis, the belief that eventually everyone will be saved. This, of course, was the same criticism that had been made of Menocchio in Friuli and of many of the people in Iberia and in Latin America that I have discussed in these pages.

By the early twenty-first century *Lumen gentium* was being subject to a more restrictive interpretation. The declaration *Dominus Iesus* (2000), issued by the Roman Congregation of the Faith, whose chief architect was the theologian Joseph Cardinal Ratzinger, emphasized the Church as the "universal sacrament of salvation." It was a statement in defense of the unique role of the Roman Catholic Church in salvation and a negation of any leveling of religious difference. With the election of Cardinal Ratzinger as Pope Benedict XVI in 2005 both Catholics and non-Catholics waited to see whether the venerable dictum *extra ecclesiam nulla salus,* the same idea that had troubled the Iberian dissidents, would again guide Rome's relations with the rest of the world.[38]

At a moment when a new religiosity, sometimes expressed as fundamental-ism and fanaticism, can be found in various religions, and when the separation or union of religion and civil authority is again in question in many countries, it is clear that there was nothing necessarily inevitable or permanent about toleration or freedom of conscience in the creation of the modern world. The growth of religious toleration in the early modern period and its triumph in the twentieth century resulted not only from the philosophical breakthroughs of learned thinkers, the self-interested calculations of statesmen, and the surge of secular and rational thought, but also from common people who, drawing on their own experiences, their own understanding of the tenets of their faith, and their own sense of justice, created a soil of tolerance in which such a policy could grow.

Notes

Abbreviations

ACC   Gracia Boix, Rafael, ed. *Autos de fe y causas de la Inquisición de Córdoba* (Córdoba: Diputación Provincial, 1983).

AHR   *American Historical Review*

CB   *Primeira visitação do Santo Ofício ás partes do Brasil. Confissoes Bahia 1591–92*. J. Capistrano de Abreu, ed. (Rio de Janeiro, 1935).

DB   *Primeira visitação do Santo Ofício ás partes do Brasil. Denunciações Bahia, 1591–92*. J. Capistrano de Abreu, ed. (Rio de Janeiro, 1925).

DCP   *Primeira visitação do Santo Ofício ás partes do Brasil. Denunciações e confissões de Pernambuco, 1593–95* (Recife: FUNDARPE, 1984).

DP   *Primeira visitação do Santo Ofício ás partes do Brasil: Denunciações Pernambuco, 1593–95* (São Paulo, 1929).

HIEA   Pérez Villanueva, Joaquín, and Bartolomé Escandell Bonet, eds., *Historia de la Inquisición en España y América* (Madrid: Biblioteca de Autores Cristianos, 1984–2000).

HEP   Bethncourt, Francisco, and Kirti Chaudhuri, eds., *História da Expansão Portuguesa*, 5 vols. (Lisbon: Círculo dos Leitores).

HP   Mattoso, José, ed., *História de Portugal*, 8 vols. (Lisbon: Estampa, 1993–94).

HRP   Moreira Azevedo, Carlos, ed., *História religiosa de Portugal*, 3 vols. (Lisbon: Círculo dos Leitores, 1998).

IG   García Fuentes, José María, *Inquisición en Granada en el siglo xvi* (Granada: Universidad de Granada, 1981).

RCM   Pérez, Llorenç, Leonard Muntaner, and Mateu Colón, eds., *El tribunal de la Inquisición en Mallorca. Relación de causas de fe* (Palma de Mallorca: Miquel Font, 1986).

SRHJ   Baron, Salo, ed., *Social and Religious History of the Jews*, 18 vols. (New York: Columbia University, 1952–93).

Archives

ACA   *Archivo de Casa de Alba (Madrid)*
ADC   *Archivo Diocesano de Cuenca*
AGN   *Archivo General de la Nación (Mexico City)*
AHN   *Archivo Histórico Nacional (Madrid)*
ANTT   *Arquivo Nacional da Torre do Tombo (Lisbon)*
BGUC   *Biblioteca Geral da Universidade de Coimbra*
BL   *British Library (London)*
BNL   *Biblioteca Nacional de Lisboa*
BNM   *Biblioteca Nacional de España (Madrid)*
BPE   *Biblioteca Pública de Évora*
IC   *Institución Colombina (Cathedral of Seville)*
SML   *Sterling Memorial Library (Yale University)*

Introduction

1. Carlo Ginzburg, *The Cheese and the Worms: The Cosmos of a Sixteenth-Century Miller*, trans. John Tedeschi and Anne Tedeschi (Baltimore, 1980). The full trial transcript is now available. See Andrea Del Col, ed., *Domenico Scandella Known as Menocchio*, trans. John Tedeschi and Anne Tedeschi (Binghamton, N.Y., 1996).

2. See Gustaf Aulén, *Christus victor: An Historical Study of the Three Main Types of the Idea of Atonement*, trans. A. G. Hebert (New York, 1951); Stephen Finlan, *Problems with Atonement: The Origins and Controversy about the Atonement Doctrine* (Collegeville, Minn., 2005). My thanks to Carlos Eire for guidance to this literature.

3. Gabriel Flynn, *Yves Congar's Vision of the Church in a World of Unbelief* (Aldershot, 2004), 66–67. See also the comments in Francis Sullivan, "The Impact of *Dominus Iesus* on Ecumenism," *America* 183 (13): 8–15.

4. Heiko Oberman, "The Travail of Tolerance and Intolerance in Early Modern Europe," in *Tolerance and Intolerance in the European Reformation*, ed. Ole Peter Grell and Bob Scribner, 13–32 (Cambridge, 1996).

5. For an example of an outstanding recent work, see John Marshall, *John Locke, Toleration and Early Enlightenment Culture* (Cambridge, 2006). For useful overviews, see Perez Zagorin, *How the Idea of Religious Toleration Came to the West* (Princeton, 2003); Henry Kamen, *The Rise of Toleration* (London, 1967).

6. See, for example, John Christian Laursen and Cary J. Nederman, eds., *Beyond the Persecuting Society: Religious Toleration before the Enlightenment* (Philadelphia, 1997); C. Nederman and J. Laursen, eds., *Difference and Dissent* (Lanham, Md., 1996); J. Laursen, ed., *Religious Toleration* (New York, 1999); Ole Peter Grell and Roy Porter,

Toleration in Enlightenment Europe (Cambridge, 2000); Ole Peter Grell and Bob Scribner, eds., *Tolerance and Intolerance in the European Reformation* (Cambridge, 1996).

7. Joseph Lecler, *Histoire de la tolérance au siècle de la Réforme*, 2 vols. (Paris, 1955); translated as *Toleration and the Reformation*, trans. T. L. Westow, 2 vols. (New York, 1960).

8. See Miguel de la Pinta Llorente, "Intolerancia y barbarie," in his *Humanismo, Inquisición* (Madrid: Editorial "Estudio Agustiniano," 1979), 91–117.

9. Henry Kamen, "Toleration and Dissent in Sixteenth-Century Spain: The Alternative Tradition," *Sixteenth Century Journal* 19 (1988): 3–23. Kamen has changed his position somewhat and now argues that Spain was no more or less tolerant than any other European nation at the time. See "Exclusão e intolerância em Espanha no início da época moderna," *Ler História* 33 (1997): 23–35. He presents a very useful overview as well in "Inquisition, Tolerance, and Liberty in Eighteenth-Century Spain," in *Toleration in Enlightenment Europe*, ed. Ole Peter Grell and Roy Porter (Cambridge, 2000), 250–58.

10. Jonathan I. Israel, *Radical Enlightenment: Philosophy and the Making of Modernity, 1650–1750* (Oxford, 2001), contains extensive discussions of toleration thought.

11. The relationship between the case study and generalization and theory is taken up in Jean-Claude Passeron and Jacques Revel, "Penser par cas: Raisonner à partir des singularités," in *Penser par cas,* ed. Jean-Claude Passeron and Jacques Revel, 9–44. Enquête 4 (Paris, 2005).

12. Jacques Revel, "Micro-analyse et construction du social," in *Jeux d'échelles: La micro-analyse à l'expérience,* ed. Jacques Revel, 15–36 (Paris, 1996).

Chapter 1. Propositions

1. Here and throughout the book I have referred to the numbering of the Ten Commandments as they appear in Exodus 2:2–17. Thus the Sixth Commandment refers to the commandment "You shall not commit adultery."

2. AHN, Inq. Leg. 2022, exp. 9. On the idea of sexual license and communalism among Protestants, see Bob Scribner, "Practical Utopias: Pre-Modern Communism and the Reformation," *Comparative Studies in Society and History* 36:4 (1994): 743–74.

3. John Arnold, *Belief and Unbelief in Medieval Europe* (London, 2006), 1–27, 216–31. The issue was nicely joined in reference to Spain in John Edwards, "Religious Faith and Doubt in Late Medieval Spain, Soria *circa* 1480–1500," *Past and Present* 120 (August 1988): 3–25, and the response by C. John Sommerville, "Religious Faith, Doubt, and Atheism," *Past and Present* 128 (August 1990): 152–55. On Spanish popular religion in the period, see Augustín Redondo, "La religion populaire espagnole au xvi siècle: un terrain d'affrontement?" *Culturas populares* (Madrid, 1986), 329–47.

4. There is an extensive theological literature on the question of heretical propositions which guided the inquisitors. Among the most important was Nicholas Eimerich and Francisco Peña, *El manual de los inquisidores* (Barcelona, 1973), which is a modern version of the sixteenth-century edition of Eimerich's fourteenth-century *Directorium Inquisitorium.*

5. I am following the explanation of Juan Antonio Alejandre and María Jesús Torquemada, *Palabra de hereje* (Seville, 1998), which is the only monograph to date dedi-

cated to the crime of propositions in a tribunal of the Inquisition, in this case, Seville in the eighteenth century. See also "La répression de délits verbaux," in *L'Inquisition espagnole au lendemain du concile de Trente,* ed. Michel Bœglin, 495–576 (Montpellier, 2003).

6. Alejandre and Torquemada, *Palabra,* 21. Discussions of the prosecution of propositions appear in all the principal studies of the Inquisition. For an excellent example of those propositions related to sexuality, see María Helena Sánchez Ortega, *La mujer y la sexualidad en el antiguo régimen* (Madrid, 1991), 179–271.

7. Maureen Flynn, "Blasphemy and the Play of Anger in Sixteenth-Century Spain," *Past and Present* 149 (1995): 29–56, includes an excellent discussion of the medieval attitudes toward blasphemy and a review of the literature on the subject.

8. These distinctions are suggested in part by Jaime Contreras, *El Santo Ofício de la Inquisición de Galicia* (Madrid, 1982), 554–64.

9. Mikhail Bakhtin, *Rabelais and His World* (Bloomington, 1984), 60–144; Umberto Eco, *The Name of the Rose* (San Diego, 1983). The possibility of real disbelief is also raised by the prosecution of propositions, which included statements denying the existence of the soul, the afterlife, or even of God. For an excellent discussion of the problem, see David Wooten, "Lucien Febvre and the Problem of Unbelief in the Early Modern Period," *Journal of Modern History* 60 (1988): 695–730.

10. Luis de Granada, *Guía de pecadores* (1556) (Madrid, 1942), as cited in Flynn, "Blasphemy," 31–32.

11. Flynn, "Blasphemy," 29–56.

12. The violation of the confessional during which priests took sexual advantage of their parishioners has been the subject of a number of recent studies. See, for example, Juan Antonio Alejandre, *El veneno de Dios* (Madrid, 1994); Stephen Haliczer, *Sexuality in the Confessional: A Sacrament Profaned* (Oxford, 1997).

13. Cited by Contreras, *El Santo Ofício,* 561–62. On the virginity of Mary, see the essay by Luiz Mott, "Maria, Virgem ou não? Quatro séculos de contestação no Brasil," *O sexo proibido* (Campinas, 1988), 131–86.

14. Henry Kamen, *The Spanish Inquisition* (New Haven, 1998), 258.

15. Francisco Fajardo Spínola, *Las víctimas del Santo Oficio* (Las Palmas, 2003), 151–92.

16. These percentages are based on my calculations from the figures provided by Jean-Pierre Dedieu, *L'administration de la foi: L'inquisition de Tolède (xvi–xvii siècle)* (Madrid, 1989), 240–41.

17. See Jaime Contreras and Gustav Henningsen, "Forty-Four Thousand Cases of the Spanish Inquisition," in *The Inquisition in Early Modern Europe,* ed. Gustav Henningsen and John Tedeschi, 100–130 (Dekalb, Ill., 1986). See the summary table of the Henningsen and Contreras study in Francisco Bethencourt, *História das inquisições* (Lisbon, 1994), 272.

18. Angel de Prado Moura, *Las hogueras de la intolerancia: La actividad represora del Tribunal Inquisitorial de Valladolid. 1700–1834* (Valladolid, 1996), 140–44, 227.

19. See William Monter, *Frontiers of Heresy: The Spanish Inquisition from the Basque Lands to Sicily* (Cambridge, 1990), 40–49.

20. This has been suggested by R. Po-Chia Hsia, *The World of the Catholic Renewal, 1540–1770* (Cambridge, 1998), 45–46. To date the principal studies of the tribunals of

the Portuguese Inquisition have devoted relatively little attention to propositions and related offenses. See António Borges Coelho, *Inquisição de Évora*, 2 vols. (Lisbon, 1987), 2:262–95; Elvira Cunha de Azevedo Mea, *Inquisição de Coimbra no século xvi* (Oporto, 1997).

21. This point is made by Antonio Bombín Pérez, *La Inquisición en el país vasco: El tribunal de Logroño, 1570–1630* (Bilbao, 1997), 144–50.

22. Ricardo García Cárcel, *Herejía y sociedad en el siglo xvi: La Inquisición en Valencia, 1530–1609* (Barcelona, 1979), 341–42.

23. For an introduction, see Bernardino Llorca, *La Inquisición española y los Alumbrados (1509–1667)* (Salamanca, 1980); Pedro Santoja, *La herejía de los Alumbrados y la espiritualidad en la España del siglo xvi* (Valencia, 2001).

24. See José C. Nieto, *Juan de Valdés and the Origins of the Spanish and Italian Reformations* (Geneva, 1970).

25. This point is made clearly by Christine Wagner, "Los luteranos ante la Inquisición de Toledo en el siglo xvi," *Hispania Sacra* 46 (1994): 473–510. An excellent summary of the suppression of Spanish Protestantism is provided by Ricardo García Cárcel and Doris Moreno Martínez, *Inquisición: Historia crítica* (Madrid, 2000), 256–75. See also the classic work of Marcel Batallion, *Erasmo y España*, 2d ed. (Mexico City, 1966). The most exhaustive study is presented in two volumes by Werner Thomas: *La repressión del protestantismo en España, 1517–1648* (Louvain, 2001), and *Los protestantes y la Inquisición en España en tiempos de Reforma y Contrarreforma* (Louvain, 2001).

26. Cf. Sarah Nalle, *God in La Mancha: Religious Reform and the People of Cuenca, 1500–1650* (Baltimore, 1983); Allyson M. Poska, *Regulating the People: The Catholic Reformation in Seventeenth-Century Spain* (Leiden, 1998); Henry Kamen, *The Phoenix and the Flame: Catalonia and the Counter-Reformation* (New Haven, 1993).

27. The case is presented in detail in Sara Nalle, *Mad for God: Bartolomé Sánchez, the Secret Messiah of Cardenete* (Charlottesville, 2001). On the complex issues of what constituted madness in early modern Europe, see the discussion in Erik Midelfort, *A History of Madness in Sixteenth-Century Germany* (Stanford, 1999), 1–79; and on the Inquisition's perception of madness, see Mara Cristina Sacristán, *Locura e Inquisición en Nueva España, 1571–1760* (Mexico City, 1992).

28. Stuart B. Schwartz, "Pecar en Colonias: Mentalidades populares, Inquisición y actitudes hacia la fornicación simple en España, Portugal y las colonias americanas," *Cuadernos de Historia Moderna* 18 (1997): 51–67. See also the overview provided in Marcel Bernos et al., *Le fruit défendu* (Paris, 1985).

29. When asked in 1595 what he really thought about the relative value of the married state versus that of religious celibacy, the soldier Antônio Pires told the Portuguese inquisitors, "I don't know, it's the *letrados* who know." Cf. Ronaldo Vainfas, *Trópico dos pecados: Moral, sexualidade, e Inquisição no Brasil*, 2d ed. (Rio de Janeiro, 1997), 250. See especially Asunción Lavrín, "Sexuality in Colonial Mexico: A Church Dilemma," in *Sexuality and Marriage in Colonial Latin America*, ed. Asunción Lavrín, 47–95 (Lincoln, 1989).

30. Sergio Ortega Noriega, "El discurso teológico de Santo Tomás de Aquino sobre el matrimonio, la familia y los comportamientos sexuales," Seminario de Historia de las Mentalidades, *El placer de pecar y el afán de normar* (Mexico City, 1988), 17–19.

31. "Simple fornication" was distinguished from "qualified fornication" (*fornicación qualificada*), which included adultery, incest, rape (*estupro*), abduction (*rapto*), and homosexual activity.

32. Bartolomé Clavero, "Delito y pecado: Noción y escala de transgresiones," in *Sexo barroco y otras transgresiones premodernas*, ed. Tomás y Valiente, B. Clavero, et al., 57–89 (Madrid, 1990).

33. Erasmus of Rotterdam's *Enchiridion militis christiani* (1504) emphasized the dangers of "filthy sensuality" and the particular dangers of women and lust, personified as Dame Lechery. See Margaret R. Miles, *Carnal Knowing: Female Nakedness and Religious Meaning in the Christian West* (Boston, 1989), 165.

34. Fray Luis de Granada, *Guía de pecadores* [1556], (Madrid, 1929). Cf. Martin de Azpilcueta Navarro, *Manual de confessores e penitentes*, 2 vols. (Coimbra, 1952). See the discussion in Lana Lage da Gama Lima, "Aprisionando o desejo: Confissão e sexualidade," in *História e sexualidade no Brasil*, ed. Ronaldo Vainfas, 67–88 (Rio de Janeiro, 1986).

35. Jean Delumeau, *Sin and Fear: The Emergence of a Western Guilt Culture, 13th–18th Centuries*, trans. Eric Nicholson (New York, 1990), 431–32. See the basic work by James A. Brundage, *Law, Sex, and Christian Society in Medieval Europe* (Chicago, 1987). On Portugal, see Angela Mendes de Almeida, "Casamento, sexualidade e pecado—os manuais portugueses de casamento dos séculos xvi e xvii," *Ler História* 12 (1988): 3–22.

36. Granada, *Guia*, lib. II, cap. vi, p. 129.

37. Kamen, *The Phoenix*, 318–20. Kamen includes an excellent review of the moralist literature on marriage. See 275–340.

38. I do not mention Portugal in this regard since there is no study to date that has examined this question, but I suspect from the evidence drawn from the statements of Portuguese colonists living in Brazil that attitudes similar to those held in Spain were common. The topic is touched on in Borges Coelho, *Inquisição de Évora*, 1:263–65.

39. Jean-Pierre Dedieu, "El modelo sexual: La defensa del matrimonio cristiano," in *Inquisición española: Poder político y control social*, 2d ed., ed. Bartolomé Bennassar, 179–219 (Barcelona, 1984); Sánchez Ortega, *La mujer*.

40. Contreras, *El Santo Oficio*, 628–29.

41. Henry Charles Lea reported the first prosecution he found to be in Seville in 1559, but seventy men were prosecuted as *fornicarios* in 1558–59. See Sánchez Ortega, *La mujer*, 24–25; Javier Pérez Escohotado, *Sexo e inquisición en España* (Madrid, 1992), 82–84.

42. Dedieu, "El modelo sexual," 285.

43. Other sexual offenses, bigamy, and solicitation made up another 21 percent (166/770) of the Lima prosecutions between 1570 and 1600. These figures are taken from B. Escandell Bonet, "El tribunal peruano en la epoca de Felipe II," in *Historia de la inquisición en España y América*, 3 vols., ed. Joaquin Pérez Villanueva and Bartolomé Escandell Bonet, 1:919–37 (Madrid, 1984–2004). The percentages for Lima reported in the table (926) are in error and have been recalculated.

44. Contreras and Henningsen, "Forty-Four Thousand Cases," 100–130. It was not Lutheranism per se but rather Anabaptists and religious radicals that presented a real

critique of traditional ideals of sexuality. See Lyndal Roper, *Oedipus and the Devil: Witchcraft, Sexuality, and Religion in Early Modern Europe* (London, 1994), 79–106.

45. Pau Simó, a soldier on the island of Minorca, said, "A man is not a Christian if he doesn't know women well." *RCM*, n. 378 (1604–05), 235–36.

46. Joana López, the wife of an innkeeper, was punished in Seville for saying, "For fornicating nobody goes to Hell." AHN, Inq. (Seville) 2075/5. The opinion was shared by Diego Hernándes de Cazarabonela, a Morisco, who said, "I don't do other sins and for putting it in and enjoying it to the fullest with whomever I want, I won't go to Hell. It's no sin." Rafael Gracia Boix, *Autos de fe y causas de la Inquisición de Córdoba* (Córdoba: Diputación Provincial de Córdoba, 1983), 54 (RC 1570).

47. AHN, Inq. (Murcia) 2022/3 relación de causa, 1583; AHN, Inq. (Seville) 2075/5 relación de causa, 1577.

48. AHN, Inq. (Toledo) 199/6. The remark about young men visiting prostitutes was made in *RCM*, n. 272 (1593), 153–54.

49. García Cárcel, *La herejía*, 344.

50. Recent studies such as Nalle, *God in La Mancha*, and Kamen, *The Phoenix*, have emphasized the effectiveness of the Church in modifying popular belief after Trent. An alternate view based on a study of Oriense, Galicia, is presented by Allyson Poska, "Regulating the People: The Catholic Reformation in Seventeenth-Century Spain" (Ph.D. diss., University of Minnesota, 1992).

51. AHN, Inq. (Toledo) 69/28 (1576).

52. A. Paz y Mélia, *Papeles de Inquisición: Catálogo y extractos*, 2d ed., Ramón Paz, ed. (Madrid, 1947), nos. 723, 733, 760, 777.

53. This point is well made in the case of Galicia by Poska, "Regulating the People," 104–05.

54. Robert McCaa, "Marriageways in Mexico and Spain, 1500–1900," *Continuity and Change* 9 (1994): 11–43. McCaa emphasizes the wide regional variations in these rates.

55. Dedieu and Vainfas believe that the Inquisition's campaign of instilling the concept of fornication as sin was relatively successful and that the reduction of prosecutions for simple fornication in the seventeenth century was a result of this success. Sánchez Ortega is less convinced and argues that the half century of prosecutions had finally convinced people to keep their opinions to themselves. Many of those accused in the seventeenth century claimed to be drunk at the time they made their statements. This was either evidence of real sentiments being expressed (in vino veritas) or a good defense since drunkenness or ignorance combined with remorse was an excellent excuse before the inquisitors. See Sánchez Ortega, *La mujer*, 202.

56. Solange Albero, "El tribunal del Santo Oficio de la Inquisición en Nueva España: Algunas modalidades de su actividad," *Cuadernos para la Historia de la Evangelización en América Latina* 4 (1989): 9–31, makes the point about the prosecution of women (17). The "essentially male" interpretation is made by Dedieu in Bennassar, *Inquisición española*, 283–94.

57. For an introduction to the theological issues, see Terrance L. Tiessen, *Irenaeus on the Salvation of the Unevangelized* (Metuchen, N.J., 1993). See also George Lindbeck, "*Fides ex auditu* and the Salvation of the Non-Christians: Contemporary Catholic and Protestant Positions," in *The Gospel and the Ambiguity of the Church*, ed. Vilmos Vajta

(Philadelphia, 1974). A review of the central doctrinal issues which preoccupied Spanish thought is found in Melquíades Andrés Martín, "Pensamiento teológico y formas de religiosidad," in *Historia de la Cultura Española "Menéndez Pidal": El Siglo del Quijote (1580–1680),* ed. José María Jover Zamora, 75–162 (Madrid, 1994).

58. Louis Capéran, *Le problème du salut des infidèles,* 2 vols. (Toulouse, 1934), traces the question from the Old Testament to the twentieth century. I have profited especially from the discussion of the issue by the Jesuit theologian Bernard Sesboüé, *Hors de l'Église pas de salut* (Paris, 2004). The older and more "rigorist" position of the Church is expressed by the Jesuit Riccardo Lombardi, *The Salvation of the Unbeliever* (London, 1956); and by the Dominican Hendrik Nys, *Le salut sans L'évangile* (Paris, 1966).

59. Francis A. Sullivan, *Salvation Outside the Church* (New York, 1992), 22–28. See also the summary in Jacques Dupuis, *Toward a Christian Theology of Religious Pluralism* (Maryknoll, N.Y., 1997), 86–96.

60. Augustine's followers, including Fulgensius of Ruspe (468–533), solidified the formulation that outside the Church there was no salvation.

61. Sesboüé, *Hors de l'Église,* 61. The author stresses the severity of Augustine's interpretation of St. Paul.

62. The debate is discussed in Julio Caro Baroja, *Las formas complejas de la vida religiosa,* 2 vols. (Madrid, 1995), 2:299–305.

63. Capéran, *Le problème,* 120. There is a useful summary of the debate in Pamela Voekel, *Alone before God: The Religious Origins of Modernity in Mexico* (Durham, 2002), 43–47.

64. The issue of predestination was, of course, a central theme during the Protestant Reformations. See Alister E. McGrath, *Reformation Thought: An Introduction* (Oxford, 1988); *The Intellectual Origins of the European Reformation* (Oxford, 1987).

65. R. Markus, "Pelagianism: Britain and the Continent," *Journal of Theological Studies* n.s. 37 (1986): 191–204; R. H. Weaver, *Divine Grace and Human Agency: A Study of the Semi-Pelagian Controversy* (Macon, Ga., 1996).

66. See the discussion in Mario Góngora, *Studies in the Colonial History of Spanish America* (Cambridge, 1975), 36–37. Cf. Melquiades Andrés Martínez, ed., *Historia de la teología española,* 2 vols. (Madrid, 1987), 2:9–21.

67. See Alister E. McGrath, *Iustitia Dei: A History of the Christian Doctrine of Justification,* 2 vols. (Cambridge, 1986). In 1997 the Catholic and Lutheran churches issued a joint declaration on the doctrine of justification.

68. Alonso Fernández de Madrigal, *Libro de las paradojas* (1437), María Teresa Herrera, ed. (Salamanca, 2000), chap. 427.

69. For a beginning on Las Casas, see Anthony Pagden, *European Encounters with the New World* (New Haven, 1993), 69–87. Personal salvation also acquired a social dimension in that the activity of a Christian in his or her society became a sign of faith. See Javier Otaola Montagne, "La idea de la salvación en la Contrarreforma," in *Formaciones religiosas en la América colonial,* ed. María Alba Pastor and Alícia Mayer, 63–80 (Mexico City, 2000).

70. Sullivan, *Salvation outside the Church?* 82–102. I have followed Father Sullivan's text closely in this discussion.

71. Alfonso de Castro, *Adversus omnes haereses* (Paris, 1564). My thanks to Martin Neswig for bringing this work to my attention.

72. A brief but useful discussion of the Jansenist movement as a Catholic heterodoxy with doctrinal and social implications is presented in Henry Kamen, *The Iron Century: Social Change in Europe, 1550–1660* (New York, 1971), 263–69.

73. *Relación de causa* (Seville, 1604–05); AHN, Inq. Leg. 2075, exp. 16. Martínez's argument emphasized the charity of God.

74. AHN, Inq. Leg. 2075, exp. 33, f. 5., cited in Michel Bœglin, *L'inquisition espagnole au lendemain du concile de Trente* (Montpellier, 2003), 511.

75. AHN, Inq. Sicilia 898, ff. 58–58v., cited in Renda, *La inquisizione in Sicilia* (Palermo, 1997), 385.

76. Robert S. Lopez, "Dante, Salvation, and the Layman," in *History and Imagination,* ed. Hugh Lloyd-Jones, Valerie Pearl, Blair Worden, 37–42 (London, 1981).

77. Carlo Ginzburg, *The Cheese and the Worms: The Cosmos of a Sixteenth-Century Miller,* trans. John and Anne Tedeschi (Baltimore, 1980). Andrea del Col believes this position to be evidence of Cathar influence on Menocchio's thought. See his *Domenico Scandella Known as Menocchio: His Trials before the Inquisition (1583–1599),* trans. John and Anne Tedeschi (Binghamton, N.Y., 1996), ix–x, 132–33. Cf. Joseph P. Consoli, *The Novellino, or One Hunderd Ancient Tales* (New York, 1997), 99.

78. See Manuela Ronquillo Rubio, *Los orígenes de la Inquisición en Canarias, 1488–1526* (Las Palmas, 1991), 240. For propositions of a similar nature later in the Canary Islands, see Fajardo Spínola, *Las víctimas del Santo Oficio,* 151–92.

79. Diego Saavedra Fajardo, *Idea de un príncipe político-cristiano* (Madrid, 1958), 3:107. See the discussion in Henry Méchoulan, "La liberté de consciente chez les penseurs juifs d'Amsterdam au xviie siècle," in *La liberté de conscience (xvi–xvii siècles),* ed. Hans R. Guggisberg, Frank Lestringant, Jean-Claude Margolin, 216–33 (Geneva, 1991).

Chapter 2. Conversos and Moriscos

1. Robert I. Burns, *Islam under the Crusaders* (Princeton, 1973), 186.

2. The bibliographies of these two scholars are overwhelming. The appropriate starting points are Claudio Sánchez-Albornoz, *Spain: A Historical Enigma,* 2 vols. (Madrid, 1975); Américo Castro, *The Spaniards: An Introduction to Their History* (Berkeley, 1971). Some idea of how more recent studies are altering the terms of debate can be seen in Robert Ignatius Burns, "Mudejar Parallel Societies: Anglophone Historiography and Spanish Context," in *Christians, Muslims and Jews in Medieval and Early Modern Spain,* ed. Mark D. Meyerson and Edward D. English, 91–124 (Notre Dame, 1999).

3. Castro's attempt to ascribe these aspects of Spanish culture to the Jews or *Conversos* was adopted by some of Spain's leading scholars. See, for example, Antonio Domínguez Ortiz, *Los judeoconversos en España y América* (Madrid, 1971). Castro's misconceptions are convincingly revealed and criticized by Benjamin Netanyahu, "The Racial Attack on the Conversos: Américo Castro's View of its Origin," in *Toward the Inquisition: Essays on Jewish and Converso History in Late Medieval Spain,* 1–42 (Ithaca, 1997). A review of the issue of *convivencia* is found in Alex Novikoff, "Between Tolerance and Intolerance in Medieval Spain: An Historiographic Enigma," *Medieval Encounters* 11:1–2 (2005): 7–36.

4. Netanyahu does a similar job of demolition, revealing a tendentious use of sources and underlying prejudices in "Sanchez-Albornoz' View of Jewish History in Spain," ibid., 126–55.

5. Andrew Hess, "The Moriscos: An Ottoman Fifth Column in Sixteenth-Century Spain," *American Historical Review* 74:1 (1968): 1–25.

6. See Benjamin Ehlers, *Between Christians and Moriscos: Juan de Ribera and Religious Reform in Valencia, 1568–1614* (Baltimore, 2006).

7. The historiography on the Moriscos is venerable and large. Perhaps the best short introduction is Antonio Domínguez Ortiz and Bernard Vincent, *Historia de los moriscos* (Madrid, 1978). A useful survey of historiography of the Moriscos is presented in María Luisa Candau Chacón, *Los moriscos en el espejo del tiempo* (Huelva, 1977). Estimates of the numbers of Moriscos expelled in 1609 vary widely, but the range falls between two hundred thousand and three hundred thousand.

8. See the figures presented by Jaime Contreras, "Los moriscos en las inquisiciones de Valladolid y Logroño," in *Les morisques et leur temps*, ed. L. Cardaillac, 477–92 (Paris, 1983). A series of quantitative studies of the various tribunals' actions against Moriscos can be seen in *Les morisques et l'inquisition*, ed. L. Cardaillac (Paris, 1990).

9. Angel Galán Sánchez, *Una visión de la 'decadencia española': La historiografía anglosajona sobre mudéjares y moriscos (siglos xviii–xx)* (Málaga, 1991). For an overview, see Richard Fletcher, *Moorish Spain* (Berkeley, 1992), 131–156.

10. The development of the *capitulaciones* in the final stages of the reconquest of Granada is presented succinctly in Miguel Angel Ladero Quesada, *Castilla y la conquista del reino de Granada* (Granada, 1987), 79–97.

11. Manuel Fernando Ladero Quesada, "Judíos y cristianos en la Zámora bajomedieval," in *Proyección histórica de España en sus tres culturas: Castilla y León, América y el Mediterráneo*, 3 vols. (Valladolid, 1993), 1:160.

12. Mark D. Meyerson, *The Muslims of Valencia* (Berkeley, 1991), 3. Meyerson's introduction provides a concise and perceptive summary of these issues, and I have drawn on it here.

13. Melquiades Andrés Martín, *Historia de la mística de la edad de oro en España y América* (Madrid, 1994), 79–80.

14. Cf. David Nirenberg, *Communities of Violence* (Princeton, 1998).

15. These points are ably made by Nirenberg, ibid., 127–200.

16. *Don Quixote,* part 1, chap. 47; also, part 2, chap. 51.

17. Relación de causa, 1604–05, AHN, Inq. 2075, exp. 16. The same sentiment was expressed in the 1650s by Juan Gómez, who was accused among other things of saying, "I swear to God that I am better than God, for he was a descendant of Jews and I am a Spaniard." See AHN, Inq. (Mexico) lib. 1065, fs. 348–50.

18. See Emilio Mitre Fernández, "Animales, vicios y herejías: Sobre la criminalización de la disidencia en el Medievo," *Cuadernos de Historia de España* (Buenos Aires) 74 (1997): 255–83; Cf. G. Fasoli, "Noi e loro," *L'uomo di fronte al mondo animale nell Alto-Medioevo*, 31st Settimana di Studi sull'Alto Medioevo (Spoleto, 1985). Denigration of Muslims and Jews was not limited to the animal epithets. See, for example, J. Battesti-Pelegrin, "A propos de la représentation du judéo-convers: Le traitement burlesque de la conversion," *Signes et marques du convers*, E'tudes Hispaniques, n. 20 (Aix-en-Provence, 1993), 95–119.

19. Louis Cardillac, "Vision simplificatrice des groupes marginaux par le groupe dominant dans l'espagne des xvi et xvii siècles," in *Les problèmes de l'exclusion en Espagne (xvi–xvii siècles)*, ed. A. Redondo, 11–49, n. 8 (Paris, 1983).

20. AHN, Inq. 2022/3, relación de causa, 1634. "Celebraban los cristianos/una fiesta en Argel un dia/y llebaban en procesión a Cristo y Santa María/y dijeron los morillos que bultillos son aquellos? respondieron los cristianos — Cristo y su madre son [,] perros."

21. The classic by Louis Cardaillac, *Morisques et Chrétiens: Un affrontement polemique, 1492–1650* (Paris, 1990), outlines the major thrust of these writings.

22. García-Arenal, *Inquisición y moriscos,*

23. Domínguez Ortiz and Bernard, *Historia,* 145–47.

24. Netanyahu, "Alonso de Espina: Was He a New Christian?" in *Toward the Inquisition,* 43–75.

25. See Julio Caro Baroja, *Los judíos en la España Moderna y Contemporanea,* 3 vols. (Madrid, 1986), 1:185–93; Domínguez Ortiz, *Los Judeoconversos,* 47–105.

26. Jerome Friedman, "Jewish Conversion, the Spanish Pure Blood Laws and Reformation: A Revisionist View of Racial and Religious Antisemitism," *Sixteenth Century Journal* 18:1 (1987): 3–29.

27. ADC, Leg. 121, n. 1633, cited in García-Arenal, *Inquisición y moriscos,* 100.

28. This point is made by Renée Levine Melammed, *Heretics or Daughters of Israel? The Crypto-Jewish Women of Castile* (New York, 1999).

29. AHN, Inq. (Toledo) Leg. 139, n. 19, f. 84v. I have depended on the summary in Haim Beinart, "The Conversos in Spain and Portugal in the 16th to 18th Centuries," in *Moreshet Sepharad: Sephardi Legacy,* ed. Haim Beinart, 3 vols., 2:43–68 (Jerusalem, 1992). Morisco women played a similar role in the preservation of Islamic teaching by hiding forbidden books in Arabic in their voluminous clothes.

30. Henry Kamen, *The Spanish Inquisition: A Historical Revision* (New Haven, 1998), 234–54, presents a summary of the extensive literature on the subject.

31. Diego de Valera, *Espejo de verdadera nobleza: Mario Penna, Prosistas castellanos del siglo XV* (Madrid, 1959).

32. Ibid., 103; Carlos del Valle R., "En los origenes del problema converso," in Torquemada, *Tratado,* 29–74. Various authors and the problem of Converso nobility in general are discussed in an excellent article by Adeline Rucquoi, "Noblesse des conversos," in *"Qu'un sang impur . . .": Les conversos et le pouvoir en Espagne à la fin du moyen âge,* ed. Jeanne Battesti Pelegrin, 89–108 (Aix-en-Provence, 1997).

33. "Libro de declaraciones de testigos sobre delitos en que entiende el Santo Oficio de la Inquisición de Soria y otras partes,"AGS, Patronato Real, Inquisición, 28–73. fs. 937–1,121.

34. This singular document has been the basis for two interesting studies. See José María Monsalvo Antón, "Herejía conversa y contestación religiosa a fines de la edad media: Las denuncias a la inquisición en el obispado de Osma," *Studia Historica* 2:3 (1984): 109–39, which emphasizes the Converso background of the accused. For a contrary view, see John Edwards, "Religious Faith and Doubt in Late Medieval Spain: Soria circa 1450–1500," *Past and Present* 120 (1988): 3–25, and the debate it inspired. Cf. John Sommerville, "Debate: Religious Faith, Doubt, and Atheism," 152–55, and Edwards's "Reply," 156–61.

35. Edwards, "Religious Faith," 16–17; cf. Monsalvo Antón, "Herejía conversa," 125.

36. Edwards, "Religious Faith," 16.

37. Monsalvo Antón, "Herejía conversa," 126.

38. Ibid.

39. Manuela Ronquillo Rubio, *Los orígenes de la Inquisición en Canarias* (Las Palmas, 1991), 240.

40. Personal communication from Henry Kamen.

41. I will use *Converso* throughout the book to mean those converted from Judaism and *Morisco* for those converted from Islam. Spanish practice, however, was to use *converso* or the alternate *confieso* in a generic sense so that it was possible to refer to a *converso de moros*.

42. David M. Gitlitz, *Secrecy and Deceit: The Religion of the Crypyo-Jews* (Philadelphia, 1996), 101.

43. Ibid., 111.

44. Ibid., 101–02.

45. Ibid., 121–24.

46. Cited in Encarnación Marín Padilla, "Relación judeoconversa durante la segunda mitad del siglo XV en Aragón: Enfermedades y muertes," *Sefarad* 43 (1983): 251–53, cited in Gitlitz, *Secrecy,* 121.

47. From Boleslao Lewin, *La inquisición en México: Racismo inquisitorial, el singular caso de María de Zárate* (Puebla, 1971), 212. See the discussion of this case in Nathan Wachtel, "Marrano Religiosity in Hispanic America in the Seventeenth Century," in *The Jews and the Expansion of Europe to the West, 1450–1800,* ed. Paolo Bernardini and Norman Fiering, 149–72 (New York, 2001).

48. Gershom Scholem, *The Messianic Idea in Judaism* (New York, 1971).

49. Gitlitz, *Secrecy,* 120.

50. Carlos Carrete Parrondo and Carolina Fraile Conde, *Los judeoconversos de Almazán, 1501–1505* (Salamanca, 1987).

51. For an adequate overview, see Baron, *A Social and Religious History of the Jews,* 15: 21–73.

52. I. S. Révah, "Aux origines de la rupture Spinozienne: Nouveaux documents sur l'incroyance dans la comunauté judéo-portugaise d'Amsterdam a l'epoque de l'excommunication de Spinoza," *Revue des Études Juives* 4th ser., v. 3 (1965): 358–429. See Brad S. Gregory, ed., *Tractatus Theologico-Politicus* (Leiden, 1991).

53. Miriam Bodian, *Hebrews of the Portuguese Nation* (Bloomington, 1997), 163–64. Jonathan Israel, *The Dutch Republic* (Oxford, 1995), 674–75.

54. Israel, *Dutch Republic,* 675, points out that Da Costa's autobiography was published in 1687 by the Christian scholar Philippus Van Limborch as part of a campaign against religious authority and in favor of toleration.

55. Yirmiyahu Yovel, *Spinoza and Other Heretics,* 2 vols. (Princeton, 1989). The relationship between Spinoza's liberalism in matters of religion and his Judaism is studied in Steven B. Smith, *Spinoza, Liberalism and the Question of Jewish Identity* (New Haven, 1997). See esp. José R. Maia Neto, "The Struggle Against Unbelief in the Portuguese Jewish Community of Amsterdam after Spinoza's Excommunication," in *Heterodoxy, Spinozism, and Free Thought in Early-Eighteenth-Century Europe,* ed. Silvia Berti, Françoise Charles-Daubert, Richard Popkin, 425–38 (Dordrecht, 1996).

56. Jonathan Israel, *Locke, Spinoza and the Philosophical Debate Concerning Toleration in the Early Enlightenment (c. 1670–c.1750)* (Amsterdam, 1999), 16–17; Smith, *Spinoza, Liberalism,* 1–26.

57. Yovel, *Spinoza and Other Heretics*, 1:159–77.

58. See the discussion in Kaplan, *From Christianity*, 222–34.

59. I. S. Révah, *Spinoza and Dr. Juan de Prado* (Paris, 1959).

60. Yosef Kaplan, *From Christianity to Judaism* (Oxford, 1989), 125–27. Kaplan provides an excellent account of the relationship between Prado and Orobio de Castro, and I follow it closely here. A more recent study that emphasizes Prado's crossing of religious boundaries is Natalia Muchnik, "Juan de Prado, o las peregrinaciones de un 'passeur de frontières,'" in *Familia, religión y negocio*, ed. Jaime Contreras, Bernardo J. García García, Ignacio Pulido, 237–68 (Madrid, 2002).

61. Ibid. There is a detailed discussion of these events and of Prado's philosophy and theology in Yovel, *Spinoza and Other Heretics*, 1:64–73.

62. Kaplan, *From Christianity*, 160–61, 176–78. Kaplan argues that as much as a dispute between Jews that the dispute between Prado and Orobio was between Spaniards. Prado represented a position of the *arbitristas*, those writers who were suggesting social reforms. His rejection of Israel's exclusive revelation paralleled *arbitrista* attacks on the emphasis of blood and honor in Spain, while Orobio's emphasis on the covenant with the Jews was a reassertion of the honor of Israel that had not been supplanted by Christian Spain despite the claims of the Church.

63. Yovel, *Spinoza and Other Heretics*, vol. 1, develops these ideas fully.

64. Perez Zagorin, *Ways of Lying: Dissimulation, Persecution, and Conformity in Early Modern Europe* (Cambridge, Mass., 1990). See esp. his treatment of Marranos, 38–62.

65. See Silvia Berti, "Scepticism and the *Traité des trois imposteurs*," in *Scepticism and Irreligion in the Seventeenth and Eighteenth Centuries*, ed. Richard Popkin and Arjo Vanderjagt, 216–29 (Leiden, 1993). For examples of the leading scholarship on the *Traité*, see *Heterodoxy, Spinozism, and Free Thought*, ed. Berti et al.

66. A recent attempt has been made to suggest that many Moriscos were, in fact, seeking to find salvation as converts to Christianity. See Amalia García Pedraza, *Actitudes ante la muerte en la Granada del siglo xvi*, 2 vols. (Granada, 2002).

67. Fernando Bouza, *Los Austrias mayores: Imperio y monarquía de Carlos I y Felipe II* in *Historia de España* (Madrid, 1996), 15:68.

68. Catherine Gaignard, *Maures et crétiens à Grenade, 1492–1570* (Paris, 1997).

69. Contact between Aragonese Moriscos and French Huguenots was not unknown. Also there was a tendency for the Moriscos to consider the "enemies of my enemies" as friends. See Louis Cardillac, "Morisques et protestants," *Al-Andalus* 36 (1971): 29–63. The classic study of the fear of the Turkish threat and of the Moriscos is Andrew Hess, "The Moriscos: An Ottoman Fifth Column in Sixteenth-Century Spain," *AHR* 74 (1968): 1–25. See also id., *The Forgotten Frontier: A History of the Sixteenth-Century Ibero-African Frontier* (Chicago, 1978).

70. For a general discussion, see John Lynch, *Spain under the Hapsburgs. 1516–1598*, 2 vols. (Oxford, 1964), 1:205–18; John H. Elliott, *Imperial Spain, 1469–1716* (New York, 1963), 228–34.

71. Henry Kamen, *The Spanish Inquisition: A Historical Revision* (New Haven, 1998), 214–29.

72. Mercedes García-Arenal, *Inquisición y moriscos: Los procesos del Tribunal de*

Cuenca (Madrid, 1978), 108–09. Similar statements were made by Moriscos tried by the Inquisition of Toledo. See Peter Dressendorfer, *Islam unter der Inquisition: Die Morisco-Prozesse in Toledo, 1575–1610* (Wiesbaden, 1971), 64.

73. Yohanan Friedmann, *Tolerance and Coercion in Islam* (Cambridge, 2003), 87–89, provides the best discussion.

74. Sara Stroumsa, *Freethinkers of Medieval Islam: Ibn al-Rawândî, Abû Bakr al-Râzî and Their Impact on Islamic Thought* (Leiden, 1999).

75. Thomas, *Los protestantes*, 480.

76. The case of Luis de Cebea of Cuenca, who on his deathbed expressed his doubts and whose son then had a Moor well versed in Islam brought to instruct his father in how to die as a Muslim, is instructive. Ibid., 109–10.

77. ADC, Leg. 91, n. 1333, cited in García-Arenal, *Inquisición y moriscos*, 109.

78. *IG*, 178. Ehlers, *Between Christians*, 105, cites the case of a Morisco, Francisco Zenequi, who in 1583 was tried by the Valencia Inquisition for holding to the belief that each can be saved in his own law.

79. Ibid.

80. Francisco Bethencourt, *História das inquisições* (Lisbon, 1994), 148.

81. *Edictos generales* (s.d.), SML, Latin American Pamphlets.

82. Bernardo Pérez de Chinchón, *Antialcorano, Diálogos Christianos: Conversión y evangelización de moriscos*, ed. Francisco Pons Fuster (Alicante, 2000), 403–15.

83. For similar statements among Conversos, see Gitlitz, *Secrecy*, 138–82.

84. Both of these cases are drawn from the Inquisition of Cuenca and are reported by García-Arenal, *Inquisición y moriscos*, 92–93.

85. AHN, Inq. (Murcia) 2033, n. 26 RC 1597.

86. Bocacho was sent to a monastery for a year for instruction and exiled from Alicante and from "places of Moors" for four years.

87. AHN, Inq. (Seville) 2075, n. 18, f. 25v. The inquisitors were anxious to explore her position, and she was subjected to torture but continued to deny under duress that she had claimed that baptism was unnecessary.

88. Boronat, *Los moriscos españoles y su expulsión*, 2 vols., Ricardo García Cárcel, ed., 2d ed. (Granada, 1992), 2:437. This is cited in a concise but penetrating discussion by Dolores Bramon, *Contra moros y judíos* (Barcelona, 1986).

89. Bramon, *Contra moros*, 194.

90. *IG*, 239. The case is discussed in Aurelia Martín Casares, "Cristianos, Musulmanes y animistas en Granada: Identidades religiosas y sincretismo cultural," in *Negros, mulatos, zambaigos*, ed. Berta Ares Queija y Alessandro Stella, 207–21 (Seville, 2000).

Chapter 3. Christian Toleration

1. Robert Ignatius Burns, "Renegades, Adventurers and Sharp Businessmen: The Thirteenth-Century Spaniard in the Cause of Islam," *Catholic Historical Review* 58:3 (1972): 341–66. The problem was an ancient one in the Mediterranean. See Steven Epstein, *Purity Lost: Transgressing Boundaries in the Eastern Mediterranean* (Baltimore, 2006), 137–72.

2. Louis Cardaillac et al., *Les morisques et l'inquisition* (Paris, 1990), 316–35.

3. Bartolomé and Lucille Bennassar, *Los cristianos de Alá: La fascinante aventura de los renegados* (Madrid, 1989); Bartolomé Bennassar, "Frontières religieuses entre Islam et chrètienté: L'expérience vécue par les 'renégats,'" in *Les frontières religieuses en Europe du xv au xvii siècle*, ed. Robert Sauzet, 71–78 (Paris, 1992); "Renégats et inquisiteurs (xvi–xvii siècles)," in *Les problèmes de l'exclusion en Espagne (xvi–xvii siècles)*, ed. A. Redondo, 105–11 (Paris, 1983); Anita González-Raymond, *La croix et le croissant: Les inquisiteurs des iles face a l'islam, 1550–1700* (Paris, 1992); Isabel M. R. Mendes Drumond Braga, *Entre a cristanidade e o islão (séculos xv–xvii): Cautivos e renegados nas franjas de duas sociedades em confronto* (Ceuta, 1998). The problem of the Portuguese renegades in the Indian Ocean is ably treated by Dejanirah Couto, "Quelques observations sur les renégats portugais en Asie au xvie siècle," *Mare liberum* 16 (1998): 57–84.

4. Braga, *Entre a cristandade*, 89.

5. Bennassar, *Los cristianos*, 494.

6. Ibid., 497–99. The case of Joan Caules was heard by the Inquisition of Mallorca in 1629.

7. ANTT, Inq. (Lisbon) 2244; Couto, "Quelques observations," 67–69.

8. His final sentence was for confession *vehementi* and one hundred lashes. See AHN, Inq. 2022 (Murcia), n. 17 (1586).

9. Rosario, *Visita da Inquisição* (1978), 26.

10. *RCM*, 1595, 161–62.

11. Caro Baroja, *Las formas complejas*, 1:271.

12. Gerónimo Graciano, *Diez lamentaciones del miserable estado de los ateistas de nuestro tiempo* [1607] (Madrid, 1959). See also Julio Caro Baroja, *De la superstición al ateismo* (Madrid 1974); id., *Las formas complejas*, 1:265–80, provides an excellent discussion critical of the idea that atheism never existed in Spain.

13. See David Wootton, "New Histories of Atheism," in *Atheism from the Reformation to the Enlightenment*, ed. Michael Hunter and David Wootton, 13–54 (Oxford, 1992). Italy has a special reputation as a place of atheistic belief, both because of its literate tradition and on the popular level. See Nicholas Davidson, "Unbelief and Atheism in Italy, 1500–1700," in *Atheism*, ed. Hunter and Wootton, 55–86.

14. Val was subjected to torture, and he did ask for pardon for denying he knew Jesus Christ and claimed he had spoken while drunk. The inquisitors had found him "very rustic" and poorly instructed. He was sentenced to two hundred lashes, appearance at an auto de fe, and a two-year seclusion in a monastery where he was to receive instruction in the faith. See Gracia Boix, *ACC RC Córdoba*, 1590, 228–29.

15. *ACC*, RC Córdoba 1574, 130.

16. There were many travelers, itinerant workers, and other "outsiders" who passed continually through the villages and towns of Spain. See David Vassberg, *The Village and the Outside World in Golden Age Castile* (Cambridge, 1996).

17. AHN, Inq. (Logroño) libro 833, f. 442–81v. The case is discussed in Bartolomé Bennassar, *Inquisición española: Poder político y control social*, 2d ed. (Barcelona, 1984), 221.

18. The anti-Morisco sentiments and actions are presented in chilling detail in José María Perceval, *Todos son Uno* (Almería, 1997).

19. María Rosa Menocal, *The Ornament of the World* (Boston, 2002), provides a

272   Notes to Pages 79–84

general statement. See also María Rosa Menocal, Raymond P. Scheindlin, Micahel Sells, eds., *The Literature of Al-Andalus* (Cambridge, 2000), which provides a recent review of the literature and the status of present scholarship in the literary field, and Jerrilyn D. Dodds, *Al-Andalus: The Art of Islamic Spain* (New York, 1992), which stresses cross-cultural contact in the arts and architecture.

20. See the classic summary by Maria Soledad Carrasco Urgoiti, *El moro de Granada en la literatura,* 2d ed. (Granada, 1989). Her continuing work in this area is collected in *El moro retado y el moro amigo* (Granada, 1996).

21. I am following Thomas E. Case, *Lope and Islam: Islamic Personages in His Comedias* (Newark, Del., 1993). See also Albert Mas, *Les Turcs dans la littérature espagnole du siècle d'or,* 2 vols. (Paris, 1967); Luce López-Baralt, *Islam in Spanish Literature: From the Middle Ages to the Present* (Leiden, 1992); Miguel Angel Teijeiro Fuentes, *Moros y turcos en la narrativa áurea* (Cáceres, 1987).

22. The play is *Las mocedades de Bernardo del Carpio* (1579), cited in Case, *Lope and Islam,* 48.

23. Emílio Solá, *Cervantes y la Berbería* (Mexico City, 1995).

24. Menocal, *Ornament,* 254–59.

25. The classic study is the chapter "El morisco Ricote o la hispana razón de estado," in *Personajes y temas del Quijote,* ed. Francisco Márquez Villanueva, 229–336 (Madrid, 1975).

26. *Don Quixote,* vol. 2, chaps. 54, 63. See also Richard Hitchcock, "Cervantes, Ricote and the Expulsión of the Moriscos," *Bulletin of Spanish Studies* 81:2 (2004): 175–85.

27. José María Monsalvo Antón, "Mentalidad antijudía en la Castilla medieval: Cultura clerical y cultura popular en la gestación y difusión de un ideario medieval," in *Xudeus e conversos na Historia,* 2 vols., ed. Carlos Barros, 1:21–84 (Santiago de Compostela, 1994). There were those who defended the "nobility" of the Jews and argued against the purity of blood statutes. See, for example, Juan de Torquemada, *Tratado contra los madianitas e ismaelitas,* ed. Carlos del Valle. R. (Madrid, 2000), edited from the 1471 MS.

28. R. Ayoun, "Les juifs d'Oran avant la conquete française," *Revue historique* 542 (1982): 375–90; Jean Federic Schaub, *Les juifs du roi d'Espagne* (Paris, 1999); B. Alonso Acero, *Orán-Mazalquivir, 1589–1639: Una sociedad española en la frontera de Berbería* (Madrid, 2000).

29. At the time of the expulsion in 1669 between 450 and 500 Jews left the city. Oran was occupied by the Ottomans from 1708 to 1732 and then retaken by Spain until 1792.

30. AHN, Inq. (Murcia) 2022 RC 1572. Sarmiento was punished with only a one-hundred-ducat fine and *abjuración de levi.*

31. AHN, Inq. (Murcia) Leg. 2022 RC 1584

32. Carlo Ginzburg, "High and Low: The Theme of Forbidden Knowledge in the Sixteenth and Seventeenth Centuries," *Past and Present* 73 (1976): 28–41.

33. Barbara Benedict, *Curiosity: A Cultural History of Early Modern Inquiry* (Chicago, 2001), 19.

34. Neil Kenny, *Curiosity in Early Modern Europe: Word Histories* (Wiesbaden, 1998), 13. See especially Edward Peters, "The Desire to Know the Secrets of the World," *Journal of the History of Ideas* (2001): 593–610.

35. AHN, Inq. (Murcia) 2022, n. 25 RC 1596. Ludena told the inquisitors that he had

not meant to imply the laws were equal, only that those who had lived as Jews and Muslims were right to die that way. He was only fined since the inquisitors found him to be a "man of little understanding."

36. Luis Coronas Tejada, *La Inquisición en Jaén* (Jaén, 1991), 167–71.

37. Ibid., 169.

38. Elliott, *Imperial Spain,* 208.

39. *RCM* (1595), 163–64.

40. It was said that "he gave signs that he wished to know what he was obliged to believe and thus demonstrated that fact during the reclusion he underwent." Ibid.

41. Govion claimed he had said these things to get out of his master's home. His master was one of the four witnesses against him. See AHN, Inq. (Murcia) 2022, n. 26.

42. *RCM* (1590), 109–10.

43. See ADC, Leg. 210, exp. 2419; cited in Sebastián Cirac Estopañan, *Catalogo de la Inquisición de Cuenca,* ed. Dimas Perez Ramirez (Madrid, 1982), 386.

44. AHN, Inq. (Toledo) Leg. 221, n. 12.

45. AHN, Inq. Leg. 1953, exp. 17, cited in Thomas, *Los protestantes,* 479.

46. AHN, Inq. lib. 1023, 302–05.

47. Ibid.

48. Adriana Romeiro, "As aventuras de um viajante no império português: Trocas culturais e tolerância religiosa no século xviii," in *O trabalho mestiço,* ed. Eduardo França Paiva and Carla Maria Junho Anastasia, 483–95 (Rio de Janeiro, 2002).

49. Parallel but somewhat distinct are the many cases of New Christians who moved back and forth between Catholicism and Judaism as they moved across national and community boundaries. They often did so as a strategy for survival without much theological concern. See David L. Graizbord, *Souls in Dispute: Converso Identities in Iberia and the Jewish Diaspora, 1580–1700* (Philadelphia, 2004), 172–76.

50. AHN, Inq. (Murcia) 2845.

51. The three *calificadores* were Fray Juan Idalgo, the ex-provincial of San Francisco, Fray Manuel Fernández Paniagua, provincial of San Francisco, and Fray Alberto Rosique, of the order of San Domingo.

52. On madness and its definition in the period, see Eric Midelfort, *History of Madness in Sixteenth-Century Germany* (Stanford, 1999); Sara Nalle, *Mad for God: Bartolomé Sánchez, the Secret Messiah of Cardenete* (Charlottesville, 2001).

53. Juan Blázquez Miguel, *La Inquisición en Albacete* (Albacete, 1985).

54. Vassberg, *The Village and the Outside World,* 173–75; Ida Altman, *Emigrants and Society* (Berkeley, 1989); *Transatlantic Ties in the Spanish Empire* (Stanford, 2000). See also the remarks on the mobility of Spanish life documented by recent historians of Spain in James Amelang, "Society and Culture in Early Modern Spain," *Journal of Modern History* 65:2 (1993): 357–74.

Chapter 4. Portugal

1. Maria Paula Marçal Lourenço, "Para o estudos da actividade inquisitorial no Alto Alentejo: A visita da Inquisição de Lisboa ao bispado de Portalegre em 1578–79," *A Cidade* 3 (1989): 109–38.

2. José Sebastião da Silva Dias, *Correntes de sentimento religioso em Portugal,* 2 vols.

(Coimbra, 1960), 1:409–57; Joaquim Romero Magalhães, "A sociedade," in *HP* 3:469–512. A recent overview of Portugal incorporating the advances in early modern religious history in general is found in Federico Palomo, *A Contra-Reforma em Portugal, 1540–1700* (Lisbon, 2006).

3. Francisco Bethencourt, "Rejeições e polémicas," *HRP* 2:77–80. See also the discussions in Elvira Cunha de Azevedo Mea, *A Inquisição de Coimbra no século xvi* (Oporto, 1997), 335–42; António Borges Coelho, *Inquisição de Évora*, 2 vols. (Lisbon, 1987), 1:279–95; Michèle Janin-Thivos Tailland, *Inquisition et société au Portugal* (Paris, 2002).

4. Denunciations and prosecutions for defense of simple fornication or for living outside of wedlock were common. See, for example, various people punished in an auto de fe in Coimbra in 1623, where Baltesar Antunes went so far as to say that not only was simple fornication not a sin but that there were confessors who had told him so. "Relação das pessoas que sacarão no auto de Fe" (Coimbra, 26 Nov. 1623) in ACA, caja 118. Cf. ANTT, Inq. Coimbra, processo 1453.

5. ANTT, Inq. Lisbon CP 232, f. 326–28.

6. Anita Novinsky, "A Inquisição portuguesa a luz de novos estudos," *Revista de la Inquisición* 7 (1998): 305.

7. Contreras and Hennigsen, "Forty-Four Thousand Cases of the Spanish Inquisition," as given in Bethencourt, *História das Inquisições*, 272–73; cf. Isabel M. R. Drumond Braga, *Os estrangeiros e a Inquisição portuguesa* (Lisbon, 2002), 265.

8. On the origins and idea of "superstition," see Jean-Claude Schmitt, *História das superstições* (Lisbon, 1997). The historiography on this topic is extensive. I have been influenced by Keith Thomas, *Religion and the Decline of Magic* (London, 1971); Jon Butler, "Magic, Astrology, and Early American Religion," *American Historical Review* 84:2 (1979): 317–46; Gary K. Waite, *Heresy, Magic and Witchcraft in Early Modern Europe* (New York, 2003); José Pedro Paiva, *Práticas e crenças mágicas* (Coimbra, 1992); Francisco Bethencourt, *O imaginário da magia* (Lisbon, 1987); Laura de Mello e Souza, *O diabo e a terra de Santa Cruz: Feitiçaria e religiosidade popular no Brasil* (São Paulo, 1986); *Inferno atlântico* (São Paulo, 1993); and esp. José Pedro Paiva, *Bruxaria e superstição num país sem "caça de bruxas,"* 2d ed. (Lisbon, 2002).

9. Paiva, *Bruxaria*, 67.

10. Rui Grillo Capelo, *Profetismo e esoterismo: A arte do prognóstico em Portugal (séculos xvii–xviii)* (Coimbra, 1994). Useful texts on the subject appear in P. G. Maxwell-Stuart, *The Occult in Early Modern Europe* (New York, 1999).

11. Paiva, *Bruxaria*, 361–67.

12. Yosef Hayim Yerulshalmi, *The Lisbon Massacre of 1506 and the Royal Image in the Shebet Yehudah* (Cincinnati, 1976).

13. The best modern study of aspects of the foundation of the Portuguese Inquisition is Maria José Pimenta Ferro Tavares, *Judaísmo e Inquisição: Estudos* (Lisbon, 1987).

14. See the discussion in Anita Novinsky, *Cristãos novos na Bahia* (São Paulo, 1973), 3–22. On the debate between I. Révah and António José Saraiva, see António José Saraiva, *The Marrano Factory*, trans. and ed. H. P. Salomon and I. S. D. Sassoon (Leiden, 2001), 235–341.

15. ANTT, Inq. Lisbon processo 6307, as cited in Geraldo Pieroni, "Outcasts from the

Kingdom: The Inquisition and the Banishment of New Christians to Brazil," in *The Jews and the Expansion of Europe to the West, 1450–1800*, ed. Paolo Bernardini and Norman Fiering, 243–51 (New York, 2001).

16. Novinsky, *Cristãos novos*, 47, provides details on the various exclusions.

17. The bibliography on the subject is extensive and continues to grow. The classic accounts of Meyer Kayserling, *Geschichte der Juden in Portugal* (Berlin, 1867); Alexandre Herculano, *História da origem e estabelecimento da Inquisicão em Portugal*, 2d ed. (Lisbon, 1975); João Lúcio de Azevedo, *História dos cristãos novos portugueses*, 2d ed. (Lisbon, 1975) have served as the starting point for a virtual explosion of new studies beginning in the 1960s.

18. For example, "Tractus de gratia et de merito a Padre Benedito Rodrigues," BPE, CXIX/2–8.

19. ANTT Inq. Lisbon, Livro dos Reduzidos 708.

20. ANTT, Inq. Lisbon, Caderno do Promotor (cited hereafter as CP) 206, f. 358. For other such statements, see Drumond Braga, *Mouriscos e cristãos*, 59–70; Ahmed Boucharb, *Os pseudo-mouriscos de Portugal no século xvi*, (Lisbon, 2004), 138.

21. ANTT, Inq. Lisbon CP 230, f. 22.

22. For Portuguese examples of the more traditional propositions, such as the proposition that sex was not a mortal sin, see ANTT, Inq. Lisboa processo 2262 (1564); 3208 (1637); 3507 (1645); 6740 (1674).

23. ANTT, Inq. Lisbon CP 265.

24. ANTT, Inq. Lisbon CP 248 (19 Nov. 1720).

25. ANTT, Inq. Évora, livro 10, ff. 250v.–252v. This case is discussed in Giuseppe Marcocci, *I custodi dell'ortodossia* (Rome, 2004), 304.

26. "Pareceres sobre se o baptismo salva os hereges que morrem na sua seita," BPE, CVII/1–26.

27. There was a considerable literature of theological instruction for the humble. See, for example, "Tratado do cuidado da salvação para humildes," BGUC Ms. 344.

28. AHN, Leg. 2106, exp. 18 (Toledo). Manso apparently sang a little *villancico:* "Dios de dioses, homen mortal . . . no nasceu para Castela, senao por Portugal." He was punished in an auto de fe in 1619 and exiled from the area of Toledo.

29. Unidentified MS. In British Library, C. R. Boxer to Malcolm Bochner (19 July 1970), correspondence in my possession. For more anti-Spanish sentiments, see AHN, Inq. Leg. 2106, exp. 17 (Toledo, 1617).

30. AHN, Inq. Leg. 1931/10 Relación de causa, Cuenca 1610.

31. ANTT, Inq. Lisbon CP 202, fs. 29–300.

32. AHN, Leg. 2105/30 Relación de causa, Toledo 1594.

33. ANTT, Inq. Lisbon CP 207.

34. ANTT, Inq. Évora, processo 4508.

35. ANTT, Inq. Lisbon CP 230, fs.152–207.

36. ANTT, Inq. Lisbon CP 207 (1620). See Novinsky, *Cristãos novos*, 52–54, which provides references to a dozen similar cases.

37. Novinsky, *Cristãos novos*, 53, n. 98, notes a MS volume entitled "Pessoas que escondiam cristãos novos para não serem presos pelo Santo Ofício."

38. ANTT, Inq. Coimbra, processo 3770, as cited in Drumond, *Os estrangeiros*, 291.

39. See João Lucio de Azevedo, *História de António Vieira*, 2d ed., 2 vols. (Lisbon, 1931).

40. Jonathan I. Israel, *European Jewry in the Age of Mercantilism, 1550–1750* (Oxford, 1985).

41. See the summary in Immanuel Wallerstein, *The Modern World System,* 3 vols. to date (New York, 1974–), 1:75–77.

42. The supposed philo-Semitism of these statesmen was sometimes exaggerated by their political opponents for political and religious motives. This has been convincingly demonstrated recently in regard to the count-duke of Olivares by Juan Ignacio Pulido Serrano, in his *Injurias a Cristo: Religión, política y antijudaísmo en el siglo xvii* (Alcalá, 2002), 37–50.

43. A. Vieira, *Obras escolhidas,* ed. A. Sergio and H. Cidade, 12 vols. (Lisbon, 1951–54), 4:15.

44. Anita Novinsky, "Padre António Vieira, the Inquisition, and the Jews," *Jewish History* 6:1–2 (1992): 151–62. On the Brazil Company, see also Leonor Freire Costa, *O transporte no Atlântico e a Companhia Geral do Comércio do Brasil (1580–1663)* (Lisbon, 2002), which demonstrates that, in fact, Vieira had little to do with the company's formation.

45. See José van den Besselaar, *António Vieira: Profecia e polêmica* (Rio de Janeiro, 2002).

46. See Susanna Akerman, "Queen Christina of Sweden and Messianic Thought," 142–61, and E. G. E. van der Wall, "A Philo-Semitic Millenarian on the Reconciliation of Jews and Christians: Henry Jessey and His 'The Glory and Salvation of Judah and Israel,' 1650,' " 161–85, both of which appear in *Sceptics, Millenarians, and Jews,* ed. David S. Katz and Jonathan I. Israel (Leiden, 1990).

47. Susanna Akerman, *Queen Christina of Sweden and Her Circle* (Leiden, 1991), 206–07; I. S. Revah, "Les Jesuites portugais contre l'Inquisition: La campagne pour la foundation de la Compagnie du Bresil," *Revista do Livro* 1 (1956): 29–53.

48. António Vieira, *Cartas do padre António Vieira,* ed. J. Lucio d'Azevedo (Coimbra, 1925), 3: xxix, p. 73.

49. Ibid, 3:34, p. 84.

50. I have analyzed this event and its historiography in Stuart B. Schwartz, "The Voyage of the Vassals: Royal Power, Noble Obligations, and Merchant Capital before the Portuguese Restoration of Independence," *American Historical Review* 96:3 (June 1991): 735–62.

51. The incident is summarized in Jorge Martins, *O senhor roubado: A inquisição e a questão judaica* (Lisbon, 2002).

52. The prophecies of Bandarra continued to fascinate Portuguese readers into the eighteenth century despite the fact that they were prohibited by the Inquisition. In 1722, Francisco Oliveira, who worked at the scale of the customshouse, was denounced for reading them, having been lent a collection by a man who served as the bailiff of the cathedral. See ANTT, Inq. Lisbon CP 283, f. 402.

53. Azevedo, *História de António Vieira,* 1:50–51.

54. António Vieira, *Defesa perante o tribunal do Santo Oficio,* ed. Hernani Cidade, 2 vols. (Salvador, 1957), 1:xi–xii.

55. Vieira, *Cartas,* 190 (Oct. 10, 1671), 366–69.

56. Ibid., 370.

57. Vicente Nogueira, a Portuguese noble who fled the Inquisition and lived in Italy, expressed considerable admiration for a new rabbi in Rome. See André Crabbé Rocha, *Cartas inéditas ou dispersas de Vicente Nogueira* (Lisbon, n.d.), 38.

58. ANTT, Inquisição de Évora, maço 64, n. 608. The case also appears summarized in the description of the auto da fe of Évora celebrated on 14 July 1624 found in ACA, caja 118, fl.101.

59. Ibid.

60. Ibid.

61. Relations of affection could break down the social barriers between Old and New Christians. The relation of Lopes and his wife was not singular. In a visit of the Inquisition to Oporto in 1570, a woman named Catherina was denounced for having said that "the New Christians are better people than the Old Christians, and that some who die for justice, die as martyrs." She was *amancebada* at the time with a New Christian merchant. See António do Rosario, *Visita da Inquisição a Entre Douro e Minho, 1570* (Braga, 1970), 53.

62. Bethencourt, *História das inquisições,* 297–99, believes that the critique of the Inquisition's campaigns against New Christians as arbitrary, self-interested, and discriminatory was essentially developed by New Christians and later picked up by others. The issue of the Inquisition's role in "creating Jews" became a central feature in the debate of the 1960s between Antonio José Saraiva and the French scholar I. S. Revah fought out in the Lisbon public press. See António José Saraiva, *Inquisição e cristãos novos* (Lisbon, 1969).

63. Testimony of Domingos Gomes (20 Nov. 1623), ANTT, Inquisição de Évora, maço 64, n. 608.

64. Lopes was originally sentenced to whipping and three years' exile to Angola, but because of his claim to noble status as the son of a town councilman (*vereador*) and to the fact that he was a large-scale merchant with capital of over 100$ *milréis,* the whipping was commuted to a fine of 20$ *milréis.* Because of his advanced age (seventy) the place of exile was changed from Angola to Castromirim in the Algarve.

65. Jacqueline Hermann, *No reino do Desejado* (São Paulo, 1998), 305–10. She notes texts such as MS 551, "Notícia da Ilha Encoberta ou Antília," and BNL, MS 503, "Relação de dois religiosos que viram a Ilha Encoberta ou Antília."

66. AHN, Inq. Lib. 1023, fs. 426–33v.

67. Hermann, *No reino,* 219–302, presents an excellent summary of the messianism of Vieira, who redirected the legend of the *encoberto* from Dom Sebastião to Dom João IV.

68. For an overview of the two visits, see Sonia A. Siqueira, *A Inquisição portuguesa e a sociedade colonial* (São Paulo, 1978), 181–305.

69. *SRHJ,* 15:188–94. The complexity of negotiation and interest groups involved in the general pardon, even on the New Christian side, is underlined by Diogo Ramada Curto, "The Stranger Within in the Time of Quijote," *Portuguese Studies* 13 (1997): 180–97.

70. ANTT, Inq. Lisboa CP 202.

71. ANTT, Inq. Lisboa CP 202, f. 645. His trial is found in ANTT, Inq. Lisbon, processo 6789.

Chapter 5. American Propositions

1. For a brief but effective overview, see Mario Góngora, *Studies in the Colonial History of Spanish America* (Cambridge, 1975), 33–66.

2. Ibid., 206–38; John Leddy Phelan, *The Millennial Kingdom of the Franciscans in the New World*, University of California Publications in History, no. 32 (Berkeley, 1956), 66–76.

3. The classic account is Lewis Hanke, *The Spanish Struggle for Justice in the Conquest of America* (Philadelphia, 1949). See also Venancio Caro, *La teología y los teólogos juristas españoles antes de la conquista de América*, 2d ed. (Salamanca, 1951); Silvio Zavala, *Filosofía de la conquista*, 2d ed. (Mexico City, 1972). Particularly useful on aspects of canon law is James Muldoon, *The Americas in the Spanish World Order* (Philadelphia, 1994).

4. Lewis Hanke, *Aristotle and the American Indians* (Chicago, 1959).

5. Francisco de Vitoria, *Doctrina sobre los Indios,* ed. Ramón Hernández-Martín (Salamanca, 1989). See also Benito Fernández Méndez, "El problema de la salvación de los 'Infieles' en Francisco de Vitoria" (Ph.D. diss., Pontifical Gregoria University, 1994).

6. Phelan, *Millennial Kingdom,* 5–7.

7. In this Las Casas followed the lead of the French theologian John Gerson, whom he cited often. See the discussion in Ramón-Jesús Queralto Moreno, *El pensamiento filosófico-político de Bartolomé de las Casas* (Seville, 1976), 31.

8. George M. Foster, *Culture and Conquest: America's Spanish Heritage* (Chicago, 1960).

9. See, for example, Anthony Pagden, *Lords of All the World* (New Haven, 1995).

10. For an excellent example of the line of argument that traces Spanish intolerance from the Old World to the New, see William Mejías-López, "Hernán Cortés y su intolerancia hacia la religión azteca en el contexto de la situación de los conversos y moriscos," *Bulletin Hispanique* 95:2 (1993): 623–46.

11. Henry Kamen, "Tradition and Dissent in Sixteenth-Century Spain: The Alternative Tradition," *Sixteenth Century Journal* 19:1 (1988): 3–23.

12. I am not unaware of the peculiar and biased nature of the Inquisition materials on which this study is based. A number of scholars (C. Ginzburg, A. Prosperi, J. Contreras) have addressed the documentary and epistemological problems inherent in these records. See especially the relevant discussion in Jaime Contreras, *El Santo Oficio de la Inquisición de Galicia* (Madrid, 1982), 571–80; Jesús M. de Bujanda, "Recent Historiography of the Spanish Inquisition (1977–1988): Balance and Perspective," in *Cultural Encounters: The Impact of the Inquisition in Spain and the New World,* ed. Mary Elizabeth Perry and Anne J. Cruz, 221–47 (Berkeley, 1991). I have also found helpful the volumes of William Monter, *Frontiers of Heresy* (Cambridge, 1990), and Ricardo García Cárcel, *Herejía y sociedad en el siglo xvi* (Barcelona, 1980). By this last author see too, "¿Son creíbles las Fuentes inquisitoriales?" in *Grafías del imaginario,* ed. Carlos Alberto González S. and Enriqueta Vila Vilar, 96–110 (Mexico City, 2003).

13. Solange Alberro, *Inquisición y sociedad en México 1571–1700* (Mexico City, 1988), 22.

14. José Toribio Medina, *Historia de la tribunal del Santo Oficio de la Inquisición de Lima,* 2 vols. (Santiago de Chile, 1887), 1:332–33n.

15. Many of the early trials in the Caribbean seem to have involved disputes between civil and religious authorities. See Luís E. González Valés, "Alonso Manso, primer obispo de Puerto Rico e inquisidor de América," in *La Inquisición en Hispanoamerica,* ed. Abelardo Levaggi, 231–51 (Buenos Aires, 1997).

16. Leon Lopétequi and Felix Zubillaga, eds., *Historia de la iglesia en la América Española* (Madrid, 1965), 373–75; Ricardo García Cárcel and Doris Moreno Martínez, *Inquisición: Historia crítica* (Madrid, 2000), 158–61.

17. See Pedro Guibovich Pérez, "Proyecto colonial y control ideológico: El establecimiento de la Inquisición en el Perú," *Apuntes* 35 (1994): 110–11; Teodoro Hampe Martínez, *Santo Oficio e historia colonial* (Lima, 1998), 9–10. On the *junta magna* of 1568 that guided Philip II's decision, see Demeterio Ramos Pérez, "La crisis indiana y la Junta Magna de 1568," *Jahrbuch für Geschichte von Staat, Wirtscsft und Gesellschaft Lateinamerikas* (1986), 23:1–61.

18. Bernard Grunberg, *L'Inquisition apostolique au Mexique* (Paris, 1998), 82. Testimony against don Carlos claimed that he had said, "Each person should live in the law that they wish [cada uno había de vivir en la ley que quisiese]." See Luis González Obregón, ed., *Proceso de Don Carlos de Texcoco* (Mexico City, 1910), 63–65.

19. Richard E. Greenleaf, "The Inquisition and the Indians of New Spain: A Study in Jurisdictional Confusion," *The Americas* 22:2 (1963): 138–66. See also José Traslosheros, "El tribunal eclesiástico y los indios en el arzobispado de México, hasta 1630," *Historia Mexicana* 51:3, no. 203 (2002): 485–517.

20. Francisco Mateos, "Ecos de América en Trento," *Revista de Indias* 6 (1945): 603–04; Severo Aparicio, "Influjo de Trento en los Concilios Limenses," *Missionalia* 29 (1972): 238.

21. The limitations on immigration are summarized in Jean-Pierre Tardieu, *L'inquisición de Lima et les hérétiques étrangers (xvie–xviie siècles)* (Paris, 1995), 19–22. Mariel de Ibáñez, *La Inquisición en México* (Mexico City, 1945), 62, notes laws of 1518 and 1522 restricting the emigration of Jews and Muslims or their descendants to the Indies.

22. Alberro, *Inquisición y sociedad,* 207. Propositions and blasphemy made up 29 percent of the Lima tribunal's activity, 24 percent of Mexico's, and 22 percent of Cartagena's prosecutions. See the tabulation in Pilar Huertas, Jesús de Miguel, Antonio Sánchez, *La Inquisición* (Madrid, 2003), 329–83.

23. The nature of social control and frequency of denunciation are discussed in Werner Thomas, *Los protestantes,* 7–50.

24. García Cárcel and Moreno Martínez, *Inquisición,* 160–61.

25. David Nirenberg, *Communities of Violence* (Princeton, 1996), 9.

26. ACC (1587), 221, José Toribio Medina, *Historia del tribunal del Santo Oficio de la Inquisición en Chile,* 2 vols. (Santiago, 1890), 1:276.

27. Aguirre also got into trouble for having said that if it came to a choice of having to exile a priest and a blacksmith, he would surely choose to keep the blacksmith since he was more valuable to the community. See the summary of the case in Medina, *Historia Chile,* 1:109–30.

28. Two recent studies are Stephen Haliczer, *Sexuality in the Confessional: A Sacrament Profaned* (Oxford, 1996); Juan Antonio Alejandre, *El veneno de Dios: La Inquisición de Sevilla ante el delito de solicitación en confesión* (Madrid, 1994). See Medina, *Historia Lima,* 1:147, 313; AHN Inq. lib. 1028, fs. 435v–441v.

29. On bigamy, see Richard Boyer, *Lives of the Bigamists: Marriage, Family, and Community in Colonial Mexico* (Albuquerque, 1994).

30. Robert McCaa, "Marriageways in Mexico and Spain, 1500–1900," *Continuity and Change* 9:1 (1994): 11–43.

31. Pierre Ragon, *Les indiens de la decouverte* (Paris, 1992), 61–63.

32. AGN, Inq. Mexico 1538, tomo 2, exp. 6, f. 201.

33. AHN, Inq. Lima, lib. 1028, f. 325 (1595).

34. For another popular manifestation of these ideas and the Inquisition's repression in Mexico, see Sergio Rivera Ayala, "Lewd Songs and Dances from the Streets of Eighteenth Century New Spain," in *Rituals of Rule, Rituals of Resistance, ed.* William H. Beezley, Cheryl English Martin, and William E. French, 27–46 (Wilmington, Del., 1994).

35. See, for example, Elias Pino Iturrieta, *Contra lujuria, castidad: Historias de pecado en el siglo xviii venezolano* (Caracas, 1992).

36. Henry Charles Lea, *A History of the Inquisition of Spain,* 4 vols. (New York, 1966), 4:147.

37. AHN, Inq. Lima, lib. 1028, fs. 393v–404v. The case is also summarized in Paulino Castañeda Delgado and Pilar Hernández Aparicio, *La Inquisición de Lima,* 3 vols. (Madrid, 1989–), 1:267–69.

38. This point is made by Lea, *History of the Inquisition of Spain,* 4:174–77.

39. G. G. Coulton, *The Plain Man's Religion in the Middle Ages* (London, 1916), 6.

40. AGN, Inq. vol. 16, fs. 205–49, cited in Bernard Grunberg, *L'Inquisition apolostique au Mexique* (Paris, 1998), 156–57.

41. AGN, Inq. vol. 10, exp. 9, fs. 335–340v.

42. Toribio Motolinía, *Memoriales: o libro de las cosas de la Nueva España,* 2d ed. (Mexico City, 1971), 311–12, n. 49. The story also appears in Alonso de Zorita, *Historia de la Nueva España* (Madrid, 1909), pt. 3, chap. 25, 556–57. Zorita and the chronicler Torquemada, however, believed that Quetzalcoatl was a charlatan.

43. "Vivir conforme a la ley de naturaleza y dictamen de la razón." Gerónimo Mendieta, *Historia eclesiastica indiana* (Mexico City, 1977), 2 vols., bk. 3, chap. 2, 1:311–13; Motolinía, *Memoriales;* Wiebke Ahrndt, *Edición crítica de la Relación de la Nueva España y de la Breve y sumaria relación escritas por Alonso de Zorita* (Mexico City, 2001).

44. AGN, Inq. vol. 112, exp. 13, fs. 386–418.

45. Federico R. Aznar Gil, "La libertad religiosa del indio en autores franciscanos del siglo xvi," *Archivo Ibero-Americano* 48:189–192 (1988): 391–440. Azuaga was author of *De iure obtentionis Regnorum Indiarum quaestiones tres.* The case is discussed in José Toribio Medina, *Historia de la tribunal del Santo Oficio de la Inquisición de México,* 2d ed., ed. Julio Jimenez Rueda (Mexico City, 1952), 32.

46. AGN, Inq. 112, exp. 13, f. 418.

47. The phrase is that of Magdalena Chocano Mena, *La fortaleza docta* (Barcelona, 2000), 344–45. She provides a good summary of the case based on the classic account by Alvaro Huerga, *Historia de los alumbrados,* 3 vols. (Madrid, 1986).

48. AHN, Inq. Libro 1964 (México), fl. 232v.–42v.

49. Jean Delumeau, *Catholicism between Luther and Voltaire: A New View of the Counter-Reformation* (London, 1977), 99–103.

50. AGN, Inq. 5 312, exp.37, fls. 167–73. The case is discussed in Antonio Ruibal Garcia, *Profetisas y solitarios* (Mexico City, 2006), 24.

51. AHN, Inq. lib. 1027; Medina, *Historia Lima*, 1:188. Cf. AHN, Inq. Leg. 2075, exp. 16. In a parallel case, the Franciscan Fray Francisco Gallen was tried in Toledo for holding that "the Law of Moses is not finished and always had its strength." ANH, Leg. 2105, n. 28.

52. Medina, *Historia México*, 360.

53. AHN, Inq. lib. 1027, fs. 237v–39.

54. Carlo Ginzburg, *The Cheese and the Worms*, trans. John and Anne Tedeschi (Baltimore, 1980), 20, 106.

55. Medina, *Historia Lima*, 1:180.

56. AHN, Inq. lib. 1064, f. 300–300v.

57. AHN, Inq. lib. 1064, f. 258.

58. AHN, Inq. lib. 1064, f. 72.

59. Wachtel, "Marrano Religiosity," 152; Nathan Wachtel, *La foi du souvenir* (Paris, 2002), 161–228. See also Lewin, *La inquisición en México* (Puebla, 1971), which publishes the trial record of María de Zárate.

60. Medina, *Historia Chile*, 1:291.

61. Anna María Spendiani et al., *Cincuenta años de la inquisición en el tribunal de Cartagena de Indias* (Bogotá, 1997).

62. Medina, *Historia Chile*, 2:71–93; see also Wachtel, *La foi*, 49–76.

63. Medina, *Historia México*, 308–09.

64. Miriam Bodian, "At the Fringes of the Reformation: 'Judaizing' Polemicist-Martyrs and the Inquisition, 1570–1670" (unpublished paper, 2001), makes the point that Inquisition publications of the autos de fe recounting the victims' obstinacy contributed to the knowledge and appreciation of their martyrdom in the Jewish communities.

65. Solange Alberro, *Inquisición y sociedad*, 467–72.

66. She was executed against the wishes of the Suprema by an overzealous inquisitor who was trying to reestablish the former importance of the Lima tribunal. See René Millar Corbacho, *La Inquisición de Lima: Signos de su decadencia, 1726–1750* (Santiago, 2005), 17–80.

67. Medina, *Historia Lima*, 2:305–06. The question of the injustice of her death was a scandal that implicated a number of inquisitors. See Jerry M. Williams, "A New Text in the Case of Ana de Castro: Lima's Inquisition on Trial," www.congreso.gob.pe.

68. Cf. AGN, Inq. vol. 119, exp. 6; ANH, Inq. 1064, fs. 115–16. His statement about Protestants in 1590 was "algunas cosas tenian buenas."

69. "En cosas de la fe hazen callar a los católicos que ante los otros son negros boçales." AHN, Inq. lib 1028, fs. 187v–88.

70. AHN, Inq. 1029, f. 219–19v; Medina, *Historia Lima*, 1:333.

71. My views on this subject have been shaped especially by the work of Robert Darnton, Roger Chartier, and Fernando Bouza Alvarez. See, for example, Robert Darnton, "First Steps Toward a History of Reading," in his *The Kiss of Lamourette: Reflections in Cultural History* (New York, 1990), 154–90; Roger Chartier, *Entre poder y placer* (Madrid, 2000); id., *El mundo como representación* (Barcelona, 1992), esp. 105–62; id., *El orden de los libros* (Barcelona, 1992), 23–40; Fernando Bouza Álvarez, *Del*

escribano a la biblioteca: La civilización escrita europea en la alta Edad Moderna (siglos xv–xvii) (Madrid, 1992); id., *Comunicación, conocimiento y memoria en la España de los siglos xvi y xvii* (Salamanca, 1999); id., *Corre manuscrito: Una historia cultural del Siglo de Oro* (Madrid, 2001).

72. See José Antonio Maraval, *La oposición politica bajo los Austrias* (Barcelona, 1972), 67.

73. I am summarizing here the results of a number of studies as presented in Antonio Viñão Frago, "Alfabetización y primeras letras (siglos xvi–xvii)," in *Escribir y leer en el siglo de Cervantes,* ed. Antonio Castillo, 39–84 (Barcelona, 1999). For Portugal, see Rita Marquillas, *A Faculdade das Letras: Lectura e escrita em Portugal no século xvii* (Bragança Paulista, São Paulo, 2003). Most studies are based on quantification of those persons who could sign their names, a research strategy which presents certain problems about functional literacy. Moreover, the collection of this information from Inquisition sources may also misrepresent or inflate the results since persons able to read were perhaps more likely to appear in its records.

74. Viñão Frago, "Alfabetización," 39–84.

75. Francisco de Quevedo, *Obras completas,* 259, cited in Maraval, "La oposición politica," 40.

76. AHN, Inq. lib. 2022 (Murcia).

77. Ángel Alcalá, *Literatura y ciencia ante la Inquisición española* (Madrid, 2001), 22. See also J. Martínez de Bujanda, "Indices de libros prohibidos del siglo xvi," *HIEA* 3:774–828. Ricardo García Cárcel, *Las Culturas del Siglo de Oro* (Madrid, 1989), 175, provides a brief summary. He comments, "Until 1790 there was not produced in Spain, Catholic Spain, any complete translation of the Holy Scripture in Spanish."

78. Manuscrito de Halle, n. 239, in Julio Sierra, *Procesos en la Inquisición de Toledo (1575–1610): Manuscrito de Halle* (Madrid, 2005), 296.

79. AGN, Inq. lib. 337, exp. Unnumbered, fs. 357–86, cited by Martin Nesvig, "Pearls before Swine: Theory and Practice of Censorship in New Spain, 1527–1640" (Ph.D. diss., Yale University, 2004), 460.

80. AGN, Inq. vol. 112, exp. 7.

81. This is an area of research that has developed rapidly in recent years. The best starting point is the reedition of Irving Leonard, *Books of the Brave,* ed. Rolena Adorno (Berkeley, 1992), in which the introduction includes an excellent bibliography. Even more recent are Pedro M. Guibovitch Pérez, *Censura, libros e inquisición en el Perú colonial* (Seville, 2003); Pedro J. Rueda Ramírez, *Negocio e intercambio cultural: El comercio de libros con América en la carrera de Indias (siglo xvii)* (Seville, 2005); Nesvig, "Pearls before Swine."

82. Magdalena Chocano Mena, *La América colonial (1492–1763): Cultura y vida cotidiana* (Madrid, 2000), 223–37.

83. Medina, *Inquisición de Lima,* 1:337, 347.

84. The story has been told many times. See, for example, Martin Cohen, *The Martyr,* 2d ed. (Albuquerque, 2003), 200.

85. AHN, Inq. lib. 1027, 445v–46v.

86. Lu Ann Homza, *Religious Authority in the Spanish Renaissance* (Baltimore, 2000), 117; Alvaro Huerga, *El proceso de la Inquisición de Sevilla contra Domingo de Baltanás* (Jaen, 1958).

87. *Concordancias de muchos passos difíciles de la divina historia* (Seville, 1555).

88. On Valtanás's ideas about New Christians, see the discussion in Albert A. Sicroff, *Los estatutos de limpieza de sangre* (Madrid, 1985), 178–79. A good summary of Valtanás's theology is found in Marcel Bataillon, *Erasmo y España,* 2d ed. (Mexico City, 1966), 543–45.

89. Paulino Castañeda Delgado and Pilar Hernández Aparicio, *Inquisición de Lima,* 3 vols (Madrid, 1989–98), 1:291.

Chapter 6. American Adjustments

1. This was not always the case. Some of the first missionaries who came into contact with peoples like the Taino of the Caribbean, who seemed to have no religion or idolatry, thought they might be closer to God than the idolaters of Peru or Mexico.

2. Susan Ramírez, *The World Turned Upside Down: Cross-cultural Contact and Conflict in Sixteenth-Century Peru* (Stanford, 1996), 134. In testimony of Joaquin, slave of don José María Saldaña, concerning a planned revolt in Bayamo, Cuba, in 1805, he was allowed to "swear by the God he worships" and stated he was "disposed to tell the truth." See AGI, Papeles de Cuba, Leg. 1649. My thanks to Ada Ferrer for this reference.

3. Jaime Lara, *City, Temple, Stage: Eschatological Architecture and Liturgical Theatrics in New Spain* (Notre Dame, 2004), 72–76.

4. Francisco Stastny, "Síntomas medievales en el 'barroco americano,'" Working paper n. 63, Instituto de Estudios Peruanos (1994), 12–13.

5. Relación de causa, 1596 (Lima), AHN, Inquisición 1028, f. 464–64v. In a similar fashion Diego Hernández de Córdoba, a Lima merchant, had intimated that the souls of Turks, Moors, and infidel Indians went to a region of air between earth and heaven. See AHN, Inq. (Lima), lib. 1027, f. 202–03.

6. Francis Borgia Steck, ed., *Motolinía's History of the Indians of New Spain* (Washington, 1951).

7. Alonso Fernández de Madrigal, *Libro de las paradojas (1437),* ed. María Teresa Herrera (Salamanca, 2000), chap. 429.

8. AHN, Inq. lib. 1027 (1579–80).

9. AHN, Inq. lib. 1028, p. 4v. (1587).

10. The peculiar cultural liminality of the first mestizo generation is an important feature of the work of the historian Berta Ares Quija. See, for example, her " 'Sang-mêlés' dans le Pérou colonial: Les defies aux contraintes des categories identitaires," in *Identités périphériques,* ed. Marie-Lucie Copete and Raúl Caplán, 25–40 (Paris, 2005); id., "Mancebas de españoles, madres de mestizos: Imágenes de la mujer indígena en el Perú colonial temprano," in *Las mujeres en la construcción de las sociedades iberoamericanas,* ed. Pilar Gonzalbo Aizpuru and Berta Ares Quija, 15–39 (Seville, 2004).

11. This is a reference to Miguel de Cervantes, *El ingenioso hidalgo Don Quijote de la Mancha,* ed. Martín de Riquer (Barcelona, 1980), book 1, part 4, chap. 32, 338–45.

12. AHN, Inq. (Lima), lib. 1027, fs. 424–26 (1583).

13. Jean-Pierre Tardieu, *Le nouveau David et la réforme du Pérou* (Bordeaux, 1992), provides the most complete account of the case, although Marcel Bataillon, "La herejía de Fray Francisco de la Cruz y la reacción antilascasiana," *Études sur Bartolomé de Las Casas* (Paris, 1966), 309–29, captures the main elements of it. The extensive trial record

has been published by Vidal Abril Castelló in a useful, if strangely organized, edition. See *Francisco de la Cruz, Inquisición,* 3 vols., Corpus Hispanorum de Pace (Madrid, 1992–96).

14. Letter of the Principal men of Xuchipilla (1570), AGN, Inq. vol. 187, exp. 2; AHN, Inq. 1064, f. 33.

15. AGN, Inq. vol. 187 exp. 2, fs. 13–106.

16. See John Martin, "Salvation and Society in Sixteenth-Century Venice: Popular Evangelism in a Renaissance City," *Journal of Modern History* 60 (1988): 205–33; Eva-Marie Jung, "On the Nature of Evangelism in Sixteenth-Century Italy," *Journal of the History of Ideas* 14 (1953): 511–27.

17. Stuart B. Schwartz and Frank Salomon, "New Peoples and New Kinds of People," in *Cambridge History of the Native Peoples of the Americas,* vol. 3 (*South America*), eds. Frank Salomon and Stuart B. Schwartz, 471–77 (Cambridge, 2002).

18. John L. Kessell, "Diego Romero, the Plains Apaches, and the Inquisition," *American West* 15:3 (1978): 12–16. Romero was charged in 1663 with various propositions and with willingly participating in an Apache ritual while on a trading expedition across the frontier.

19. Francisco Núñez de Pineda y Bascuñán, *Cautiverio feliz y razón individual de las guerras dilatadas del Reino de Chile,* ed. Alejandro Lipsutz and Alvaro Jara (Santiago, 1973).

20. See Ana María Lorandi, *Spanish King of the Incas* (Pittsburgh, 2005).

21. Medina, *Historia Chile,* 1:278.

22. Herbert S. Klein, "The African Slave Trade to 1650," in *Tropical Babylons: Sugar and the Making of the Atlantic World,* ed. Stuart B. Schwartz, 201–36 (Chapel Hill, 2004).

23. Isacio Pérez Fernández, *Fray Bartolomé de Las Casas, O.P.: De defensor de los indios a defensor de los negros,* Monumenta Histórica Iberoamericana de la Orden de Predicadores, 8 (Salamanca, 1995), 150–51.

24. A. J. R. Russell-Wood, "Iberian Expansion and the Issue of Black Slavery: Changing Portuguese Attitudes, 1440–1770," *American Historical Review* 83:1 (1978): 16–42.

25. Cited by Robin Blackburn, *The Making of New World Slavery* (London, 1997), 152. For the civil, canonical, and scriptural justifications, see also Jesús María García Añoveros, *El pensamiento y los argumentos sobre la esclavitud en Europa en el siglo xvi y su aplicación a los indios americanos y a los negros africanos* (Madrid, 2000).

26. The statements of slaves about slavery are naturally difficult to find. Manuel Francisco Zapata was a Wolof slave living in Panama and working as a mason and had lived for awhile as a corsair in North Africa; he said that if back in those days he had found the white man who had sold him into slavery he would have taken his revenge for the misfortunes he had suffered. He was sentenced in 1716 in Cartagena de Indias. AHN, Leg. 5349/5.

27. Oliveira had been a Dominican. He left the order and later ran afoul of the Portuguese Inquisition for a number of propositions that smacked of Erasmian thought. See Henrique Lopes de Mendonça, *O padre Fernando Oliveira e a sua obra nautica* (Lisbon, 1898). On Oliveira's maritime thought, see Inácio Guerreiro and Francisco Contente Domingues, eds., *Fernando Oliveira e seu tempo: Humanismo e arte de navegar no*

Renascimento europeu (1450–1650) (Cascais, 1999). On early antislavery thought in Spain and Portugal, see also Russell-Wood, "Iberian Expansion," 36–37.

28. Fernão Oliveira, *A arte de guerra no mar* (Lisbon, 1983), esp. chap. 11, "Qual he guerra justa?" On Oliveira, also see C. R. Boxer, *The Church Militant in Iberian Expansion, 1440–1770* (Baltimore, 1978), 30–36; Harold Livermore, "Padre Oliveira's Outburst: Slave-Trade and the Portuguese Empire," *Portuguese Studies* 17 (2001): 22–41.

29. There is a modern edition. Alonso de Sandoval, *Un tratado sobre la esclavitud,* ed. Enriqueta Vila Vilar (Madrid, 1987). See also Margaret M. Olsen, *Slavery and Salvation in Colonial Cartagena de Indias* (Gainesville, 2004), who uses postmodern and postcolonial theory to analyze Sandoval's text.

30. IC, 60–1-5, Relación de auto de fe de Cartagena de Indias (1613–14).

31. The case is summarized in the *relación de causa* published in Spendiani et al., *Cincuenta años,* 275–79.

32. Ibid.

33. Medina, *Historia Lima,* 1:52–55, reprints the information in the printed *relación* of the auto de fe of 15 November 1573. See also Jean Pierre Tardieu, *L'inquisition de Lima et les hérétiques étrangers* (Paris, 1995), 64.

34. The question of madness is explored in depth in H. C. Erik Midelfort, *A History of Madness in Sixteenth-Century Germany* (Stanford, 1999). More specifically on the Inquisition's treatment of madness, see María Cristiana Sacristán, *Locura e inquisición en Nueva España, 1571–1760* (Mexico City, 1992).

35. The site is located in the neighborhood of Chacra Rios. See *Inventario de monumentos arqueológicos del Perú* (Lima, 1985), site 65.

36. The shared or collective nature of early modern Hispanic culture is emphasized forcefully by Luis E. Rodríguez-San Pedro and José Luis Sánchez-Lora, *Los siglos xvi–xvii,* Historia de España 3er. Milenio (Madrid, 2000), 207–28.

37. For a recent overview of the extensive but inconclusive literature on this topic, see Carlos Eire, "The Concept of Popular Religion," in *Local Religion in Colonial Mexico,* ed. Martin Nesvig, 1–35 (Albuquerque, 2006). An older but perceptive overview is Peter Burke, "Popular Piety," in *Catholicism in Early Modern History: A Guide to Research,* ed. John O'Malley, 113–31 (St. Louis, 1988).

38. William Christian, Jr., *Local Religion in Sixteenth-Century Spain* (Princeton, 1981), 146–80; "Catholicisms," in *Local Religion,* ed. Nesvig, 259–68. See also Augustín Redondo, "La religion populaire espagnole au XVI siècle: Un terrain d'affrontement," in *Culturas populares,* ed. Casa de Velázquez, 329–49 (Madrid, 1986).

39. Adriano Prosperi, *Tribunali della coscienza* (Turin, 1996), is an excellent example of an extensive literature. See also Paolo Prodi and Carla Penuti, eds., *Disciplina dell'anima, disciplina del corpo e disciplina della società tra medioevo ed età moderna* (Bologna, 1994).

40. Cf. Nalle, *God in La Mancha;* Kamen, *The Phoenix and the Flame;* Poska, *Regulating the People.*

41. Adriano Prosperi, *America e apocalisse e altri saggi* (Pisa, 1999); Eire, "The Concept of Popular Religion," 28.

42. Christian, *Local Religion,* 147–48.

43. A classic formulation of this relationship is Keith Thomas, *Religion and the Decline of Magic* (London, 1973), 301–34.

44. John Butler, *Awash in a Sea of Faith* (Cambridge, Mass., 1990), 25; see also his "Magic, Astrology, and Early American Religious Heritage, 1600–1760," *American Historical Review* 84:2 (1979): 317–46.

45. This literature is vast, but essential starting points for understanding the cultural and religious contact between Native Americans and Spaniards are Serge Gruzinski, *La colonization de l'imaginaire* (Paris, 1988); Carmen Bernand and Serge Gruzinski, *De la idotatría: Una arqueología de las ciencias religiosas* (Mexico City, 1992); Sabine MacCormack, *Religion in the Andes* (Princeton, 1991).

46. Laura A. Lewis, *Hall of Mirrors: Power, Witchcraft, and Caste in Colonial Mexico* (Durham, 2003), 121–23. An excellent discussion of the relationship between the supernatural and religiosity in New Spain is found in Antonio Rubial García, *Profetisas y solitarios* (Mexico City, 2006), 224–34.

47. AGN, Inq. vol. 348, exp. 4 (1624), cited in Lewis, *Hall of Mirrors,* 123–27. Cf. AGN Inq. vol. 435, fs. 74–75v.

48. See Fermín del Pino, "Demonología en España y América: Invariantes y matices de la práctica inquisitorial y la misionera," in *El Diablo en la Edad Moderna,* ed. María Tauset and James Amelang, 277–95 (Madrid, 2004). On the devil in the Spanish Indies, see Fernando Cervantes, *The Devil in the New World* (New Haven, 1994); "The Devils of Querétaro: Scepticism and Credulity in Late Seventeenth-Century Mexico," *Past and Present* 130 (1991): 51–69. See also Lisa Sousa, "The Devil and Deviance in Native Criminal Narratives from Early Mexico," *The Americas* 59:2 (2002): 161–79. For a fascinating Caribbean case of an exorcism, see Fernando Ortiz, *Historia de una pelea cubana contra los demonios* (Havana, 1973). On the general problem of the devil in the New World, see Laura de Mello e Souza, *Inferno atlântico: Demonologia e colonização, séculos XVI–XVIII* (São Paulo, 1993). Jorge Cañizares-Esguerra, *Puritan Conquistadors* (Stanford, 2006), argues that Puritans in New England were just as liable as the Spanish Catholic missionaries to see the devil in America.

49. The work of Serge Gruzinski has been particularly important is detailing this process of cultural interchange in Mexico and then projecting his findings as a more global process. See his *The Conquest of Mexico: The Incorporation of Indian Societies into the Western World, 16th–18th Centuries* (Cambridge, Mass., 1993); and the more succinct discussion in Carmen Bernand and Serge Gruzinski, *Histoire du Nouveau Monde: Les métissages* (Paris, 1993), 286–328. Cf. Serge Gruzinski, *Les quatre parties du monde* (Paris, 2004).

50. This point is made in the penetrating essay by Anthony Grafton and Ingrid Rowland, "The Witch Hunter's Crusade," *New York Review of Books* 49:14 (2002): 68–70.

51. I mention here some of the works that have most influenced my thinking on this issue: Roger Chartier, *Cultural History between Practices and Representations* (Cambridge, 1988); id., "Religión campesina y ortodoxia católica," in *El juego de las reglas: Lecturas,* 147–61 (Buenos Aires, 2000); Peter Burke, *Popular Culture in Early Modern Europe,* 2d ed. (Aldershot, England, 1994); Anne Jacobson Schutte, "Carlo Ginzburg," *Journal of Modern History* 48:2 (1976): 296–315; James Sharpe, "Popular Culture in the Early Modern West," in *Companion to Historiography,* ed. Michael Bentley, 361–76 (London, 1997); Chandra Mukerji and Michael Schudson, "Popular Culture," *Annual Review of Sociology* 12 (1986): 47–66; Stuart Clark, "French Historians and Early Modern Popular Culture," *Past and Present* 100 (1983): 62–99.

52. This is cited and discussed in Magdalena Chocano Mena, *La fortaleza docta: Elite letrada y dominación social en México colonial (siglos xvi–xvii)* (Barcelona, 1999), 309.

53. Richard Greenleaf, "Persistence of Native Values: The Inquisition and the Indians of Colonial Mexico," *The Americas* 50:3 (1994): 351–76; id., "The Inquisition and the Indians of New Spain: A Study in Jurisdictional Confusion," *The Americas* 22:2 (1965): 138–66. See also Jorge Klor de Alva, "Colonizing Souls: The Failure of the Indian Inquisition and the Rise of Penitential Discipline," in *Cultural Encounters: The Impact of the Inquisition in Spain and the New World,* ed. Mary Elizabeth Perry and Anne J. Cruz, 3–22 (Berkeley, 1991).

54. The redefinition of idolatry as superstition and its consideration as a venial sin can be seen in Alonso de la Peña Montenegro, *Itinerario para párrocos de indios,* 2 vols. (Madrid, 1995), 1:458–83. For examples of Indians prosecuted by episcopal courts, see Medina, *Historia México,* 370–71. An edict of the Provisorato of Mexico issued in 1769 provides a detailed list of Indian religious deviations. See Medina, *Historia México,* 372–78.

55. Although the concept of *nepantla* was Mesoamerican, it has been applied creatively by Nicholas Griffiths, *The Cross and the Serpent* (Norman, 1996), 15–16, to the Andean situation.

56. William B. Taylor, *Magistrates of the Sacred* (Stanford, 1996), 47–73; Nancy M. Farriss, *Maya Society under Colonial Rule* (Princeton, 1984), 286–319.

57. Serge Gruzinski and Nathan Wachtel, "Cultural Interbreedings: Constituting a Majority as a Minority," *Comparative Studies in Society and History* 39:2 (1997): 231–50.

58. Felipe Salvador Gilij, *Ensayo de historia Americana, o sea historia natural, civil y sacra de los reinos y las provincias españolas de Tierra Firme en la América Meridional,* 3 vols., trans. Antonio Tovar (Caracas, 1987), 2:313, 3:116. See the discussion in Lourdes Giordani, "Speaking Truths or Absurdities: The Religious Dialogues between Father Gilij and His Indian Contemporaries (18th century Venezuela)," Paper presented to Latin American Studies Association (Washington, 1995).

59. Kenneth Mills, *Idolatry and Its Enemies: Colonial Andean Religion and Extirpation, 1640–1750* (Princeton, 1997), 243–66; Sabine McCormack, *Religion in the Andes: Vision and Imagination in Early Colonial Peru* (Princeton, 1991), 383–433.

60. Mills, *Idolatry,* 75. See also Kenneth Mills, "The Limits of Religious Conversion in Mid-Colonial Peru," *Past and Present* 145 (1994): 84–121; id., "The Naturalization of Andean Christianities," in *The Cambridge History of Christianity,* vol. 6, *Reformation and Expansion, 1500–1660,* ed. Po-Chia Hsia, 508–39 (Cambridge, 2007).

61. On the devotion of the Virgin of Ocotlán, a cult sponsored by the Franciscans in the sixteenth century, see Rodrigo Martínez Baracas, *La secuencia tlaxcalteca: Orígenes del culto a Nuestra Señora de Ocotlán* (Mexico City, 2000), 11–40.

62. Lara, *City, Temple, Stage,* 171–74.

63. Fernando Cervantes, "The Impact of Christianity in Spanish America," *Bulletin of Latin American Research* 14:2 (1995): 201–10.

64. Gruzinski and Wachtel, "Cultural Interbreedings," 248–49.

65. Mills, *Idolatry,* 281–82.

66. My thanks to Eric van Young for his personal suggestions in this regard. See Eric van Young, *The Other Rebellion* (Stanford, 2001).

Chapter 7. Brazil

1. BNM, MS 9394, "Papeles varios . . . Portugal."

2. Ronaldo Vainfas, *Trópico dos pecados* (Rio de Janeiro, 1997), 19–39; Laura de Mello e Souza, *O diabo,* 38–40; Maria de Lourdes Correia Fernandes, "Da reforma da Igreja à reforma dos cristãos," *HRP* 2:15–47.

3. Caio Bosci presents data indicating that 950 people were denounced in the two visits. Those accused of Judaism (207) were 22 percent of the total, a percentage far below the figures for Judaizers of between 65 and 83 percent of those prosecuted in Portuguese tribunals. In the Brazilian visits, sodomy, bigamy, and sorcery/witchcraft/ superstition each made up about 5 percent of the accusations, but the accusations for blasphemy/irreverence and doctrinal error made up over 35 percent of the denunciations. See Caio Bosci, "Estuturas eclesiásticas e inquisição," *HRP,* 2:429–55.

4. Mello e Souza, *O diabo,* 40–44.

5. José Justino Andrade e Silva, *Colleção chronológico da legislação portuguesa (1603–1700)* (Lisbon, 1854–59), 3:50 (22 July 1622).

6. BL, Egerton 323, f. 97–97v. The Council of Portugal recommended in 1622 that the bishop of Salvador serve as inquisitor with the assistance of the judges of the Bahian Court of Appeals, but the inquisitor-general of Portugal claimed that the bishop could not do the task, and he asked for a separate inquisitor for Brazil paid for by the crown. Although he did not use this source, the best summary of the issue is Bruno Feitler, *Inquisition, juifs et nouveaux-chétiens au Brésil* (Louvain, 2003), 64–67.

7. In the *sertão* of Piaui it was reported that a cross stood before the door of every home. ANTT, Inq. Lisboa CP 270, f. 186.

8. There were apparently other visits of the Inquisition for which there is only fragmentary evidence, including at least one to Rio de Janeiro in 1627 and another to Maranhão in 1731. See Lina Gorenstein, "A tercera visitação do Santo Ofício às partes do Brasil (século xvii)," in *A inquisição em xeque,* ed. Ronaldo Vainfas, Bruno Feitler, Lana Lage, 25–32 (Rio de Janeiro, 2006).

9. The classic description of this case is João Capistrano de Abreu, "Atribulações de um donatário," in *Caminhos antigos e povoameno do Brasil,* 2d ed., 41–57 (Rio de Janeiro, 1960).

10. The text is cited in ibid., 57. The original is ANTT, Inq. Lisbon 8821.

11. The trial of João de Bolés is published in *Anais da Biblioteca National de Rio de Janeiro* 25 (1904). An excellent summary of the case and analysis using the Jesuit correspondence is presented by Adriana Romeiro, "Todos os caminhos levam ao ceu: Relações entre cultura popular e cultura erudite no Brasil do século xvi" (M.A. thesis, Universidade de Campinas, 1991).

12. Luiz Walter Coelho Filho, *A capitania de São Jorge e a década do açúcar* (Salvador, 2000). Elaine Sanceau, *Captains of Brazil* (Porto, 1965), 167–70.

13. ANTT, Inq. Lisbon, processo 1682 (1584).

14. The authorship and genre of the *Viaje de Turquía* has been long disputed. Modern scholarship has suggested the author was the Spanish physician Andrés de Laguna, but other possible authors have also been suggested. See the excellent critical edition of Marie-Sol Ortola, *Viaje de Turquía* (Madrid, 2000), which accepts and then expands on

the argument of Marcel Bataillon, *Le docteur Laguna auteur du Voyage en Turquie* (Paris, 1958).

15. ANTT, Inq. Lisbon, 1682.

16. Bento Teixeira has been the subject of extensive analysis by literary scholars. These paragraphs are based on the summaries of his life presented by Costa Pôrto, *Nos tempos do visitador* (Recife, 1968), 189–95; and Adriana Romeiro, "Todos os caminhos," 167–87.

17. See Jaques LeGoff, *The Birth of Purgatory*, trans. Arthur Goldhammer (Chicago, 1984).

18. *DB, 1591–93*, 363.

19. ANTT, Inq. Lisbon CP 207, fs.29–30.

20. ANTT, Inq. Lisbon CP 232, fls. 1–80.

21. Vainfas, *Trópico;* Mello e Souza, *O diabo;* Romeiro, "Todos os caminhos"; and Janete Ruiz de Macedo, "Ideologia e controle no Brasil colonial, 1540–1620" (Ph.D. diss., Universidad de León, 1999) are excellent analyses of popular religion in Brazil, emphasizing the first century but in the case of Mello e Souza extending the story into the eighteenth century. Luiz Mott, *Rosa Egypciaca: Uma santa Africana no Brasil* (Rio de Janeiro, 1993), also deals with the eighteenth century.

22. *DCP*, 86; 415.

23. *DCP*, 28; Vainfas, *Trópico*, 59–69. I have written more extensively on this question in Schwartz, "Pecar en colonias," 51–67.

24. See, for example, the confessions of Cristóvão Bulhões, Rodrigo Martins, Manoel Branco, and Gonçalo Fernandes in *CB*, 1591, 87–89, 93–95, 96–97, 104–05.

25. Manuel de Faria e Sousa, *Asia portuguesa*, 3 vols. (Lisbon, 1675).

26. These figures come from the best analysis of the movement, Ronaldo Vainfas, *A heresia dos índios* (São Paulo, 1995), 231. Of course, the primary participants were Indians, and at one stage there were perhaps as many as three thousand in the Jaguaripe movement, but the Inquisition was less interested in them and thus their relative absence in the denunciations and confessions to the tribunal.

27. *DB 1591–93,* 283–85. This case is examined thoroughly by Romeiro, "Todos os caminhos."

28. Ibid. There was some suggestion that Aranha's father may have been a New Christian, but the Inquisition gave no attention to the possibility that his ideas may have been those of a Judaizer. Cf. Francisco Marquez Villanueva, " 'Nascer y morir como bestias' (criptojudaísmo y criptoaverroísmo)," in *Inquisição: Ensaios sobre mentalidade, heresies e arte,* ed. Anita Novinsky and Maria Luiza Tucci Carneiro, 11–34 (São Paulo, 1992).

29. Eddy Stols, "Convivências e conivências luso-flamengas na rota do açúcar," *Ler História* 32 (1997): 119–47.

30. ANTT, Inq. Lisbon CP 265, fs. 214–16.

31. ANTT, Inq. Lisbon CP 270, f. 399–399v.

32. Rebecca Catz, ed., *The Travels of Mendes Pinto* (Chicago, 1989); John Christian Laursen, "Irony and Toleration: Lessons from the Travels of Mendes Pinto," *Critical Review of International Social and Political Philosophy* 6:2 (2002): 21–40.

33. ANTT, Inq. Lisbon CP 283, f. 51–51v. On the work of Fernao Mendes Pinto, see Catz, *Travels.*

34. Novinsky, *Cristãos novos na Bahia,* 57–102, is the classic statement of this position.

35. Angela Vieira Maia, *A sombra do medo: Cristãos Velhos e cristãos Novos nas capitanias do açúcar* (Rio de Janeiro, 1995), 97–139, following the lead of Novinsky, *Cristãos novos na Bahia*, presents interesting evidence of interaction. I have calculated the percentages of exogamy from Vieira Maia's somewhat confusing tables, 243–45, which summarize the information in the 1591–93 visit.

36. Ronald J. Raminelli, "Tempo das visitações: Cultura e sociedade em Pernambuco e Bahia: 1591- 1620" (M.A. thesis, University of São Paulo, 1990), 142–51.

37. Jonathan Schorsch, "Jews, Judaism, Blacks and Christianity According to the Early Modern Inquisitions" (unpublished paper). See also his *Jews and Blacks in the Early Modern World* (Cambridge, 2004).

38. *DB,* Livro de confessões e retificações Bahia, 1618, 362.

39. Ibid., 362–64.

40. The literature on Dutch toleration is extensive. For a short introduction, see Henry Méchoulan, *Amsterdam au temps de Spinoza, Argent et liberté* (Paris, 1990). On Brazil, see the summary article by Ronaldo Vainfas, "La Babel religiosa: Católicos, calvinistas, conversos y judíos en Brasil bajo loa dominación holandesa (1630–54)," in *Familia, religión y negocio,* ed. Jaime Contreras et al., 321–42 (Madrid, 2002).

41. This story has now been detailed in Frans Leonard Schalkwijk, *Igreja e estado no Brasil holandês* (Recife, 1986).

42. José Antônio Gonsalves de Mello, *Tempo dos flamengos* (Rio de Janeiro: José Olímpio, 1947), 134.

43. Adriaen van der Dussen, *Relatório sôbre as capitanias conquistadas no Brasil pelos holandeses* (1639), ed. José Antônio Gonsalves de Mello (Rio de Janeiro, 1947).

44. Anita Novinsky, "Uma devassa do Bispo Dom Pedro da Silva, 1635–37," *Anais do Museu Paulista* 22 (1968): 217–85. The original document is in ANTT, Inq. Cadernos do promotor, n. 19.

45. Manuel Calado, *O valeroso lucideno* (1648), 2 vols. (Belo Horizonte, 1987). See the discussion in C. R. Boxer, *Dutch in Brazil* (Oxford, 1957), 298–99.

46. Boxer, *Dutch in Brazil,* 267–69, provides a biography of Moraes, a Brazilian-born Jesuit who changed from Catholic priest to secular Calvinist, married, lived in Leiden for a while, and returned to Brazil and to the Catholic faith. Although his case is particularly colorful, it was not that uncommon for individuals, even clerics, to move back and forth between religions. On New Christians who became Jews and then returned to the Church, see David L. Graizbord, *Souls in Dispute: Converso Identities in Iberia and the Jewish Diaspora* (Philadelphia, 2004); Isabel M. R. Mendes Drumond Braga, "Uma estranha diáspora rumo a Portugal: Judeus e cristãos-novos reduzidos à fé católica no século xvii," *Sefarad* 62 (2002): 259–74.

47. José António Gonsalves de Mello, *João Fernandes Vieira: Mestre-de-campo do Terço de Infantaria de Pernambuco,* 2d ed. (Lisboa, 2000), 47–49; Boxer, *Dutch in Brazil,* 273–76.

48. Gonsalves de Mello, *Tempo dos flamengos,* 141–43.

49. Feitler, *Inquisition,* 83–85.

50. Nassau was a practicing Calvinist who saw the king of Spain as a primary enemy of Christian faith, and he also supposedly held negative opinions about Jews according to his chroniclers. See Schalkwijk, *Igreja e estado,* 87. On his measures on behalf of freedom

of conscience of the Portuguese and in defense of their interests, see Gaspar Barléu, *História dos feitos recentemente praticados durante oito anos no Brasil* (Belo Horizonte, 1974), 53.

51. Nassau's personal negative attitude toward the Jews is suggested in the anti-Semitic remarks of the former Spanish priest turned Calvinist minister Vicente Joaquin Soler. See his correspondence edited by B. N. Teensma, *Dutch Brazil: Vincent Joachim Soler's Seventeen Letters* (Rio de Janeiro, 1999), 74.

52. Manuel Calado, *O valeroso lucideno*, 1:165–74.

53. D. Margarida to Cabido da Sé of Miranda (1639) in Schalkwijk, *Igreja e estado*, 237.

54. This point was made by the Portuguese ambassador Francisco de Sousa Coutinho. See Boxer, *Dutch in Brazil*, 262.

55. Evaldo Cabral de Mello, *Rubro veio: O imaginário da Restauração pernambucana*, 2d ed. (Rio de Janeiro, 1997); *Olinda restaurada*, 2d ed. (Rio de Janeiro, 1998), 381–447.

56. Saul Levy Mortera, "Providencia de Dios con Ysrael y verdad y eternidad de la ley de Moseh y Nullidad de los demas leyes," trans. A. Wiznitzer, *Jewish Social Studies* 16:112–13.

57. Anita Novinsky, *Cristãos novos*, 129–33.

58. ANTT, Inq. Lisbon CP 270, f. 87 (29 Dec. 1705). The case is also mentioned in James Sweet, *Recreating Africa* (Chapel Hill, 2004), 153.

59. On the calundus, the most important work has been done by Laura de Mello e Souza, "Revsitando o calundu," in *Ensaios sobre a intolerancia,* ed. L. Gorenstein and M. L. Tucci Carneiro, 293–318 (São Paulo, 2002), and her *The Devil and the Land of the Holy Cross* (Austin, 2004), 167–72, 234–37. See also the following basic articles: Luiz Mott, "O calundu angola de Luiza Pinta: Sabará, 1739," *Revista IAC* (Ouro Preto) (1994): 73–82; João José Reis, "Magia Jeje na Bahia: A invasão do calundu de Pasto de Cachoeira, 1785," *Revista Brasileira da História* 8:16 (1988): 57–81.

60. Nuno Marques Pereira, *O peregrino da America* (Lisbon, 1722). See the discussion in Laura de Mello e Souza, *The Devil*, 194–95. See also Sweet, *Recreating Africa,* 144–60.

61. Marques Pereira, *O peregrino da America,* 160.

62. ANTT, Inq. Lisboa CP 268, f. 156

63. ANTT, Inq. Lisboa CP 270, f. 416.

64. Mello e Souza, *The Devil,* 171.

65. This point is made specifically for Minas Gerais by Donald Ramos, "A influência africana e cultura popular em Minas Gerais: Um comentário sobre a interpretação da escravidão," in *Brasil: Colonização e escravidão,* ed. M. B. Nizza da Silva, 142–62 (Rio de Janeiro, 1999). Cf. Jon Butler, *Awash in a Sea of Faith* (Cambridge, Mass., 1990), 25–36.

66. My argument is guided here by Paiva, *Bruxaria e superstição,* 95–164; Mello e Souza, *The Devil,* 93–178; Thomas, *Religion,* 179–209; and Gary K. Waite, *Heresy, Magic and Witchcraft in Early Modern Europe* (New York, 2003), 11–51.

67. ANTT, Inq. Lisboa CP 270, f. 41–42v.

68. Stuart Clark, "Inversion, Misrule and the Meaning of Witchcraft," *Past and Present* 87 (1980): 98–127.

69. Ibid.

70. ANTT, Inq. Lisboa CP 254, f. 146 (que não servia mais que de tomar as fazendas).

71. ANTT, Inq. Lisboa CP 265.

72. There are two fine studies of this case that emphasize different aspects of Henne-quim's heresy: Adriana Romeiro, *Um visionário na corte de D. João V* (Belo Horizonte, 2001); and Plínio J. Freire Gomes, *Um herege vai ao paraíso* (São Paulo, 1997).

73. ANTT, Inq. Lisboa, maço 1119, n. 15520.

74. Important experimentation by the Italian Francesco Redi was published in 1668 suggesting that the doctrine of spontaneous generation was false. See Matthew R. Good-rum, "Atomism, Atheism, and Spontaneous Generation of Human Beings: The Debate Over a Natural Origin of the First Humans in Seventeenth-Century Britain," *Journal of the History of Ideas* (2002): 207–24.

75. The Jesuit Padre Simão de Vasconcelos (1597–1671) wrote a number of works on the Jesuit order in Brazil. He is particularly remembered as an exponent of a utopian vision of Brazil and for his assertion that St. Thomas had visited Brazil in the early days of Christianity.

76. See Beatriz Helena Domingues, "Jesuits in Brazil and Seventeenth-Century Euro-pean Modern Philosophy and Science: Continuities or Discontinuities," www.la.utexas.edu/research/paisano/BDHtext.html.

77. Paiva, *Bruxaria e superstição,* 95–164.

78. Gaspar Cardoso de Sequeira, *Thesouro de prudentes, novamente tirado a lus* (Lisboa, 1612). There were subsequent editions in 1626, 1651, three in 1675, 1700, and 1702.

79. Timothy D. Walker, *Doctors, Folk Medicine and the Inquisition* (Leiden, 2005), 88–153.

Chapter 8. From Tolerance to Toleration in the Eighteenth-Century Iberian Atlantic World

1. My brief analysis of Olavide is based primarily on Guillermo Lohman Villena, *Pedro Peralta Barnuevo y Pablo de Olavide: Biblioteca de Hombres del Perú* (Lima, 1964); Richard Herr, *The Eighteenth-Century Revolution in Spain* (Princeton, 1958), 209–11; Marcelin Defourneaux, *Pablo de Olavide, ou l'afrancesado* (Paris, 1959); Luis Perdices Blas, *Pablo de Olavide (1725–1803) El Ilustrado* (Madrid, 1992); Manuela Moreno Mancebo, "Breve biografía de Olavide," in *Inquisición española: Nuevas aproxima-ciones,* Centro de Estudios Inquisitoriales (Madrid, 1987), 257–96. The case was also fully discussed in the traditional studies of the Inquisition, where, in Lea, *History of the Inquisition,* 4:308–11, Olavide receives a sympathetic discussion, while in Menéndez Pelayo, *Historia de los heterodoxos,* 2:682–700, the author's ridicule is tempered only by the fact that Olavide later returned to the Church.

2. Perdices Blas, *Pablo de Olavide,* provides the fullest analysis of this stage of his career.

3. AHN, Inq. 3733, n. 80 (Corte).

4. Perez Zagorin, *How the Idea of Religious Toleration Came to the West* (Princeton, 2003), 248–67; Jonathan Israel, "Spinoza, Locke, and the Enlightenment Battle for Tol-eration," in *Toleration in Enlightenment Europe,* ed. Ole Peter Grell and Roy Porter, 102–13 (Cambridge, 2000).

5. Alphonse Dupront, *Qu'est-ce que les Lumières?* (Paris, 1996), 137–230. He draws extensively on René Pomeau, *Le religion de Voltaire* (Paris, 1956). See also Harry C. Payne, *The Philosophes and the People* (New Haven, 1976), 65–93.

6. Jonathan I. Israel, *Radical Enlightenment* (Oxford, 2001), 528–40.

7. Francisco Sánchez Blanco, *La mentalidad ilustrada* (Madrid, 1999), 275.

8. Richard Herr, "The Twentieth Century Spaniard Views the Spanish Enlightenment," *Hispania* 45:2 (1962): 183–93; Stephen Haliczer, "La Inquisición como mito y como historia: Su abolición y el desarrollo de la ideología política española," in *Inquisición española y mentalidad inquisitorial,* ed. Ángel Alcalá, 496–517 (Barcelona, 1984). Particularly important is Doris Moreno, *La invención de la Inquisición* (Madrid, 2004).

9. The classic histories of the Spanish Enlightenment are Herr, *The Eighteenth Century Revolution;* Jean Sarrailh, *L'Espagne éclairée de la seconde moitié du XVIIIᵉ siècle* (Paris, 1954); and Francisco Sánchez Blanco, *El absolutismo y las luces en el reinado de Carlos III* (Madrid, 2002); Jesús Pérez Magallón, *Construyendo la modernidad: La cultura española en el tiempo de los novatores (1675–1725)* (Madrid, 2002).

10. Ana Cristina Araújo, *A cultura das luzes em Portugal: Temas e problemas* (Lisbon, 2003), provides an overview of intellectual life. Kenneth Maxwell, *Pombal: Paradox of the Enlightenment* (Cambridge, 1995), concentrates on political affairs but provides a general cultural context.

11. Ángel de Prado Moura, *Las hogueras de la intolerancia* (Valladolid, 1996), 132.

12. Histories of atheism, like those of toleration, concentrate on a few important thinkers and their texts. A good introduction to the question is found in David Wooton, "New Histories of Atheism," in *Atheism from the Reformation to the Enlightenment,* ed. Michael Hunter and David Wooton, 13–54 (Oxford, 1992).

13. ANH, Inq. Leg. 3733/73 (Corte).

14. Enrique Gacto Fernández, *Cantabria y la inquisición en el siglo xviii* (Santander, 1999), 136–40. The note accompanying this reference cites many cases of this type in the last years of the eighteenth century. See also Manuel Arana Mendíaz, *El tribunal de la inquisición de Canarias durante el reinado de Carlos III* (Las Palmas, 2000).

15. Medina, *Historia México,* 349; AHN, Leg. 1730, n. 24 (1758).

16. Alejandre and Torquemada, *Palabra de hereje,* 76–77, cites this and similar statements. See also AHN, Inq. Leg. 5349–3 (Cartagena).

17. García Cárcel and Moreno Martínez, *Inquisición,* 319–41.

18. Maria Adelaide Salvador Marques, "Pombalismo e cultura media: Meios para um diagnóstico através da Real Mesa Censória," in *Como interpretar Pombal?* (Lisbon, 1983), 185–214.

19. Luiz Carlos Villalta, "As licenças para posse e lectura de livros proibidos," in *De Cabral a Pedro I: Aspectos da colonização portuguesa no Brasil,* ed. Maria Beatriz Nizza da Silva, 235–45 (Oporto, 2001).

20. The term *libertine* was first used by Calvin in 1554 in his attack on irreligiosity and disregard for morality. See the discussion by Adauto Novaes, "Por que tanta libertinagem?" in *Libertinos, libertários,* ed. Adauto Novaes, 9–20 (São Paulo, 1996).

21. José A. Ferrer Benimeli, "La inquisición frente a masonería e ilustración," in *Inquisición española y mentalidad inquisitorial,* ed. Ángel Alcalá, 463–96 (Barcelona, 1984). See his fundamental works *Masonería, Iglesia e Ilustración,* 4 vols. (Ma-

drid, 1976–77), and *Los archivos secretos vaticanos y la Masonería* (Caracas, 1976).

22. Ferrer Benimeli, "La inquisición," 494; García Cárcel and Moreno Martínez, *Inquisición*, 314–16.

23. Lea, *History of the Inquisition*, 4:176–77.

24. For recent work in this area, see Enrique Gacto Fernández, ed., *Inquisición y censura: El acoso a la inteligencia en España* (Madrid, 2006).

25. The treaty of alliance between Spain and England in 1604 has been identified as the first example of such grants of pragmatic toleration in Iberia. See Antonio Domínguez Ortiz, "El primer esbozo de tolerancia religiosa en la España de los Austrias," in *Instituciones y sociedad en la España de los Austrias,* 185–91 (Barcelona, 1985). The treaty of the period of the Portuguese Restoration after 1640 provided for limited freedom of conscience while one was in Portuguese territory so long as no public display was made and there was no affront to Catholic practice.

26. The complex situation of English merchants in Portugal and their ability to practice their religion together in the home of the consul is detailed in L. M. E. Shaw, *Trade, Inquisition, and the English Nation in Portugal, 1650–1690* (Manchester, 1989), 119–34.

27. Herr, *The Eighteenth Century Revolution,* 386. Cf. AHN, Inq. Leg. 2845 (Murcia).

28. Joachim Whaley, *Religious Toleration and Social Change in Hamburg, 1529–1819* (Cambridge, 1985), 3–5. On the failure of Spain to produce a theory of toleration, see Henry Kamen, "Inquisition, Toleration and Liberty in Eighteenth-Century Spain," in *Toleration in Enlightenment Europe,* ed. Ole Peter Grell and Roy Porter, 250–58 (Cambridge, 2001).

29. Guillaume Thomas François Raynal, *L'histoire philosophique des Deux Indes* (Paris, 1774). Most scholars believe that Denis Diderot collaborated in the authorship of this work. A Spanish edition in five volumes appeared in Madrid after 1784. Raynal's work was widely read and cited throughout Spanish America by the generation involved in the movements for independence.

30. See "Projeto de un novo regimento para o Santo Ofício por Pascoal José de Melo," José Eduardo Franco and Paulo de Assunção, *As metamorfoses de um polvo* (Lisbon, 2004), 510.

31. Gilberto Fuezalida Guzmán, *La tolerancia de la Iglesia y la Inquisición* (Santiago de Chile, 1916), 25.

32. Enrique Álvarez Cora, "Iusnaturalismo racionalista y censura del Santo Oficio," in *Inquisición y censura,* ed. Gacto Fernández, 233–81; Francisco de Paula Vera Urbano, "La libertad religiosa en el pensamiento católico según los tratados de teología moral y la literatura polémica del siglo xviii," *Revista de Estudios Histórico-Jurídicos* 25 (2003): 445–74.

33. See Manuel de Aguirre, *Cartas y discursos del Militar Ingenuo al Correo de los Ciegos de Madrid,* ed. A. Elorza (San Sebastián, 1974), 306–30, esp. 311. See also Elorza, "La Inquisición y el pensamiento ilustrado," 8.

34. García Cárcel and Moreno Martínez, *Inquisición,* 314.

35. Menéndez Pelayo, *Historia,* 2:1081.

36. Still useful is Manoel Cardozo, "The Internationalism of the Portuguese Enlightenment: The Role of the *Estrangeirado,* c. 1700–1750," in *The Ibero-American Enlighten-

ment, ed. A. Owen Aldridge, 141–210 (Urbana, 1971). See also the entry "Estrangeirados" in the *Dicionário da História de Portugal,* Joel Serão, ed., 4 vols. (Lisbon, 1963–71), 1:122–29.

37. Janin-Thivos Tailland, *Inquisition et société au Portugal,* 137–38, provides a statistical analysis of the tribunal of Évora.

38. Luis da Cunha, *Instruções políticas,* ed. Abílio Diniz Silva (Lisbon, 2001), is an excellent critical edition.

39. Ibid., 218–56.

40. Ibid., 267.

41. Frédéric Max, "Un écrivan français des lumières oublié: Francisco Xavier de Oliveira (1701–83)," *Revue d'Histoire et de Philosophie Religieuses* 75:2 (1995): 193–98. See also the preface by Aquilino Ribeiro to Cavaleiro de Oliveira, *Cartas familiares,* 3d ed. (Lisbon, 1982), vii–xxv.

42. Silva, "Da festa barroca à intolerancia ilustrada," 14–16.

43. Araújo, *A cultura das luzes,* 93.

44. James Wadsworth, "Agents of Orthodoxy: Inquisitional Power and Prestige in Colonial Pernambuco, Brazil," (Ph.D. diss., University of Arizona, 2002), 296–318.

45. Boleslao Lewin, *Confidencias de los criptojudíos en las cárceles del Santo Oficio* (Buenos Aires, 1975), 78.

46. ANTT, Inq. Lisbon, CP 268, fs. 216–24; AHN Leg. 3733, n. 23 (1754).

47. Hilário Franco Júnior, *Cocanha: A história e um país imginário* (São Paulo, 1998), 227–33.

48. ADC, Inq. Leg. 522/6740.

49. On Voltaire's particularly negative views of Spain, see Alfonso de Salvio, "Voltaire and Spain," *Hispania* 7:2 (1924): 69–110.

50. Kamen, *The Iron Century,* 254.

51. The question of toleration in France has produced an enormous literature, one that expanded significantly after the fourth centenary of the Edict of Nantes in 1998. For an example, see Guy Saupin, Rémy Fahbre, Marcel Launay, eds., *La Tolérance: Colloque international de Nantes* (Rennes, 1998). I have found particularly perceptive Barbara de Negroni, *Intolérances: Catholiques et protestants en France, 1560–1787* (Paris, 1996).

52. Ibid.; see also Whaley, *Religious Toleration,* 2–6; Brian Eugene Strayer, *Huguenots and Camisards as Aliens in France, 1598–1789* (Lewiston, N.Y., 2001), 17–21.

53. Israel, *Radical Enlightenment,* 515–41.

54. The phrase is from Herbert Butterfield, "Toleration in Early Modern Times," *Journal of the History of Ideas* 38:4 (1977): 573–79. See also Avihu Zakai, "Orthodoxy in England and New England: Puritans and the Issue of Religious Toleration, 1640–1650," *Proceedings of the American Philosophical Society* 135:3 (1991): 401–41. On attitudes toward the Jews, see Justin Champion, "Toleration and Citizenship in Enlightenment England: John Tolland and the Naturalization of the Jews, 1714–1753," in *Toleration in Enlightenment Europe,* ed. Ole Peter Grell and Roy Porter, 133–56 (Cambridge, 2000).

55. Stephen Pincus, "The First Modern Revolution: The Revolution of 1688–89 in England" (MS).

56. John Redwood, *Reason, Ridicule, and Religion: The Age of Enlightenment in England (1660–1750)* (Cambridge, Mass., 1976), 79–85.

57. ANTT, Inq. Lisbon CP 207, fs. 29–30.

58. Medina, *Historia Lima*, 2:239. He was sent to Lima, subjected to torture, and confessed. He was sentenced to loss of all property and three years of exile.

59. Leandro Fernández de Moratin, *Apuntaciones sueltas de Inglaterra*, ed. Ana Rodríguez Fisher (Madrid, 2005). My thanks to Antonio Feros for this reference.

60. This problem is examined in some detail in Jean-Pierre Tardieu, *L'Inquisition de Lima et les héretiques étrangers* (Paris, 1995).

61. The memorial is undated. A copy can be found in BPE, CVIII-212.

62. Carlos González Batista, "Conversiones judaicas en Coro durante la época española," http://investigacion.unefm.edu.ve/croizatia.

63. Medina, *Historia México*, 360. In a similar fashion Rufino José Maria, a Yoruba Muslim arrested in Recife in 1853, defended his religion before a Brazilian magistrate who claimed that only Christianity was a true religion. José Maria stated that people are brought up in different faiths and on the question of which is best, "only at the end of the world will this be decided." See João José Reis, Flávio dos Santos Gomes, and Marcus J. M. de Carvalho, "Rufino José Maria: Aventuras e desventuras de um malé entre Africa e o Brasil, c. 1822–1853." Paper presented to symposium "L'expérience coloniale: Dynamiques des échanges dans les espaces Atlantiques à l'époque de l'esclavage" (Nantes, 2005).

64. AHN, Inq. Leg. 5349, n. 4 (Cartagena)

65. AHN, Inq. Leg. 5349/4 (Cartagena), relación de causa, 1710–15.

66. J. Martínez Bujanda, "Indices de libros prohibidos del siglo xvi," in *Historia de la Inquisición en España y América,* 3:808–22.

67. AHN, Inq. Leg. 5349. For a closely parallel case of another "seeker" of religious truth who was undecided about the validity of Protestant or Catholic belief, see Nicholas Griffiths, "The Best of Both Faiths: The Boundaries of Religious Allegiance and Opportunism in Early Eighteenth-Century Cuenca," *Bulletin of Hispanic Studies* 77 (2000): 13–39.

68. AHN, Inq. Leg. 5349/ 7 (1716).

69. Ibid. "Que era cierto aver buelto a leer los libros por la afición que les tenía, y que si esto era ser herege y apostatar, era asi."

70. This argument is made by Gregory Hanlon, *Confession and Community in Seventeenth-Century France: Catholic and Protestant Coexistence in Acquitaine* (Philadelphia, 1993), 6–8.

71. Ibid. There is the parallel case of José Ricor, a French surgeon resident in New Granada originally denounced in Guayama, Venezuela, by a Catalan capuchin in the Orinoco missions because of liberal statements. The missionary feared that in that region among "soldiers and ignorant people" he might plant "bad seeds of doctrine." Ricor had spoken against the clerical establishment and stated that after the king of England expelled the monks and nuns, England had become a great nation. He also said that "all the religions are good and that outside the Roman Church anyone could be saved in their religion." Eventually arrested in Cali, his investigation revealed that he owned twenty books in different languages and that he had lived as a corsair for awhile, having traveled to Martinique, Curacao, and Isla Margarita before settling on the plains of Casanare. He was sentenced to work in a hospital and then arrested a second time in Popayán for defending Conversos as "good Christians." See AHN, Inq. Leg. 1621, exp. 16.

72. José Pardo Tomás, *Ciencia y censura: La Inquisición española y los libros científicos en los siglos xvi y xvii* (Madrid, 1991), 183–89.

73. AHN, Inq. Leg. 1730/34 (Mexico). The case is also mentioned in Ferrer Benimeli, *Los archivos secretos*, 541, and in Medina, *Historia México*, 357–58.

74. ANTT, Inq. Lisbon CP 319, f. 300.

75. ANTT, Inq. Lisbon CP 318, fs. 6–7.

76. ANTT, Inq. Lisbon CP319, f. 275–85v.

77. ANTT, Inq. Lisbon CP 319, f. 19–19v. (2 Jan. 1779).

78. This is noted in Wadsworth, "Agents of Orthodoxy," 309.

79. In 1669, Luís de Crasto of Rio de Janeiro, a New Christian whose relatives had been arrested, was denounced for saying that the Inquisition "served only to take away property" (não servia mais que de tomar as fazendas). See ANTT, Inq. Lisbon CP 254, f. 1.

80. ANTT, Inq. Lisbon CP 319, f. 378.

81. ANTT, Inq. Lisbon 2825. The evidence being inconclusive, his case was dismissed.

82. ANTT, Inq. Lisbon CP 319, f. 445.

83. Antonio Elorza, "La Inquisición y el pensamiento ilustrado," www.geocities.com/urunuela34/inquisicion/pensamento ilustrado.htm.

84. These figures are reported in Francisco Bethencourt, "A Inquisição," *HRP*, 2:95–131. If those burned in effigy are also included, the percentage rises to over 6 percent. If the Goa tribunal's activities are included, the total for all the Portuguese Inquisitions is 28,066 persons sentenced, of which 1,817 were sentenced to be burned. See Wadsworth, "Agents of Orthodoxy," 66.

85. Herr, *The Enlightenment*, 408.

86. This summary is based on Bethencourt's chapter "A Abolição," in *História das inquisições*, 341–59.

87. Cited in Moreno, *La invención*, 242. This was the statement of Bishop Francisco Javier de Mier y Campillo.

88. Juan Antonio Llorente, *Histoire critique de l'Inquisition d'Espagne*, 4 vols. (Paris, 1817–18), is the most famous of them. Although the historian Menéndez Pelayo branded Llorente as a "double traitor," as a priest and as a Spaniard, for his criticisms, in fact, he was not the only ecclesiastic to attack the tribunal. Exiled Jesuits, regalist Jansenists, and illuminist clerics all found reasons to criticize the tribunal. See Gérard Dufour, "Eclesiásticos adversarios del Santo Oficio al final del Antiguo Régimen," in *Inquisición y sociedad*, ed. Angel del Prado Moura, 157–91 (Valladolid, 1999).

89. Michèle Duchet, *Anthropologie et histoire au siècle des lumières*, 2d ed. (Paris, 1995); Louis Sala-Molins, *Les misères de lumières* (Paris, 1992). See the discussion in Laurent Dubois, "An Enslaved Enlightenment: Rethinking the Intellectual History of the French Atlantic." Paper presented to symposium "La experience coloniale: Dynamiques des échanges dans les espaces Atlantiques à l'époque de l'esclavage" (Nantes, 2005).

90. Jean-Marc Masseaut, "La Franc-Maçonnerie dans la traité atlantique. Un paradox des Lumières." Paper presented to symposium "La experience coloniale: Dynamiques des échanges dans les espaces Atlantiques à l'époque de l'esclavage" (Nantes, 2005).

91. Juan Antonio Alejandre, "El Santo Oficio contra dos poemas antiinquisitoriales,"

in *Inquisición y censura: El acoso a la inteligencia en España,* ed. Enrique Gacto Fernández (Madrid, 2006), 475–99

92. Ricardo García Cárcel, "Prólogo," in Moreno, *La invención,* 9–20, provides an excellent discussion of the differing types of toleration and argues that the Inquisition itself was given to pragmatic tolerance when it suited its political or religious objectives.

Chapter 9. Rustic Pelagians

1. Whaley, *Religious Toleration,* 2–3.

2. Andrea del Col, "Shifting Attitudes in the Social Environment toward Heretics: The Inquisition of Friuli in the Sixteenth Century," *Ketzerverfolgung im 16. und frühen 17. Jahrhundert,* Wolfenbütteler Forschungen (Wiesbaden, 1992), 65–86.

3. The historiography is extensive. See, for example, Denis Crouzet, *Les Guerriers de Dieu: La Violence au temps des troubles de religion, vers 1525–vers 1610* (Paris, 1990).

4. Lecler, *Toleration and the Reformation,* 6–7; Malcolm C. Smith, "Early French Advocates of Religious Freedom," *Sixteenth Century Journal* 25:1 (1994): 29–51.

5. Smith, "Early French Advocates," 36. The letter came in the name of the king but was probably written by L'Hôpital.

6. Strayer, *Huguenots and Camisards,* 21–26.

7. Keith Luria, "Separated by Death? Burials, Cemeteries, and Confessional Boundaries in Seventeenth-Century France," *French Historical Studies* 24:2 (2001): 185–222.

8. Hanlon, *Confession and Community,* 119.

9. Keith Cameron, Mark Greengrass, and Penny Roberts, eds., *The Adventure of Religious Pluralism in Early Modern France* (Bern, 2000).

10. Olivier Christin, *La paix de religion* (Paris, 1997), 21–33.

11. On the changing status of the reformed churches across Europe, see Philip Benedict, *Christ's Churches Purely Reformed* (New Haven, 2002), 423–29.

12. Christopher Marsh, *Popular Religion in Sixteenth-Century England* (New York, 1998), 184–93.

13. There were numerous subsequent editions. See also Peter Iver Kaufman, *Thinking of the Laity in Late Tudor England* (Notre Dame, 2004).

14. See Christopher Haigh, "The Taming of the Reformation: Preachers, Pastors, and Parishioners in Elizabethan and Early Stuart England," *History* 85:280 (2000): 572–88.

15. Barry Reay, *Popular Cultures in England, 1550–1750* (New York, 1998), 75.

16. The term is attributed to Patrick Collinson without a specific citation in Haigh, "The Taming of the Reformation," 582. On popular religion, see Patrick Collinson, *The Religion of the Protestants* (Oxford, 1982), 189–242.

17. Medina, *Historia Chile,* 1:284. "La fe era cosa muerta sin caridad y que ambas virtudes eran lo mismo."

18. Christopher Hill, *The World Turned Upside Down* (London, 1972); id., *Liberty against the Law* (London, 1996).

19. Thomas Edwards, *Gangraena* (London, 1646). Ann Hughes, *Gangraena and the Struggle for the English Revolution* (Oxford, 2004), provides an extended analysis of the work and of its complex history of publication.

20. Hill, *The World Turned Upside Down,* 87. Peter Linebaugh and Marcus Rediker,

The Many-Headed Hydra (Boston, 2000), provides many examples of the mixing of social, political, and religious radicalism in an Atlantic context.

21. John Coffey, "Puritanism and Liberty Revisited: The Case for Toleration in the English Revolution," *Historical Journal* 41:4 (1998): 961–85. Wilbur K. Jordan, *The Development of Religious Toleration in England*, 4 vols. (Cambridge, Mass., 1932–40), is the essential starting point for modern studies of English religious pluralism.

22. Zakai, "Orthodoxy in England and New England," 401–41.

23. Steven Pincus, "The First Modern Revolution: The Revolution of 1688–89 in England" (MS), makes the point that despite antipapal rhetoric the climate for toleration of Catholics after the revolution was positive.

24. The statement was made by Sir John Reresby in 1688 and is cited in Christopher Hill, *Century of Revolution, 1603–1714*, 2d ed. (New York, 1980), 211. See the important study by John Coffey, *Persecution and Toleration in Protestant England (1558–1689)* (New York, 2000).

25. Roy Porter, *The Creation of the Modern World* (New York, 2000), 108.

26. Teófanes Egido, "El año 1559 en la Historia de España," in *Sociedad, tolerancia y religión*, ed. Santiago del Cura Elena, 11–25 (Burgos, 1996).

27. John Bossy, *Peace in the Counter-Reformation* (Cambridge, 1998).

28. In another hundred cases of those prosecuted for Protestanism where relativist remarks were made, eighty-seven of those tried were foreigners, most of them French. See Thomas, *Los protestantes*, 478–83.

29. I emphasize again that there are probably many more statements of religious relativism made by New Christians but that in the Inquisition proceedings such statements by a Converso or Morisco would lead to charges of apostasy rather than to accusations for heretical propositions. Thus in a sample drawn from cases of heretical propositions, Conversos and Moriscos are underrepresented.

30. Most would have accepted the Christocentric nature of Spanish religion but would have differed from the majority in believing that salvation was exclusively for those in the Church. See Jean-Pierre Dedieu, "L'hérésie salvatrice: La pédagogie inquisitoriale en Nouvelle Castille aux xvi siècle," in *Les frontières religieuses en Europe du xv au xvii siècle*, ed. Robert Sauzet, 79–88 (Paris, 1992).

31. Isaiah Berlin, *Four Essays on Liberty* (New York, 1970), 122–31. Berlin says of this idea, "It is scarcely older, in its developed state, than the Renaissance or the Reformation. Yet its decline would mark the death of civilization, of an entire moral outlook" (129).

32. I base this summary on Bethencourt, *História das inquisições*, 341–59; García Cárcel and Moreno Martínez, *Inquisición*, 82–102.

33. Joaquín de Finestrad, *El vasallo instruido*, ed. Margarita González (Bogotá, 2000).

34. See, for example, *Apología de la intolerancia religiosa* (Caracas, 1811). This anonymous text is a refutation of a letter published by an Irishman, Wlliam Burke, in the *Gaceta de Caracas* on 19 March 1811.

35. John Lloyd Mecham, *Church and State in Latin America* (Chapel Hill, 1934), 43–46.

36. Ibid., 3–37.

37. Miguel de Unamuno, *San Manuel Bueno, mártir*, ed. Mario J. Valdés, 24th ed. (Madrid, 1980), 143.

38. Anthony Grafton, "Reading Ratzinger: Benedict XVI, the Theologian," *New Yorker* (July 25, 2005), 41–49. *Dominus Iesus,* VI, par. 22, quoting Pope John Paul II, *Redemptoris mission,* states, "This truth of faith does not lessen the sincere respect which the Church has for all the religions of the world, but at the same time, it rules out, in a radical way, that mentality of indifferentism 'characterized by a religious relativism which leads to the belief that one religion is as good as another one.' "

Glossary

(all terms are Spanish unless otherwise noted)

amancebado living together as man and wife; *amancebamiento*, the institution of concubinage

auto de fe "act of faith," ceremony in which those condemned by the Inquisition have their sentences pronounced, followed by punishment

benzedeiro (Port.) blesser; a person who knows prayers for curing, amatory, and other purposes

calificador assessor, usually with theological training, provided evaluations of the heretical content of evidence for the Inquisition

calundu (Port.) African religious ceremonies or rites

chinas, chinillas term for Indian women in Chile

comisario commissary, an agent of the Inquisition, usually a cleric, in towns with no tribunal of the Holy Office

Converso any convert but usually applied to converts from Judaism

convivencia conviviality; description of the relations between Muslims, Christians, and Jews in medieval Spain

Cristão novo (Port.) New Christian; a convert from Judaism or the descendant of one

cruzado (Port.) a Portuguese coin worth four hundred *réis*

de levi (Lat.) form of inquisitorial sentence indicating lesser crime and punishment

de vehementi (Lat.) form of inquisitorial sentence indicating serious crime and punishment

doctrina a parish of Indians under the guidance of a missionary priest

elches (Port.) a renegade (*renegado*)

encomienda a grant of Indians whose labor or tribute was owed theoretically in return for the provision of religious instruction and protection by the holder, or *encomendero engenho* (Port.) sugar mill and, by extension, a sugar plantation; the owner of a plantation bore the title *senhor do engenho*

familiar a lay associate or assistant of the Inquisition

fitra (Arab.) inborn sense of religiosity

gentio (Port.) gentiles; term applied to unconverted Indians and other non-Europeans

hato an estate for raising cattle, a term used mostly in the Spanish Caribbean region

hidalgo a gentleman; *fidalgo* (Port.)

huaca Andean term indicating spirituality or divinity of a place, object, or thing; used by the Spanish to designate monuments or burial sites considered holy by the native peoples; *huaquero*, someone who excavates and robs these places

mameluco (Port.) term used in Brazil to describe people born of Indian–white unions

marrano term of disputed origins; literally, a swine, used for Conversos

mestizo Spanish term for offspring of Indian–white unions; *mestiço* (Port.)

morador (Port.) colonist or settler

Morisco convert to Christianity from Islam and descendants; *Mourisco* (Port.)

mudéjar Muslim living under Christian rule

polé (Port.) a pulley arrangement used to torture victims by dislocating their arms; *roldana* (Span.)

Provisorato an ecclesiastical court that handled cases involving Native Americans since they were exempt from the jurisdiction of the Inquisition

saludador (Port.) folk healer, sorcerer

sertão (Port.) the backlands or interior

taqiyya (Arab.) conformity permitted to Muslims living under another religion as a strategy of dissimulation

vecino a citizen of a municipality

Select Bibliography

Primary Sources

Barrionuevo de Peralta, Jerónimo de. *Avisos del Madrid de los Austrias*. Edited by José María Díez Borque. Madrid: Editorial Castalia, 1996.

Casas, Bartolomé de las. *Historia de las Indias,* 3 vols. Mexico City: Fondo de Cultura Económica, 1951.

Castro, Alfonso de. *Adversus omnes haereses*. Paris, 1564.

Cervantes, Miguel de. *El ingenioso hidalgo Don Quijote de la Mancha*. Edited by Martín de Riquer. Barcelona: Planeta, 1980.

Cunha, Luis da. *Instruções políticas*. Edited by Abílio Diniz Silva. Lisbon: Comissão Nacional para as Comemorações dos Descobrimentos Portugueses, 2001.

Eimeric, Nicolau, and Francisco Peña. *El manual de los inquisidores*. Translated from the Latin and edited by Luis Sala-Molins. Translated from the French by Francisco Martín. Barcelona: Muchnik, 1996.

Gilij, Felipe Salvador. *Ensayo de historia Americana, o sea historia natural, civil y sacra de los reinos y las provincias españolas de Tierra Firme en la América Meridional*. Translated by Antonio Tovar. 3 vols. Caracas: Biblioteca de la Academia Nacional de la Historia, 1987.

Granada, Luis de. *Guía de Pecadores*. Edited by Luis G. Alonso Getino. 4th ed. Madrid: Aguilar, 1962.

Peña Montenegro, Alonso de. *Itinerario para párrocos de indios*. 2 vols. Madrid: Consejo Superior de Investigaciones Científicas, 1995.

Pérez de Chinchón, Bernardo. *Antialcorano, Diálogos Christianos (Conversión y evan-*

gelización de moriscos). Edited by Francisco Pons Fuster. Alicante: Universidad de Alicante, 2000.

Saavedra Fajardo, Diego. *Idea de un príncipe político-cristiano*. Edited by Vicente García Diego. 4 vols. Madrid: Espasa-Calpe, 1958.

Sandoval, Alonso de. *Un tratado sobre la esclavitud*. Edited by Enriqueta Vila Vilar. Madrid: Alianza, 1987.

Torquemada, Juan de. *Tratado contra los madianitas e ismaelitas*. Edited by Carlos del Valle R. Madrid: Aben Ezra, 2000.

Vitoria, Francisco de. *Doctrina sobre los Indios*. Edited by Ramón Hernández-Martín. Salamanca: Editorial San Esteban, 1989.

Modern Works

Adorno, Rolena. "Colonial Reform or Utopia? Guaman Poma's Empire of the Four Parts of the World." In *Amerindian Images and the Legacy of Columbus,* edited by René Jara and Nicholas Spadaccini, 346–74. *Hispanic Issues,* vol. 9. Minneapolis: University of Minnesota Press, 1992.

Alberro, Solange. *Inquisición y sociedad en México 1571–1700*. Mexico City: Fondo de Cultura Económica, 1988.

———. "La sexualidad manipulada en Nueva España: Modalidades de recuperación y de adaptación frente a los tribunales eclesiasticos." In *Familia y sexualidad en Nueva España,* 238–57. Mexico City: Fondo de Cultura Económica, 1982.

———. "El tribunal del Santo Oficio de la Inquisición en Nueva España: Algunas modalidades de su actividad." *Cuadernos para la Historia de la Evangelización en América Latina* 4 (1989): 9–31.

Alejandre, Juan Antonio. *El veneno de Dios: La Inquisición de Sevilla ante el delito de solicitación en confesión*. Madrid: Siglo XXI, 1994.

———, and María Jesús Torquemada. *Palabra de hereje: La Inquisición de Sevilla ante el delito de proposiciones*. Seville: Universidad de Sevilla, 1998.

Allen, Don Cameron. *Doubt's Boundless Sea: Skepticism and Faith in the Renaissance*. Baltimore: Johns Hopkins University Press, 1964.

Almeida, Angela Mendes de. "Casamento, sexualidade e pecado—os manuais portugueses de casamento dos séculos xvi e xvii." *Ler História* 12 (1988): 3–22.

Amelang, James. "Society and Culture in Early Modern Spain." *Journal of Modern History* 65:2 (1993): 357–74.

Andrés Martín, Melquíades. "Pensamiento teológico y formas de religiosidad." In *Historia de la Cultura Española "Menéndez Pidal": El Siglo del Quijote (1580–1680),* edited by José María Jover Zamora, 75–162. Madrid, 1994.

———, ed. *Historia de la teología española*. 2 vols. Madrid: Fundación Universitaria Española, 1987.

———. *Historia de la mística de la edad de oro en España y América*. Biblioteca de Autores Cristianos. Madrid: EDICA, 1994.

Aranda Mendíaz, Manuel. *El Tribunal de la Inquisición de Canarias durante el reinado de Carlos III*. Las Palmas: Universidad de Las Palmas de Gran Canaria, 2000.

Araújo, Ana Cristina. *A cultura das luzes em Portugal*. Lisbon: Livros Horizonte, 2003.

[Archivo Historico Nacional]. *Catálogo de las causas contra la fe sagrada seguidas ante el tribunal del Santo Oficio de la Inquisición de Toledo.* Madrid, 1903.

Arnold, John H. *Belief and Unbelief in Medieval Europe.* London: Hodder Arnold, 2005.

Ascia, Luca de. "Fadrique Furió Ceriol fra Erasmo e Machiavelli." *Studi Storici* 40:2 (1999): 551–84.

———. "Fadrique Furió Ceriol: Consigliere del principe nella Spagna di Filippo II." *Studi Storici* 40:4 (1999): 1037–87.

Azevedo, Carlos Moreira, ed. *História religiosa de Portugal.* 3 vols. Lisbon: Circulo dos Leitores, 2000.

Azevedo, João Lucio de. *História dos cristãos novos portugueses.* Lisbon: Livraria Clássica, 1921.

———. *História de António Vieira.* 2d ed. 2 vols. Lisbon: A. Teixeira, 1931.

Bakhtin, Mikhail. *Rabelais and His World.* Bloomington: University of Indiana Press, 1984.

Barbosa Sánchez, Araceli. *Sexo y conquista.* Mexico City: UNAM, 1994.

Barros, Carlos. "El otro admitido: La tolerancia hacia los judios en la edad media gallega." In *Sociedad, tolerancia y religión,* edited by Santiago del Cura Elena, 85–113. Burgos: Caja de Ahorros Municipal de Burgosl, 1996.

———, ed. *Xudeus e conversos na historia.* 2 vols. Santiago de Compostela: La Editorial de la Historia, 1994.

Bataillon, Marcel. *Erasmo y España.* 2d ed. Mexico City: Fondo de Cultura Económica, 1966.

Baudot, George. *La pugna franciscana por México.* Mexico City: Alianza Editorial Mexicana, 1990.

———. "Amerindian Image and Utopian Project: Motolinia and Millenarian Discourse." In *Amerindian Images and the Legacy of Columbus,* edited by René Jara and Nicholas Spadaccini, 375–400. Hispanic Issues, vol. 9. Minneapolis: University of Minnesota Press, 1992.

Bell, Aubrey, F. G. "Liberty in Sixteenth-Century Spain." *Bulletin of Spanish Studies* 10 (1933): 164–79.

Benedict, Barbara. *Curiosity: A Cultural History of Early Modern Inquiry.* Chicago: University of Chicago Press, 2001.

Bennassar, Bartolomé. "Frontières religieuses entre Islam et chrètienté:L'expérience vécue parles 'renégats.' " In *Les frontières religieuses en Europe du xv au xvii siècle,* edited by Robert Sauzet, 71–78. Paris: Librairie Philosophique J. Vrin, 1992.

———. "Renégats et inquisiteurs (xvi–xvii siècles)." In *Les problèmes de l'exclusion en Espagne (xvi-xvii siècles),* edited by A. Redondo, 105–11. Paris: Publications de la Sorbonne, 1983.

———, and Lucile Bennassar. *Los cristianos de Alá: La fascinante aventura de los renegados.* Madrid: Nerea, 1989.

Beonio-Brocchieri, Mariateresa Fumagalli. "The Feminine Mind in Medieval Mysticism." In *Creative Women in Medieval and Early Modern Italy,* edited by E. A. Matter and J. Coakley, 19–33. Philadelphia: University of Pennsylvania Press, 1994.

Berksvens-Stevelinck, C., J. Israel, and G. H. M. Posthumus Meyjes, eds. *The Emergence of Tolerance in the Dutch Republic.* Leiden: Brill, 1997.

Bernand, Carmen, and Serge Gruzinski. *De la idolatría: Una arqueología de las ciencias religiosas.* Mexico City: Fondo de Cultura Económica, 1992.

Berti, Silvia. "At the Roots of Unbelief." *Journal of the History of Ideas* 56:4 (1995): 555–75.

Bethencourt, Francisco. "Les hérétiques et l'inquisition portugaise: Représentations et pratiques de persécutions." *Ketzerverfolgung im 16. und frühen 17 Jahrhundert. Wolfenbütter Forshungen* 51 (1992): 103–17.

———. *História das Inquisições.* Lisbon: Circulo dos Leitores, 1994.

———. "Portugal: A Scrupulous Inquisition." In *Early Modern European Witchcraft,* edited by Bengt Ankarloo and Gustav Henningsen, 404–22. Oxford: Clarendon, 1990.

———. *O imaginário da magia.* Lisbon: Universidade Aberta, 1987.

Blackburn, Robin. *The Making of New World Slavery.* London: Verso, 1997.

Blázquez Miguel, Juan. *La inquisición en Cataluña.* Toledo: Arcano, 1990.

Bleznik, David. "Fadrique Furió Ceriol: Political Thinker of Sixteenth Century Spain." Ph.D. diss., Columbia University, 1954.

Bodian, Miriam. "At the Fringes of the Reformation: "Judaizing" Polemicist-Martyrs and the Inquisition, 1570–1670." Unpublished paper, 2001.

Bœglin, Michel. *L'Inquisition espagnole au lendemain du concile de Trente: Le tribunal du Saint-Office de Séville, 1560–1700.* Montpellier: Université de Montpellier III, 2005.

Bombín Pérez, Antonio. *La Inquisición en el país vasco: El tribunal de Logroño, 1570–1630.* Bilbao: Universidad del País Vasco, 1997.

Borja Gómez, Jaime Humberto. *Rostros y rastros del demonio en la Nueva Granada.* Bogotá: Editorial Ariel, 1998.

Boronat y Barrachina, Pascual. *Los moriscos españoles y su expulsión.* 2d ed. 2 vols. Edited by R. García Cárcel. Granada: Universidad de Granada, 1992.

Bosch Gajano, Sofia. "Identità religiose, motelli culturali, funzioni economiche: Diversità e alterità nell'Europa mediovale del secoli xi–xiv." In *Rapports entre Juifs, Chrétiens et Musulmans,* edited by Johannes Irmscher, 161–72. Amsterdam: Verlag Adolf M. Hakkert, 1995.

Boucharb, Ahmed. *Os pseudo-mouriscos de Portugal no século xvi.* Lisbon: Hugin, 2004.

Boxer, C. R. *The Church Militant in Iberian Expansion, 1440–1770.* Baltimore: Johns Hopkins University Press, 1978.

———. *The Dutch in Brazil, 1624–1654.* Oxford: Clarendon, 1957.

Boyer, Richard. *Lives of the Bigamists: Marriage, Family, and Community in Colonial Mexico.* Albuquerque: University of New Mexico Press, 1994.

Braga, Isabel M. R. de Mendes Drumond. *Os estrangeiros e a Inquisição portuguesa.* Lisbon: Hugin, 2002.

———. *Mouriscos e cristãos no Portugal quinhentista.* Lisbon: Hugin, 1999.

Brundage, James A. *Law, Sex, and Christian Society in Medieval Europe.* Chicago: University of Chicago Press, 1987.

Bujanda, Jesús M. de. "Recent Historiography of the Spanish Inquisition (1977–1988): Balance and Perspective." In *Cultural Encounters: The Impact of the Inquisition in*

Spain and the New World, edited by Mary Elizabeth Perry and Anne J. Cruz, 221–47. Berkeley: University of California Press, 1991.

———. "Indices de libros prohibidos del siglo xvi." *HIEA,* 3:774–828.

Burke, Peter. "The Cultural History of Dreams." In *Varieties of Cultural History.* Ithaca: Cornell University Press, 1997.

———. "Learned Culture and Popular Culture in Renaissance Italy." *Revista de História* 125–26 (1992): 53–64.

Burns, Robert Ignatius. "Renegades, Adventurers and Sharp Businessmen: The Thirteenth-Century Spaniard in the Cause of Islam." *Catholic Historical Review* 58:3 (1972): 341–66.

———. *Islam under the Crusaders.* Princeton: Princeton University Press, 1973.

———. "Mudejar Parallel Societies: Anglophone Historiography and Spanish Context." In *Christians, Muslims and Jews in Medieval and Early Modern Spain,* edited by Mark D. Meyerson and Edward D. English, 91–124. Notre Dame: University of Notre Dame Press, 1999.

Butler, Jon. "Magic, Astrology, and Early American Religion." *American Historical Review* 84:2 (1979): 317–46

Cabantou, Alain, et al., eds. *Homo religiosus: Autour de Jean Delumeau.* Paris: Fayard, 1997.

———. *Blasphemy: Impious Speech in the West from the Seventeenth to the Nineteenth Centuries.* New York: Columbia University Press, 2001.

Campagne, Fabián. *Homo catholicus: Homo superstitiosus.* Buenos Aires: Miño y Dávila, 2002.

Candau Chacón, María Luisa. *Los moriscos en el espejo del tiempo.* Huelva: Universidad de Huelva, 1977.

Canossa, Romano. *Sessualità e inquisizione in Italia tra cinquecento e seicento.* Roma: Sapere, 2000.

Capelo, Rui Grillo. *Profetismo e esoterismo: A arte do prognóstico em Portugal (séculos xvii–xviii).* Coimbra: Minerva, 1994.

Capéran, Louis. *Le problème du salut des Infidèles.* 2 vols. Toulouse: Grand Séminaire, 1934.

Cardaillac, Louis, et al. *Les morisques et l'inquisition.* Paris: Publisud, 1990.

———. *Morisques et Chrétiens, un affrontement polémique (1492–1650).* 2d ed. Zaghouan, Tunisia: Centre d'études et de recherches ottomanes, morisques et de documentation et d'information, 1995.

Cardozo, Manoel. "The Internationalism of the Portuguese Enlightenment: The Role of the *Estrangeirado,* c. 1700–1750." In *The Ibero-American Enlightenment,* edited by A. Owen Aldridge, 141–210. Urbana: University of Illinois Press, 1971.

Caro, Venancio. *La teología y los teólogos juristas españoles antes de la conquista de América.* 2d ed. Salamanca, 1951.

Caro Baroja, Julio. *Las formas complejas de la vida religiosa.* 2 vols. Madrid: Galaxia Gutemberg and Círculo de Lectores, 1995.

Carrasco Urgoiti, Maria Soledad. *El moro de Granada en la literatura.* 2d ed. Granada: Universidad, 1989.

Case, Thomas. *Lope and Islam: Islamic Personages in His Comedias.* Newark, Del.: Juan de la Cuesta, 1993.

Castañeda Delgado, Paulino, and Pilar Hernández Aparicio. *La Inquisición de Lima.* 3 vols. Madrid: Deimos, 1989–98.

Castro, Américo. *The Spaniards: An Introduction to Their History.* Berkeley: University of California Press, 1971.

Castro, Dinorah. *A mulher submissiva: Tese da faculdade de medicina da Bahia no século xix.* Salvador: Press Color, 1996.

Cervantes, Fernando. "The Impact of Christianity in Spanish America." *Bulletin of Latin American Research* 14:2 (1995): 201–10.

Chantraine, G. "La doctrine catholique de la tolérance au xvi siècle." In *Naissance et affirmation de l'idee de tolerance, xvi et xviii siècle,* organized by Michelle Péronnet, 1–18. Montpellier: Université Paul Valéry, 1987.

Chincilla Aguilar, Ernesto. *La Inquisición en Guatemala.* Guatemala City: Ministerio de Educación Pública, 1953.

Chocano Mena, Magdalena. *La fortaleza docta.* Barcelona: Ediciones Bellaterra. 2000.

———. *La América colonial (1492–1763): Cultura y vida cotidiana.* Madrid: Editorial Síntesis, 2000.

Christin, Olivier. *La paix de religión.* Paris: Seuil, 1997.

Clavero, Bartolomé. "Delito y pecado: Noción y escala de transgresiones." In *Sexo barroco y otras transgresiones premodernas,* edited by F. Tomás y Valiente, B. Clavero, et al., 57–89. Madrid: Alianza, 1990.

Coelho, António Borges. *Inquisição de Évora.* 2 vols. Lisbon: Caminho, 1987.

Coffey, John. *Persecution and Toleration in Protestant England, 1558–1689.* London: Longman, 2000.

Contreras, Jaime. "Los moriscos en las inquisiciones de Valladolid y Logroño." In *Les morisques et leur temps,* edited by L. Cardaillac, 477–92. Paris: CNRS, 1983.

———. *El Santo Oficio de la Inquisición de Galicia.* Madrid: Akal, 1982.

———, and Gustav Henningsen. "Forty-Four Thousand Cases of the Spanish Inquisition." In *The Inquisition in Early Modern Europe,* edited by Gustav Henningsen and John Tedeschi, 100–130. Dekalb: Northern Illinois University Press, 1986.

Coote, Lesley. *Prophecy and Public Affairs in Later Medieval England.* York: York Medieval Press, 2000.

Coulton, G. G. *The Plain Man's Religion in the Middle Ages.* London: Simpkin, Marshall, Hamilton, Kent, 1916.

Crahay, R. "Le problème du pluralisme confessionnel dans les Pays Bas à la fin du xvi siècle: Les embarras de Juste Lipse (1589–1596)." In *Naissance et affirmation de l'idee de tolerance, xvi et xviii siècle,* organized by Michelle Peronnet, 1–18, 157–88. Montpellier: Université Paul de Valéry, 1987.

Cruz, Anne J., and Mary Elizabeth Perry. *Culture and Control in Counter-Reformation Spain.* Minneapolis: University of Minnesota Press, 1992.

Davidson, Nicholas. "Unbelief and Atheism in Italy, 1500–1700." In *Atheism from the Reformation to the Enlightenment,* edited by M. Hunter and D. Wootton, 13–54. Oxford: Clarendon Press, 1992.

Dedieu, J.-P. "L'Hérésie salvatrice: La pédagogie inquisitoriale en Nouvelle Castille au xvi siècle." In *Les frontières religieuses en Europe du xv au xvii siècle,* edited by Robert Sauzet, 79–88. Paris: Librairie Philosophique J. Vrin, 1992.

——. *L'administration de la foi: L'inquisition de Tolède (xvi–xvii siècle).* Madrid: Casa de Velásquez, 1989.

——. "El tribunal de la Inquisición: Encarnación de la intolerancia?" In *Dogmatismo e intolerancia,* edited by Enrique Martínez Ruiz and Magdalena de Pazzis Pi, 107–25. Madrid: Actas, 1997.

——. "The Inquisition and Popular Culture in New Castile." In *Inquisition and Society in Early Modern Europe,* edited by Stephen Haliczer, 129–46. London: Croom Helm, 1987.

——. " 'Christianization' in New Castile: Catechism, Communion, Mass, and Confirmation in the Toledo Archbishopric, 1540–1650." In *Culture and Control in Counter-Reformation Spain,* edited by Anne J. Cruz and Mary Elizabeth Perry, 1–24. Hispanic Issues vol. 7. Minneapolis: University of Minnesota Press, 1992.

Defourneaux, Marcelin. *Pablo de Olavide, ou L'afrancescado.* Paris: Presses Universitaires de France, 1959.

Delumeau, Jean. *Sin and Fear: The Emergence of a Western Guilt Culture, 13th-18th Centuries.* Translated by Eric Nicholson. New York: St. Martin's Press, 1990.

——. *Catholicism between Luther and Voltaire: A New View of the Counter-Reformation.* London: Burns and Oates, 1977.

Del Col, Andrea. *Domenico Scandella detto Menocchio.* Pordenone: Edizioni Biblioteca dell'Immagine, 1990.

Deleito y Piñuela, José. *La mala vida en la España de Felipe II.* Madrid: Alianza, 1987.

Domínguez Ortiz, Antonio. *Autos de la Inquisición de Sevilla.* Seville: Ayuntamiento de Sevilla, 1981.

——. "El primer esbozo de tolerancia religiosa en la España de los Austrias." In *Instituciones y sociedad en la España de los Austrias.* Barcelona: Ariel, 1985.

——, and Bernard Vincent. *Historia de los moriscos.* Madrid: Revista de Occidente, 1978.

Duchet, Michèle. *Anthropologie et histoire au siècle des lumières.* 2d ed. Paris: Albin Michel, 1995.

Dubois, Laurent. "An Enslaved Enlightenment: Rethinking the Intellectual History of the French Atlantic." Unpublished paper presented at "La experience coloniale: Dynamiques des échanges dans les espaces Atlantiques à l'époque de l'esclavage." Nantes, 2005.

Dufour, Gérard. "Eclesiásticos adversaries del Santo Oficio al final del Antiguo Régimen." In *Inquisición y sociedad,* edited by Angel del Prado Moura, 157–91. Valladolid: Universidad de Valladolid, 1999.

Dupront, Alphonse. *Qu'est-ce que les Lumières?* Paris: Gallimard, 1996.

Dupuis, Jacques. *Toward a Christian Theology of Religious Pluralism.* Maryknoll, N.Y.: Orbis Books, 1997.

Eco, Umberto. *The Name of the Rose.* San Diego: Harcourt Brace Jovanovich, 1983.

Edwards, Jonathan. "Religious Faith and Doubt in Late Medieval Spain: Soria circa 1450–1500." *Past and Present* 120 (1988): 3–25.

——. "The Beginnings of a Scientific Theory of Race? Spain, 1450–1600." In *Rapports entre Juifs, Chrétiens et Musulmans,* edited by Johannes Irmscher, 179–98. Amsterdam: Verlag Adolf M. Hakkert, 1995.

Egido, Teófanes. "La defensa de los conversos." In *Dogmatismo e intolerancia,* edited by Enrique Martínez Ruiz and Magdalena de Pazzis Pi, 191–208. Madrid: Actas 1997.

———. "El año 1559 en la historia de España." In *Sociedad, tolerancia y religión,* edited by Elena Santiago del Cura, 11–26. Burgos: Caja de Ahorros Municipal de Burgos, 1996.

Ehlers, Benjamin. *Between Christians and Moriscos: Juan de Ribera and Religious Reform in Valencia 1568–1614.* Baltimore: Johns Hopkins University Press, 2006.

Elorza, Antonio. *La ideología liberal en la Illustración española.* Madrid: Editorial Tecnos, 1970.

———, ed. *Pan y toros y otros papeles sediciosos de fines del siglo xviii.* Madrid: Editorial Ayuso, 1971.

———. "La Inquisición y el pensamiento ilustrado." www.geocities.com/urunuela34/inquisicion.

Epstein, Steven. *Purity Lost: Transgressing Boundaries in the Eastern Mediterranean.* Baltimore: Johns Hopkins University Press 2006.

Fajardo Spínola, Francisco. *Las víctimas del Santo Oficio.* Las Palmas: Gobierno de Canarias, 2003.

Farriss, Nancy M. *Maya Society under Colonial Rule.* Princeton: Princeton University Press, 1984.

Fasoli, G. "Noi e loro." In *L'uomo di fronte al mondo animale nell Alto-Medioevo.* 31st Settimana di Studi sull'Alto Medioevo. Spoleto: Presso de la Sede del Centro, 1985.

Feitler, Bruno. *Inquisition, juifs et nouveaux-chétiens au Brésil.* Louvain: Presses Universitaires Louvain, 2003.

Ferreira da Cunha, Norberto. *Elites e académicos na cultura portuguesa setecentista.* Lisbon: Imprensa Nacional, 2000.

Ferrer Benimeli, José A. "La inquisición frente a masonería e ilustración." In *Inquisición española y mentalidad inquisitorial,* edited by Ángel Alcalá, 463–96. Barcelona: Ariel, 1984.

———. *Masonería, Iglesia e Ilustración.* 4 vols. Madrid: Fundación Universitaria Española, 1976–77.

———. *Los archivos secretos vaticanos y la Masonería.* Caracas: Universidad Católica "Andres Bello," 1976.

Ferretti, Sérgio, "Notas sobre o sincretismo religioso no Brasil: Modelos, limitações possibilidades." *Tempo* 6:11 (2001): 13–26.

Few, Martha. *Women Who Live Evil Lives: Gender, Religion, and the Politics of Power in Colonial Guatemala.* Austin: University of Texas Press, 2002.

Flynn, Maureen. "Blasphemy and the Play of Anger in Sixteenth-Century Spain." *Past and Present* 149 (1995): 29–56.

Foster, George M. *Culture and Conquest: America's Spanish Heritage.* Chicago: Quadrangle Books, 1960.

Franco, José Eduardo, and Paulo de Assunção. *As metamorfoses de um polvo: Religião e política nos regimentos da Inquisição portuguesa.* Lisboa: Prefácio, 2004.

Furió Ceriol, Fadrique. *El consejo y consejeros del príncipe.* Edited by Diego Sevilla Andrés. Valencia: Institución Alfonso el Magnánimo, 1952.

Gacto Fernández, Enrique. *Cantabria y la inquisición en el siglo xviii.* Santander: Fundación Marcelino Botín, 1999.

Gama Lima, Lana Lage da. "Aprisionando o desejo: Confissão e sexualidade." In *História e sexualidade no Brasil,* edited by Ronaldo Vainfas, 67–88. Rio de Janeiro: Graal, 1986.

García Cárcel, Ricardo. *Herejía y sociedad en el siglo XVI.* Barcelona: Ediciones Península, 1980.

———. "¿Son creíbles las fuentes inquisitoriales?" In *L'inquisizione romana: Metodologia delle fonti e storia istituzionale,* edited by Andrea del Col and Giovanna Paolin, 103–16. Trieste: Edizioni Università di Trieste and Circolo Culturale Menocchio, 2000.

———, and Doris Moreno Martínez. *Inquisición: Historia crítica.* Madrid: Temas de Hoy, 2000.

García Villoslada, Ricardo. *Historia de la Iglesia en España.* 5 vols. in 7. Biblioteca de Autores Cristianos. Madrid: EDICA, 1979–82.

Gil, Juan. *Los conversos y la inquisición sevillana.* 4 vols. Seville: Universidad de Sevilla, 2000.

Giles, Mary, ed. *Women in the Inquisition: Spain and the New World.* Baltimore: Johns Hopkins University Press, 1999.

Gill, Anthony. "The Political Origins of Religious Liberty: Initial Sketch of a General Theory." In *Political Origins of Religious Liberty* (in press).

Gill, Katherine. "Women and the Production of Religious Literature in the Vernacular, 1300–1500." In *Creative Women in Medieval and Early Modern Italy,* edited by E. A. Matter and J. Coakley, 64–104. Philadelphia: University of Pennsylvania Press, 1994.

Ginzburg, Carlo. *The Cheese and the Worms.* Translated by John and Anne Tedeschi. Baltimore: Johns Hopkins University Press, 1980.

———, and Adriano Prosperi. *Giochi di Pazienza: Un seminario sul "Beneficio di Cristo."* Turin: Einaudi, 1975.

Giordani, Lourdes. "Speaking Truths or Absurdities: The Religious Dialogues between Father Gilij and His Indian Contemporaries (18th-century Venezuela). Paper presented to Latin American Studies Association. Washington, D.C., 1995.

Gitlitz, David M. *Secrecy and Deceit: The Religion of the Crypto-Jews.* Philadelphia: Jewish Publication Society, 1996.

Given, James B. *Inquisition and Medieval Society.* Ithaca: Cornell University Press, 1997.

Góngora, Mario. *Studies in the Colonial History of Spanish America.* Cambridge: Cambridge University Press, 1975.

Gorenstein, Lina, and Maria Luiza Tucci Carneiro, eds. *Ensaios sobre a intolerância.* São Paulo: Universidade de São Paulo, 2002.

Graizbord, David L. *Souls in Dispute: Converso Identities in Iberia and the Jewish Diaspora, 1580–1700.* Philadelphia: University of Pennsylvania Press, 2004.

Greenleaf, Richard E. "The Inquisition and the Indians of New Spain: A Study in Jurisdictional Confusion." *The Americas* 22:2 (1963): 138–66.

———. "Persistence of Native Values: The Inquisition and the Indians of Colonial Mexico." *The Americas* 50:3 (1994): 351–76.

Grell, Ole Peter, and Bob Scribner. *Tolerance and Intolerance in the European Reformation.* Cambridge: Cambridge University Press, 1996.

———, and Roy Porter, eds. *Toleration in Enlightenment Europe.* Cambridge: Cambridge University Press, 2000.

Griffiths, Nicholas. "Popular Religious Scepticism and Idiosyncrasy in Post-Tridentine Cuenca." In *Faith and Fanaticism: Religious Fervour in Early Modern Spain,* edited by Lesley K. Twomey, 95–128. Aldershot: Ashgate, 1997.

Grunberg, Bernard. *L'inquisition apostolique au Mexique.* Paris: L'Harmattan, 1998.

Gruzinski, Serge. "L'Amerique espagnole dans le miroir du Brasil portugais." *Arquivos do Centro Cultural Calouste Gulbenkian* 42 (2001): 119–33.

——. *The Conquest of Mexico: The Incorporation of Indian Societies into the Western World.* Translated by E. Corrigan. Cambridge: Polity Press, 1994.

——, and Nathan Wachtel. "Cultural Interbreedings: Constituting a Majority as a Minority." *Comparative Studies in Society and History* 39:2 (1997): 231–50.

Guerreiro, Inácio, and Francisco Contente Domingues, eds. *Fernando Oliveira e sue tempo: Humanismo e arte de navegar no Renascimento europeu (1450–1650).* Cascais: Patrimonia, 1999.

Guggisberg, Hans, Frank Lestringant, and Jean-Claude Margolin. *La liberté de conscience (xvi–xvii siècles).* Geneva: Droz, 1991.

Guibovich Pérez, Pedro. "Proyecto colonial y control ideológico: El establecimiento de la Inquisición en el Perú." *Apuntes* 35 (1994): 110–11.

——. *Censura, libros e inquisición en el Perú colonial.* Seville: Diputación de Sevilla, Universidad de Sevilla, CSIC, 2003.

Haliczer, Stephen, ed. *Inquisition and Society in Early Modern Europe.* London: Croom Helm, 1987.

——. *Sexuality in the Confessional: A Sacrament Profaned.* Oxford: Oxford University Press, 1997.

Halperin-Donghi, Tulio. *Un conflicto nacional. Moriscos y cristianos viejos en Valencia.* Valencia: Institución Alfonso el Magnánimo, 1980.

Hampe Martínez, Teodoro. *Santo Oficio e historia colonial.* Lima: Ediciones del Congreso del Perú, 1998.

Hanke, Lewis. *Aristotle and the American Indians.* Chicago: Henry Regnery, 1959.

——. *The Spanish Struggle for Justice in the Conquest of America.* Philadelphia: American Philosophical Society, 1949.

Harris, A. Katie. *From Muslim to Christian Granada: Inventing a City's Past in Early Modern Spain.* Baltimore: Johns Hopkins University Press, 2007.

Henriques, Ursula. *Religious Toleration in England, 1787–1833.* Toronto: University of Toronto Press, 1961.

Heras Santos, Juan de las. *La justicia penal de los Austrias en la Corona de Castilla.* Salamanca: Universidad de Salamanca, 1991.

Herr, Richard. *The Eighteenth-Century Revolution in Spain.* Princeton: Princeton University Press, 1958.

——. "The Twentieth Century Spaniard Views the Spanish Enlightenment" *Hispania* 45:2 (1962): 183–93.

Herrera Sotello, F. "Ortodoxia y control social en México en el siglo xvii: El Tribunal del Santo Oficio." Ph.D. diss., Universidad Complutense, 1982.

Higgs, David. "O Santo Ofício da Inquisição de Lisboa e a 'Luceferina Assembléia' do Rio de Janeiro na década de 1790." *Revista do Instituto Histórico e Geográfico Brasileiro* 412 (2001): 239–384.

Hsia, Po-Chia. *The World of the Catholic Renewal, 1540–1770.* Cambridge: Cambridge University Press, 1998.

Hunter, Michael, and David Wootton, eds. *Atheism from the Reformation to the Enlightenment.* Oxford: Clarendon Press, 1992.

——, and Henk van Nierop. *Calvinism and Religious Toleration in the Dutch Golden Age.* Cambridge: Cambridge University Press, 2002.

Illanes, José Luis, and Josep Ignasi Saranyana. *Historia de la teología.* Biblioteca de Autores Cristianos. Madrid: EDICA, 1995.

Ingram, Martin. *Church Courts, Sex and Marriage in England, 1570–1640.* Cambridge: Cambridge University Press, 1987.

Irmscher, Johannes, ed. *Rapports entre Juifs, Chrétiens et Musulmans.* Amsterdam: Verlag Adolf M. Hakkert, 1995.

Israel, Jonathan. "Locke, Spinoza and the Philosophical Debate Concerning Toleration in the Early Enlightenment (c. 1670–c. 1750)." *Mededelingen van de Afdeling Letterkunde,* Royal Netherlands Academy of Sciences, n.s. no. 62 (1999): 5–19.

——. *The Dutch Republic.* Oxford: Oxford University Press, 1995.

——. *Radical Enlightenment: Philosophy and the Making of Modernity, 1650–1750.* Oxford: Oxford University Press, 2001.

Jiménez Monteserín, Miguel. *Sexo y bien común.* Cuenca: Ayuntamiento de Cuenca and Instituto Juan de Valdés, 1994.

Jung, Eva-Marie. "On the Nature of Evangelism in Sixteenth-Century Italy." *Journal of the History of Ideas* 14 (1953): 511–27.

Kamen, Henry. "Toleration and Dissent in Sixteenth-Century Spain: The Alternative Tradition." *Sixteenth-Century Journal* 19 (1988): 3–23.

——. *The Iron Century.* New York: Praeger, 1971.

——. *Nacimiento y desarrollo de la tolerancia en la Europa moderna.* Madrid: Alianza, 1967.

——. "Exclusão e intolerância em Espanha no início da época moderna." *Ler História* 33 (1997): 23–35.

——. "Inquisition, Tolerance, and Liberty in Eighteenth-Century Spain." In *Toleration in Enlightenment Europe,* edited by Ole Peter Grell and Roy Porter, 250–58. Cambridge: Cambridge University Press, 2000.

——. *The Spanish Inquisition: A Historical Revision.* New Haven: Yale University Press, 1998.

——. *The Phoenix and the Flame: Catalonia and the Counter-Reformation.* New Haven: Yale University Press, 1993.

Kaplan, Yosef. *From Christianity to Judaism.* Oxford: Oxford University Press, 1989.

Kenny, Neil. *Curiosity in Early Modern Europe: Word Histories.* Wiesbaden: Harrassowitz Verlag, 1998.

Klein, Herbert S. "The African Slave Trade to 1650." In *Tropical Babylons: Sugar and the Making of the Atlantic World,* edited by Stuart B. Schwartz, 201–36. Chapel Hill: University of North Carolina Press, 2004.

Klor de Alva, Jorge. "Colonizing Souls: The Failure of the Indian Inquisition and the Rise of Penitential Discipline." In *Cultural Encounters: The Impact of the Inquisition in Spain and the New World,* edited by Mary Elizabeth Perry and Anne J. Cruz, 3–22. Berkeley: University of California Press, 1991.

Lapeyre, Henri. *Géographie de l'Espagne morisque.* Paris: SEVPEN, 1959.

Largomarsino, David. "Furió Ceriol y la 'Pragmatica de las Cortesias' de 1586." *Estudis* 8 (1979–80): 87–104.

Laurensen, John Christian, ed. *Religious Toleration.* New York: St. Martin's Press, 1999.

Lea, Henry Charles. *A History of the Inquisition of Spain.* 4 vols. New York: AMS Press, 1966.

Lecler, Joseph. *Histoire de la tolérance au siècle de la Réforme.* 2 vols. Paris, 1955. Translated as *Toleration and the Reformation* by T. L. Westow. 2 vols. New York: Associated Press, 1960.

Levine, Alan. *Early Modern Skepticism and the Origins of Toleration.* Lanham: Lexington Books, 1999.

Lewin, Boleslao. *Confidencias de los criptojudíos en las carceles del Santo Oficio.* Buenos Aires: Boleslao Lewin, 1975.

———. *La inquisición en México.* Puebla: José Cajica, 1971.

Lindbeck, George. "*Fides ex auditu* and the Salvation of the Non-Christians: Contemporary Catholic and Protestant Positions." In *The Gospel and the Ambiguity of the Church,* edited by Vilmos Vajta. Philadelphia: Fortress Press, 1974.

Lohman Villena, Guillermo. *Pedro Peralta Barnuevo y Pablo de Olavide: Biblioteca de Hombres del Peru.* Lima: Editorial Universitaria, 1964.

Lombardi, Riccardo. *The Salvation of the Unbeliever.* London: Burns and Oates, 1956.

Lopetegui, Leon, and Felix Zubillaga, eds. *Historia de la Iglesia en la América Española.* Madrid: Biblioteca de Autores Cristianos, 1965.

Lopez, Robert. "Dante, Salvation, and the Layman." In *History and Imagination,* edited by Hugh Lloyd-Jones, Valerie Pearl, Blair Worden, 37–42. London: Duckworth, 1981.

López-Baralt, Luce. *Islam in Spanish Literature: From the Middle Ages to the Present.* Leiden: Brill, 1992.

Losada, Angel. "En la España del siglo XV, la voz de un eminente teólogo español se alza contra la acusación de 'deicidio': Alfonso Fernández de Madrigal, 'El Tostado.'" In *Encuentros en Sefarad,* edited by Francisco Ruiz Gomez and Manuel Espadas Burgos. Ciudad Real: Instituto de Estudios Manchegos, 1987.

Lourenço, Maria Paula Marçal. "Para o estudos da actividade inquisitorial no Alto Alentejo: A visita da Inquisição de Lisboa ao bispado de Portalegre em 1578–79." *A Cidade* 3 (1989): 109–38.

MacCormack, Sabine. *Religion in the Andes: Vision and Imagination in Early Colonial Peru.* Princeton: Princeton University Press, 1991.

Magalhães, Joaquim Romero. "A sociedade." In *História de Portugal,* 3:469–512.

Maravall, José Antonio. "Trabajo y exclusión: El trabajador manual en el sistema social español de la primera modernidad." In *Les problèmes de l'exclusion en Espagne (xvi–xvii siècles),* edited by A. Redondo, 135–59. Paris: Publicacions de la Sorbonne, 1983.

Margolin, Jean-Claude. "La tolérance et ses limites d'après Érasme." In *Homo Religiosus: Autour de Jean Delumeau,* 628–36. Paris: Fayard, 1997.

Mariel de Ibáñez, Yolanda. *La Inquisición en México.* Mexico City: [Imprenta Barrie], 1945.

Markus, R. "Pelagianism: Britain and the Continent." *Journal of Theological Studies* n.s. 37 (1986): 191–204.

Márquez Villanueva, Francisco. "La criptohistoria morisca (Los otros conversos)." In *Les problèmes de l'exclusion en Espagne (xvi–xvii siècles)*, edited by A. Redondo, 77–94. Paris: Publications de la Sorbonne, 1983.

———. *Personajes y temas del Quijote.* Madrid: Taurus, 1975.

———. *El problema morisco (desde otras laderas).* Madrid: Libertarias, 1991.

Marsh, Christopher W. *The Family of Love in English Society, 1550–1630.* Cambridge: Cambridge University Press, 1994.

———. *Popular Religion in Sixteenth-Century England.* New York: St. Martin's Press, 1998.

Marshall, John. *John Locke, Toleration and Early Enlightenment Culture.* Cambridge: Cambridge University Press, 2006.

Martin, John. "Salvation and Society in Sixteenth-Century Venice: Popular Evangelism in a Renaissance City." *Journal of Modern History* 60 (1988): 205–33.

Martín, Josep Lluís, org. "La Inquisició a debat." *Manuscrits* 13 (1995): 31–55.

Martín Casares, Aurelia. "Cristianos, Musulmanes y animistas en Granada: Identidades religiosas y sincretismo cultural." In *Negros, mulatos, zambaigos,* edited by Berta Ares Queija and Alessandro Stella, 207–21. Seville: Escuela de Estudios Hispano-Americanos, 2000.

Martínez Baracas, Rodrigo. *La secuencia tlaxcalteca: Orígenes del culto a Nuestra Señora de Ocotlán.* Mexico City: Instituto Nacional de Antropología e Historia, 2000.

Martínez Ruiz, Enrique, and Magdalena de Pazzis Pi, eds. *Dogmatismo e intolerancia,* Madrid: Actas, 1997.

Mas, Albert. *Les Turcs dans la littérature espagnole du siècle d'or.* 2 vols. Paris: Institut d'études hispaniques, 1967.

Masseaut, Jean-Marc. "La Franc-Maçonnerie dans la traite atlantique: Un paradox des Lumières." Paper presented at "La experience coloniale: Dynamiques des échanges dans les espaces Atlantiques à l'époque de l'esclavage." Nantes, 2005.

Max, Frédéric. "Un écrivan français des lumières oublié: Francisco Xavier de Oliveira (1701–83)." *Revue d'Histoire et de Philosophie Religieuses* 75:2 (1995): 193–98.

Maxwell, Kenneth. *Pombal: Paradox of the Enlightenment.* Cambridge: Cambridge University Press, 1995.

Maxwell-Stuart, P. G. *The Occult in Early Modern Europe.* New York: St. Martin's Press, 1999.

McCaa, Robert. "Marriageways in Mexico and Spain, 1500–1900." *Continuity and Change* 9:1 (1994): 11–43.

McGrath, Alister E. *Iustitia Dei: A History of the Christian Doctrine of Justification.* 2 vols. Cambridge: Cambridge University Press, 1986.

———. *Reformation Thought: An Introduction.* Oxford: Oxford University Press, 1988.

———. *The Intellectual Origins of the European Reformation.* Oxford: Oxford University Press, 1987.

Mea, Elvira Cunha de Azevedo. *A Inquisição de Coimbra no século xvi.* Oporto: Fundação Eng. António de Almeida, 1997.

Méchoulan, Henri. *Razón y alteridad en Fadrique Furió Ceriol.* Madrid: Editorial Nacional, 1973.

———. "La liberté de conscience chez les penseurs juifs d'Amsterdam au xviie siècle." In

La liberté de conscience (xvi–xvii siècles), edited by Hans R. Guggisberg, Frank Lestringant, Jean-Claude Margolin, 216–33. Geneva: Droz, 1991.

———. *Le sang de l'autre ou l'honneur de dieu.* Paris: Fayard, 1979.

Medina, José Toribio. *Historia del tribunal del Santo Oficio de la Inquisición en Chile.* 2 vols. Santiago: Ercilla, 1890.

———. *Historia de la tribunal del Santo Oficio de la Inquisición de Lima.* 2 vols. Santiago de Chile: Gutenberg, 1887.

———. *Historia de la tribunal del Santo Oficio de la Inquisición de México.* 2d ed. Edited by Julio Jimenez Rueda. Mexico: Ediciones Fuente Cultural, 1952.

Mejías-López, William. "Hernán Cortés y su intolerancia hacia la religión azteca en el contexto de la situación de los conversos y moriscos." *Bulletin Hispanique* 95:2 (1993): 623–46.

Mello e Souza, Laura de. *O diabo e a terra de Santa Cruz: Feitiçaria e religiosidade popular no Brasil.* São Paulo: Companhia das Letras, 1986.

———. *Inferno atlântico.* São Paulo: Companhia das Letras, 1993.

Mendonça, Enrique Lopes de. *O padre Fernando Oliveira e a sua obra nautica.* Lisbon, 1898.

Mensching, Gustav. *Toleration and Truth in Religion.* Translated by H. J. Klimkeit. University: University of Alabama Press, 1971.

Miles, Margaret R. *Carnal Knowing: Female Nakedness and Religious Meaning in the Christian West.* Boston: Beacon Press, 1989.

Mills, Kenneth. *Idolatry and Its Enemies: Colonial Andean Religion and Extirpation, 1640–1750.* Princeton: Princeton University Press, 1997.

———. "The Limits of Religious Conversion in Mid-Colonial Peru." *Past and Present* 145 (1994): 84–121.

———. "The Naturalization of Andean Christianities." In *The Cambridge History of Christianity.* Vol. 6, *Reformation and Expansion, 1500–1660,* edited by Po-Chia Hsia, 508–39. Cambridge: Cambridge University Press, 2007.

Mitre Fernández, Emilio. "Animales, vicios y herejías: Sobre la criminalización de la disidencia en el Medievo." *Cuadernos de Historia de España* (Buenos Aires) 74 (1997): 255–83.

Monsalvo Antón, José María. "Herejia conversa y contestación religiosa a fines de la edad media: Las denuncias a la inquisición en el obispado de Osma." *Studia Historica* 2:3 (1984): 109–39.

———. "Mentalidad antijudia en la Castilla medieval: Cultura clerical y cultura popular en la gestación y difusión de un ideario medieval." In *Xudeus e conversos na Historia,* edited by Carlos Barros, 1:21–84. Santiago de Compostella: De la Historia, 1994.

Midelfort, Erik. *A History of Madness in Sixteenth-Century Germany.* Stanford: Stanford University Press, 1999.

Monter, William. "Anticlericalism and the Early Spanish Inquisition." In *Anticlericalism in Late Medieval and Early Modern Europe,* edited by Peter A. Dykema and Heiko A. Oberman, 237–42. Leiden: Brill, 1993.

———. *Frontiers of Heresy.* Cambridge: Cambridge University Press, 1990.

Mott, Luiz. "Maria, Virgem ou não? Quatro séculos de contestação no Brasil." In *O sexo proibido,* 131–86. Campinas: Papirus, 1988.

——. "O sexo cativo: Alternativas eróticas dos Africanos e seus descendentes no Brasil escravista." Mimeo, Congresso International sobre a Escravidão. São Paulo, 1988.

Muldoon, James. *The Americas in the Spanish World Order.* Philadelphia: University of Pennsylvania Press, 1994.

——. "Medieval Canon Law and the Conquest of the Americas." *Jahrbuch für Geschichte Lateinamerikas* 37 (2000): 9–25.

Mullett, Michael. *Radical Religious Movements in Early Modern Europe.* London: Allen and Unwin, 1980.

Nalle, Sara. "Popular Religion in Cuenca on the Eve of the Catholic Reformation." In *Inquisition and Society in Early Modern Europe,* edited by Stephen Haliczer, 67–87. London: Croom Helm, 1987.

——. *Mad for God: Bartolomé Sánchez, the Secret Messiah of Cardenete.* Charlottesville: University of Virginia Press, 2001.

——. *God in La Mancha: Religious Reform and the People of Cuenca, 1500–1650.* Baltimore: Johns Hopkins University Press, 1983.

Nederman, Cary J. , and John Christian Laurensen. *Difference and Dissent: Theories of Toleration in Medieval and Early Modern Europe.* Lanham: Rowman and Littlefield, 1996.

Nesvig, Martin. "Pearls before Swine: Theory and Practice of Censorship in New Spain, 1527–1640." Ph.D. diss., Yale University, 2004.

Nieto, José C. *Juan de Valdés and the Origins of the Spanish and Italian Reformations.* Geneva: Droz, 1970.

Nirenberg, David. "Conversion, Sex, and Segregation: Jews and Christians in Medieval Spain." *American Historical Review* 107:4 (2002): 1065–93.

——. *Communities of Violence.* Princeton: Princeton University Press, 1996.

——. "Mass Conversion and Genealogical Mentalities: Jews and Christians in Fifteenth-Century Spain." *Past and Present* 174 (2002): 3–41.

Novaes, Adauto. "Por que tanta libertinagem." In *Libertinos, libertários,* edited by Adauto Novaes, 9–20. São Paulo: Companhia das Letras, 1996.

Novinsky, Anita. *Cristãos novos na Bahia.* São Paulo: Editorial Perspectiva, 1973.

——. "A Inquisição portuguesa a luz de novos estudos." *Revista de la Inquisición* 7 (1998): 297–307.

——. "Marranos and the Inquisition: On the Gold Route in Minas Gerais, Brazil." In *The Jews and the Expansion of Europe to the West, 1450–1800,* edited by Paolo Bernardini and Norman Fiering, 215–41. New York: Berghan Books, 2001.

Nys, Hendrik. *Le salut sans l'évangile.* Paris: Cerf, 1966.

Olsen, Margaret M. *Slavery and Salvation in Colonial Cartagena de Indias.* Gainesville: University Press of Florida, 2004.

O'Malley, John. *Catholicism in Early Modern History: A Guide to Research.* Center for Reformation Research. Ann Arbor: Edwards Brothers, 1988.

Ortega Noriega, Sergio. "Teología novohispana sobre el matrimonio y comportamientos sexuales." In *De la santidad a la perversión.* Mexico City: Grijalbo, 1986.

Pagden, Anthony. *Lords of All the World.* New Haven: Yale University Press, 1995.

——. *European Encounters with the New World.* New Haven: Yale University Press, 1993.

Paiva, José Pedro. *Bruxaria e superstição num país sem 'caça às bruxas.* 2d ed. Lisbon: Editorial Notícias, 2002.

———. *Práticas e crenças mágicas.* Coimbra: Minerva, 1992.

———. "Inquisição e visitas pastorais. Dois mecanismos complementares de controle social?" *Revista de História das Ideias* 15 (1993): 85–102.

———. "Os bispos e a Inquisição portuguesa (1536–1613)." *Lusitania Sacra,* 2d series, 15 (2003): 43–76.

———. "A diocese de Coimbra antes e depois do Concilio de Trento: D. Jorge de Almeida e D. Afonso Castelo Branco." Coimbra, Nov. 2003.

Palomo, Federico. *A contra-reforma em Portugal, 1540–1700* (Lisbon: Livros Horizonte, 2006).

Pardo Tomás, José. *Ciencia y censura: La Inquisición española y los libros científicos en los siglos xvi y xvii.* Madrid: Consejo Superior de Investigaciones Científicas, 1991.

Passeron, Jean-Claude, and Jacques Revel. *Penser par cas.* Paris: EHESS, 2005.

Payne, Harry C. *The Philosophes and the People.* New Haven: Yale University Press, 1976.

Penna, M. *La parabola dei tre anelli e la toleranza del Medio Evo.* Torino, 1953.

Pérez, Joseph. "Política y religión en tiempos de Felipe II." *Las sociedades Ibéricas y el mar a finales del siglo xvi.* 6 vols. Madrid: Pabellón de España , 1998), 2:223–35.

Pérez Fernández, Isacio. *Fray Bartolomé de Las Casas, O.P.: De defensor de los indios a defensor de los negros.* Vol. 8, Monumenta Histórica Iberoamericana de la Orden de Predicadores. Salamanca: Editorial San Esteban, 1995.

Pérez, Llorenç, Lleonard Muntaner, and Mateu Colom, eds. *El tribunal de la Inquisición en Mallorca: Relación de causas de fe, 1578–1806.* 1 vol to date. Palma de Mallorca: Miquel Font, 1986.

Pérez Magallón, Jesús. *Construyendo la modernidad: La cultura española en el tiempo de los novatores (1675–1725).* Madrid: Consejo Superior de Investigaciones Científicas, 2002.

Pérez Muñoz. Isabel. *Pecar, delinquir y castigar: El tribunal eclesiastico de Coria en los siglos xvi y xvii.* Cáceres: Diputación Provincial de Cáceres, 1992.

Peronnet, Michelle, org. *Naissance et affirmation de l'idée de tolerance, xvi et xviii siècle.* Montpellier: Université Paul Valéry, 1987.

Peters, Edward M. "Transgressing the Limits Set by the Fathers: Authority and Impious Exegesis in Medieval Thought." In *Christendom and Its Discontents: Exclusion, Persecution, and Rebellion, 1000–1500,* edited by Scott L. Waugh and Peter D. Diehl, 338–62. Cambridge: Cambridge University Press, 1996.

———. "The Desire to Know the Secrets of the World." *Journal of the History of Ideas* 62:4 (2001): 593–610.

Phelan, John Leddy. *The Millennial Kingdom of the Franciscans in the New World.* University of California Publications in History, no. 32. Berkeley: University of California Press, 1956.

Pincus, Stephen. "The First Modern Revolution: The Revolution of 1688–89 in England." MS.

Pino Iturrieta, Elias. *Contra lujuria, castidad: Historias de pecado en el siglo xviii venezolano.* Caracas: Alfadil, 1992.

Pinto Crespo, Virgilio. "Thought Control in Spain." In *Inquisition and Society in Early Modern Europe*, edited by Stephen Haliczer, 171–88. London: Croom Helm, 1987.

Plumb, J. H. "Reason and Unreason in the Eighteenth-Century English Experience." In *the Light of History*, 3–24. Boston: Houghton Mifflin, 1973.

Po-Chia Hsia, R. *The World of the Catholic Renewal, 1540–1770*. Cambridge: Cambridge University Press, 1998.

Porter, Roy. *The Creation of the Modern World*. New York: W. W. Norton, 2000.

Poska, Allyson M. *Regulating the People: The Catholic Reformation in Seventeenth-Century Spain*. Leiden: Brill 1998.

Prado Moura, Angel de. *Las hogueras de la intolerancia: La actividad represora del Tribunal Inquisitorial de Valladolid (1700–1834)*. Valladolid: Junta de Castilla y León, 1996.

Prosperi, Adriano. "L'Europa cristiana e il mondo: Alle origini dell'idea di missione." *Dimensioni e problemi della ricerca storica* 2 (1992): 190–220.

———. *Tribunali della coscienza*. Turin: Einaudi, 1996.

———. "América y Apocalipsis." *Teología y Vida* 44 (2003): 196–208.

Rabb, Theodore K. "Religious Toleration during the Age of Reformation." In *Politics, Religion, and Diplomacy in Early Modern Europe*, edited by Malcolm R. Thorp and Arthur J. Slavin, eds., 305–21. Sixteenth-Century Essays and Studies 27. Kirksville, Mo.: Sixteenth-Century Journal Publishers, c. 1994.

Ragon, Pierre. *Les indiens de la decouverte*. Paris: L'Harmattan, 1992.

———. *Les amours indiennes, ou l'imaginaire du conquistador*. Paris: A. Colin, 1992.

Ramos Pérez, Demetrio. "La crisis indiana y la Junta Magna de 1568." *Jahrbuch für Geschichte von Staat, Wirtschaft und Gesellschaft Lateinamerikas* 22 (1986): 1–61.

Reay, Barry, ed. *Popular Culture in Seventeenth-Century England*. London: Croom Helm, 1985.

———. "Popular Religion." In *Popular Culture in Seventeenth-Century England*, edited by Barry Reay, 91–128. London: Croom Helm, 1985.

———. *Popular Cultures in England, 1550–1750*. London: Longman, 1998.

Redwood, John. *Reason, Ridicule, and Religion: The Age of Enlightenment in England (1660–1750)*. Cambridge: Harvard University Press, 1976.

Redondo, Augustín, ed. *Les problèmes de l'exclusion en Espagne (xvi–xvii siècles)*. Travaux du "Centre de Recherche sur l'Espagne des xvi et xvii siècles." Paris: Publications de la Sorbonne, 1983.

———. "La religion populaire espagnole au xvi siècle: Un terrain d'affrontement?" In *Culturas populares*, 329–47. Madrid: Casa de Velázquez and Universidad Complutense, 1986.

Reher, David. *Town and Country in Pre-Industrial Spain: Cuenca, 1550–1870*. Cambridge: Cambridge University Press, 1990.

Reis, João José, Flávio dos Santos Gomes, and Marcus J. M. de Carvalho. "Rufino José Maria: Aventuras e desventuras de um Malé entre Africa e o Brasil, c. 1822–1853." Paper presented to "L'expérience coloniale: Dynamiques des échanges dans les espaces Atlantiques à l'époque de l'esclavage." Nantes, 2005.

Renda, Francesco. *L'inquisizione in Sicilia*. Palermo: Sellerio, 1997.

Rivera Ayala, Sergio. "Lewd Songs and Dances from the Streets of Eighteenth-Century

New Spain." In *Rituals of Rule, Rituals of Resistance,* edited by William H. Beezley, Cheryl English Martin, and William E. French, 27–46. Wilmington, Del.: Scholarly Resources, 1994.

Romero Magalhães, Joaquim. "A sociedade." In *História de Portugal,* 3:469–512.

Révah, I. S. *Spinoza and Dr. Juan de Prado.* Paris: Mouton, 1959.

Ribas, Rogério de Oliveira. "O Islam na diáspora: Crenças mouriscas em Portugal nas fones inquisitoriais quinhentistas." *Tempo* 6:11 (2001): 45–66.

Rocha, André Crabbé. *Cartas inéditas ou dispersas de Vicente Nogueira.* Lisbon, n.d.

Romeiro, Adriana. "As aventuras de um viajante no império português: Trocas culturais e tolerância religiosa no século xviii." In *O trabalho mestiço,* edited by Eduardo França Paiva and Carla Maria Junho Anastasia, 483–95. Rio de Janeiro: Ana Blume, 2002.

———. *Um visionário na corte de Dom João V.* Belo Horizonte: UFMG, 2001.

Roncancio Parra, Andrés. *Indice de documentos de la inquisición de Cartegena de Indias.* Bogotá: Instituto Colombiano de Cultura Hispánica, 2000.

Ronquillo Rubio, Manuela. *Los orígenes de la Inquisición en Canarias.* Las Palmas: Cabildo Insular de Gran Canaria, 1991.

Roper, Lyndal. *Oedipus and the Devil: Witchcraft, Sexuality, and Religion in Early Modern Europe.* London: Routledge, 1994.

Roselló Vaquer, Ramón, and Jaume Bover Pujol. *El sexe a Mallorca.* Palma de Mallorca: Miquel Font, 1992.

Rowland, Robert. "Inquisição, intolerância e exclusão." *Ler História* 33 (1997): 9–22.

Rueda Ramírez, Pedro J. *Negocio e intercambio cultural: El comercio de libros con América en la carrera de Indias (siglo xvii).* Seville: Diputación de Sevilla, Universidad de Sevilla, CSIC, 2005.

Russell-Wood, A. J. R. "Iberian Expansion and the Issue of Black Slavery: Changing Portuguese Attitudes, 1440–1770." *American Historical Review* 83:1 (1978): 16–42.

Sacristán, María Cristina. *Locura e Inquisición en Nueva España, 1571–1760.* Mexico City: Fondo de Cultura Económica, 1992.

Sala-Molins, Louis. *Les misères de lumières.* Paris: R. Lafont, 1992.

Salvador Marques, Maria Adelaida. "Pombalismo e cultura media: Meios para um diagnóstico através da Real Mesa Censória." In *Como interpreter Pombal?* 185–214. Lisbon: Brotéria, 1983.

Salvio, Alfonso de. "Voltaire and Spain." *Hispania* 7:2 (1924): 69–110.

Sánchez-Albornoz, Claudio. *España, un enigma histórico.* 2 vols. Buenos Aires: Editorial Sudamericana, c. 1956. Translated as *Spain, A Historical Enigma* by Colette Joly Dees and David Sven Seher. 2 vols. Madrid: Fundación Universitaria Española, 1975.

Sánchez Blanco, Francisco. *La mentalidad ilustrada.* Madrid: Taurus, 1999.

———. *El absolutismo y las luces en el reinado de Carlos III.* Madrid: Macial Pons, 2002.

Sánchez Ortega, María Helena. *La mujer y la sexualidad en el antiguo regimen.* Madrid: Akal, 1991.

Santoja, Pedro. *La herejía de los Alumbrados y la espiritualidad en la España del siglo xvi: Inquisición y sociedad.* Valencia: Generalitat Valenciana, 2001.

Saraiva, António José. *The Marrano Factory.* Translated and edited by H. P. Salomon and I. S. D. Sassoon. Leiden: Brill, 2001.

Saranyana, Josep-Ignasi, *Teología profética americana.* Pamplona: Universidad de Navarra, 1991.

Sarrailh, Jean. *L'Espagne éclairée de la seconde moitié du XVIIIᵉ siècle.* Paris: Librairie C. Klincksieck, 1954.

Saupin, Guy, Rémy Fabre, and Marcel Launay, eds. *La Tolérance: Colloque international de Nantes.* Rennes: Presses Universitaires de Rennes, 1998.

Sauzet, Robert, ed. *Les frontières religieuses en Europe du xv au xvii siècle.* Paris: Librairie Philosophique J. Vrin, 1992.

Schmitt, Jean-Claude. *História das superstições.* Lisbon: Forum da História, 1997.

Scholem, Gershom. *The Messianic Idea in Judaism.* New York: Schocken Books, 1971.

Schwartz, Stuart B. "Pecar en colonias: Mentalidades populares, Inquisición y actitudes hacia la fornicación simple en España, Portugal y las colonias americanas." *Cuadernos de Historia Moderna* 18 (1997): 51–67.

Scribner, Bob. "Practical Utopias: Pre-Modern Communism and the Reformation." *Comparative Studies in Society and History* 36:4 (1994): 743–74.

Sesboüé, Bernard. *Hors de l'Église pas de salut.* Paris: Desclée de Brouwer, 2004.

Sierra, Julio. *Procesos en la Inquisición de Toledo (1575–1610): Manuscrito de Halle.* Madrid: Editorial Trotta, 2005.

Silva Dias, José Sebastião da. *Correntes de sentimento religioso em Portugal.* 2 vols. Coimbra: Universidade de Coimbra, 1960.

Sina, Mario, ed. *La tolleranza religiosa: Indagini storiche e riflessioni filosofiche.* Milan: Università Cattolica del Sacro Cuore, 1991.

Siqueira, Sonia. "O pecado na Bahia nos séculos xvi e xvii." Anais do IV Congresso da História da Bahia. 2 vols. 1:147–74. Salvador: Instituto Geográfico e Histórico da Bahia, 2001.

———. *A Inquisição portuguesa e a sociedade colonial.* São Paulo: Editorial Atica, 1978.

Smith, Steven B. *Spinoza, Liberalism and the Question of Jewish Identity.* New Haven: Yale University Press, 1997.

Solá, Emílio. *Cervantes y la Berbería.* Mexico City: Fondo de Cultura Económica, 1995.

Sommerville, John. "Religious Faith, Doubt, and Atheism." *Past and Present* 128 (August 1990): 152–55.

Spendiani, Anna María, et al. *Cincuenta años de la inquisición en el tribunal de Cartagena de Indias.* Bogotá: Centro Editorial Javeriano, 1997.

Strayer, Brian E. *Huguenots and Camisards as Aliens in France, 1598–1789.* Lewiston, N.Y.: Edward Mellen, 2001.

Sullivan, Francis A. *Salvation Outside the Church.* New York: Paulist Press, 1992.

Surtz, Ronald. "Morisco Women, Written Texts, and the Valencian Inquisition." *Sixteenth Century Journal* 32:2 (2001): 421–33.

Sweet, James H. *Recreating Africa.* Chapel Hill: University of North Carolina Press, 2003.

Tailland, Michèle Janin-Thivos. *Inquisition et société au Portugal.* Paris: Fundação Calouste Gulbenkian, 2002.

Tardieu, Jean-Pierre. *L'Inquisición de Lima et les herétiques étrangers (xvie–xviie siècles).* Paris: Harmattan, 1995.

Taylor, William B. *Magistrates of the Sacred.* Stanford: Stanford University Press, 1996.

Thomas, Keith. *Religion and the Decline of Magic.* London: Weidenfeld and Nicolson, 1971.

Thomas, Werner. *La repressión del protestantismo en España, 1517–1648.* Louvain: Leuven University Press, 2001.

———. *Los protestantes y la Inquisición en España en tiempos de Reforma y Contrarreforma.* Louvain: Leuven University Press, 2001.

Tiessen, Terrance L. *Irenaeus on the Salvation of the Unevangelized.* Metuchen, N.J.: Scarecrow Press, 1993.

Tomás y Valiente, Francisco. "Ensayo para una historia de la tolerancia, sus formas, sus contrarios y sus límites." In *Sociedad, tolerancia y religión,* edited by Santiago del Cura Elena, 29–42. Burgos, 1996.

Toulouse-Le Mirail, Université de. *Penseurs hétérodoxes du monde hispanique.* Toulouse, 1974.

Traslosheros, José. "El tribunal eclesiástico y los indios en el arzobispado de México, hasta 1630." *Historia Mexicana* 51:3, n. 203 (2002): 485–517.

Trinkhaus, Charles. "The Problem of Free Will in the Renaissance and the Reformation." *Journal of the History of Ideas* 10:1 (1949): 51–62.

Turner, Ralph V. " 'Descendit ad Infernos': Medieval Views of Christ's Descent into Hell and the Salvation of the Ancient Just." *Journal of the History of Ideas* 27:2 (1966): 173–94.

Vaillancourt, P. L. "Clémence et tolérance dans quelques traités politiques à l'automne de la Renaissance." In *Naissance et affirmation de l'idee de tolerance, xvi et xviii siècle,* organized by Michelle Peronnet, 117–30. Montpellier: Université Paul Valéry, 1987.

Vainfas, Ronaldo. *Trópico dos pecados: Moral, sexualidade e Inquisição.* Rio de Janeiro: Nova Fronteira, 1997.

———. *Os protagonistas anônimos da história.* Rio de Janeiro: Campus, 2002.

Vera Urbano, Francisco de Paula. "La libertad religiosa en el pensamiento católico según los tratados de teología moral y la literatura polémica del siglo xviii." *Revista de Estudios Histórico-Jurídicos* 25 (Valparaíso, Chile): 445–74.

Villads Jensen, Kurt. "Christian Reading of the Quran before and after 1300." In *Rapports entre Juifs, Chrétiens et Musulmans,* edited by Johannes Irmscher, 173–78. Amsterdam: Verlag Adolf M. Hakkert, 1995.

Viñao Frago, Antonio. "Alfabetización y primeras letras (siglos xvi–xvii)." In *Escribir y leer en el siglo de Cervantes,* edited by Antonio Castillo, 39–84. Barcelona: Gedisa, 1999.

Vivanti, C. *Lotta politica e pace religiosa in Francia fra Cinque e Seicento.* Torino: Einaudi, 1963.

Vizuete Mendoza, J. Carlos, and Palma Martínez-Burgos García, eds. *Religiosidad popular y modelos de identidad en España y América.* Cuenca: Universidad de Castilla–La Mancha, 2000.

Voekel, Pamela. *Alone before God: The Religious Origins of Modernity in Mexico.* Durham: Duke University Press, 2002.

Wachtel, Nathan. "Marrano Religiosity in Hispanic America in the Seventeenth Century." In *The Jews and the Expansion of Europe to the West,* edited by P. Bernardini and N. Fiering, 149–71. New York: Berghahn, 2001.

———. *La foi du souvenir.* Paris: Seuil, 2002.

Wadsworth, James. "Joaquim Marques de Araújo: o poder da inquisição em Pernambuco no fim do período colonial." In *De Cabral a Pedro I,* edited by Maria Beatriz Nizza da Silva, 309–20. Oporto: Universidade Portucalense, 2001.

———. "Agents of Orthodoxy: Inquisitional Power and Prestige in Colonial Pernambuco, Brazil." Ph.D diss., University of Arizona, 2002.

Wagner, Christine. "Los luteranos ante la Inquisición de Toledo en el siglo xvi." *Hispania Sacra* 46 (1994): 473–510.

Walker, Timothy D. *Doctors, Folk Medicine and the Inquisition.* Leiden: Brill, 2005.

Waught, Scott L., and Peter D. Diehl, eds. *Christendom and Its Discontents.* Cambridge: Cambridge University Press, 1996.

Weaver, R. H. *Divine Grace and Human Agency: A Study of the Semi-Pelagian Controversy.* Patristic Monograph Series 15. Macon, Ga.: Mercer University Press, 1996.

Whaley, Joachim. *Religious Toleration and Social Change in Hamburg, 1529–1819.* Cambridge: Cambridge University Press, 1985.

Wilson, Stephen. *The Magical Universe: Everyday Ritual and Magic in Pre-Modern Europe.* London: Hambledon and London, 2000.

Wooton, David. "New Histories of Atheism." In *Atheism from the Reformation to the Enlightenment,* edited by Michael Hunter and David Wooton, 13–54. Oxford: Clarendon Press, 1992.

———. "Lucien Febvre and the Problem of Unbelief in the Early Modern Period." *Journal of Modern History* 60 (1988): 695–730.

———. "Unbelief in Early Modern Europe." *History Workshop Journal* 20:1 (1985): 85–100.

Yerulshalmi, Yosef Hayim. *The Lisbon Massacre of 1506 and the Royal Image in the Shebet Yehudah.* Cincinnati: Hebrew Union College, 1976.

Yovel, Yirmiyahu. *Spinoza and Other Heretics.* 2 vols. Princeton: Princeton University Press, 1989.

Zagorin, Perez. *Ways of Lying: Dissimulation, Persecution, and Conformity in Early Modern Europe.* Cambridge: Harvard University Press, 1990.

Zaid, Rhoda. "Popular Discontent and Unsung Heroes: The Holy Office of the Inquisition in Cuenca, 1550–1590." Ph.D. diss., University of California: Los Angeles, 1991.

Zavala, Silvio. *Filosofía de la conquista,* 2d ed. Mexico City: Fondo de Cultura Económica, 1972.

Zuñiga, Jean-Paul. *Espagnols d'Outre-Mer.* Paris: École des Hautes Études en Sciences Sociales, 2002.

Index

Numbers in italics indicate figures.

DATE DUE

DEMCO, INC. 38-2931